croatia

FODOR'S TRAVEL PUBLICATIONS
NEW YORK • TORONTO • LONDON • SYDNEY • AUCKLAND

WWW.FODORS.COM

Contents

KEY TO SYMBOLS

✚ Map reference
✉ Address
☎ Telephone number
🕐 Opening times
💷 Admission prices
🚌 Bus/tram number
🚉 Train station
⛴ Ferry/boat
🚗 Driving directions
ℹ Tourist office
🎫 Tours
📖 Guidebook
🍽 Restaurant
☕ Café
🍸 Bar
🏬 Shop
🚻 Toilets
🛏 Number of rooms
🚭 No smoking
❄ Air conditioning
🏊 Swimming pool
🏋 Gym
❓ Other useful information
🛍 Shopping
🎭 Entertainment
🎶 Nightlife
⚽ Sports
✪ Activities
♡ Health and Beauty
❂ For Children
▷ Cross reference
★ Walk/drive start point

HOW TO USE THIS BOOK

Understanding Croatia is an introduction to the country, its geography, economy and people. **Living Croatia** gives an insight into Croatia today, while **Story of Croatia** takes you through the country's past.

For detailed advice on getting to Croatia—and getting around once you are there—turn to **On the Move**. For useful information, from weather to emergency services, go to **Planning**.

Out and About gives you the chance to explore Croatia through walks, drives and organized tours.

The **Sights**, **What to Do,** and **Eating and Staying** sections are divided geographically into six regions, which are shown on the map on the inside front cover. These regions always appear in the same order. Towns and places of interest are listed alphabetically within each region.

Map references for the **Sights** refer to the atlas section at the end of the book or to the town plans. For example, Split has the reference ✚ 297 F7, indicating the page on which the map is found (297) and the grid square in which Split sits (F7).

3

UNDERSTANDING CROATIA

The young Republic of Croatia (Republika Hrvatska) is a fascinating blend of Balkan, Central European and Mediterranean cultures. Born in 1991 out of the collapse of the former Yugoslavia, it is fast emerging as one of Europe's most beguiling holiday destinations. Historic towns and cities have become lively cultural centres, none more so than Dubrovnik, spectacularly risen from the ashes of war. Ruled at various times in its history by Rome, Venice, Vienna, Budapest and Belgrade, Croatia has adopted influences from them all. On the Adriatic coast and islands, craggy mountains loom over a sparkling blue sea with some of the cleanest waters and best sailing in Europe. This is a land of vivid colours—green pines, purple lavender, golden stone, azure sea and bright Mediterranean sky.

THE CROATS

The Croats were a Slavic race who migrated to the Balkans in the 7th century AD at the same time as the Serbs. Before that Croatia was occupied by Illyrian hill tribes, including the Histri in present-day Istria and the Liburnians in Kvarner Bay. It had also been part of the Roman empire, one of whose greatest emperors, Diocletian (cAD245–313), was born in Dalmatia. During its medieval golden age, Croatia was a nation ruled by its own dukes and kings. Legend states that the last king cursed Croatia to a millennium of foreign rule. In fact, it took just over 900 years for the 'thousand-year dream' of Croatian independence to be realized.

NEVER MIND THE BALKANS

Until 1991, Croatia was part of Yugoslavia, with Serbia, Montenegro, Macedonia, Bosnia-Herzegovina and Slovenia. Together with others such as Albania, Bulgaria and Greece, these countries are often referred to as the Balkans. While this is geographically correct—the Balkan peninsula extends from the Adriatic to the Black Sea—it is politically controversial.

Croatia has always looked north and west rather than south and east, and its leaders refer to it as a Central European rather than a Balkan country. This is partly to distance it from Serbia, but also because the word balkanization implies fragmentation into small, ungovernable states. The divisions in the Balkans can be traced to the partition of the Roman empire, its boundary roughly along today's borders of Croatia and Bosnia-Herzegovina. Famously described by Pope Leo X as 'the ramparts of Christendom', Croatia has always tended to see itself as a nation on the front line of civilizations, and the last bastion of Catholic Europe before the Orthodox and Muslim worlds of the Balkans. For this reason, the term Balkan is loaded with historical symbolism and visitors should be wary of using it.

THE HOMELAND WAR

It is impossible to understand Croatia without reference to the Domovinski Rat (Homeland War), a war of independence from Yugoslavia from 1991 to 1995 (▷ 22–23). At that time Croatia was also involved in a bloody three-way conflict in Bosnia-Herzegovina.

The war has left an indelible mark on Croatia and continues to dominate political debate, especially the issue of alleged war criminals and war crimes tribunal at The Hague. Nationalism is still a potent force in Croatia and visitors should exercise caution when expressing opinions on the war.

There are few visible signs of war damage on the coast, but bombed-out houses and abandoned villages are a common sight near the Bosnian and

The official language is Croatian (Hrvatski), a branch of the Serbo-Croat languages of the Balkans. However, largely for political reasons, it is now treated as distinct from Bosnian and Serbian. Croatian uses the Latin script while Serbia uses Cyrillic, but many words are otherwise identical. Most young people speak a foreign language, usually English, German or Italian, and there is a significant Italian-speaking minority in Istria.

Launching a boat in Istria; strolling in Dubrovnik; the Croatian flag flies over Zagreb's parliament complex; a view from Dubrovnik's city walls (left to right). The Dalmatian coast (opposite)

Serbian borders, especially in Vukovar and the Krajina region of northern Dalmatia. Landmines are still a problem in remote areas—over 400 people have been killed by mines since the end of the war—so keep to main roads and footpaths and heed warning signs.

PEOPLE
The 2001 census shows Croatia to have just under 4.5 million inhabitants, of whom almost 1 million live in Zagreb. The next biggest cities are Split, Rijeka and Osijek. Around 90 per cent of the population are Croats and 4 per cent are Serbs. Before 1991, some 15 per cent were Serbs, but many left during the war, at a time when many Croat refugees arrived from Bosnia-Herzegovina. Several million Croats live abroad, with large communities in the USA, Canada, Australia, Great Britain and Germany.

Religion is divided along ethnic lines, with 88 per cent Roman Catholic, 4 per cent Serbian Orthodox and 1 per cent Muslim. Although church attendance is low, there has been a revival of popular religion since independence and there are strong links between Catholicism and nationalism.

THE COUNTRY
Croatia is shaped like a boomerang, with one blade pointing south along the Adriatic coast and the other pointing east across the fertile Pannonian plain. For much of its length, the coast is sheltered by mountains that rise steeply from the sea. The Dinaric range separates Croatia from Bosnia-Herzegovina. Of its 1,185 islands, around 50 are permanently inhabited.

NATIONAL PARKS

UNESCO WORLD HERITAGE SITES

CROATIA AT A GLANCE

Zagreb is the political and cultural capital of Croatia, home to around 20 per cent of the population. With elegant Austro-Hungarian cafés, grand boulevards and Viennese Secession architecture, it is often compared to Vienna.

Inland Croatia stretches from the Kvarner highlands to the River Danube via the fertile Slavonia plains. Apart from the Plitvice Lakes, tourism has yet to make an impact. The areas bordering Bosnia and Serbia suffered badly in the war.

Istria (Istra) is a peninsula in the northern Adriatic. Once occupied by Italy, it reflects a strong Italian influence. Pula has well-preserved Roman monuments, while the west coast has some of the biggest resorts in Croatia.

Kvarner is a large bay separating Istria from Dalmatia, including Croatia's two largest islands, Cres and Krk. The smaller islands of Lošinj and Rab are popular with visitors, and Rijeka is a busy port beneath the Gorski Kotar mountains.

Dalmatia (Dalmacija) is a long, narrow coastal region, with hundreds of islands and a beautiful shoreline. The main cities are Zadar, Šibenik and Split, and there is a historical Venetian influence in its coastal and island towns.

Dubrovnik and Beyond includes the gem of the Croatian coast, Dubrovnik, a walled city brilliantly restored after devastation during the Homeland War and other sights within day-trip distance of Dubrovnik.

CROATIA'S REGIONS

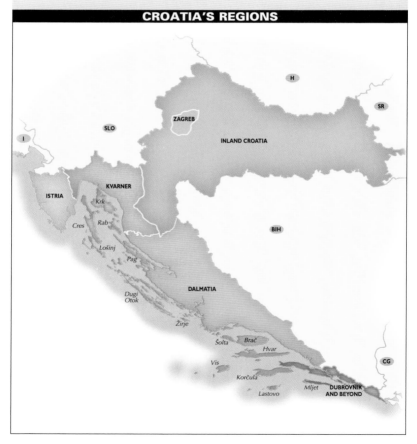

The best of
Croatia

ZAGREB

Gornji Grad (▷ 52) Take the funicular to the top of the city for churches and museums on cobbled streets.
Hrvatsko Narodno Kazalište (▷ 51) Spend an evening amid the Habsburg splendour of the National Theatre.
Medvednica (▷ 56) Take the cable-car to the summit of Zagreb's mountain for fresh air, walks and views.
Tkalčićeva (▷ 202) Join the beautiful people for an evening *korzo* (stroll) on Zagreb's prettiest street.
Trg Bana Jelačića (▷ 59) Soak up city life and enjoy people-watching from a café table on the main square.

INLAND CROATIA

Lonjsko Polje (▷ 66–67) See black storks and relax for a night in a wooden cottage by the River Sava.
Plitvička Jezera (▷ 70–73) Follow boardwalk trails around the lakes and waterfalls of this famous national park.
Varaždin (▷ 76–79) Stroll through the streets admiring the baroque architecture of Croatia's former capital.
Vukovar (▷ 75) Ponder the horror and futility of war in this once beautiful town on the River Danube.
Zdjelarević (▷ 237) Spend the night at Croatia's first wine hotel, in the rural heartland of Slavonia.

ISTRIA

Brijuni (▷ 86–87) Explore Tito's presidential playground on a day trip to these surreal islands off the Istrian coast.
Motovun (▷ 90) Discover exquisite fortified hilltop towns such as Motovun and Grožnjan (▷ 88).
Pula (▷ 94–97) Imagine gladiators and Christians being thrown to the lions at the magnificent Roman arena.
Rovinj (▷ 98–101) Dip your feet in the sea while sipping cocktails at Istria's most attractive seaside resort.
Zigante (▷ 240) Feast on Istrian truffles and local wine in this truffle-themed restaurant in Livade.

KVARNER

Caput Insulae, Cres (▷ 216–217) Explore the stone labyrinth on an eco-trail from Beli.
Opatija (▷ 107) Relive the *fin-de-siècle* days of the Austro-Hungarian empire on the Lungomare seafront.
Platak (▷ 186–187) Ski in winter with a view of the sea, or walk in the highlands of the Gorski Kotar in summer.
Rab (▷ 108–109) Uncover the layers of history on a stroll through one of Croatia's most appealing island towns.
Rijeka (▷ 110–111) Delve into the story of the Glagolitic alphabet (▷ 19) at an exhibition in the university library.

Trg Bana Jelačića, Zagreb; traditional wooden farmhouse, Lonjsko Polje; tour boat, Brijuni; Roman remains, Rab (top to bottom)

The best of
Croatia

DALMATIA

Korčula (▷ 120–123) See a performance of the *moreška* sword dance and stroll around the Venetian town.
Kornati (▷ 126) Cruise through the remote and eerily beautiful islands of this archipelago near Zadar.
Krka (▷ 124–125) Swim beneath the cascades, then take a boat trip through the dramatic Krka canyon.
Morske Orgulje, Zadar (▷ 141) Sit on the steps at sunset with a symphony of nature from the sea organ below.
Split (▷ 132–137) Wander around the remains of the palatial retirement home of Roman emperor Diocletian.

DUBROVNIK AND BEYOND

Elafitski Otoci (▷ 156) Take the ferry to these peaceful islands, with their sandy beaches and gentle walks.
Gradske Zidine (▷ 148–149) Everyone does it, but you simply have to make the circuit atop the city walls.
Lokanda Peskarija (▷ 247) Dine on fresh fish, salad and chilled white wine at a table beside the harbour.
Stradun (▷ 152–153) Sit at a pavement (sidewalk) café and watch the crowds on this beautiful street.
Summer Festival (▷ 198) See Shakespeare's *Hamlet* performed at Fort Lovrijenac.

TOP TEN EXPERIENCES

Charter your own yacht and sail among the Dalmatian islands, tying up at a different port each night.
Drive the Magistrala highway between Dubrovnik and Split, one of Europe's most spectacular coast roads.
Get away from it all with a night in a farmhouse in Istria, Slavonia or the Zagorje, dining on local food.
Go island-hopping on the excellent network of local ferries (▷ 38).
Look out for concerts in magical outdoor settings— every town has a summer festival.
Sip *prošek* (sweet red wine) on a summer evening by the sea, on the café-lined Riva (waterfront promenade) to be found in all coastal towns.
Take a walk in the mountains in summer, enjoying cool breezes, stunning scenery and magnificent sea views.
Taste *pršut* (cured ham) with *paški sir* (Pag cheese), olives and crusty bread—heaven on a plate.
Throw off your clothes and go as nature intended on one of Croatia's many nudist beaches—if you are ever going to shed your inhibitions, this is the place to do it.
Unwind and give in to the spirit of *fijaka*—a feeling of indolent pleasure, best captured in lazy days by the sea.

Skradinski Buk falls in Krka; along Dubrovnik's Stradun; Opuzen fruit; walking to the Dragon's Cave, Brač (top to bottom)

Living Croatia

Pilgrims at Our Lady of the Snows, Marija Bistrica (right)

Participants in the Sinjska Alka festival (above and far left)

A New
Nation

No visitor to Croatia can fail to notice the Croats' immense pride in their country since independence in 1991. Symbols of nationhood are everywhere, from the ubiquitous red, white and blue tricolour flying from government buildings to the checkered *hrvatski grb* seen on everything from policemen's uniforms to soccer shirts. Streets and squares once named after Tito (▷ 20) now carry names of Croatian nationalist heroes. Soccer fans wave banners proclaiming 'Proud to be Croat'. Traditional festivals are being revived, and the language is now always *hrvatski* (Croatian), rather than Serbo-Croat. Another sign of resurgent nationalism is the growth in support for the Catholic church, after its decades of marginalization under communism. According to the 2001 census, some 88 per cent of Croatia's population are Roman Catholics, a rise of 12 per cent in ten years. In part, this reflects post-war demographic changes, the majority of Orthodox Serbs having fled to Bosnia, but it also shows that many Croats embrace Catholicism as a symbol of national identity.

Money Talks

Even the currency is a political statement in Croatia. Officially introduced in October 1993, the kuna takes its name from the pine-marten, whose furs were traded in medieval times. Critics, however, saw it as a throwback to an earlier era of nationalism, recalling that the kuna had last been used by the Fascist Ustaše regime which occupied Croatia during World War II. The 1-, 2- and 5-kuna coins feature an image of the pine-marten on one side, with a nightingale, tuna and brown bear respectively on the reverse. Banknotes are adorned with Croatian poets, dukes, politicians and iconic landmarks, such as the Eltz Palace at Vukovar and the King Tomislav statue in Zagreb. Ironically, for all its controversy and symbolism, the kuna is already on the way out. Croatia will introduce the euro by 2012.

Mirko Norac with generals Marakac and Gotovina (above).
Model Jodie Kidd wearing a Gharani Štrok design (left).
The emblem of Hajduk Split soccer team
features the *hrvatski grb* (right)

Model Modern Croat

The businessman Goran Štrok is typical of the new breed of Croatian expatriate entrepreneurs who are investing their cash in the rebuilding of their country. Born in Zagreb in 1947, this son of one of Tito's generals was a professional motor-racing driver, winning seven national championships before moving to London in 1977. In 1995, he bought his first hotel in Rijeka and now owns a chain of smart Croatian hotels, the flagship being the restored Dubrovnik Palace. It was opened in 2004 by President Stjepan Mesić, after a €45 million investment. Štrok's wife Renata is an interior designer and his daughter Vanja is one of the fashion duo Gharani Štrok, with such clients as Madonna and Nicole Kidman. The Štroks support charitable projects in Croatia—Goran set up the Izidor Štrok Memorial Fund in memory of his father, and Renata sponsors children who were orphaned in the Homeland War.

Knights in Armour

The ugly side of Croatian nationalism occasionally rears its head, especially in former war zones that still have an undercurrent of anti-Serb hostility. The medieval Sinjska Alka festival (▷ 194) in the Dalmatian town of Sinj is a heady brew of patriotism and religious fervour, in an area with a large military presence where memories of the war are still fresh. In 2001 the event was taken over by supporters of General Mirko Norac, a local soldier who was elected Duke of Sinjska Alka, despite being dismissed from the Army and accused of war crimes for which he was later sentenced to 12-years in prison. In his support, the local *alkari* (knights) returned the traditional gift sent by Croatian president Stjepan Mesić, who responded by cutting off state funding for the festival until 2005. The event went ahead with supporters chanting Norac's name and waving flags and insignia of the Ustaše period.

Check Mate

The red and white checkerboard known as the *hrvatski grb* (Croatian shield) is one of the oldest national symbols in Europe, dating back at least 500 years. According to mythology, its origins lie in a game of chess, in which a 10th-century Croatian king defeated a Venetian prince to preserve Croatia's freedom. The shield is at the centre of the national flag, topped by a crown made up of five smaller shields representing the historic coats of arms of Croatia, Dubrovnik, Dalmatia, Istria and Slavonia. This potent symbol of nationalism is often derided by opponents because of its associations with the Ustaše régime, but it has been used by Croatian rulers of every political complexion, from Austrian emperors and Serbian kings to Communist Yugoslavia.

Brown bear with cubs (right).
Prickly pear in a Botanical
garden on Lokrum (below)

The Great
Outdoors

It may seem hard to believe amid the bustle of Zagreb or on the crowded Adriatic beaches in summer, but Croatia is still largely a wilderness country. Around 40 per cent of the landmass is taken up with karst limestone mountains, while another 30 per cent is forests of oak, pine, beech, spruce and fir. Add pristine lakes, unpolluted rivers and hundreds of desert islands, and what you have is a giant outdoor adventure playground. At weekends Croatians flee the cities to go hiking in the mountains, or hunting and fishing in the forests and rivers. Adrenaline addicts get their fix from rafting, canoeing, kayaking, caving and climbing. In summer people go camping in alpine huts or sail their yachts to remote islands; in winter, at the first sign of snow, they pack up their skis and head for the hills. It is not only humans who enjoy Croatia's spectacular natural landscapes. Among the wildlife to be found in the forest and mountain regions of Croatia are lynx, wolves, wild boar, red and roe deer, pine-marten, golden eagles, peregrine falcons and brown bears.

Bear Necessities

Once brown bears roamed over much of the planet, but today they are reduced to a few pockets of Europe and North America. The brown bear is one of the largest living land carnivores on earth, weighing up to 300kg (660lb). There are an estimated 400 bears in Croatia, mostly in the Gorski Kotar and Velebit massifs. They are typically shy, coming down to the lower slopes at night to hunt. Although protected within national parks, bears can be legally hunted in Croatia and are prized for meat, medicinal uses and fur. Travellers may be shocked to see smoked bear salami and paté on sale in shops. It is forbidden to hunt mothers and young bear cubs, but inevitably some do get killed. The Refugium Ursorum bear sanctuary at Kuterevo, near Otočac, supports bear cubs orphaned as a result of poaching (▷ 188).

A naturist beach (right). Croatia's own dog, the Dalmatian (below)

Croatia has some great hiking country (below)

Naturism sign (right)

Spotted Dogs

The black and white spotted dogs known as Dalmatians were immortalized in the 1961 Disney film *101 Dalmatians*, based on the children's story by Dodie Smith (1896–1990), in which the wicked Cruella de Vil kidnaps Dalmatian puppies to make a fur coat. However, the Dalmatian is much more than a cuddly cartoon character. In 1994 the World Canine Federation officially recognized Croatia's claim to be the origin of the breed. First seen in ancient Egyptian and Greek art, the Dalmatian was popular as a carriage dog in 19th-century England, running alongside horses to protect carriages and their occupants from attack. They were also used in the Balkans by bands of *Roma* (gypsy) musicians and circus performers, and have been adopted as mascots by fire stations across the USA. A little-known fact is that the puppies are born white all over; the distinctive black spots develop later.

The Naked Truth

One sign of Croatia's back-to-nature approach is its laid-back attitude to nudity. The first naturist beach opened in 1934 on the island of Rab, and today there are more than 30 official resorts, plus many where nudity is tolerated. In the 1960s Yugoslavia was the first country to commercialize naturism, and the Istrian coast was heavily promoted in Germany and Austria as a naturist destination. Koversada, which opened in 1961 on an islet off Vrsar, has become Europe's biggest nudist colony, accommodating 7,000. Beaches where naturism is encouraged are indicated by the letters FKK (*freikörperkultur* or 'free body culture') but in practice clothing is optional at most remote beaches and islands. Visitors can go to the harbour at any popular resort in summer and find boatmen offering trips to nudist beaches. More information on naturism in Croatia is available at www.cronatur.com

Bottlenose Dolphins

If dolphins are a sign of a healthy marine environment, then the waters around Cres and Lošinj are some of the cleanest in the Mediterranean. The Adriatic Dolphin Project in Veli Lošinj has identified and photographed around 160 individual bottlenose dolphins, whose behaviour is closely monitored by researchers. Among the biggest threats to the survival of dolphins here are overfishing, which forces them to hunt farther afield for food, and the engine noise from motorboats, which has a disrupting effect on their navigational senses. In 2006 the Croatian government announced the establishment of the Lošinj Dolphin Reserve off the coasts of Cres and Lošinj, the first such protected area in the Mediterranean. If you want to help, Blue World (▷ 187) offer 'adopt a dolphin' sponsorship or you could join one of the volunteer research programmes in summer. Swimming with dolphins is illegal in Croatia.

Dražen Petrović faces the USA's Michael Jordan at the Barcelona Olympics (below)

Bulgaria's Iliev challenges Croatia's Dado Pršo during a World Cup qualifier in Sofia (above)

Sporting Heroes

For a country of 4.5 million people which has been in existence for less than 20 years, Croatia has achieved a remarkable level of sporting success. Sport is seen by many Croats as a source of national pride and a way of gaining international recognition. Ask a 10-year-old boy in Germany or Britain what he knows about Croatia, and he will probably reel off the names of soccer stars such as Dado Pršo, Igor Tudor and brothers Robert and Niko Kovač, or tennis players Ivan Ljubičić and Mario Ančić, heroes of the Davis Cup-winning team of 2005. Since first entering the Olympic Games as an independent nation in 1992, Croatia has won medals in tennis, basketball, water polo, swimming, weightlifting, rowing and skiing, with Janica Kostelić (▷ 15) becoming the most successful female skier ever. The greatest results have come in handball, at which Croatia traditionally excels. Croatian athletes made up the bulk of the Yugoslav handball team which won the first Olympic gold medal at Munich in 1972, and Croatia went on to win handball gold at Atlanta in 1996 and Athens in 2004.

Golden Boots

In 1998, playing in their first World Cup, the Croatian national soccer team finished third, going out in the semi-finals to the hosts, and eventual champions, France. The star was Davor Šuker of Real Madrid and Croatia, winner of the Golden Boot for the World Cup's leading scorer (six goals in seven games). He now runs a soccer academy in Zagreb. The Croatian captain was Zvonimir Boban, who played for AC Milan for nine years. Since his retirement he has gained a history degree at Zagreb University and been a commentator for Croatian and Italian TV. He also owns a restaurant in Zagreb. Although the Vatreni (Fiery Ones) have not reached those heights since 1998, Croatia continues to be a major force in world soccer and qualified for the World Cup in 2002 and 2006.

Janica Kostelić triumphs at Val d'Isère in 2002 (above).
Goran Ivanišević wins Wimbledon in 2001 (left)

From Refugee to Champion

Born in 1979 in Banja Luka, Bosnia, Ivan Ljubičić faced a disrupted childhood when his family was forced to flee to Croatia in 1992 as a result of ethnic cleansing by Bosnian Serbs. Thirteen years later he virtually single-handedly won for Croatia the Davis Cup, the world's premier international men's team tennis tournament. With first round victories over Americans Andre Agassi and Andy Roddick, he won seven of his eight singles matches and all of his doubles during the year, culminating in defeating Slovakia in the final. One of his teammates was Goran Ivanišević, formerly the most famous sportsman in Croatia after winning at Wimbledon as a wild card entry in 2001. Known for striking good looks and an erratic temperament, he had reached, but lost, the final three times in the 1990s. Typically, perhaps, he came back to win when everybody least expected it.

Born to Ski

Despite the lack of high-class winter sports facilities, Croatia has produced probably the greatest female skier of all time. Born in Zagreb in 1982, Janica Kostelić took her first tentative steps on the slopes of Medvednica when she was just three years old. At 16 she competed in the Nagano Winter Olympics, finishing eighth in the combined downhill and slalom. In 2002 at Salt Lake City, she created Olympic history, becoming the first Alpine skier to win four medals in a single Olympic Games, including gold in the slalom, giant slalom and combined. Following knee operations, serious illness and the removal of her thyroid gland, she took part in the 2006 Winter Olympics in Turin, winning another gold in the combined event and silver in the Super-G to become the most successful female skier in Olympic history. Her brother Ivica also got in on the act, taking silver in the men's combined event.

Basketball Giant

The great propensity of the Croats to grow tall gives them a considerable advantage when it comes to basketball, and no one made better use of his height than the 195cm (6ft 5in) Dražen Petrović (1964–93), a legendary player who has achieved iconic status since his death in a car crash at the age of 28. Born in Šibenik, Petrović first made his name playing for Cibona of Zagreb, where he once scored an astounding 112 points in a single game. Later he represented the Portland Blazers and the New Jersey Nets in the American NBA (National Basketball Association) and led Croatia to a silver medal in the 1992 Olympics, behind the USA 'Dream Team'. Petrović is still idolized by fans in Zagreb, and the Cibona stadium is named after him. He was posthumously admitted to the Basketball Hall of Fame and is honoured with a memorial in the Olympic park at Lausanne, in Switzerland.

Polo and sailing are popular celebrity pursuits (below)

A view from the scenic Bol to Murvica road, Brač (above). Goran Ivanišević and Tanja Dragović on Hvar Island in 2005 (right)

Adriatic Jet Set

With over a thousand uninhabited islands, Croatia's Adriatic coastline is perfect for escaping the attentions of the paparazzi, especially if you are rich enough to have your own private yacht. In recent years it has become the destination of choice for royalty, film stars and A-list celebrities seeking Mediterranean seclusion. Hollywood actor John Malkovich has been spotted cruising the Adriatic from his villa near Dubrovnik; fellow star Sharon Stone is rumoured to be eyeing up an island, and Princess Caroline of Monaco already owns an island off the Istrian coast. Billionaire soccer club owner Roman Abramovich attracted admiring glances when he moored his luxury yacht off Lokrum in summer 2005.

Anyone for Polo?

The Brijuni islands (▷ 86–87) off the west coast of Istria have been attracting the rich and famous since becoming the favoured resort of the Habsburg aristocracy in the dying days of the Austro-Hungarian empire. During the Communist era Brijuni was Tito's private retreat, where he entertained movie stars appearing at the Pula Film Festival, such as Richard Burton, Elizabeth Taylor and Sophia Loren. In an attempt to revive Brijuni's exclusive image, Italian fashion house Brioni reintroduced the sport of polo in 2004, after a 70-year absence. The Brioni Polo Classic is now an annual event, with specially imported polo ponies and guests arriving by yacht and private jet. Brijuni has recovered its cachet and is once again the place to be seen in Croatia in summer.

The Right Formula

Bernie Ecclestone (born 1930), Formula One motor-racing supremo, and his Croatian wife Slavica Malić (born 1958), a former Armani model, regularly spend summers in Croatia, cruising the Adriatic on their luxury yacht. In 2001 they flew Wimbledon champion Goran Ivanišević (▷ 15) in their private plane on his triumphant return to his home town of Split.

The Story
of Croatia

At the Crossroads of *Empires*

The partition of the Roman empire into east and west in AD395 redrew the map of the Balkans, creating a fault line which still exists today as the boundary of the Catholic and Orthodox worlds. When Slavic tribes migrated to the Balkans in the 7th century the Croats settled on the coast, while the Serbs occupied the interior. Croatia's golden age began in 925, when Tomislav was crowned its first king, and ended with the death of King Zvonimir in 1089. According to legend, Zvonimir was murdered by Croat nobles, and swore on his deathbed that Croatia would be ruled by foreigners for a thousand years. After entering a union with Hungary in 1102, Croatia spent the next eight centuries torn between powerful neighbours, with Austria-Hungary to the north, Ottoman Turkey to the south and Venice, which controlled much of Istria, Kvarner and Dalmatia, to the west. The Habsburg emperors formed the Vojna Krajina (Military Frontier) and recruited Serb soldiers from Bosnia to defend it against the Turks—a decision that was to have far-reaching consequences as it established the presence of a large Serbian minority in Croatia.

Ragusa

Medieval Dubrovnik was the republic of Ragusa (1358–1808), a city state with a fleet to rival Venice and possessions stretching from Lastovo to the Bay of Kator. Wealth bought freedom, paying Turkish, Hungarian and Austrian rulers to leave it alone, and artists, mathematicians, poets, philosophers, architects and playwrights all flourished here. The nominal ruler, the rector, elected each month by all male nobles, was confined to the Rector's Palace during his term of office. Ragusa was abolished and taken into the French Illyrian prov-inces by Napoleon, then ceded to Austria in 1815. Much of the ruling class, rather than serve under a foreign power, took a vow of celibacy.

The Minčeta Tower, part of Dubrovnik's fortifications (right)

AD395

Statue of Tomislav in Zagreb (top).
Roman amphitheatre at Pula (right).
The historic walled city of Dubrovnik (below)

A Feudal Conspiracy

During the Middle Ages, power, wealth and influence in Croatia rested in the hands of two aristocratic families, granted large estates by the Hungarian and Austrian kings as a reward for military service against the Turks. The Frankopan and Zrinski families supplied several Croatian *bans* (governors) and owned more than 40 castles, from Krk to the Hungarian border. Related by marriage, the two dynasties died out at the same time after a conspiracy by Petar Zrinski (1621–71) and his brother-in-law Fran Krsto Frankopan (1643–71) against the Austrian emperor. When the plot was discovered the two men were summoned to Vienna and publicly beheaded, and their properties in Croatia confiscated. In 1919 their bodies were transferred to Zagreb cathedral. The two conspirators are now proudly displayed on the 5kn banknote. In 2002, a family claiming to be descendants of the Frankopans signed a contract allowing them to return to one of their castles near Karlovac.

Renaissance Man

The 19th century saw a flowering of Croatian language, arts and literature in the movement known as the Croatian National Revival, accompanied by growing political support for Croatian independence. A key figure was Josip Juraj Strossmayer (1815–1905), bishop of his home diocese of Đakovo for 55 years until his death. As leader of the National Party from 1860 to 1873, he advocated *Jugoslavenstvo*—the unity of all southern Slavs, including Croats and Serbs, within the Austro-Hungarian empire. In the light of what has happened since, this may seem an idea doomed to failure, but at the time many Croats saw an alliance with Serbia as the best way of standing up to Vienna. Strossmayer saw no conflict between Croatian nationalism and support for the concept of Yugoslavia. As well as being a priest and politician, he was an art collector and lover of Lipizzaner horses and fine wine. He also spoke several languages fluently and helped to found the University of Zagreb.

Slavic Script

One notable feature of the early Croatian state was the use of the Glagolitic script, devised in the 9th century by Macedonian brothers Cyril and Methodius to present the scriptures in the Slavic languages of the Croats and Serbs. Based on the ancient Greek alphabet, it featured around 40 characters in intricate geometric forms. The 10th-century bishop of Nin, Grgur Ninski, clashed repeatedly with the Pope after Ninski championed the use of the Glagolitic alphabet and Croatian language to replace Latin in church. Glagolitic was widely used in Istria and Kvarner, where it survived as recently as the 19th century. It was also the forerunner of the Cyrillic alphabet, still used in Serbia and Macedonia today. There is a permanent exhibition of Glagolitic writings in the university library at Rijeka (▷ 110).

Glagolitic script on a tablet in Roč (right)

1918

Women wearing traditional Croatian dress in Dubrovnik (left). Statue of Jelačić on Trg Bana Jelačića in Zagreb (below)

Brotherhood and Disunity

World War I began in the Balkans with the assassination of Austrian Archduke Franz Ferdinand by a Serb gunman in the Bosnian capital Sarajevo. Thus Croatia entered the war on the Austro-Hungarian side, but there was a growing southern Slav consciousness and many Croats saw their future with Serbia. When the Habsburg empire collapsed in 1918 Croatia entered the Kingdom of Serbs, Croats and Slovenes under the Serbian monarch in Belgrade. Despite becoming Yugoslavia (Land of the Southern Slavs) in 1929, the kingdom was effectively run by Serbs. In 1934, on a visit to France, King Aleksandar was assassinated by Croatian nationalists of the Fascist Ustaše movement. In 1941 Yugoslavia was invaded by Germany and Italy, who established a puppet regime in Croatia under Ustaše leader Ante Pavelić. The Ustaše were opposed both by royalist Serbian Chetniks and Tito's Partisan liberation army, which gained control of Yugoslavia in 1945. After Tito's death in 1980 Yugoslavia fell apart as Slobodan Milošević (1941–2006) fought disastrous wars in Croatia, Bosnia and Kosovo in his quest for a Greater Serbia.

Tito's Yugoslavia

Born in Kumrovec, Josip Broz Tito (1892–1980) had a Croatian father and a Slovenian mother. Joining the Austro-Hungarian military as a conscript, he was imprisoned by the Russians, and, inspired by Bolshevik ideals, fought with the Red Army on his release. Returning to Yugoslavia, he rose rapidly through the Communist Party and, after leading the Partisans to victory in 1945, became president for life. He formed six socialist republics, linked by the slogan 'brotherhood and unity', and his unique form of communism rejected both western capitalism and the Soviet model. Tito held Yugoslavia together for 35 years; a measure of his achievement is that after his death, brotherhood and unity quickly gave way.

Tito's photograph in the Tito Museum, Brijuni (left)

1918

Bronze sculpture by Meštrović in Zagreb (top)

Ivan Generalić's self portrait in the Naive Art Museum, Zagreb (above)

The Ustaše

The occupying powers in World War II set up the NDH (Independent State of Croatia), ostensibly a Croatian nationalist regime but really a puppet state of Nazi Germany, with Ustaše leader Ante Pavelić as Poglavnik (Führer). It encompassed most of present-day Croatia and Bosnia-Herzegovina, but the Dalmatian coast was largely ceded to Italy. The Ustaše unleashed a reign of terror across Croatia, with thousands of Serbs and Jews murdered at concentration camps such as Jasenovac (▷ 63). It was official policy to eliminate Serbs from Croatia by deporting a third, killing a third and converting the rest to Catholicism. The spectre of the Ustaše continues to haunt politics here, and accounts for the fear felt by many Croatian Serbs at the revival of Croatian nationalism. President Franjo Tuđman (▷ 23) was accused of rehabilitating the Ustaše and pandering to extremist sympathies when he questioned the number of deaths at Jasenovac and allowed the return of Ustaše insignia.

Ivan Meštrović

Talented Ivan Meštrović (1883–1962) was undeniably one of the greatest sculptors of the 20th century. At the age of 15 he was apprenticed to a stonemason in Split and spent much of the next two decades abroad in Vienna, Paris and Rome. Returning to Croatia, he was later imprisoned by the Ustaše and spent his final years living in exile in the USA. Meštrović worked in wood, bronze and stone, with influences ranging from Balkan history and religion to classical Greek sculpture and the work of his mentor, Auguste Rodin (1840–1917). In 1952 he presented his house and studio in Zagreb (▷ 54) and his summer villa in Split (▷ 137) to the nation. His public works include monuments to Grgur Ninski in Split (▷ 135) and Bishop Strossmayer (▷ 58) in Zagreb, as well as his family mausoleum at Otavice (▷ 128).

Sculptor Ivan Meštrović (left)

A Turbulent Priest

The Blessed Alojzije Stepinac (1898–1960) is a much-loved but deeply controversial figure. As Archbishop of Zagreb in 1941, he initially gave his blessing to the Ustaše régime, but although he continued to view the Ustaše leaders as patriots, he is said to have cried when he learnt of the horrors of Jasenovac (▷ 63) and personally intervened to save the lives of many Jews. Arrested on Tito's orders in 1946, he was charged with collaboration and sentenced to 16 years in prison. After five years in Lepoglava prison he spent the rest of his life under house arrest in Krašić (▷ 63) and is buried in Zagreb Cathedral. In 1952 Pope Pius XII appointed Stepinac a cardinal, causing Tito to break diplomatic relations with the Vatican. Beatified in 1998, he is revered by many Croats, though questions remain about the role of the church during the war and its links with the Ustaše régime.

1991

Franz Ferdinand and his wife lie in state after their assassination (below left)

Dr. Pavelić with members of the Ustaše youth in 1941 (left)

Alojzije Stepinac (right)

War and Peace

In 1990 the first multi-party elections for over 50 years resulted in victory for Franjo Tuđman's HDZ (Croatian Democratic Union). Alarmed by Tuđman's nationalist rhetoric, Croatia's minority Serb population began organizing resistance, supported by the Yugoslav army. When Croatia declared independence from Yugoslavia in 1991, rebel Serbs established the Republic of the Serbian Krajina at Knin. Soon, almost a third of Croatia was in Serbian hands, including a swathe of Northern Dalmatia, cutting road and rail links between Zagreb and Split and leaving Croatia's unity dependent on a ferry crossing from Pag. Croats were murdered or driven from their homes in an operation known as *etničko čišćenje* (ethnic cleansing). Serbs living in Croatian areas were subject to revenge attacks and the fighting escalated into all-out war, with at least 10,000 killed between 1991 and 1995. The Homeland War ended in August 1995, when Croatian forces led by Ante Gotovina captured the Krajina in Operation Oluja (Storm) and over 200,000 Serbs fled across the border, but parts of Slavonia remained under UN control and were only returned to Croatia in 1998.

The Battle for Vukovar

One of the first acts of the Homeland War was the massacre of 12 Croatian policemen by Serbian paramilitaries in the Vukovar suburb of Borovo Selo in May 1991. From August to November, this small town was besieged by the Yugoslav army, with a volunteer force of under 2,000 trying to hold out against at least 40,000 troops, 600 tanks and 100 planes. During the three-month battle at least 2,000 Croat civilians were killed, along with many Serbian soldiers. The most shocking incident occurred a day after the fall of the town, when 200 wounded were taken from Vukovar hospital and executed in a field before being buried in a mass grave at Ovčara.

Yugoslav tanks on the move (left)

1991

Minefield warning sign (top).
Detail of Croatian Parliament plaque,
Zagreb (below)

The Siege of Dubrovnik

The war in Croatia came to the world's attention through television footage of shells raining down on the medieval walls in Dubrovnik. From October 1991 to May 1992 the city came under constant attack from the Yugoslav army, aided by Montenegrin reservists and Bosnian Serbs from the nearby hills. Around 80 per cent of houses in the old town took direct hits, 45 bombs landed on Stradun and over 80 civilians were killed. Many people retreated to their cellars, without adequate food, water or electricity. Unlike other key battlegrounds in Croatia, Dubrovnik had no significant Serbian minority and was of no obvious strategic interest. There has long been suspicion that both sides manipulated the siege of Dubrovnik for their own ends. The Serbs saw it as a chance to destroy Croatia's tourist industry and strike at a powerful historic and cultural symbol; the Croats used it as an opportunity to rally international opinion to the defence of a World Heritage city.

Father of the Nation

Croatia's war leader was Dr. Franjo Tuđman (1922–99), who, as the first president of independent Croatia, is widely seen as the father of the nation. A former Communist who fought with the Partisans and became a general in Tito's army, he was later expelled from the party and imprisoned for anti-Yugoslav activity. By 1990 he had emerged as a hardline nationalist, famously declaring during the election campaign:'I am glad that my wife is neither a Serb nor a Jew.' He was criticized for his authoritarian tendencies and his role in the Bosnian war, but he is still a hero to many Croats—though had he lived, it is likely that he would have ended up in the dock in The Hague, on trial for war crimes alongside his old adversary Slobodan Milošević.

Franjo Tuđman (left)

A Dentist from Knin

Milan Babić (1956–2006) was a provincial dentist whose Serbian parents were nearly murdered by a Croatian Ustaše neighbour before he was born. In 1990 he was elected President of the Municipal Assembly of Knin and leader of the Serbian Democratic Party. He became president of the Republic of the Serbian Krajina and one of the architects of the ethnic cleansing of Croatian villages. In 1995 he fled to become a chicken farmer in Belgrade. Seven years later he surrendered to the international war crimes tribunal at The Hague, testifying in court against his former mentor Slobodan Milošević. Babić is one of the few convicted war criminals to show remorse, telling the tribunal he felt a 'deep sense of shame' and begging his 'brother Croats' to forgive him. 'These crimes and my participation in them can never be justified,' he said. Jailed for 13 years for crimes against humanity, he committed suicide in 2006.

1999

Milošević at the Elysée Palace in 1995 (right).
Milan Babić on trial in The Hague (below)

Vukovar suffered severe damage from Yugoslav shelling in 1991 (left)

WAR AND PEACE 23

Into the Future

Croatian politics has settled down since the death of President Tuđman, with the parties campaigning on the economy and taxation rather than nationalism. Nevertheless, the government's cooperation with the UN war crimes tribunal remains a source of controversy, with many Croats accusing leaders of betraying national heroes for the sake of international acceptance. In 2003 the former Communist Ivica Račan of the Social Democratic Party was replaced as prime minister by Ivo Sanader of the HDZ, who has led his party away from nationalism toward mainstream European Christian democracy. Talks with the European Union met delays in 2005 over the failure to arrest Ante Gotovina (▷ right), but Croatia is on course to join the EU and NATO around 2010.

A Mesić of Peace

If Franjo Tuđman was a natural war leader, Stjepan (Stipe) Mesić, president of Croatia since 2000, is the man for peace. A former Communist mayor, he was actually the last president of Yugoslavia before it collapsed in 1991. In 1994 he split with Tuđman over the war in Bosnia-Herzegovina, and formed the Croatian People's Party. Elected as president following Tuđman's death, he was branded a traitor by nationalists for being a witness at The Hague. He has also encouraged the return of Serbian refugees. Re-elected for a second five-year term in 2005, Mesić hopes to crown his presidency by leading Croatia into the EU.

Hero or Villain?

The arrest of General Ante Gotovina (born 1955) on the Spanish island of Tenerife in December 2005 brought crowds onto the streets in Croatia. To many Croats, especially veterans of the Homeland War, he is regarded as a patriotic hero who liberated Croatia from Serbian aggression. To prosecutors at The Hague, he is a war criminal who allowed his troops to murder and deport Croatian Serbs during Operation Storm in 1995. The arrest highlighted the dilemmas for the Croatian government in its dealings with the war crimes tribunal, as it attempts to tread a delicate balance between international obligations and public opinion. In 2006 a Croatian film director announced plans to make a movie (with the lead role played by his son-in-law Goran Višnjić, star of the television drama *ER*) about General Gotovina.

2000–Today

Ivo Sanader at the UN (left).
Ivica Račan in 2001 (above).
Stjepan Mesić is sworn in (right)

On the Move

ARRIVING

Arriving by Air

Croatia is well served by flights from other European countries, with major international airports at Zagreb, Split and Dubrovnik having flights all year. Pula, Rijeka and Zadar airports are busiest in summer, with many charter flights and a growing number of budget airlines. All airports have facilities including currency exchange, ATMs and car hire, while bigger terminals at Zagreb, Split and Dubrovnik have banks, post offices, cafés and shops. There is also an airport at Osijek, mostly for domestic flights, and international airfields on Brač and Lošinj, used by smaller planes.

SCHEDULED FLIGHTS
The national carrier, Croatia Airlines, flies to Zagreb from major European cities including Amsterdam, Berlin, Brussels, Frankfurt, London, Milan, Munich, Paris, Rome, Sarajevo, Vienna and Zurich. It also operates connecting flights from Zagreb to regional airports, and direct international services to Pula, Rijeka, Split and Dubrovnik in summer (tel 020 8563 0022, UK; www.croatiaairlines.hr).

From the UK, British Airways flies from Gatwick and Manchester to Dubrovnik and from Gatwick to Split. Other airlines with direct flights from Europe include Aer Lingus, Air France, Alitalia, Austrian Airlines, CSA, KLM, Lufthansa, Malev and SAS.

There are currently no direct flights to Croatia from North America. Travellers from outside Europe should fly to a European city such as London and pick up a connecting flight.

BUDGET AIRLINES
The low-cost airline revolution has reached

GETTING INTO CITIES FROM THE AIRPORT			
AIRPORT	**ZAGREB (ZAG)**	**PULA (PUY)**	**RIJEKA (RJK)**
INFORMATION	Tel 01 456 2222 www.zagreb-airport.hr	Tel 052 530105 www.airport-pula.hr	Tel 051 842132 www.rijeka-airport.hr
LOCATION	15km (9.5 miles) south of Zagreb at Pleso	8km (5 miles) northeast of Pula	30km (19 miles) south of Rijeka on the island of Krk
BY BUS	Croatia Airlines shuttle buses depart every 30–60 minutes from 7am–8pm, with later buses linked to flight arrival times. The bus terminates at Zagreb's main bus station, from where tram 6 goes to the city centre. Journey time: 30 minutes Price: 30kn	None	Autorolej buses meet incoming flights for the transfer to Jelačićev Trg in the city centre. Journey time: 40 minutes Price: 25kn
BY TAXI	Approximately 200kn to downtown Zagreb	Approximately 80kn to city centre	Approximately 250kn to city centre

Croatia, with a growing number of budget carriers operating flights, particularly to the coastal airports in summer. Routes change with the seasons and prices vary from day to day, so you should shop around online for the best deals or look on an internet search engine such as www.skyscanner.net

Budget airlines flying to Croatia from the UK include Easyjet from Bristol and Luton to Rijeka and Gatwick to Split; Flybe from Birmingham to Dubrovnik and Split; Fly Globespan from Edinburgh and Glasgow to Pula; and Wizz Air from Luton to Split and Zagreb. European budget airlines to Croatia include German Wings and Hapag Lloyd

The arrivals hall at Zagreb airport (above)

BUDGET AIRLINES WEBSITES	
Easyjet	www.easyjet.com
Flybe	www.flybe.com
Fly Globespan	www.flyglobespan.com
German Wings	www.germanwings.com
Hapag Lloyd Express	www.hlx.com
Norwegian Air Shuttle	www.norwegian.no
Ryanair	www.ryanair.com
Sky Europe	www.skyeurope.com
SN Brussels	www.flysn.com
Wizz Air	www.wizzair.com

ZADAR (ZAD)	SPLIT (SPU)	DUBROVNIK (DBV)
Tel 023 205800 www.zadar-airport.hr	Tel 021 203555 www.split-airport.hr	Tel 020 773377 www.airport-dubrovnik.hr
8km (5 miles) southeast of Zadar	25km (16 miles) west of Split near Trogir	20km (12 miles) south of Dubrovnik at Čilipi
Croatia Airlines shuttle buses coincide with flight arrival times for the transfer to the city bus station and ferry port. Journey time: 15 minutes Price: 25kn	Croatia Airlines shuttle buses coincide with flight arrival times. The bus terminates at the east end of the Riva, close to the ferry port. Journey time: 30 minutes Price: 30kn Local bus 37 from Trogir runs every 20 minutes throughout the day, passing the airport on its way to Split. Journey time: 45 minutes Price: 15kn	Croatia Airlines and Atlas shuttle buses coincide with flight arrival times. The buses terminate at the main bus station at Gruž, and also stop by the entrance to the old town at Pile Gate. Journey time: 30 minutes Price: 35kn
Approximately 100kn to city centre	Approximately 250kn to city centre	Approximately 200kn to Dubrovnik and 100kn to Cavtat

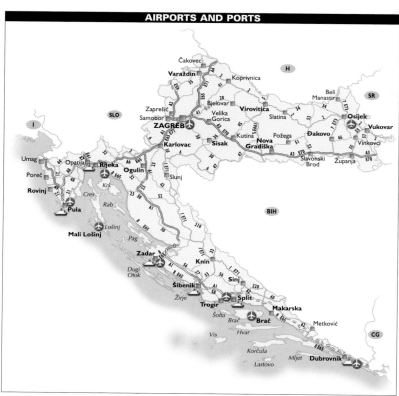

AIRPORTS AND PORTS

ON THE MOVE

Express from Germany; SN Brussels from Belgium; Norwegian Air Shuttle from Norway; and Sky Europe from Hungary, Poland, the Czech Republic and Slovakia. This list is likely to grow significantly over the next few years, so watch for new airlines and routes.

Europe's largest budget airline, Ryanair flies from London Stansted to Pula and usually offers the cheapest fares on flights from Stansted to Italy's Adriatic coast. You can fly to Ancona, Bari, Pescara,

Trieste or Venice and continue by ferry or bus.

CHARTER FLIGHTS
During the busy summer season tour operators have charter flights to Croatia from a number of regional airports across Europe. Although many of the seats are booked by the tour operators for passengers on their package holidays, it is often possible to buy seat-only tickets on these flights. Among the major operators of charter flights to Croatia are Holiday Options and Thomson in the UK.

Arriving by Sea

The many ferry services linking Croatia to Italy across the Adriatic Sea are a convenient option for travellers driving across Europe or those taking budget flights to Italy. Most ferry ports are right in the city centre, and standing on deck watching the ship sail into the harbour is undoubtedly the most romantic way to arrive in Croatia. Main year-round routes are Ancona to Zadar, Ancona to Split and Bari to Dubrovnik. Additional seasonal services include fast ferries from Venice to Istria in summer.

CAR FERRIES

Jadrolinija has overnight car and passenger ferries from Ancona to Zadar (8 hours), Ancona to Split (10 hours) and Bari to Dubrovnik (8 hours). In summer there are also services from Pescara to Split (6–12 hours), Pescara to Stari Grad (9 hours), Ancona to Stari Grad (12 hours) and Ancona to Korčula (15 hours). These ferries link with the main Jadrolinija coastal route between Rijeka and Dubrovnik.

SEM Blueline operates year-round car ferries from Ancona to Split, with seasonal services to Stari Grad and Vis. Car ferries are also run by Azzurra Line to Dubrovnik from Bari. From June to September both Sanmar and SNAV offer high-speed jetfoil services from Pescara to Stari Grad (3.5 hours) and Split (5 hours). SNAV also run catamarans from Ancona to Split (4.5 hours), much faster than traditional car ferries, but you can't go on deck.

PASSENGER FERRIES

In summer Venezia Lines operates high-speed catamarans from Venice to Pula, Poreč, Rovinj, Rabac, Opatija and Mali Lošinj, with sailing times of between 2 and 4 hours. Mostly for pedestrians, it is possible to take cars and motorcycles on the routes from Venice to Pula and Rovinj. This company has passenger services from Rimini to Pula, Poreč and Mali Lošinj, and from Ravenna to Poreč.

Emilia Romagna offers high-speed catamarans in summer from the Italian ports of Pesaro, Ravenna and Rimini to Pula, Rovinj, Mali Lošinj, Hvar and Dugi Otok. Mia Tours operates fast boats in summer from Ancona to Zadar and Hvar.

PRACTICALITIES

● Foot passengers can usually buy tickets on arrival, but for vehicles, particularly at peak times, it is best to book, direct with the company or at www.traghettionline.net.
● Large car ferries have a full range of facilities: restaurants, bars, shops cabins, reclining seats and couchettes.
● The port at Dubrovnik is at Gruž, 4km (2.5 miles) west of the old town; take bus 1A or 1B to Pile.

USEFUL TELEPHONE NUMBERS AND WEBSITES		
FERRY COMPANY	TELEPHONE	WEBSITE
Jadrolinija	+385 051 666111	www.jadrolinija.hr
SEM Blueline	+385 021 352553	www.bli-ferry.com
Azzurra Line	+39 080 592 8400	www.azzurraline.com
Sanmar	+39 085 451 0873	www.sanmar.it
SNAV	+39 071 207 6116	www.snav.it
Venezia Lines	+39 041 242 4000	www.venezialines.com
Emilia Romagna	+39 054 767 5157	www.emiliaromagnalines.it
Mia Tours	+385 023 254300	www.miatours.hr

Arriving by Land

ON THE MOVE

Croatia shares land borders with Slovenia, Hungary, Bosnia-Herzegovina, Serbia and Montenegro. The majority of border crossings are open 24 hours a day. Travellers arriving from Slovenia and Hungary can expect minimal delays at the border, but be prepared for long delays and extensive checks of paperwork if entering from Bosnia, Serbia or Montenegro.

BY CAR

Drivers entering Croatia must show their driver's licence, car registration documents and insurance certificate (green card). International driving licences are not valid in Croatia, but EU and other national driver's licences are valid for six months. If you are bringing your own car or motorcycle, it is essential to arrange insurance and obtain the relevant documents from your insurance company before you leave home.

If you hire a car outside Croatia you will need to show rental documents at the border. It is important to check that the insurance covers Croatia. Because of the number of visitors arriving in Croatia via low-cost flights to Italy, car rental agencies in Trieste and Venice are used to this situation and will usually stamp your documents at no extra cost to confirm that your insurance is valid in Croatia. If you book online be sure to read the small print regarding insurance in other countries.

It is compulsory for all drivers to carry a first-aid kit, warning triangle, reflective jacket and set of replacement bulbs. You are also strongly advised to carry snow chains in winter, particularly if travelling in mountain and highland regions. Car hire companies usually supply these at no extra charge.

Before arriving you should familiarize yourself with the section on Driving in Croatia (▷ 32–35) as some regulations differ from neighbouring countries. In particular, all drivers should be aware that dipped (low beam) headlights are compulsory at all times and that driving with any alcohol in the system is strictly forbidden.

Roadside assistance and repairs are available from the Hrvatski Autoklub 24 hours a day by calling 987. A charge is made for this service. Alternatively, take out European breakdown cover before you leave home with an organization like the Automobile Association (AA). Car hire firms provide their own breakdown/rescue service.

BY BUS

Croatia is served by international bus services from across Europe. Most buses arrive at the central bus station in Zagreb. There are also daily services from the Italian city of Trieste to Poreč, Pula, Rovinj, Opatija, Rijeka, Zadar, Split and Dubrovnik. Travellers to Croatia can fly to Trieste, take a local bus from the airport to the city bus station and pick up a connection from there.

BY TRAIN

There are direct rail links to Zagreb from Budapest, Ljubljana, Munich, Venice and Vienna, and indirect links from other European cities. The Inter Rail and Eurail passes are valid for journeys both to and within Croatia. Border formalities are completed on the train.

EMERGENCY TELEPHONE NUMBERS	
Police	92
Fire	93
Ambulance	94
All emergencies	112
Roadside assistance	987 (+385 1 987 from a mobile phone)

GETTING AROUND

Croatia has a comprehensive and well-integrated public transportation network. Bus and train stations in the main towns and cities are generally close together, and buses also link with ferry timetables, making it easy to switch from one mode of transport to another. Most of the sights in this book are accessible by public transport, but to get the most out of your visit, consider hiring a car to explore the countryside, national parks and out-of-the-way areas.

BY CAR

Driving in Croatia is mostly straightforward once you have got used to the cavalier attitude to overtaking (passing) of many Croatian drivers. Speed limits and the ban on drink-driving are strictly enforced by the police, so stick to the law whatever the locals do. Much of the time the roads are pleasantly free of traffic, though major routes to the Adriatic coast get clogged up on summer weekends and the single-lane Magistrala coast road is a nightmare in July and August. New motorways from Zagreb to Rijeka and Split have reduced journey times to the coast and linked Croatia into the European route network. Although motorways are less scenic than many of the alternatives, they are also much faster and the volume of traffic regulated by the high cost of tolls.

BY BUS

Buses are the most common form of public transport in Croatia, and range from luxury air-conditioned vehicles on inter-city and long-

distance routes to rickety old buses linking remote villages. A plethora of private companies cover virtually the entire country. It is possible to get just about anywhere by bus, though you may need to change buses along the way and some remote destinations are served very infrequently. Bus journeys between the mainland and the islands include travel by ferry. Larger cities such as Zagreb, Split, Dubrovnik, Rijeka and Osijek have their own municipal bus and tram services.

BY TRAIN

Croatia's rail network is concentrated in the north and east of the country. There are no trains to

Dubrovnik and few trains to other coastal cities. Train travel in inland Croatia is safe and comfortable, but tends to be slower than the equivalent journey by bus.

BY FERRY

The only way to reach the outlying islands is by ferry. Most ferries are operated by Jadrolinija, together with various local companies. Car and passenger ferries run throughout the year, with extra services in summer. During the peak holiday months of July and August long lines build up at the ferry ports so it is essential to arrive in good time if you plan to take a car on the ferry.

ORGANIZED TOURS

Local tour operators in the main towns and resorts offer a wide variety of organized excursions. Although these invariably work out more expensive than doing your own thing, they make a good alternative to public transport if you want to visit remote areas, such as the Plitvice Lakes, without hiring a car.

Driving in Croatia

Driving is the quickest and easiest method of travelling around Croatia, and the only way to reach remote villages and mountain areas. Roads vary from well-maintained motorways (highways) to dirt roads.

ON THE MOVE

BRINGING YOUR OWN VEHICLE

Before bringing your car or motorcycle to Croatia, ensure that it is properly serviced and that you have adequate insurance and breakdown cover. For more details, see Arriving By Land (▷ 30).

CAR RENTAL

● International car rental chains have offices at airports, ports and city centres. You will also find local companies in main towns and resorts. Rental can be arranged through travel agents and hotels.

● It is usually cheaper to book in advance. The best deals are available online, through websites or at www.holidayautos.com. Definitely book in advance if you need a car for the duration of your visit or want to collect it on arrival at the airport. If you only want a car for a few days, it may be better to wait until you arrive, when you have a better idea of where you want to go.

● Extras such as child seats, luggage racks and snow chains should be booked in advance.

● You will need to show a passport, national driver's licence and credit card. The credit card deposit will be used as security in case you return the vehicle damaged or without fuel.

● The minimum age is usually 21, or 25 for larger vehicles, and you must have held a valid licence for at least two years.

● Check that you have adequate insurance. Your rental agreement should include the minimum legal requirements for third-party insurance, but you are strongly advised to take out CDW (collision damage waiver) and theft protection. Without these, you will be liable for the full repair or replacement

cost in the event of accident or theft.

● Insurance policies usually include an excess of around €400, meaning that you will pay the first part of any claim. You may be offered a waiver for an additional payment.

● If you plan to drive into neighbouring countries, make sure the insurance covers you for this. Some policies exclude driving in Serbia and Montenegro. If you rent a car outside Croatia, check that the insurance is valid in Croatia and get confirmation of this on the rental documents.

● Check the condition of the vehicle before driving it and get the rental company to note damage.

● Check the procedure for returning the car. Most companies have designated parking at airports. Always return the keys and documents to the office inside the airport—never to anyone in the car park (parking lot) claiming to be an employee of the car rental company.

SPEED LIMITS

● 50kph (31mph) in built-up areas
● 90kph (56mph) outside built-up areas
● 110kph (68mph) on expressways
● 130kph (80mph) on motorways

- Most cars are supplied with a full tank of fuel and should be returned full.
- Always keep your passport, driver's licence and rental documents with you; never leave them unattended in the car.

RULES OF THE ROAD

- Drive on the right and overtake (pass) on the left.
- At roundabouts give way to cars from the left.
- The minimum driving age is 18.
- Children under 12 must sit in a rear seat.
- It is illegal to use a mobile phone while driving.
- Dipped (low beam) headlights must be on at all times.
- The driver and all passengers must wear safety belts.
- Moped and motorcycle drivers and passengers must wear safety helmets.
- Speed limits (▷ 32) are strictly enforced. There is a minimum speed limit of 40kph (25mph) on motorways.
- Croatia's drink-driving laws are the strictest in Europe. The regulation zero percentage of alcohol in the blood means that it is illegal to drive after even low consumption of alcohol. Never drink and drive, and allow at least 24 hours for any alcohol to leave the system.
- The police can impose fixed on-the-spot fines, ranging from 300kn for driving without headlights to 3,000kn for speeding or drink-driving. Fines must be paid into a bank within eight days and the police may hold your passport until you do so.

DRIVING DISTANCES

The chart below shows the distances in kilometres of a car journey between key destinations in Croatia.

	Đakovo	Dubrovnik	Karlovac	Knin	Makarska	Nova Gradiška	Ogulin	Osijek	Pula	Rijeka	Rovinj	Šibenik	Sinj	Sisak	Split	Trogir	Varaždin	Virovitica	Vukovar	Zadar
Dubrovnik	850																			
Karlovac	297	553																		
Knin	540	310	243																	
Makarska	684	166	387	144																
Nova Gradiška	104	705	195	395	539															
Ogulin	342	540	45	230	374	240														
Osijek	37	887	334	577	721	125	379													
Pula	527	703	230	388	537	425	206	564												
Rijeka	421	597	124	282	431	319	100	458	106											
Rovinj	512	688	215	373	522	410	191	549	43	91										
Šibenik	596	288	299	56	122	451	286	633	431	325	416									
Sinj	605	245	308	65	79	460	295	642	453	347	438	80								
Sisak	202	605	95	295	439	100	140	239	325	219	310	351	360							
Split	634	228	337	94	62	489	324	671	475	369	460	60	29	389						
Trogir	634	250	317	74	84	489	324	671	460	354	445	38	51	369	22					
Varaždin	218	683	130	373	517	200	175	235	360	254	345	429	438	145	467	447				
Virovitica	110	724	214	414	558	113	259	127	444	338	429	657	666	119	695	695	108			
Vukovar	52	902	349	592	736	156	394	35	579	473	564	648	657	254	686	686	270	162		
Zadar	530	369	233	102	203	385	188	567	327	221	312	71	154	285	145	113	363	447	582	
Zagreb	248	603	50	293	437	150	95	285	280	174	265	349	358	65	387	367	80	165	306	283

Fuel station in Novi Vinodolski (above)

CAR RENTAL AGENCIES		
NAME	**TELEPHONE**	**WEBSITE**
Avis	062 222226	www.avis.com.hr
Budget	01 480 5688	www.budget.hr
Europcar	01626 5008	www.europcar.hr
Hertz	01 456 2635	www.hertz.hr
National	01 6215924	www.nationalcar.hr
Sixt	01 665 1599	www.sixt.hr

TOLL FEES	
Zagreb–Varaždin	23kn
Zagreb–Rijeka	56kn
Zagreb–Zadar	105kn
Zagreb–Split	157kn
Krk bridge	30kn
Mirna bridge	14kn
Učka tunnel	28kn
(All prices correct as of August 2006)	

MAJOR ROUTES
Motorways (Highways)
● Croatia has a rapidly developing system of motorways (*autoceste*) linked into the European route network. All have at least two traffic lanes plus an emergency lane in each direction. Overhead electronic signs display traffic information, such as temperature, wind velocity and temporary speed limits. There are regular service areas (*odmorište*).

● The A1 motorway, also known as the Dalmatina, connects Zagreb with Split (380km/236 miles). Completed in 2005, it is a remarkable feat of engineering, with two tunnels of around 5.6km (3.5 miles) beneath the Velebit and Mala Kapela mountains. It will extend south to Ploče by 2008 and Dubrovnik by 2012.

● The A3 motorway runs west from Zagreb to the Slovenian border and east to the Serbian border. This is the Croatian section of the Autocesta, the major route across the former Yugoslavia, linking Zagreb with Ljubljana and Belgrade. It forms part of European route E70.

● Other motorways include the A2 from Zagreb to the Slovenian border via Krapina; A4 from Zagreb to the Hungarian border via Varaždin; and A6 from Zagreb to Rijeka. The A7 links Rijeka with the Slovenian border at Rupa and will soon join the A1.

● The A8 and A9 form the 'Istrian ypsilon', a Y-shaped motorway network linking Rijeka, Pula and Slovenia.

● Projects under way include a motorway from Zagreb to Sisak, and a north–south motorway across Slavonia linking Hungary and Bosnia via Osijek and Đakovo.

Main Roads
● The D1 is the old main road from Zagreb to Split via Karlovac, the Plitvice Lakes, Knin and Sinj. This follows a scenic route through the Lika and Krajina regions, but is single-lane each way.

● The D2 runs across northern Croatia from Varaždin to Osijek, with one lane in each direction.

● The D8, also known as the Magistrala or Adriatic Highway, follows the coast for 600km (372 miles) from Rijeka to Dubrovnik. A stunning drive, it gets very busy in summer and there are few opportunities for overtaking. It forms part of European route E65.

The Neum corridor
Between Ploče and Dubrovnik, the Magistrala

travels through a short section of Bosnia-Herzegovina for 9km (5.5 miles) around the Bosnian town of Neum. There are minimal formalities at the border, but have your passport and vehicle documents ready and check that your insurance covers you. The only way of avoiding this is to take a ferry from Ploče to Trpanj, but plans to build a bridge from Ploče to Pelješac by 2010 will make it possible to drive from Zagreb to Dubrovnik within Croatia.

Tolls

● A toll is payable on all motorways, with the exception of the southern ring road around Zagreb, which links the various parts of the motorway network together.

● Collect a ticket on entering the motorway and pay at the toll booth on exit. Tolls can be paid in Croatian kunas, euros or by major credit cards.

● The A8 and A9 in Istria are largely toll-free, except for the Učka tunnel linking Rijeka with Istria and the bridge over the River Mirna between Poreč and Novigrad.

● There is also a toll for using the road bridge between Rijeka and Krk.

ACCIDENTS AND BREAKDOWNS

● If you are involved in an accident, you must call the police. If driving a rental car, failure to get a police report will invalidate your insurance and you will be liable for the full cost of repairs.

● Hrvatski Autoklub provides a breakdown service with a fixed scale of charges. Mechanics can carry out minor repairs at the roadside or transfer you and your vehicle up to 200km (125 miles) after an accident or breakdown.

TRAFFIC INFORMATION

Hrvatski Autoklub provides a 24-hour information service (tel 01 464 0800) covering traffic and weather, ferry times and road closures.

FUEL

● Petrol (gas) stations open daily from 7am to 8pm; many stay open until 10 in summer. At motorway service areas, on main roads and in major cities, petrol stations open 24 hours.

● Most petrol stations are staffed by attendants, but some are self-service.

● Fuel includes Eurosuper 95, Superplus 98 and Eurodiesel.

● The majority of petrol stations accept payment by credit card.

PARKING

● Car parking can be a problem in towns and cities, especially between June and September. Most towns have car parking (lots) just outside the historic centre.

● On-street parking is indicated by blue lines. Pay cash at the meter and display the ticket clearly.

● You can pay parking by SMS (text message) in some cities. Send a text with your registration number without spaces to the telephone number on the meter and you will receive confirmation that your mobile phone account has been debited.

● Check the details of any parking restrictions. In some towns parking is free between October and May, while in others there is a charge all year.

● Do not be tempted to park illegally, especially in large cities. Your car will probably be towed away and the fee for getting it back will be expensive.

TIPS

● Try to avoid driving in big cities.

● There are few fuel stations on the islands, so fill up before you go.

● Carry snow chains in winter, particularly if travelling in mountain regions.

● Be suspicious of anyone indicating that you have a problem with your car, or flagging you down by the roadside, as thieves have been known to operate in this way. If you are concerned, drive on.

Buses

Long-distance bus travel in Croatia is fast, reliable and efficient, and a good way to meet local people. Modern, air-conditioned buses travel between the major cities, while local routes serve outlying towns and villages. Services are run by a variety of private companies, with competition keeping prices low and standards high.

BUYING TICKETS

● Major cities have large, central bus stations, always open, with such facilities as left luggage (baggage check), toilets and ATMs.
● Departures are usually displayed on a board. Major routes have hourly services, but some may only be served once a day or once a week.
● Buy a ticket from one of the ticket windows. The ticket should show the destination, departure time, platform and seat numbers and name of the bus company.
● At some bus stations different companies have their own ticket windows, so compare times and prices before you buy.
● Tickets are valid for a particular bus, not for the route. Round-trip tickets usually work out cheaper, but mean you must travel with the same company in both directions.
● Children under 12 usually travel for half-price and under 4s travel free, though this may vary.
● On popular routes it is worth booking your seat a day or two in advance, but this is usually only possible if you get on in the city where the bus originates.
● To join an inter-city bus at a point on its route, buy a ticket when the bus arrives or pay the driver.

PRACTICALITIES

● Smoking is banned.
● Large items of luggage go in the hold (small fee).
● Not all buses have toilets, but comfort breaks are taken every two hours.
● On journeys to islands ticket prices include the ferry crossing.

LOCAL BUSES

● Major cities have municipal bus networks, extending to the suburbs and including popular tourist routes.
● In Rijeka and Split local buses depart from a suburban bus station, not the main inter-city station.
● Tickets can be bought from the driver but may be cheaper if bought in advance from a kiosk. Tickets must be validated at the start of your journey by punching them in the machine behind the driver.

INTER-CITY ROUTES

FROM	TO	TIME	SINGLE FARE
Dubrovnik	Korčula	3 hours	85kn
Dubrovnik	Split	4 hours	120kn
Dubrovnik	Zagreb	11 hours	180kn
Pula	Rijeka	2 hours	65kn
Rijeka	Rab	3 hours	103kn
Zadar	Zagreb	4 hours	100kn
Zagreb	Osijek	4 hours	110kn
Zagreb	Samobor	30 minutes	20kn
Zagreb	Split	6 hours	90kn
Zagreb	Varaždin	2 hours	56kn

MAIN BUS STATIONS

CITY	TELEPHONE
Zagreb	060 313333
Pula	052 502997
Rijeka	060 302010
Zadar	023 211555
Split	060 327777
Dubrovnik	060 305070

Trains

Croatia's rail network was developed in the days of the Austro-Hungarian empire to link Zagreb with other parts of the empire to the north. As a result, train travel in Croatia is largely restricted to the north and east of the country, making it most useful for journeys to and from Zagreb. There are no trains to Dubrovnik, and only slow branch lines to Dalmatian coastal cities such as Šibenik and Zadar. Travelling by train is generally slower but marginally cheaper than making the equivalent journey by bus. The exception is the high-speed rail link from Zagreb to Split, with modern, well-equipped trains complete with personal headphones and laptop connections making the journey in under six hours.

WHERE TO START

The central railway station in Zagreb is a magnificent Austro-Hungarian edifice, built in 1892 as a stop on the Orient Express. Now restored, it has a currency exchange, newsagents, ATMs and left luggage (baggage check).

TRAIN AND TICKET TYPES

● *Putnički* (passenger trains) are slow trains that stop at every station. All seating is second-class, unreserved and non-smoking. The only facilities are toilets.

● *Brzi* (express) and Inter-City trains are much faster, stopping only at major stations, and usually have first- and second-class carriages, with a choice of smoking or non-smoking. Booking is recommended, and is compulsory on certain rush-hour services. Trains are modern, comfortable and have air-conditioning and toilets, with buffet cars on some trains.

● First-class tickets cost 50 per cent more than the standard second-class.

● A return fare is usually twice the cost of one-way, but a few Inter-City routes offer cheaper returns.

● Children under 12 travel half price and under 4s travel free.

● Overnight trains from Zagreb to Split you can pay extra for a berth in a sleeping car or couchette.

RAIL PASSES

● Inter Rail, available to citizens of European countries, offers unlimited second-class travel in 30 countries for up to a month. Croatia is in Zone D, together with Hungary, Poland, Slovakia, the Czech Republic, and Bosnia-Herzegovina.

● Eurail is for people living outside Europe and offers unlimited first-class travel in 25 European countries for anything from 15 days to three months. There is also a second-class option for travellers under 26.

● European residents can buy a Euro Domino pass in their home country, giving unlimited rail travel in Croatia for between three and eight days in a given calendar month. This is only worth doing if you plan to travel extensively by rail.

INFORMATION

Timetables are available at main railway stations, or contact Hrvatske Željeznice (Croatian Railways). Tel 060 333444; www.hznet.hr

GLOSSARY	
CROATIAN	**ENGLISH**
blagajna	ticket office
dolazak	arrival
odlazak	departure
putnički	slow train
vozni red	timetable

INTER-CITY ROUTES			
FROM	TO	TIME	SINGLE (SECOND-CLASS)
Zagreb	Osijek	3–4 hours	102kn
Zagreb	Split	5–6 hours	147kn
Zagreb	Varaždin	2–3 hours	50kn

Ferries

Ferries are an essential part of Croatia's transport network and the only way to reach the Adriatic islands. Car and passenger ferries run throughout the year, providing a lifeline for islanders and an enjoyable experience for visitors.

CAR FERRIES

● Most routes are operated by Jadrolinija (tel 051 666111; www.jadrolinija.hr), which has offices in Rijeka, Zadar, Split, Dubrovnik and on the major islands.

● SEM Blueline (tel 021 352553; www.splittours.hr) competes with Jadrolinija on the busy Split–Supetar route, with three ferries a day in winter and more in summer at prices around 20 per cent lower than Jadrolinija.

● In a few places, the service is provided by a local company, such as Rapska Plovidba, which runs to the island of Rab.

● The majority of routes link the islands directly with the mainland, making them less useful for island-hopping.

Exceptions are the summer service from Baška (Krk) to Lopar (Rab) and the year-round service from Korčula to Lastovo.

● Split is the major point of departure for the Dalmatian islands, with ferries to Brač, Hvar, Korčula, Lastovo, Šolta and Vis. The large, modern passenger terminal has ticket offices, toilets, parking and ATMs.

● The nearest islands to the mainland can be reached by short hops of 20–40 minutes from ports directly opposite the island. Routes include Brestova to Porozina (Cres), Jablanac to Mišnjak (Rab) and Orebić to Dominće (Korčula). In summer these provide an almost continuous roll-on, roll-off service, with

departures at least hourly during the day. Buses from Rijeka and Dubrovnik use these ferries on their way to Cres, Lošinj, Rab and Korčula.

● Jadrolinija also operates a coastal ferry from Rijeka to Dubrovnik via Split, Stari Grad and Korčula. The frequency varies from twice a week in winter to daily in summer. Boats leave Rijeka in the evening, travelling overnight to Split (10 hours) and continuing by day to Dubrovnik (20 hours).

TIMETABLES AND TICKETS

● Jadrolinija publishes timetables twice a year, covering June to September and October to May. They are available at Jadrolinija offices and ferry ports. A basic service operates all the year, with more frequent departures in summer.

● Tickets for departures from Split can be bought at the Jadrolinija ticket office inside the terminal or from kiosks outside the terminal building.

● Tickets for most island ferries can be bought at kiosks on the quayside around 30 minutes before departure.

FARES			
FROM	**TO**	**PASSENGER**	**CAR**
Baška	Lopar	37kn	225kn
Brestova	Porozina	16kn	108kn
Drvenik	Sućuraj	12kn	86kn
Dubrovnik	Lopud	15kn	n/a
Dubrovnik	Sobra	38kn	259k
Orebić	Dominće	12kn	58kn
Split	Stari Grad	38kn	259kn
Split	Supetar	28kn	127kn
Split	Vela Luka	42kn	374kn
Split	Vis	41kn	270kn

All prices correct for high season 2006

JADROLINIJA OFFICES

PORT	TELEPHONE
Rijeka	051 211444
Zadar	023 254800
Split	021 338333
Dubrovnik	020 418000
Supetar	021 631357
Stari Grad	021 765048
Korčula	020 715410
Vis	021 711032

● It is possible to buy tickets in advance, but this does not guarantee a reservation. Foot passengers can always get onto the boat, but cars must join a line. At busy times, especially in July and August, you should aim to arrive at the harbour at least two hours before departure. If the ticket office is not open, park your car in the line and wait.

● There are separate charges for passengers and vehicles, including cars, motorcycles and bicycles. You must buy a ticket for all passengers, including the driver. Children aged 3 to 12 pay half price. The cost of tickets rises by around 20 per cent between June and September.

● Tickets for the coastal route can be booked in advance. Accommodation ranges from deck passage to couchettes and private cabins. Prices are quoted in euros but can be paid in Croatian kuna. A journey from Rijeka to Dubrovnik in high season costs 250kn for deck passage and 670kn for a berth in a two-bed inside cabin with shower and toilet, plus 670kn for a car. Cabin prices include breakfast, and other meals can be booked in advance. There is a 20 per cent discount for return journeys. Foot passengers can break their journey for up to a week at no extra charge, provided their ticket is validated by the purser at each stop.

PRACTICALITIES

● Ferries on the major routes from Rijeka, Split and Dubrovnik begin embarkation 1–2 hours before sailing. Most island ferries embark around 10–15 minutes prior to departure, but it is best to arrive well before this.

● There are limited facilities at most ports. As well as a Jadrolinija ticket booth, there may be a café and newspaper kiosk.

● Most ferries have a café on board for hot and cold drinks and snacks.

The main coastal ferry from Rijeka to Dubrovnik has a full restaurant.

● Smoking is only permitted on deck.

FAST FERRIES

● Jadrolinija operates high-speed catamarans all year to the islands of Rab, Cres, Lošinj, Brač, Hvar, Korčula and Lastovo. High-speed services are also run by SEM Blueline (Split to Vis), Krilo Express (Split to Hvar and Korčula), and Atlantagent (Dubrovnik to Mljet).

● Catamarans take foot passengers only. They tend to be quicker than conventional ferries, but are more expensive and you cannot go on deck to enjoy the view, which is one of the pleasures of travelling by ferry. Smoking is not permitted.

● Most of these services are subsidised by the state and the timetable is geared to the needs of islanders, usually with one departure from the island in early morning and a return service in late afternoon. This makes them useful for day-trips from the islands to the mainland, but means an overnight stay if you are travelling to the islands. An exception is the daily Dubrovnik to Mljet catamaran (▷ above).

● In summer taxi and excursion boats from the main harbours and resorts offer day-trips to islands and island-hopping trips.

Getting Around in Zagreb

Zagreb has an efficient and integrated public transportation system, operated by ZET. The city centre is served by trams, while buses link Zagreb with the outlying suburbs.

TRAMS

● Trams run every 5–10 minutes from 4am to midnight. Lines 3 and 8 operate weekdays only.

● A network map is displayed at all stops. The busiest interchange is Trg Bana (Josipa) Jelačića, with seven different lines.

● The route number and destination are displayed at the front of the tram.

● Night trams run every 30–40 minutes from midnight to 4am. Most useful is No. 31, from Črnomerec to Savski Most.

● Beware of pickpockets on crowded trams.

USEFUL TRAM LINES

2 Črnomerec–rail station–bus station–Savišće

6 Črnomerec–Trg Bana Jelačića–rail station–bus station–Sopot

11 Črnomerec–Trg Bana Jelačića–Maksimir–Dubec

12 Ljubljanica–Trg Maršala Tita–Trg Bana Jelačića–Maksimir–Dubrava

BUSES

● Buses serve districts beyond the city centre. Most suburban bus routes begin at the end of tram lines. Bus stations and the destinations they serve are shown on the tram map.

● Buses for Mirogoj depart in front of the cathedral; for Samobor from the main bus station and Črnomerec, at the end of tram lines 2, 6 and 11; for Velika Gorica from behind the railway station.

● Smoking is not allowed on buses or trams.

Tickets and Passes

● Bus and tram tickets can be bought from the driver, but are cheaper in advance from ZET or newspaper kiosks, found in Trg Bana Jelačića and all major transport termini.

● A ticket for Zone 1 costs 6.5kn in advance and 8kn from the driver. This covers the tram network and most local buses, and is valid for 90 minutes. A one-day pass, valid until 4am, costs 18kn and also includes the funicular.

● A ticket for Zone 2 costs 13kn in advance and 16kn from the driver and covers journeys to Velika Gorica.

● Children under 6 and people over 65 travel free.

● Tickets must be validated in the machine behind the driver. Passes must be validated the first time of use and shown on request.

● Fines of 150kn are levied for travelling without a ticket or with a non-validated ticket.

● The Zagreb Card, from tourist offices, costs 90kn and gives unlimited travel on buses, trams, the funicular and Medvednica cable-car for 72 hours.

FUNICULAR AND CABLE-CAR

● A funicular railway (*uspinjača*), built in 1890, connects the upper and lower towns, departing from Tomićeva every 10 minutes from 6.30am to 9pm for Gornji Grad. A single ticket costs 3kn.

● The Sljeme cable-car (*žičara*) makes the 20-minute trip to the summit of Medvednica from near the Dolje tram terminus, leaving on the hour from 8am to 8pm. A single fare costs 11kn, a return 17kn.

TAXIS

● There are taxi ranks outside the Croatian National Theatre on Trg Maršala Tita, south of Trg Bana Jelačića at junction of Gajeva and Teslina, and north of Trg Bana Jelačića near the cathedral.

● You can get a taxi 24 hours a day by dialling 970 or 01 661 0200.

● Fares are metered, with a basic fare of 19kn, plus 7kn per km and 3kn per item of luggage (more on Sundays, public holidays and from 10pm–5 am).

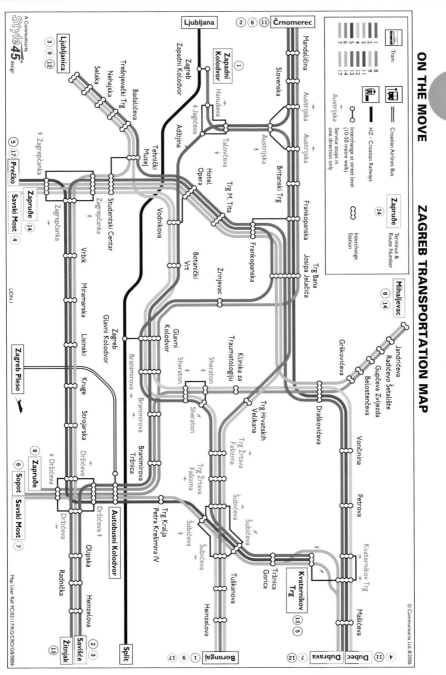

ON THE MOVE

ZAGREB TRANSPORTATION MAP

© Communicarta Ltd. 8/2006

Map User Ref: 9C/021/7/KG/CRO/GB/0806

UDN.1

A Communicarta
Style 45 design

Getting Around in Dubrovnik

The old town of Dubrovnik is easily explored on foot, and traffic is banned within the city walls. Buses connect the old town with the hotels on the Lapad peninsula, and boat trips link Dubrovnik with nearby islands.

BUSES

● Buses are operated by Libertas. The city bus network is concentrated to the west of the old town, with buses leaving from a terminus outside Pile Gate for Gruž harbour and the Lapad and Babin Kuk peninsulas.

● Timetables are shown at bus stops and available from tourist offices. On busy routes, buses run every 15–20 minutes from 6am to midnight.

● A single ticket costs 8kn from news kiosks or Libertas counters at the bus station and Pile Gate, or 10Kn on the bus. You need the exact money as drivers don't give change.

● Tickets must be validated in the machine beside the driver as you board.

● Buses for Cavtat leave from the long-distance bus station at Gruž harbour.

● Smoking is not allowed on buses.

● Beware of pickpockets on crowded buses.

TAXIS

● There are taxi ranks outside Pile and Ploče gates, at Gruž harbour, the bus station and on the main street of Lapad.

● You can get a taxi 24 hours a day by dialling 970

or calling the Pile taxi rank, tel 020 424343.

● Fares are metered, and the basic fare is 25kn, plus 8kn per km, with additional charges at night.

FERRIES

● Ferries and catamarans to the Elafiti Islands and Mljet depart from the harbour at Gruž.

● Taxi and excursion boats depart from the Old Port for Cavtat and Lokrum in summer.

● Between June and September Nova (tel 020 313599; www.nova-dubrovnik.com) operates

a fast shuttle service between Dubrovnik and the Elafiti Islands, as well as boats to Lokrum and a daily shuttle between Gruž harbour and the old town, which stops at various hotels on the Lapad peninsula. Sample fares are 15kn from the Old Port to Lokrum, 60kn from the Old Port to Gruž, 60kn from Gruž to Lopud and 30kn from Lopud to Šipan. Children under 7 travel free. You can also buy a one-day pass for 150kn and there are various family and weekly passes available.

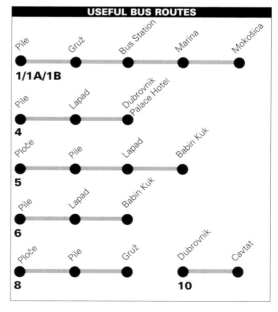

USEFUL BUS ROUTES

Pile	Gruž	Bus Station	Marina	Mokošica

1/1A/1B

Pile	Lapad	Dubrovnik Palace Hotel

4

Ploče	Pile	Lapad	Babin Kuk

5

Pile	Lapad	Babin Kuk

6

Ploče	Pile	Gruž	Dubrovnik	Cavtat

8   **10**

● Between April and October an old-fashioned rowing boat ferry (*barkariol*) makes the morning journey across the bay from Lapad to Gruž, as it has done for more than 100 years. Although it only saves a short walk, this is a delightfully nostalgic trip. The journey lasts 10 minutes and costs 5kn.

CAR PARKING

● There are car parks (parking lots) open 24 hours a day outside Pile Gate (10kn/hour) and the northern entrance to the city walls (5kn/hour).

● There is also a long-term car park at Gruž harbour, where you can leave your car for 40kn per day and travel into the city by bus.

● The nearest free parking to the old town is at Gradac, outside Pile Gate, though you will be very lucky to find a space here.

● Do not be tempted to park illegally, especially in the vicinity of the old town, as your car will be clamped or towed away and you will pay a hefty fee for its return.

Bicycling in Croatia

Croatia has a wealth of unspoilt countryside, coastal scenery and wild mountainous landscapes that are perfect for exploring on two wheels. Options range from challenging mountain-bike trails in the national parks to gentle bicycle touring on the islands.

TAKING YOUR OWN BICYCLE

● Service your bicycle before you go and take spare lights, reflectors and tyres, which may not be available in Croatia.

● Check that your airline will carry a bicycle.

● Check your insurance policy covers bicycling in Croatia, including personal accidents.

FAMILY TRAILS

These flat, easy bicycle trails are located in places of scenic beauty, with bicycle rental facilities available in summer.

● Lake Jarun, Zagreb
● On the island of Veli Brijun
● Zlatni Rt forest park, Rovinj
● Around the shores of Vransko Jezero, Pakoštane
● Around the shores of Veliko Jezero, Mljet
● Park Prevlaka, Dubrovnik

BICYCLE RENTAL

● Tourist offices and hotels can give details of local bicycle rental outlets.

● Most coast and island resorts have at least one bicycle rental shop. You can also rent from hotels and travel agents.

● Typical charges are 20kn per hour or 100kn per day, with discounts for longer rentals.

SAFETY

● Bicycles are forbidden on motorways and drivers on main roads do not always pay attention to cyclists. Take particular care on the busy Magistrala coast road.

● Check lights, brakes, reflectors and tyres each time you set off.

● Wear bright reflective clothing and a bicycle helmet. Children under 16 must always wear a helmet or face a fine.

RESOURCES

● For trails around Zagreb and Samobor, visit www.pedala.hr

● Get *Istra Bike*, with maps and routes, from tourist offices.

● *Kvarner by Bike* has 19 Croatian bicycle routes.

BICYCLING HOLIDAYS IN CROATIA

COMPANY	TELEPHONE	WEBSITE
Explore	+44 0870 333 4001	www.explore.co.uk
Pure Adventures	+1 480 905 1235	www.pure-adventures.com
Saddle Skedaddle	+44 0191 2651110	www.skedaddle.co.uk
2 Wheel Treks	+44 01483 271212	www.2wheeltreks.co.uk

VISITORS WITH A DISABILITY

Croatia has greatly improved its recognition of the needs of people with disabilities. Following a war in which many people were disabled, around 10 per cent of the population are officially registered as disabled, and war veterans in particular are treated with dignity and respect. Most people will go out of their way to help visitors with disabilities. Although changes have been made to accommodate the needs of visitors with disabilities, many public buildings and the majority of public transportation services are still not accessible to wheelchair users. Many sights are often located in historic town centres, where cobbled streets and steps are particularly unfriendly for wheelchairs.

BEFORE YOU GO

● Ask your tour operator or airline about the facilities they can provide. Although most airlines will transport wheelchairs free of charge and most airports have wheelchair transfer on arrival, this may have to be booked in advance.

● Be clear about your needs and discuss them in detail with your hotel or tour operator before you book. The majority of recently built or renovated hotels are adapted for disabled visitors, but older hotels may not even have ramps.

GETTING AROUND ZAGREB

● The city of Zagreb offers a free dial-a-ride service for wheelchair users in a fleet of adapted vehicles. Companions must pay a fare. The service must be booked at least one day in advance, or on Friday for travel the following Saturday, Sunday or Monday (tel 01 299 5956).

● Old-style buses and trams are being phased out in favour of the new low-floor type which provide wheelchair access. Most buses are now accessible, and the first low-floor trams came into service in 2005.

● The funicular railway between the upper and lower towns is fully wheelchair-accessible.

GETTING AROUND CROATIA

● Airports, bus and train stations in the major cities have wheelchair access, including to toilets.

● Buses, trains and ferries are not generally adapted for travellers with disabilities. Getting on and off ferries can be a problem as most boats do not have ramps, but the steward and crew will usually help out.

● Taxis are ordinary cars and are rarely adapted for travellers with disabilities. However, if you specify your needs when booking, a larger vehicle may be provided.

● There are designated disabled parking spaces in most towns and cities.

● In Zagreb and other large cities low-level public phone kiosks are provided.

USEFUL ORGANIZATIONS

CROATIA

SOIH (Association of Organizations of Disabled People in Croatia)

Savska 3, Zagreb

Tel 01 482 9394

www.soih.hr

UK

Tourism for All

Tel 0845 124 9974

www.tourismforall.org.uk

USA

SATH (Society for Accessible Travel and Hospitality)

Tel 212 447 7284

www.sath.org

This chapter is divided into six regions, which are shown on the map on the inside front cover. Places of interest are listed alphabetically within each region. Major sights are listed at the start of each region.

The Sights

ZAGREB

As Croatia's capital and biggest city, Zagreb is the heartbeat of the nation. One in four of the country's population lives here, enjoying a wide variety of restaurants and shops and a vibrant cultural scene throughout the year. The city is also home to some splendid late 19th-century Austro-Hungarian architecture.

MAJOR SIGHTS

Zagreb

Trg Bana Jelačića 11 ☎ 01 481 4051 🕔 Jul–15 Sep Mon–Fri 8.30am–9pm, Sat 9–5, Sun 10–2; Sep 16–end May, Mon–Fri 8.30–8, Sat 9–5, Sun 10–2
www.zagreb-touristinfo.hr • Excellent site in Croatian and English, updated daily with details of exhibitions and cultural events.

SEEING ZAGREB

Zagreb lies between the Medvednica mountain to the north and the River Sava to the south. Its centre is in two parts—Gornji Grad (Upper Town) and Donji Grad (Lower Town)—which meet at the main square, Trg Bana Jelačića. Gornji Grad, reached by a charmingly old-fashioned funicular which rattles up the hill from Ilica, is easily explored on foot. The sights of Donji Grad are more spread out, with the city's biggest museums set in gardens and parks.

If you are going to be here for a few days it is worth buying a Zagreb Card from the tourist office or airport arrivals hall. It costs 90kn for 72 hours for unlimited public transport plus discounts at museums, theatres, cinemas, restaurants, shops and tours.

BACKGROUND

The origins of modern Zagreb can be traced back to 1094, when King Ladislav founded a bishopric at Kaptol. In 1242 the Hungarian King Bela IV established a free royal city at Gradec, across the Medveščak stream from Kaptol. The settlements were surrounded by walls and towers and there were frequent battles between the two. Even today, there is continuing rivalry between Gradec, source of political power, and Kaptol, the religious centre.

The two were united in 1850 as the city of Zagreb, and the second half of the 19th century saw rapid expansion. Trg Bana Jelačića took on its present shape, and Donji Grad was laid out in a grid with wide boulevards and parks. Much of the city had to be rebuilt after an earthquake in 1880 and many of the grand buildings date from this time.

Since 1991 Zagreb, capital of an independent Croatia, has become a lively, self-confident, modern city, combining Central European architecture with a laid-back Mediterranean lifestyle.

THE SIGHTS

HOW TO GET THERE

❌ **Airport**
Pleso airport, 16km (10 miles) south of city, with regular shuttle buses to centre

🚌 **Bus station**
The bus station is 1.6km (1 mile) southwest of the centre; tram 6 to Trg Bana Jelačića

🚆 **Railway station**
The main railway station is a short walk south of Trg Bana Jelačića

TIPS

● Don't spend all your time in museums; it can be just as rewarding to soak up the café life on Trg Bana Jelačića or join the evening promenade along Tkalčićeva.

● Get hold of a copy of *Zagreb In Your Pocket*, a free magazine published every two months with reviews of restaurants, clubs, bars and shops. It is available in tourist offices and hotels.

● Zagreb is just as lively in winter as in summer. Go in December for Christmas markets, roast chestnuts and mulled wine, but be sure to wrap up warm against the cold.

DON'T MISS

GORNJI GRAD
Stroll around the cobbled streets of Gradec, the original nucleus of the city (▷ 52–55)

MUZEJ GRADA ZAGREBA (ZAGREB CITY MUSEUM)
Take a walk through 2,000 years of history at this museum (▷ 57)

TRG BANA JELAČIĆA
Soak up the café life in Zagreb's central square, then join the evening promenade along Tkalčićeva (▷ 59)

ZAGREB

0   400 m
0   400 yds

GORNJI GRAD

Muzej Grada Zagreba

Medvednica, Mirogoj

Miklou-šiceva

Degen

KAPTOL

Prirodoslovni Muzej

Atelier Meštrović
Markov Trg

Sv Marka   Sabor   Kam

Kamenita Vrata

Hrvatski Povijesni Muzej

Hrvatski Muzej Naivne Umjetnosti

Katarinin Trg

Sv Katerina

Trg A Stepinca

Dolac

Katedra

Strossm Šetalište

Kula Lotrščak   Uspinjača

Pod zidom

Britanski Trg

Arnoldova

ILICA

ILICA

Trg Bana Jelačića

Cesarčev

Trg Petra Preradovića

Bogovićeva

JURIŠIĆEV

AMRUŠEVA

Dalmatin

Varšavska

N TESLE

Arheološki Muzej

PRILAZ GYURE DEŽELIĆA

Trg Maršala Tita

Hrvatsko Narodno Kazalište

Trg Nikole Šubića Zrinskog

R BOŠKOV

Muzej Za Umjetnost i Obrt

KLAIĆEVA

A HEBRANGA

Strossmayerova Galerija Starih Majstora

Rooseveltov Trg

Etnografski Muzej

DONJI GRAD

Strossmayerova Trg

Muzej Mimara

Mažuranićev Trg

KRŠRJAGOVA

BARUNA TRENKA

Zagrebačko Kazalište Lutaka

Marulićev Trg

Trg Kralja Tomislava

VODNIKOVA

MIHANOVIĆEVA

Botanički Vrt

Grgurova

ŽELJENIČKI KOLODVOR

Tehnički Muzej

Trnjanska ce

A Hebranga	B3	Crnatkova	A4	Grgurová	C4	K Državslava D3
Amruševa	C3	Crvenog Križa	E3	Grškovica	C1	K Jelene E4
Antuna Bauera	E2	Dalmatin	A3	Gundulićeva	B3	Klaićeva A3
Arnoldova	A2	Degen	C1	Habdelic	B2	K L Posav E3
A Šenoina	D4	Demetrova	B1	Haulikova	C4	K Mislava D3
Babonićeva	E1	Dežmanova	B2	Heinzelova	F2	Kneza D3
Bakačeva	C2	Domagojeva	D4	Horvatovac	E1	Kneza Branimira D4
Barčićeva	E3	Đorđićeva	D3	Hrvoj	E3	Kneza Višeslava E3
Baruna Trenka	C3	Dubravkin put	B1	I Kukuljevica	A2	Kralja Zvonimira E3
Berislavićeva	C3	Dvornicićeva	C1	Ilica	B2	Križanićeva D3
Bogišićeva	F3	Erdödyjeva	E4	Ivana Gorana Kovacica	B1	Krležin Gvozd B1
Bogovićeva	C2	Fijanova	F1	J Draškovica	D2	Kršrjagova A3
Borne	D3	Filipoviceva	F1	Jukiceva	A4	Kružićeva E4
Branjugova	D2	F Račkog	D3	Jurievska	C1	Kuhačeva F2
Brescenskog	E3	Fra F Grabovća	F3	Juripra	C2	Kumićićeva B4
Brozova	A4	Frankopanska	B3	Jurkovićeva	E2	Laginjina E2
Bulic	E3	Gajdekova	D1	Jurišiceva	C2	Lasčinska F1
Bunićeva	F4	Gajeva	C3	J Žerjavica	B3	Ljudevita Posavskog F3
Čačkovićeva	E1	Golubovac	B1	Kam	B2	Lopašiceva E3
Cešarceva	C2	Gotovca	E2	Kaptol	C2	Makančeva F2

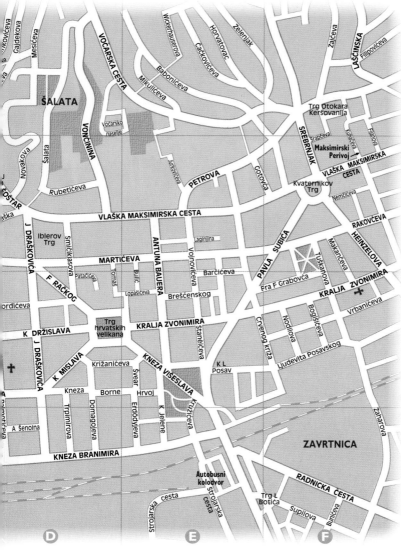

THE SIGHTS

The Lapidarium features a collection of Roman stone monuments (above). An example of Greek vase painting (left)

ARHEOLOŠKI MUZEJ (ARCHAEOLOGICAL MUSEUM)

This wide-ranging museum contains artefacts spanning over 5,000 years of Croatian history.

RATINGS

Cultural interest	●●●●
Good for kids	●●●
Historic interest	●●●●

BASICS

✚ 48 C3
✉ Trg Nikole Šubića Zrinskog 19
☎ 01 487 3101
🕐 Tue–Fri 10–5, Sat–Sun 10–1
💰 Adult 20kn, child 10kn
🚋 Tram 6,13
☕ Lapidarium courtyard café
🏛 👫

www.amz.hr
Informative site with detailed notes on the collections and an online shop selling reproductions and gifts.

TIP

● Don't miss the Lapidarium in the museum courtyard, with a collection of Roman stone monuments from the 1st to 4th centuries AD. In summer the courtyard doubles up as a pleasant outdoor café.

In a late 19th-century palace overlooking Zrinjevac park, chronological exhibits start on the top floor with the prehistory collection. The wealth of objects is an indication of the rich cultures in Croatia before the arrival of the Greeks, Romans and Slavs. Pride of place goes to the Vučedol culture, which thrived in Vukovar around 2,500BC, including the Vučedolska Golubica (Vučedol Dove), a three-legged vessel in the shape of a bird decorated with geometric patterns. Look out too for the Idol of Dalj, from the 14th century BC.

THE ZAGREB MUMMY

Also on the top floor is the Egyptian collection, with sarcophagi and burial goods from ancient Egyptian tombs. The star attraction is the Zagreb Mummy, brought back from Egypt by Croatian noble Mihael Barić in 1848. When examined, it was found that its linen shroud contained the world's longest surviving Etruscan script, from the 4th century BC, thought to be a liturgical calendar.

ROMAN TO MEDIEVAL

The second-floor galleries contain several fine Roman sculptures, including the head of a girl from Salona, beautifully carved in marble in the 3rd century BC. The medieval collection includes the earliest known Croatian stone carving, an altarpiece dated AD888 and inscribed with the name of prince Branimir.

The Croatian National Theatre is an outstanding example of baroque architecture and an important showcase for the arts

Zagreb's stunning Katedrala contains many works of art

ETNOGRAFSKI MUZEJ (ETHNOGRAPHIC MUSEUM)

➕ 48 B3 ✉ Trg Mažuraniça 14 ☎ 01 482 6220 ⏰ Tue–Thu 10–6, Fri–Sun 10–1 💷 Adult 15kn, child 10kn; free on Thu 🚃 Tram 12,13,14,17 🎫 🚹
www.etnografski-muzej.hr

In a Viennese Secession trades hall dating from 1904, this museum features folk costumes and crafts from Croatia and abroad. The first floor is devoted to Croatian folk culture, particularly traditional costume from the late 19th and early 20th centuries. Look out for golden embroidery from Slavonia, silk embroidery from the Konavle region, and beautiful lace costumes from Pag. The collection also includes jewellery, musical instruments, agriculture and rural crafts. The ground floor has non-European items, with many objects brought back by explorers Mirko and Stjepan Seljan, brothers from Karlovac, such as Native American headdresses, African masks, Aboriginal bark paintings and samurai swords.
Don't miss The building is one of Zagreb's finest examples of art nouveau.

GORNJI GRAD

See pages 52–55.

HRVATSKO NARODNO KAZALIŠTE (CROATIAN NATIONAL THEATRE)

➕ 48 B3 ✉ Trg Maršala Tita 15 ☎ 01 482 8532 🚃 Tram 12,13,14,17
www.hnk.hr

With trumpet-blowing angels on the balcony and classical columns adorning a mustard-coloured façade, the ostentatiously baroque Croatian National Theatre is in the tradition of grand Central European opera houses. Designed by the Viennese architects Ferdinand Fellner and Hermann Helmer, it was opened by Franz Josef I on a state visit in 1895. The main auditorium is a riot of baroque details, with plush furnishing and sculpted cherubs, while the first-floor hall, with a balcony overlooking the square, has ceiling frescoes and busts of distinguished actors. This is the most prestigious venue in Croatia for ballet, opera and drama, and it is well worth attending a performance if you get the chance (▷ 173). Outside the theatre is a sculpture by Ivan Meštrović, a group of interesting bronze figures known as *Zdenac Života* (Well of Life).

KATEDRALA (CATHEDRAL)

➕ 48 C2 ✉ Kaptol 31 ☎ 01 481 4727 ⏰ Mon–Sat 10–5, Sun 1–5; for Mass at other times 🚹 Free

The cathedral's twin spires are the tallest structures in Zagreb, at 105m (344ft). The first church was begun on this site in 1094, but today's neo-Gothic structure was largely built by Hermann Bollé (1845–1926) after the 1880 earthquake. The baroque marble pulpit is a survivor from the 17th century, while the 1846 stained-glass windows in the sanctuary are the oldest in Croatia. Behind the main altar, a sarcophagus contains an effigy of Cardinal Stepinac (▷ 21), which attracts a steady stream of pilgrims. His actual tomb is in the north wall, with a relief by Ivan Meštrović depicting the archbishop kneeling before Christ. Near here is the sacristy, with some rare 13th-century frescoes, and the treasury of precious objects including an embroidered cloak of King Ladislav, founder of the Zagreb diocese in 1094. The statue outside the cathedral, with the Virgin at the head of a column surrounded by gilded angels, is by Anton Fernkorn (1813–78).

THE SIGHTS

KNJIŽNICA
GORNJI GRAD

Gornji Grad

The oldest part of Zagreb, on a wooded hill, is an attractive district of old houses, leafy lanes and cobbled streets. With several interesting sights, this is a great place for a stroll.

Roofs tiled in shield patterns (above)

Quaint architectural details abound (above and opposite)

View from Kula Lotrščak (above). A narrow alley (below)

RATINGS	
Historic interest	●●●●
Photo stops	●●●●
Walkability	●●●●

BASICS
✚ 48 B1
🚋 Funicular from Tomićeva

SEEING GORNJI GRAD

The easiest way of getting to Gornji Grad is on the *Uspinjača* (funicular railway) which leaves from Tomićeva every 10 minutes from 6.30am to 9pm. In continuous operation since 1893, this was the city's first form of public transport and it continues to be held in great affection by the people of Zagreb. It takes less than a minute to make the ascent, but it saves a steep climb up the steps. If you do want to walk, you can take the staircase alongside the funicular tracks or head up Radićeva from the northwest corner of Trg Bana Jelačića and enter through Kamenita Vrata. Gornji Grad itself is compact and best explored on foot.

HIGHLIGHTS

KULA LOTRŠČAK

✚ 48 B2 ✉ Strossmayerovo Šetalište 9 ☎ 01 485 1768
🕐 Apr–end Oct Tue–Sun 11–8 ✋ Adult 10kn, child 5kn
Kula Lotrščak (Burglars' Tower) is the only surviving part of the 13th-century fortifications that once enclosed the free royal city of Gradec. Its name reflects the *campana latrunculorum* (bell of thieves) which used to chime from the watchtower each night to signify the closing of the city gates. The modern equivalent is the Grič cannon, fired from the tower at noon each day by a cannoneer in military uniform. Climb the spiral staircase to see the ceremony take place, then go up to the observation platform for views over the city.

TRG SVETOG MARKA/MARKOV TRG
(ST. MARK'S SQUARE)
✚ 48 B2

St. Mark's Square is the symbolic heart of power in Croatia, surrounded by key state institutions including the Sabor (Parliament), Banski Dvor (seat of the Croatian government) and Ustavni Sud (the highest constitutional court). At the centre of the square is St. Mark's church, dating from the 13th century. The church was rebuilt in the late 19th century by Hermann Bollé, with the addition of colourful mosaic roof tiles featuring the historic coats of arms of Croatia, Slavonia, Dalmatia and Zagreb. Also of note are the Gothic south portal and the sculptures by Ivan Meštrović inside the church.

HRVATSKI POVIJESNI MUZEJ
(CROATIAN HISTORY MUSEUM)
✚ 48 B2 ✉ Ulica Matočeva 9 ☎ 01 485 1900 🕐 Mon–Fri 10–5, Sat–Sun 10–1 💰 Adult 10kn, child 5kn; free on Mon 🏛 👫
www.hismus.hr

TIPS

● Time your visit to coincide with the noon firing of the Grič cannon. However, if you are nervous about loud noises or have small children with you, it is best to avoid midday.
● Pod Gričkim Topom (▷ 235), near the upper funicular station, makes a good spot for lunch with views over Donji Grad from the terrace.

HRVATSKI PRIRODOSLOVNI MUZEJ (CROATIAN NATURAL HISTORY MUSEUM)

✚ 48 B1 ✉ Ulica Demetrova 1 ☎ 01 485 1700 🕓 Tue–Fri 10–5, Sat–Sun 10–1 ✋ Adult 15kn, child 7kn
www.hpm.hr

Fossils, rocks, stuffed animals and birds are displayed in old-fashioned cabinets. The museum also holds the original remains of Krapina Man (▷ 82), but these are not on display and can only be seen by appointment.

Set in one of the finest baroque townhouses in Zagreb, built in 1764 as the palace of the Vojković-Orsić family, this museum has temporary exhibitions on themes from Croatian history. A pair of solid oak doors leads into the entrance hall, designed to provide space for carriages to turn around. From here, climb the steps to the first-floor ballroom and private apartments for a glimpse into the lifestyle of aristocratic families in 18th-century Zagreb.

ATELIER MEŠTROVIĆ

✚ 48 B1 ✉ Ulica Mletačka 8 ☎ 01 485 1123 🕓 Tue–Fri 10–6, Sat–Sun 10–2 ✋ Adult 20kn, child 10kn 🏛 👫
www.mdc.hr/mestrovic

The sculptor Ivan Meštrović (▷ 21) lived in this house from 1924 to 1942 and it has been preserved as a museum of his work, with more than 100 sculptures in wood, bronze and stone. Pieces on display range from large-scale works in the garden to intimate portraits of his family and a beautiful walnut carving of a *Mother and Child* (1942). On the second floor are plaster reliefs of Meštrović, his mother and father, wife, son and daughter, designed for the bronze doors of the family mausoleum at Otavice (▷ 128). The originals were destroyed during the 1991–5 war, making these surviving copies all the more valuable.

CRKVA SVETA KATARINE/SV KATERINA (ST. CATHERINE'S CHURCH)

✚ 48 C2 ✉ Katarinski Trg

Depending on your taste, you will either find this church beautiful or completely over the top. Built by Jesuit priests between 1620 and 1632, it is considered the city's baroque masterpiece. The ceiling and walls

A stone lion watches over the old town; the funicular; visitors at the entrance to the Kamenita Vrata (left to right)

are covered in pink stucco adorned with angels and plant motifs, while behind the main altar is a fresco of St. Catherine by Slovenian artist Kristofor Andrija Jelovšek. The gleaming white façade was remodelled after the 1880 earthquake and features statues of Mary and the four evangelists in niches.

KAMENITA VRATA (STONE GATE)
✚ 48 C2

The Stone Gate is all that remains of the four original entrance gates to the medieval city. According to legend, when fire swept through this district in 1731 destroying most of the wooden houses, a painting of the Virgin was found unharmed in the ashes and a shrine was built to house it. The image is kept behind a wrought silver grid inside the gate, attracting large numbers of pilgrims who pause here to pray and light candles.

BACKGROUND

In 1242, following a Tatar assault on Zagreb, King Bela IV established a free royal city on Gradec hill. In a document known as the Golden Bull, he granted privileges to the citizens of Gradec, including the right to trade and hold markets, but in return he required them to build defensive walls around the city. Since the 16th century, Gradec has been the seat of government in Croatia. The walls were pulled down in the 17th century. The term Gornji Grad (Upper Town) usually refers to Gradec, but also includes the neighbouring district of Kaptol, which lies across the Medveščak stream on the site of today's Tkalčićeva.

HRVATSKI MUZEJ NAIVNE UMJETNOSTI (CROATIAN NAIVE ART MUSEUM)
✉ Ulica Ćirila i Metoda 3
☎ 01 485 1911 ◉ Tue–Fri 10–6, Sat–Sun 10–1 ✋ Adult 10kn, child 5kn
www.hmnu.org

The Croatian naive art movement began in the village of Hlebine (▷ 62), and this museum features paintings and sculptures by artists including Ivan Generalić (1914–92) and his son Josip (1936–2004).

MUZEJ GRADA ZAGREBA
See page 57.

Woodland section of the Medvednica Nature Park

Ornate memorials and the burial places of many famous Croatians can be seen in Mirogoj cemetery

MAKSIMIRSKI PERIVOJ (MAKSIMIR PARK)

➕ Off map 49 F2
✉ Maksimirska Cesta 🚊 Tram 11,12 🔲 🏛

Opened in 1794, this is one of Europe's oldest public parks and is named after its founder, Bishop Maksimilian Vrhovec (1752–1827). With lakes, meadows, oak woods, pavilions, sculptures and bridges, it is a lovely place to stroll. A wide avenue leads to the *vidikovac*, a three-storey belvedere built in 1843 which now houses a summer café. Near here is the zoo (tel 01 230 2198; May–end Sep daily 9–8, Oct–end Apr 9–4; www.zoo.hr). A path from the belvedere leads to Mogila, an artificial hill of soil from more than 100 places in Croatia, beneath which are buried items of cultural heritage. The hill is topped by a statue of a falcon, and the Croatian flag and coat of arms. Opposite the main entrance, Maksimir Stadium is the home of Dinamo Zagreb and the national football team.

MEDVEDNICA

➕ 290 E2 ℹ Park Prirode Medvednica, Bliznec, tel 01 458 6317 🚊 Tram 8,14 to Mihaljevac then 15 to Dolje www.pp-medvednica.hr

The wooded mountain overlooking the city makes a popular retreat for the people of Zagreb, who come here to hike in summer and ski in winter. Getting there is part of the fun, on the *žičara* (cable-car) which makes the dramatic 20-minute journey to the summit (daily 8–8). From the Dolje tram terminus, walk through the tunnel and climb through the woods to reach the lower cable-car station. It is also possible to walk up in about two hours, or take the cable-car up and walk down. The cable-car drops you beneath the summit of Sljeme (1,033m/3,388ft), from where there is an extensive network of trails. An easy path leads to the Church of Our Lady of Sljeme, built in 1932 at a height of 1,000m (3,280ft) to commemorate the millenium of the medieval Croatian kingdom. A longer hike goes to the 13th-century fortress at Medvedgrad, with its Altar of the Homeland and an eternal flame honouring the Croatian victims of war. Other sights include the reconstructed Zrinski silver mine (Sat–Sun 10–4) and the underground Veternica cave (guided tours only, Apr–end Oct Sat–Sun).

MIROGOJ

➕ 48 C1 🕐 Daily 8–6 🚌 106 from Kaptol

This cemetery was designed by Hermann Bollé, who built the arcades at the entrance. With tombs and memorials by famous sculptors such as Ivan Rendić, Ivan Meštrović and Antun Augustinčić, this is virtually an open-air museum of 19th and 20th-century Croatian sculpture. Look in the arcade to the right for the tomb of Stjepan Radić (1871–1928), the assassinated leader of the Croatian Peasants Party and campaigner for independence. Behind the chapel, the black granite tomb of Franjo Tuđman (▷ 23) attracts many visitors, who lay candles and flowers there. Thousands of citizens are buried here too, with each tombstone bearing the symbols of their religion, and others engraved with the red star of Tito's Partisans.

Don't miss The memorial park for the victims of the Homeland War lies outside the gates. Beneath the park, the Zid Boli (Wall of Pain), is a pile of bricks each representing a missing person. Built by the victims' families on a street corner in central Zagreb, it was moved here in 2005.

Detail from this old parchment shows even lettering (above).
An ancient map on show in the City Museum (right)

MUZEJ GRADA ZAGREBA (ZAGREB CITY MUSEUM)

An entertaining journey through a thousand years of the city's history.

The Zagreb City Museum tells the city's story using models, maps, photographs and original artefacts. The building itself is one of the main exhibits, based in the 17th-century convent of the nuns of St. Clare. Iron Age remains excavated in the basement form the opening galleries, including a reconstructed blacksmith's workshop from the first century BC. The museum also incorporates parts of Popov Toranj (Priests' Tower), a 13th-century fortress at the northern gate of Gradec, which has housed the city observatory since 1903.

THE EARLY YEARS

The ground-floor concentrates on early history. Room 4 contains a copy of Felician's Charter (1134), the first recorded document to mention Zagreb, while Room 5 has a copy of the Golden Bull (1242) in which Bela IV established the royal city of Gradec. The oldest coat of arms of Zagreb, carved in stone in 1499, is in Room 9.

CITY LIFE

The first-floor galleries follow Zagreb's development through such themes as parks and promenades, clubs and societies, theatres, shops and domestic life. Highlights include the silver hammer used by Franz Josef I at the opening of the Croatian National Theatre (Room 35) and a reconstructed bathing shed (Room 40). The finale is a sobering display of furniture and crockery from the presidential palace broken by Yugoslav rockets in October 1991.

THE SIGHTS

RATINGS

Good for kids	● ● ● ○
Historic interest	● ● ● ●
Photo stops	● ● ● ○

BASICS

✚ 48 C1
✉ Ulica Opatička 20
☎ 01 485 1361
🕐 Tue–Fri 10–6, Sat–Sun 10–1
💰 Adult 20kn, child 10kn
📷 80kn
🎫 Free tours, Sat–Sun 11am
🍴 Stara Vura
▣ 🏛 👥

www.mdc.hr/mgz
Comprehensive site covering the history of the museum and a detailed guide to collections.

TIPS

● Allow at least a couple of hours, with a break for lunch in the Stara Vura restaurant.
● Look out for the pillar in the reception area, displaying old museum posters. This is an original from 19th-century Zagreb and similar examples can still be seen in the city today.

An example of Venetian glass in the Mimara Museum

George and the Dragon in front of the Umjetnost i Obrt

Madam Recamier by Gros, in the Strossmayer Gallery

THE SIGHTS

MUZEJ MIMARA

🏛 48 A3 ✉ Rooseveltov Trg 5 ☎ 01 482 8100 🕐 Tue–Wed, Fri–Sat 10–5, Thu 10–7, Sun 10–2 👣 Adult 20kn, child 10kn 🚊 Tram 12,13,14,17 ▢ 🏛 🏃

This extensive museum reflects the eclectic tastes of Ante Topić Mimara (1898–1987), a Croatian businessman who acquired art from around the world, which he donated to the state shortly before his death. Born in Korusča, Mimara first left his homeland during World War I; it was in Rome in 1918 that his collection began with an ancient Christian chalice, made in Alexandria in the 3rd century AD. Over the years, his collection grew to encompass Egyptian antiquities and glassware, Chinese porcelain and jade, Turkish carpets, Spanish tapestries, Italian Renaissance sculpture and paintings by European masters including Rembrandt, Rubens and Raphael. Among the highlights is *The Bather* by Pierre Auguste Renoir (1841–1919).

Don't miss Room 17 has a 14th-century carved ivory English hunting horn; Room 26 has the 17th-century carved ivory sceptre used by Polish kings.

MUZEJ ZA UMJETNOST I OBRT (ARTS AND CRAFTS MUSEUM)

🏛 48 B3 ✉ Trg Maršala Tita 10 ☎ 01 488 2111 🕐 Tue–Sat 10–7, Sun 10–2 👣 Adult 20kn, child 10kn 🚊 Tram 12,13,14,17 🚋 11 and 5 🍴 ▢ 🏛 🏃 www.muo.hr

Like the Muzej Mimara (▷ left), this museum offers a broad sweep through the arts, but Croatia and Central Europe are the theme. Founded in 1880 to preserve traditional arts and crafts and housed in a Hermann Bollé neo-Renaissance palace, the collections include furniture, ceramics, textiles, clocks and watches, paintings and sculpture, musical instruments, and graphic and industrial design. Of particular interest is the religious art collection, with polychrome wooden sculptures from the 15th to 18th centuries and an altarpiece of the Madonna from the church of Remetinec, near Varaždin.

STROSSMAYEROVA GALERIJA STARIH MAJSTORA (STROSSMAYER GALLERY OF OLD MASTERS)

🏛 48 C3 ✉ Trg Nikole Šubića Zrinskog 11 ☎ 01 489 5117 🕐 Tue 10–1, 5–7, Wed–Sun 10–1 👣 Adult 10kn, child 5kn 🚊 Tram 6,13 www.hazu.hr

This collection of paintings is in the Academy of Sciences and Arts, in an Italian Renaissance-style building commissioned by Josip Juraj Strossmayer (1815–1905) and opened in 1884. As well as being Bishop of Đakovo, Strossmayer was a key figure in 19th-century Croatian politics and a patron of the arts, and his personal collection of European art from the 15th to 19th centuries forms the core of this gallery. Heavily biased towards religious painting with a handful of portraits, landscapes and rural scenes, the collection includes artists from the Italian, Dutch and Flemish schools, among them Carpaccio, Fra Angelico and El Greco. Look for a St. Mary Magdalene by El Greco (Room 5) and a self-portrait by Jean Fragonard (Room 9). Behind the building is a statue of Strossmayer by Ivan Meštrović.

Don't miss The entrance lobby has the original Bašćanska Ploča (Baška Stone), an 11th-century tablet with one of the oldest examples of Glagolitic script.

Street life and people-watching on Trg Bana Jelačića (above). A statue of Jelačić presides over the main square (below)

TRG BANA JELAČIĆA

Café life is the rule on Zagreb's central square, a vibrant hive of activity from morning to night.

Trg Bana Jelačića lies at the meeting point of the upper and lower towns, and is the heart and soul of Zagreb. Originally a fairground and market place, it has been the main square since 1850. At first, it was called Manduševac after the spring on its eastern side, which is now a pretty fountain but until 1878 supplied the city with water. The current name dates from 1866, when the statue of Josip Jelačić was erected.

THE STATUE
An equestrian statue of Josip Jelačić (1801–59), by Anton Fernkorn, is at the square's centre. Appointed by Vienna as *ban* (governor) of Croatia, Jelačić was a popular figure who abolished slavery and united Croatia, Slavonia and Dalmatia into a single state. He became an icon of Croatian nationalism, particularly during the Communist era when the statue was removed and the square renamed Trg Republike (Republic Square). In 1990 it was restored to its pedestal following a petition and now acts as a rallying point for political demonstrations and a meeting place for young people at the start of the evening *korzo* (stroll) along nearby Tkalčićeva.

THE MARKET
An archway behind the statue leads to Dolac (Mon–Sat 6–2, Sun 6–12), the city's main market since 1930. The raised outdoor terrace is where farmers sell fresh fruit, vegetables and home-made cottage cheese. Meat and fish are sold at indoor market halls, and there are flower stalls on nearby Ulica Splavnica.

RATINGS
Café life	● ● ● ● ●
Photo stops	● ● ●
Specialist shopping	● ● ●

BASICS

🞧 48 C2
🛈 Trg Bana Jelačića 11
☎ 01 481 4051
🕓 Jul–15 Sep Mon–Fri 8.30am–9pm, Sat 9–5, Sun 10–2; Sep 16–end May Mon–Fri 8.30–8, Sat 9–5, Sun 10–2
🚋 Tram 1,6,11,12,13,14,17

TIPS
● The best way to enjoy Trg Bana Jelačića is from one of the café terraces. Mala Kavana is a good choice.
● The streets around Trg Bana Jelačića are the main venues for the evening *korzo* (promenade)—especially Tkalčićeva to the north and Bogovićeva to the south.

INLAND CROATIA

Overlooked by many in favour of the coast, continental Croatia has varied landscapes, from the gently rolling hills of the Zagorje to the floodplains of the River Danube. There are fine baroque cities at Osijek and Varaždin, as well as Croatia's greatest natural attraction, the waterfalls of Plitvice Lakes National Park.

MAJOR SIGHTS

THE SIGHTS

Old buildings in Čakovec are evidence of the long history of this small town, which is dominated by a large castle

The imposing red-brick cathedral in Đakovo

ČAKOVEC

✚ 290 E1 ⛨ Trg Kralja Tomislava 1, tel 040 313319; Mon–Fri 8–4, Sat 8–1 🚌 From Varaždin and Zagreb 🚂 From Varaždin and Zagreb www.tourism-cakovec.hr

Čakovec, 16km (10 miles) north of Varaždin and near the Hungarian border, was the northern stronghold of the Zrinski dynasty, aristocrats and soldiers who were granted the town in 1547 for their services to the Habsburg emperor. It was Nikola Šubić Zrinski (1508–66), a former governor of Croatia, who began the castle that dominates the town. His great-grandson, Nikola (1620–64), was killed in a wild boar hunt and is recalled in a memorial in the nearby park. The restored castle is now the Muzej Međimurja (Tue–Fri 10–3, Sat–Sun 10–1; adult 15kn, child 10kn), a museum with exhibits ranging from archaeology and local history to Carnival masks, modern art and a reconstruction of an old pharmacy. The town centre is based around Trg Kralja Tomislava, an elongated main square leading to wide pedestrianized shopping streets. Look for the Zrinski coat of arms above the portal of the parish

church. Čakovec is the main town of Međimurje, a fertile region of farmland between the Mura and Drava rivers. The village of Štrigova is known for its excellent white wines. **Don't miss** The former trades hall (1908), a striking red-brick building, now contains the city library. It is on the main square opposite the tourist office.

ĐAKOVO

✚ 293 J3 ⛨ Ulica Kralja Tomislava 3, tel 98 338 675; Mon–Fri 8–3 🚌 From Osijek and Slavonski Brod www.tz-djakovo.hr

The approach to Đakovo is dominated by the twin spires of its neo-Gothic cathedral, 84m (275ft) tall and towering over the city. The cathedral was built between 1866 and 1882 for Bishop Josip Strossmayer (▷ 19) and as you explore the city, it can start feeling like a Strossmayer memorial theme park. His tomb lies in the crypt, his statue stands outside, the city park is named after him and there is also a small museum (Mon–Fri 8–6, Sat 8–1.30) devoted to his life. Ulica Hrvatskih Velikana—known as the *korzo*—runs north from the cathedral to the small whitewashed church of Svi Svetih (All Saints),

housed in a converted 16th-century Turkish mosque. A short walk from the centre leads to the Lipizzaner stud farm (tel 031 813286; www.ergela-djakovo.hr; visits by appointment), founded in 1506 to breed white horses for the imperial court in Vienna.

HLEBINE

See page 62.

ILOK

✚ 293 K3 ⛨ Trg Nikole Iločkog 2, tel 032 590020; Mon–Fri 9–4 🚌 From Osijek and Vukovar

The easternmost town in Croatia sits above a bend in the River Danube, with views across the river to the Serbian city of Novi Sad. Ilok is built around a 14th-century fortress, within whose walls is the parish church of Sveti Ivan Kapistran, a Franciscan priest who died defending the town from the Turks. For more than 100 years, Ilok was part of the Ottoman empire and you can see the remains of a Turkish bath in the castle. The nearby hills of Fruška Gora have been known for their vineyards since Roman times. After a lull, the vineyards are productive again and the wine harvest fair in September is a joyous occasion.

A Dance in the Mountains by *Ivan Generalić*, one of the leading exponents of naive art in Croatia

BASICS

🞣 291 F1
🛈 Trg Ivana Generalića 1, Koprivnica, tel 048 836139; Mon–Fri 8–4, Sat 8–12

www.generalic.com
Online gallery and shop run by Goran Generalić, with biographies of three generations of artists from the same family.

TIPS

● A map outside Galerija Hlebine shows the location of around 20 studios in the village, all of which can be visited to see and buy.
● Galerija Koprivnica (tel 048 622564; Tue–Fri 10–1, 5–8, Sat–Sun 10–1), on the main square in Koprivnica, also has exhibitions of naive art.
● There are no restaurants in Hlebine, but Pivnica Kraluš in Koprivnica serves filling fare at reasonable prices (▷ 236).

HLEBINE

This small rural village is known throughout Croatia as the birthplace of naive art.

The Croatian naive art movement began in the 1930s when the artist Krsto Hegedušić (1901–75) returned from Paris to find villagers in Hlebine producing colourful scenes of rural life reminiscent of the French primitive painter Henri Rousseau (1844–1910). The first generation of naive artists, such as Ivan Generalić (1914–92), Mirko Virius (1889–1943) and Franjo Mraz (1910–81), were self-taught, but Hegedušić developed their technique and exhibited their works in Zagreb.

FROM FATHER...

Galerija Hlebine (tel 048 836075; Mon–Fri 10–4, Sat 10–2; adult 10kn, child 5kn) in the village has exhibitions of work by local artists. One room is devoted to Ivan Generalić, considered the father of naive art. It reveals the development of his style, from youthful portraits and landscapes to experiments with fantasy and magical realism. The highlight is a striking triptych of Christ crucified among the snows of Hlebine.

...TO SON

Ivan's son Josip (1936–2004) also worked in Hlebine and his home is now the Galerija Josip Generalić (tel 048 836071; visits by appointment). Among his works are portraits of his father, plus fanciful images of Sophia Loren and The Beatles in Hlebine. Also here is Ivan's house and studio, now a small museum with photographs and posters from exhibitions. The family tradition is continued by grandson Goran (born 1971), who has an online gallery in nearby Koprivnica.

The memorial at Jasenovac concentration camp

Children enjoying an archery lesson in the grounds of Dubovac castle, which overlooks the town of Karlovac

JASENOVAC

🚩 291 F3 ℹ️ Jasenovac Memorial Museum, tel 044 672033 🚃 From Zagreb www.jusp-jasenovac.hr

Jasenovac was the site of a notorious concentration camp run by the Ustaše regime during the Independent State of Croatia (1941–5). No one knows how many people were murdered here, but estimates range from 50,000 to over 100,000. The majority of victims were ethnic Serbs, but others included Jews, Roma (gypsies), Bosnian Muslims and Croats opposed to the regime. The camp was razed to the ground, and in its place now stands a large concrete lotus flower. The monument was designed by Bogdan Bogdanović (born 1922), a Serbian artist and former mayor of Belgrade who now lives in exile in Vienna. The walkway to the monument is constructed out of railway sleepers; nearby stands an old cattle train, similar to those that transported inmates to the camp. During the 1991–5 war Jasenovac was occupied by Serbian troops and the Memorial Museum was looted, with many exhibits ending up in Belgrade. There are now plans to return as many of the

items as possible and a new museum is under construction and scheduled to open by 2007.

KARLOVAC

🚩 295 D3 ℹ️ Ulica Petra Zrinskog 3, tel 047 600606; Jun–end Sep Mon–Fri 8–3, Sat 9–1, 5–8; Oct–end May Mon–Fri 8–3, Sat 9–12 🚃 From Zagreb 🚃 From Zagreb www.karlovac-touristinfo.hr

Karlovac was established at the junction of four rivers in 1579 as a military base on the southern border of the Austro-Hungarian empire, and named Karlstadt after Charles, Archduke of Habsburg. The walls that once surrounded the citadel in the shape of a six-pointed star were torn down in the 19th century, but their outline can still be seen in the tree-lined promenades encircling the town. The 2.5km (1.5-mile) circuit makes a pleasant walk, through green parks overlooking a moat. The prettiest section is along Šetalište Tuđmana, where there is a restored 19th-century theatre, Zorin Dom. Inside the walls, the old town keeps its baroque feel, particularly around the central square, Trg Bana Jelačića, with its 1691 plague pillar topped by a

statue of the Virgin. The nearby Gradski Muzej (Mon–Fri 7–3, Sat–Sun 10–12) has displays of local history, archaeology and folk costumes. Just 5km (3 miles) south of the town, at the confluence of the Korana and Mrežnica rivers, Turanj was the frontline of the Homeland War. An open-air memorial museum displays tanks and anti-aircraft guns from the war. There are plans for a permanent museum on this site.

KOPAČKI RIT

See page 64.

KRAŠIĆ

🚩 295 D3 ℹ️ Krašić 101, tel 01 627 0910; Tue and Fri 8–12

This small village in the Kupčina river valley has become an important place of pilgrimage to Cardinal Alojzije Stepinac (▷ 21). Stepinac grew up in Krašić and held his first Mass here. He also spent the last years of his life in Krašić, under house arrest following his release from Lepoglava prison. His apartment behind the church is a now a memorial museum. The large statue of Stepinac in front of the parish church was erected in 1998 on the centenary of his birth; crowds flock here every year on his birthday (8 May).

A tranquil sunset at Kopački Rit Nature Park (above).
Visitors on a boardwalk trail through the wetlands (left)

RATINGS

Good for kids	● ● ●
Outdoor pursuits	● ● ●
Photo stops	● ● ● ●

BASICS

✚ 293 J2
✉ Park Prirode Kopački Rit, Kopačevo
☎ 031 752320
🕐 Daily 9–5
💶 Apr–end Oct: adult 60kn, child 45kn including boat trip; Nov–end Mar: adult 40kn, child 20kn

🍴 💻 🅿 🏛 🚻

www.kopacki-rit.com
Sophisticated site in Croatian, Hungarian and English, with maps and information on fauna and flora.

TIPS

● Mosquitoes can be a problem in summer, so wear long sleeves and trousers and use insect repellent.
● If you want to stay overnight, several families in the village of Bilje offer cheap rooms in private houses.

KOPAČKI RIT

The nature park at the confluence of the Danube and Drava rivers harbours an extraordinary variety of wildlife.

The floodplain of the River Danube, on the borders of Croatia, Hungary and Serbia, is a significant wetland habitat, and around 180sq km (70sq miles) is protected as Kopački Rit Nature Park. Among the wildlife here are 44 species of fish, 11 species of amphibians including frogs, 10 species of reptiles, 55 species of mammals and more than 140 species of nesting birds. Less appealing are the 7 species of mosquito that terrorize unwitting visitors in summer.

SEEING THE PARK
The visitor centre is close to Kopačevo, 3km (2 miles) from Bilje and 12km (7.5 miles) from Osijek. Get there by heading north from Osijek towards Hungary, turning right at the crossroads in Bilje and following signs to the park. The staff can issue maps of footpaths and bicycle trails. From April to October, the best introduction is to take a boat trip on Lake Sakadaš, on an old steamer that departs from a dock near the entrance. Take some binoculars to see herons, cormorants and geese as you travel through the marshes. Among other birds to nest here are white-tailed eagles, black storks, little egrets and the endangered ferruginous duck.

IN THE WOODS
Deeper in the park, you encounter swathes of willow and oak forest, home to populations of red deer, wild boar and wild cats. The best place to walk is in the oak woods around the old hunting lodge at Tikveš.

The exterior of Tito's birthplace in the village of Kumrovec (above) and a bronze statue of the politician (right)

KUMROVEC

The village in which Tito was born is now an enjoyable open-air museum of rural life.

Kumrovec is just like any other Zagorje village, with whitewashed, thatched wooden cottages and a stream running through the middle. What makes it different is that this is where the Yugoslav leader Tito was born in 1892. His parents, Franjo and Marija Broz, had a blacksmith's workshop here and lived in the first brick house in the village. A statue of Tito by local artist Antun Augustinčić (1900–79) stands outside.

THE MUSEUM

The origins of the Staro Selo (Old Village) museum go back to 1953, when the Broz family house was opened as a branch of the Ethnographic Museum in Zagreb. Much later, after Tito's death, the museum expanded to take over the entire village. Some 40 buildings, including farmhouses, barns, pigsties and wells have been reconstructed to recreate the conditions Tito knew at the end of the 19th century. There are stables, potteries and a toymaker's workshop. From April to October, craftspeople demonstrate rural activities such as cider-making and weaving, and sell *štrukli* (cottage cheese parcels) in the old wine-cellar Zagorski Klet.

THE VILLAGE

All of the buildings have been restored in situ, with the result that Kumrovec has the feel of a real village rather than a museum piece. When restoration was taking place in the 1980s, a few families refused to leave their houses; they go about their everyday lives among the renovated cottages and actors in folk costume.

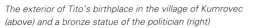

RATINGS	
Good for kids	●●●●●
Historic interest	●●●
Photo stops	●●●●

BASICS

✛ 290 D2
✉ Staro Selo, Kumrovec
☎ 049 225830; 500477 (guided tours)
🕐 Apr–end Sep daily 9–7; Oct–end Mar daily 9–4
✋ Adult 20kn, child 10kn
🚌 From Zagreb
🍴 🛈 🅿 🏛 👫

www.mdc.hr/kumrovec
The history of the museum, plus notes on rural architecture in Croatian and English.

TIP

● Take a walk along the main street of the village to see the school that Tito attended from 1900 to 1905.

Lonjsko Polje

The marshy floodplains of the River Sava provide a refuge for numerous migrant birds, including the much-loved white storks that nest here in spring and summer.

Much of the region is underwater in the winter

A stork on the roof of a farmhouse

Horses grazing in the fertile meadows of the park

SEEING LONJSKO POLJE

Although the Lonjsko Polje Nature Park occupies an area of over 500sq km (193sq miles), the main sights are strung out along the 70km (44-mile) road that follows the east bank of the River Sava from Sisak to Jasenovac. The park headquarters is in Krapje, but there is also an information office in Čigoć (open throughout the year), where you can pick up leaflets and maps. The best time to visit is between April and August, when storks nest on the roofs and the meadows are carpeted with wild flowers; from November to March, much of the Lonjsko Polje is under water.

HIGHLIGHTS

ČIGOĆ

🛈 Čigoć 26, tel 044 715115; Daily 8–4 🔲 🔲
Čigoć has been designated the first European Stork Village because of its large population of white storks, who arrive each spring to build their nests and stay here until departing for Africa in late summer. You can see storks in other villages—notably Mužilovčica—but the greatest concentration is in Čigoć. During the season, almost every house in the village has a stork's nest on the roof. The information office, housed in a typical wooden cottage at the centre of the village, has details of local walks, including a 30-minute stroll through the forest and a two-hour hike along the flood dyke. Also in Čigoć is the Sučić ethnographic museum, with collections of textiles, embroidery, and farming

Winter fuel (left)

A herdsman with his pigs in the flooded wetlands (below)

and fishing tools displayed in a family house (tel 044 715184; included in price of park entry ticket).

KRAPJE

🛈 Krapje 1, tel 098 222086; Apr–end Oct, daily 8–4 📅 👪
The village of Krapje is known for its traditional Posavina oak houses, with steep-sided roofs and wooden staircases to the first floor. Some of these houses are more than 200 years old. There has been a move to restore traditional cottages in the Lonjsko Polje and some families in the village offer rooms to visitors. Just outside Krapje, Krapje Đol was Croatia's first ornithological reserve and provides a nesting ground for waterfowl such as herons and spoonbill.

BACKGROUND

Established in 1990, the Lonjsko Polje Nature Park is the largest protected wetland area in Croatia and is included on the Ramsar list of internationally important wetland habitats. Much of it consists of the flood plain of the River Sava. When the waters rise each winter, the low-lying meadows flood, becoming filled with waterlilies as well as carp and frogs which provide nourishing food for migrant storks. The Lonjsko Polje also acts as a valuable flood defence system for Zagreb, which would otherwise be threatened by the rising waters of the Sava. The farmers of the Lonjsko Polje still use traditional farming methods. Sturdy Posavina horses roam freely on the marshes, and spotted Turopolje pigs (an indigenous breed unique to this region) live in the oak forests, feeding off wild acorns.

<table>
<tr><td>TIPS</td></tr>
</table>

● Mosquitoes can be a problem in summer, so wear long sleeves and trousers and protect yourself with insect repellent.
● If you plan to go walking in this area, remember that it can be flooded at any time of year and good boots are essential.

A traditional wooden farmhouse (opposite)

Osijek

The biggest city in eastern Croatia is a relaxing place of
avenues and parks, built around an 18th-century
fortress on the south bank of the River Drava.

*The plague monument in
Holy Trinity Square*

*A winter view of the church
of SS Peter and Paul*

*The plague monument (above right);
detail of the sculptures (above left)*

BASICS

✚ 293 J2

ℹ Županijska 2, tel 031
203755; Mon–Fri 7–4, Sat 8–12;
also at Trg Križanićeva 6, Tvrđa

🚌 From Đakovo, Vukovar and
Zagreb

🚆 From Zagreb

www.tzosijek.hr
Official site of the city tourist
board, with maps and listings.

SEEING OSIJEK

Osijek is divided between the fortress at Tvrđa and
the 19th-century district of Gornji Grad. With its
baroque churches and grand public buildings,
Tvrđa has the character of an open-air museum,
while Gornji Grad houses most of the hotels,
restaurants and shops. The two are linked by
Europska Avenija, a fine avenue of art nouveau
townhouses served by tram 1 during the day. The
two districts are also linked by a riverside path.

HIGHLIGHTS

TRG SVETOG TROJSTVA
(HOLY TRINITY SQUARE)

The central square of Tvrđa is lined with fine public
buildings dating from the early 18th century. At the
centre of the square is a beautiful baroque plague
column, erected in 1729 by the widow of General
Maksimilijan Petraš, who had died in a plague
epidemic. This monument was offered to God in the
hope that he would deliver Osijek from the plague.

MUZEJ SLAVONIJE (MUSEUM OF SLAVONIA)

✉ Trg Svetog Trojstva 6 ☎ 031 208501 🕐 Tue–Sun 10–1
💵 Adult 13kn, child 7kn 🏛 🏃

The former magistrates court is now the Museum of
Slavonia, with collections of archaeology, geology,
coins and metallurgy. The archaeological exhibits
include finds from the Roman colony of Mursa as
well as bronze jewellery from the 15th century BC.

The metallurgy section has a fascinating variety of household items from the 19th and 20th centuries.

GALERIJA LIKOVNIH UMJETNOSTI (GALLERY OF FINE ARTS)

✉ Europska Avenija 9 ☎ 031 213587 🕐 Tue–Fri 10–6, Sat–Sun 10–1 👍 Adult 10kn, child 5kn 🎫 👪

The city art gallery occupies a Renaissance mansion,

Plague monument statues (left)

Clock detail on the bell tower of the Church of St. Michael (above)

TIPS

● Car parking in the city centre is a nightmare; it is easier to leave your car in one of the side streets around Tvrđa.
● To explore both Tvrđa and Gornji Grad, walk one way along the riverbank and return by tram, or follow the walk on pages 208–209.
● You can make a tour of Osijek on a 1926 vintage tram, complete with costumed driver and conductor.
There are also plans to introduce horse-drawn carriage rides for tourists.

and holds changing exhibitions, some of which feature the works of the 19th-century Osijek school.

CRKVA SV PETRA I PAVLA (CHURCH OF SS PETER & PAUL)

This neo-Gothic red-brick church, built in 1894 as a rival to the cathedral at Đakovo (▷ 61), is known in the city as the cathedral, although it is only a parish church. At 90m (295ft) tall, its tower is higher than those at Đakovo and it dominates the heart of Gornji Grad.

BACKGROUND

On the south bank of the River Drava near its confluence with the Danube, Osijek has always been strategically important. Destroyed by the Ottomans in 1526, it was recaptured by Austrian troops in 1687. In 1712, they began building Tvrđa, a magnificent baroque garrison town with barracks and government buildings, churches, schools and houses, with defensive walls and gates. The walls were demolished in 1926. After bombardment in the 1991–5 war, Osijek has been restored and Tvrđa has recovered its easy-going atmosphere.

Plitvička Jezera (Plitvice Lakes)

The Plitvice Lakes National Park has spectacular natural scenery.

A visitor stops to watch the fish in one of the lakes

Stunning scenery around one of the park's lakes

Trout thrive in the clear waters of the lakes here

RATINGS	
Outdoor pursuits	●●●○
Photo stops	●●●●●
Walkability	●●●●●

BASICS

✚ 290 D5
✉ Plitvička Jezera
☎ 053 751132; 751015 (hotel reservations)
🕐 May—end Oct daily 8–8; Nov—end Apr daily 9–5
💶 Jul—end Aug: adult 100kn, child (7–18) 60kn; May—end Jun and Sep—end Oct: adult 85kn, child 50kn; Nov—end Apr: adult 55kn, child 30kn; two-day ticket available May—end Oct: adult 100–130kn
🚌 From Zagreb
🍴 🚌 🅿 🏛 👫

www.np-plitvicka-jezera.hr
Well-designed site with maps, information on flora and fauna, plus nature-themed games and puzzles in Croatian and English.

Visitors following a scenic path through the Plitvice

SEEING THE PLITVICE LAKES

Plitvice Lakes National Park is 75km (47 miles) south of Karlovac, on the old main road from Zagreb to Split. The park is signposted from the A1 motorway; you can also get there from the coast by taking the mountain roads that climb inland from the Kvarner Bay towns of Senj and Karlobag. Among the public transport options, regular Zagreb–Split buses stop at the entrance to the park, and there are also two daily departures from Zagreb, leaving in early morning and returning in late afternoon to allow you a full day at the lakes. In addition, tour operators offer organized excursions to Plitvice from resorts in Istria, Kvarner and Northern Dalmatia.

Visiting independently gives you the chance to explore the park at your own pace, or even to stay overnight and enjoy the colours of dawn and dusk and the peace after the day-trippers have left. On the other hand, it is a long drive from the coast and for many people an organized tour will be the best option. Although you could spend several days here, it is so well geared up for day-trippers that you can see the main sights in a few hours.

Of the two park entrances, Ulaz 1 is close to Veliki Slap and the lower lakes, while Ulaz 2 gives access to the upper lakes. In practice you can use either entrance, as the admission price includes shuttle bus and boat rides in summer, allowing you to explore the lower and upper lakes in a single day. Wooden boardwalks and footbridges travel around

The lakes are lovely at any time of year, but take on a different character with the seasons. Spring (May–Jun) is a good time to visit for birdsong, wild flowers and rushing water as the winter snows melt, increasing the flow over the falls. Summer (Jul–Aug) is the busiest time, when it can be hard to avoid the crowds. Autumn (Sep–Oct) is when the colours begin to turn on the trees. Throughout the winter months (Nov–Apr), the park is frequently covered in snow; the national park buses and boats do not operate, and the foot-paths are sometimes closed to visitors. Some people think that this is the loveliest time of all.

THE SIGHTS

Among the larger mammals to inhabit the park are wolves, foxes, lynx, badgers, pine marten, roe deer and brown bear. You are unlikely to see any of these, though you stand the best chance in the early-morning, twilight or just after dusk. Some of these species are seriously endangered. There are thought to be fewer than 50 wolves living in Croatia, and around 60 pairs of lynx, who returned to Plitvice in 1980 after an absence of 80 years. You are far more likely to see some of the 70 species of nesting birds who have made Plitvice their home, including the black wood-pecker, mountain titmouse and mountain owl.

and between the lakes, passing above and beneath the waterfalls for spectacular views. With a map, you can work out your own route, but there are also a number of colour-coded itineraries, clearly sign-posted and designed to take between two and six hours using buses, boats and on foot. Note that the shuttle buses and boats do not operate between November and April.

HIGHLIGHTS

VELIKI SLAP
Veliki Slap (Big Waterfall) is an apt description for the most famous sight in the park, where the Plitvica stream empties into the River Korana by plunging 70m (230ft) over a cliff. This is also the easiest sight to see, with an observation terrace overlooking the waterfall just inside Ulaz 1. From here, paths continue down to the foot of the cascade; you can climb to the top for views over the falls, or follow the lakeside trail past Kaluđerovac, Gavanovac and Milanovac lakes to arrive at the dock for the boat trip across Jezero Kozjak.

THE LAKES
The lakes at Plitvice are formed from travertine (a mixture of moss and eroded limestone) and fed by numerous rivers, brooks and streams. There are 16 major lakes altogether, joined by waterfalls which force them to descend more than 150m (490ft) from Prošćansko Jezero, the highest lake, to the River Korana. The colour of the lakes varies from turquoise to emerald green, reflecting the forests and the wild flowers that grow on the cliffs. A network of footpaths criss-crosses the lakes, allowing you to get up close.

To explore off the beaten track, head for the more remote upper lakes. Take the shuttle bus from Ulaz 2 to the Labudovac falls at the head of Prošćansko Jezero. From here, you can make a complete circuit of the lake on foot, or follow a path up into the mountains to the source of the spring. Alternatively, stay on the red trail along the shores of Okgruljak, Galovac and Gravinsko until you reach Jezero Kozjak, the largest lake, where you can catch a boat downstream towards Veliki Slap. The circuit takes about six hours.

BACKGROUND

Established in 1949, Plitvice Lakes is the oldest national park in Croatia; its ecological importance was underlined when it was awarded UNESCO World Heritage status in 1979. The park occupies an area of almost 300sq km (116sq miles), with the biggest lake, Jezero Kozjak, lying at 535m (1,755ft) above sea level. Although the lakes and waterfalls are the main attractions, most of the park consists of karst limestone covered in forests of beech, fir, pine and maple. This unique ecosystem attracts a wide range of fauna and flora. The rivers and lakes teem with trout, newts, frogs, toads, salamanders, lizards and water snakes. Around 140 species of birds have been identified, including black stork and several varieties of woodpecker. Brown bears, wolves and lynx inhabit the mountains. The now peaceful environment of Plitvice is a far cry from 31 March 1991, when, in the so-called Bloody Easter incident, forces of the Republic of the Serbian Krajina took over the park and Croatian policeman Josip Jović became the first casualty of the Homeland War.

Spectacular waterfalls (above).
Enjoying a boat tour (above left)

TIPS

● Go early or late in the day to see the park at its best: There are fewer visitors about, the light is better for photography and you have more chance of seeing animals.
● Take an extra layer of clothing whatever the time of year; it can be surprisingly cool in summer and bitterly cold in winter.

Old houses in the town of Samobor (above).
Samoborska kremšnita *is a popular local custard tart (left)*

SAMOBOR

This pretty country town has become a favourite weekend destination for the people of Zagreb.

With a stream running through the middle and a square lined with baroque 19th-century townhouses, over-looked by a Habsburg yellow onion-domed church, Samobor is a delight. Just 20km (12.5 miles) from the capital and served by regular buses, this is where the people of Zagreb come for a weekend break. Most visitors seem to spend their time in cafés, enjoying Samobor's delicious custard tart, *samoborska kremšnita*. The best place to try it is at Kavana Livadić (Trg Kralja Tomislava 1), which opened in 1800 and is still the social hub, with its elegant salons and summer patio.

MUSIC AND ART

During the 19th century, Samobor was at the heart of the Croatian National Revival in politics, music and the arts. A key figure was Ferdo Livadić (1799–1879), composer of the patriotic song *Još Hravatska nij Propala* (Croatia Has Not Fallen Yet). His home is now the town museum, Gradski Muzej (tel 01 336 1014; Tue–Fri 9–3, Sat–Sun 9–1; adult 8kn, child 5kn), with archaeology and geology displays, 19th-century portraits and furniture, and occasional piano recitals. A scale model shows how Samobor looked in 1764; the only surviving buildings are the Livadić manor house and the parish church. Above the church, Muzej Marton (Jurjevska 7, tel 01 332 6426; Sat–Sun 10–1 in summer; adult 20kn, child 15kn) was Croatia's first private museum when it opened in 2003, with collections of Austro-Hungarian furniture, porcelain, glass, paintings and clocks displayed in a 19th-century mansion.

RATINGS

Good for food	●●●○
Photo stops	●●●○
Specialist shopping	●●●○

BASICS

✚ 290 D2
🛈 Trg Kralja Tomislava 5, tel 01 336 0044; Mon–Fri 8–7, Sat 9–7, Sun 10–7
🚌 From Zagreb

www.samobor.hr
The official website of the town, currently in Croatian only.

TIPS

● Restaurants in Samobor sell garlic sausages accompanied by local mustard. You can buy mustard at the Filipec family shop, just off the main square (▷ 178).
● Walk off the calories by taking Ulica Svete Ane behind the church and climbing through the woods to the ruined castle, Stari Grad.

The Franciscan monastery at Slavonski Brod

War-damage in the town of Vukovar, scene of a siege and the mass murder of many of its inhabitants in the 1991–2 war

SLAVONSKI BROD

🔹 292 H3 🔹 Trg Pobjede 30, tel 035 445765; Jul–end Aug daily 7am–7.30pm, rest of year Mon–Sat 7am–7.30pm; also an information kiosk at Tvrđava, 15 Jun–15 Sep 🔹 From Đakovo, Osijek and Zagreb 🔹 From Zagreb
www.tzgsb.hr

This busy town on the north bank of the River Sava grew up around its star-shaped Tvrđava (fortress), built in 1715 to guard the historic Vojna Krajina (Military Frontier) between the Habsburg and Ottoman empires. Today, the river forms a natural border between Bosnia and Croatia. Slavonski Brod suffered extensive shelling during the Homeland War and the damage to the Tvrđava is clearly visible. A section of the restored fortress houses the Galerija Ružić (tel 035 411510; Tue–Fri 9–1, 5–8, Sat–Sun 10–2), with sculptures by Branko Ružić (1919–97) displayed in the former casemates. A short walk along the riverbank leads to the 18th-century Franciscan monastery, with a beautiful baroque cloister. The nearby Muzej Brodskog Posavlja (Regional Museum) was damaged during the war and is currently under restoration.

VARAŽDIN

See pages 76–79.

VELIKA GORICA

🔹 290 E3 🔹 Ulica Matije Slatinskog 11, tel 01 622 2378; Mon–Fri 8–4 🔹 268 from Zagreb
www.tzvg.hr

When you arrive at Zagreb airport, you are actually landing in Velika Gorica, which would be Croatia's seventh largest city were it not effectively a suburb of Zagreb. To get there, walk through the tunnel beneath the railway station in Zagreb and catch the bus, which leaves every 10 minutes. The farmers' market in a hall beside the bus station is a reminder that this is the main town of the rural Turopolje region. The bright orange building with street-level arcades on the edge of the central park is the former town hall, built in 1765. It is now the Muzej Turopolja (tel 01 622 1325; Tue–Fri 9–4, Sat–Sun 10–1), with collections of archaeology, folk costumes and local history.
Don't miss Velika Gorica is known for its wooden chapels, built out of local oak. The simple 18th-century Kapela Ranjenog Isusa (Chapel of the Wounded Christ) is dramatically floodlit at night.

VUKOVAR

🔹 293 K3 🔹 Strossmayerova 15, tel 032 442889; Mon–Fri 7–3 🔹 From Osijek

Vukovar is a name that evokes strong feelings across Croatia. Until 1991, this was a peaceful provincial town; now it has become synonymous with the suffering of war. For three months, the people of Vukovar held out under siege from heavily armed Serbian forces. At least 2,000 people were killed and thousands more are missing, believed to be buried in mass graves. When the town finally fell, the surviving Croats fled and most have never returned. Vukovar today is a shadow of its former self. The baroque Eltz Palace, now the Town Museum (tel 032 441270; Mon–Fri 7–3), has been stripped of its treasures and its façade is littered with holes. The only reason to go to Vukovar is to contemplate the horrors of war and pay tribute to the victims at the large white cross by the Danube. The memorial cemetery, just outside town on the road to Ilok, contains the graves of the defenders of Vukovar and rows of unmarked white crosses recalling the bodies that were never found.

Varaždin

This delightful city to the north of Zagreb contains the most perfect baroque architectural ensemble in Croatia, while street artists, musicians and festivals give it a relaxed, easy-going feel.

Old buildings add to the character of Varaždin

Detail of a carving on the cathedral door

The 16th-century Town Hall on the main square

SEEING VARAŽDIN

The easiest way to see Varaždin is on a day trip from Zagreb. Buses make the journey in under two hours, though the three-hour train ride offers constantly changing views over the rolling countryside of the Zagorje. Cars cannot be taken into the city centre and the best place to leave them is at the free car park outside the cemetery. The centre is compact and easily explored on foot. The finest baroque palaces and churches are concentrated in the traffic-free streets around Trg Kralja Tomislava. As you walk look out for architectural details.

HIGHLIGHTS

TRG KRALJA TOMISLAVA

The main square is dominated by the town hall, whose present appearance dates from 1791 when the clock tower was added. Above the entrance, look for the coat of arms of Varaždin, with a red-and-white striped shield watched over by an angel. This is one of the oldest surviving coats of arms in Europe, first used in 1464 and revived in 1990. On the east side of the square, Kavana Korzo is the city's most popular meeting place, while the nearby Palača Drašković briefly acted as the Croatian parliament building. On the western side, take a close look at Kraš, a confectionery shop in the former Casa Jaccomini. A bare-breasted mermaid hangs above the door; inside, the stucco decorations on the ceiling include the initials of owner Daniela Jaccomini and the date 1777.

RATINGS

Historic interest	●●●●
Photo stops	●●●●
Walkability	●●●●

BASICS

✚ 290 E1
ℹ Ulica Padovca 3, tel 042 210987; Apr–end Oct Mon–Fri 8–7, Sat 8–4, Sun 10–1; Nov–end Mar Mon–Fri 8–4, Sat 10–1
🚆 From Zagreb
🚌 From Zagreb

www.tourism-varazdin.hr
The official tourism portal of the city.

Detail of the foot of the Grgur Ninski bronze statue in the town (opposite)

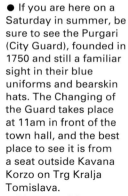

Varaždin (below) has a wealth of baroque architecture (right)

TIPS

● If you are here on a Saturday in summer, be sure to see the Purgari (City Guard), founded in 1750 and still a familiar sight in their blue uniforms and bearskin hats. The Changing of the Guard takes place at 11am in front of the town hall, and the best place to see it is from a seat outside Kavana Korzo on Trg Kralja Tomislava.

● You can pick up a good guidebook to Varaždin for 39kn from the tourist office.

BAROQUE PALACES

The entire city centre is an open-air museum of baroque architecture, but two of the best examples are found side by side on Franjevački Trg, just off the main square. Palača Patačić, with its cream-coloured rococo façade, was built in 1764 and was the social centre of 18th-century Varaždin; next door is the peach-coloured palace of the county governor, dating from 1768. Across the street, outside the Franciscan monastery church, is a bronze statue of Grgur Ninski by Ivan Meštrović—a smaller version of the one in Split (▷ 135).

URŠULINSKA CRKVA (URSULINE CHURCH)

✉ Uršulinska Ulica 3

The Ursuline sisters arrived in Varaždin in 1703 at the invitation of Countess Magdalena Drašković, the owner of the castle, whose own daughter was an Ursuline nun. The single-nave baroque church was built between 1707 and 1712, but the most striking feature is the tower, which was added in 1726. Slender and tall, pink and white, with a fresco set into the niche and topped by an onion-dome, it acts as a city landmark just outside the castle gates.

STARI GRAD (OLD CASTLE)

✉ Strossmayerovo Šetalište ☎ 042 212918 ☻ Apr–end Oct Tue–Sun 10–6; Nov–end Mar Tue–Fri 10–5, Sat–Sun 10–1 ✋ Adult 20kn, child 10kn 📖 70kn 🏛 👫

Set in a Renaissance palace surrounded by a medieval

moat, the old castle dominates Varaždin. Get there by crossing the drawbridge and passing through the 16th-century watchtower. From here, you can follow the promenade around the protective earth ramparts, now an attractive park. The castle itself, with a beautiful galleried courtyard at the centre, is home to the city museum, whose exhibits include the town magistrate's mace and seal from 1464 and a charter signed by Ferdinand II of Austria in 1621 granting legal rights to Varaždin's tailors. The upper floor galleries display furniture from different periods, revealing the changing tastes of the nobility from the 16th to 20th centuries.

A flower cart; the tower of St. John the Baptist church; the old castle; a pretty street lamp (below, left to right)

A balcony leads to the chapel of Sveti Lovre (St. Lawrence) and the adjoining sacristy, set in a circular defence tower.

GROBLJE (CEMETERY)

✉ Hallerova Aleja ☎ 042 330316 🕓 May–end Sep daily 7am–9pm; Oct–end Apr daily 7–5 ✋ Free

Situated on the outskirts of Varaždin, 500m (550 yards) west of the castle, the peaceful town cemetery is a lovely place, with wide avenues planted with beech, birch and magnolia amid the tombstones and statuary. Herman Haller, who designed the cemetery in 1905, was determined that rather than being sad and gloomy, it should be uplifting for all who visited it and the result is a beautiful memorial garden for the people of Varaždin.

BACKGROUND

Varaždin was founded in 1181 and was declared a free and royal city by King Andrija II in 1209, more than 30 years before Zagreb. In 1756 it became the seat of the Croatian governor and parliament, and in 1767 a decree by Empress Maria Teresa of Austria made Varaždin the capital of the tripartite kingdom of Croatia, Slavonia and Dalmatia. Its status as capital lasted less than 10 years, until a fire—said to have been started by a peasant boy who tripped over a pig and dropped the cigarette he was carrying into a haystack—destroyed 80 per cent of the town in 1776. Rebuilt from scratch, the resulting town is a harmonious blend of late 18th-century baroque architecture that is unrivalled in the whole country.

MORE TO SEE

GALERIJA STARIH I NOVIH MAJSTORA (GALLERY OF OLD AND NEW MASTERS)

✉ Trg Stančića 3 ☎ 042 214172 🕓 Apr–end Oct Tue–Sun 10–6; Nov–end Mar Tue–Fri 10–3, Sat–Sun 10–1 ✋ Adult 20kn, child 10kn

Paintings from minor European artists including the Rubens and Canaletto schools are displayed in the baroque Sermage palace, opposite the castle drawbridge.

ENTOMOLOŠKI MUZEJ (ENTOMOLOGICAL MUSEUM)

✉ Franjevački Trg 6 ☎ 042 210474 🕓 Apr–end Oct Tue–Sun 10–6; Nov–end Mar Tue–Fri 10–3, Sat–Sun 10–1 ✋ Adult 20kn, child 10kn

A remarkable display of thousands of insects in the 18th-century palace of the Herczer family.

Zagorje

This bucolic region of gently rolling hills dotted with picture-book castles and churches is known throughout Croatia for its beauty.

Sheaves of wheat in the farmland, Zagorje *A plaque on the castle wall at Trakošćan* *Onion domes of a church, Zagorje (above left). A lake in the region (above right)*

RATINGS

Good for food	●●●
Historic interest	●●●
Photo stops	●●●●

BASICS

✚ 290 D2
🛈 Zagrebačka 6, Krapinske Toplice, tel 049 233653; Mon–Fri 8–4

www.tz-zagorje.hr
Website of the Zagorje Tourist Board, in Croatian only.

TIP

● A delicacy of the Zagorje region is the *licitarsko srce*, a gingerbread heart decorated with red icing and displayed in the home rather than eaten. You can buy them at shops in the church square at Marija Bistrica.

A statue of Jesus at Our Lady of the Snows, Marija Bistrica (opposite)

SEEING ZAGORJE

The Zagorje (highlands) occupies the area north of Zagreb between the Medvednica mountain range and the Slovenian border. The sights are spread out across the region, and there are only a few main roads so you will need to allow plenty of time. Buses connect Zagreb with Krapina and Marija Bistrica, but to get the most out of the Zagorje you will need your own car. It is possible to make a circuit of the Zagorje in a single day (▷ 206–207), but to explore the region in depth and visit the castles at Veliki Tabor and Trakošćan, consider staying overnight at one of the growing number of farmhouses offering rural accommodation.

HIGHLIGHTS

TRAKOŠĆAN

✚ 290 E1 ☎ 042 796422 ⏰ Apr–end Oct daily 9–6; Nov–end Mar daily 9–3 💰 Adult 20kn, child 10kn 📖 Guidebook 50kn, miniguide 10kn 🚻 📇 👪
www.mdc.hr/trakoscan
A castle in Croatia usually means a stately country house, but Trakošćan is everyone's idea of what a proper castle should look like, standing proud on a wooded hillside with white walls and crenellated towers reflected in an artifical lake. Begun in the 13th century as part of the defence network of what was then the Zagorje principality, the castle takes its present romantic appearance from a 19th-century restoration by the Drašković family. They were granted

The castle at Veliki Tabor; rural landscape; part of the 12 Stations of the Cross at Our Lady of the Snows, Marija Bistrica (below, left to right)

the estate by the Habsburg emperor in 1584 as a reward for military service and it remained in their possession until it was confiscated by the state and turned into a museum in Tito's Yugoslavia. Cross the drawbridge and climb the steep path to the castle, where exhibits reflect the lifestyles of the Austro-Hungarian nobility, with family portraits, tapestries, hunting trophies, firearms, ceramic braziers and furniture, including a splendid 19th-century card table. Don't miss the study of Julijana Erdödy-Drašković (1847–1901), the first recognized female painter in Croatia, whose piano is preserved alongside her

MORE TO SEE

KUMROVEC
See page 65.

GALERIJA AUGUSTINČIĆ
✉ Trg Antun Mihanovića 10, Klanjec ☎ 049 550343 🕐 Apr–end Sep daily 9–5; Oct–end Mar, Tue–Sun 9–3 💷 Adult 20kn, child 10kn www.mdc.hr/augustincic
Sculptures by Antun Augustinčić (▷ 65) on display in the village of Klanjec.

BELEC
A minor road from Zlatar leads to the village of Belec and the church of Sveta Marije Snježne (St. Mary of the Snows). This 18th-century church is one of the finest baroque creations in Croatia, a riot of extravagant detail with sculpted angels and saints, and frescoes by Ivan Ranger (1700–53), all newly restored to their former glory.

paintings of rural life. Afterwards, you can walk around the lakeshore or take a boat out on the lake.

VELIKI TABOR
✚ 290 D2 ✉ Desinić ☎ 049 343963 🕐 Apr–end Sep daily 10–5; Oct–end Mar daily 9–3 💷 Adult 10kn, child 5kn www.veliki-tabor.hr
Standing on a hill 334m (1,095ft) high with views across the Zagorje, the castle at Veliki Tabor is the finest surviving example of a late medieval fortress in Croatia. It was built during the 16th century by the Ratkay family, who lived here for almost 300 years. The castle is pentagonal, with four semicircular towers around an arcaded courtyard. Inside is a museum containing halberds and pikes, but the real attractions are the views. Following the demise of the Ratkay family, the castle changed hands several times; during World War II it was run as an orphanage by Franciscan nuns. It became a museum in 1993 but it is still in a poor state of repair and restoration is likely to be ongoing for some time.

MUZEJ KRAPINSKOG PRAČOVJEKA (MUSEUM OF EVOLUTION)
✉ Šetalište Sluge, Krapina ☎ 049 371491 🕐 Apr–end Sep daily 9–5; Oct–end Mar Tue–Sun 9–3 💷 Adult 20kn, child 10kn www.krapina.com
The region's main town of Krapina is best known for the discovery of *Homo krapinensis*, a Neanderthal human who lived here some 30,000 years ago and whose bones were found in a cave on the Hušnjakovo hill in 1899. The originals are kept in the Croatian Natural History Museum in Zagreb (▷ 54), but the on-site museum has reproductions of human

skulls, together with prehistoric tools and a full skeleton of a cave bear. Walk up the hill behind the museum to see the cave itself, marked by lifesize sculptures of humans and animals. The museum offers guided tours. A major new interactive museum is currently under construction and is scheduled to open by 2007.

Religious items on sale (left) at Our Lady of the Snows church (below)

MARIJA BISTRICA

✚ 290 E2 🚇 Zagrebačka, tel 049 468380; Apr–end Oct daily 7–5; Nov–end Mar Mon–Fri 7–3 🚌 From Zagreb
www.marija-bistrica.hr

The Church of Our Lady of the Snows at Marija Bistrica is the most important pilgrimage site in Croatia. The object of veneration is the Black Madonna, a dark wooden statue of the Virgin and Child, probably dating from the 15th century. According to tradition, the statue was walled into the church by the parish priest to protect it from Turkish invaders and was discovered in 1684 when a miraculous beam of light revealed its hiding place. In 1935 the Black Madonna was proclaimed Queen of the Croats by the Archbishop of Zagreb. The present church was built in 1883 by Hermann Bollé, architect of Zagreb cathedral. Pope John Paul II made the pilgrimage here in 1998 to announce the beatification of Cardinal Alojzije Stepinac (▷ 21); the square in front of the church is now named after the pontiff. Climb the Via Crucis (Way of the Cross) on the hill behind the church for good views.

BACKGROUND

Ruled as an independent principality from the 13th to 15th centuries, the Zagorje region contains more than 40 castles and mansions, due to its strategic location between Zagreb, Slovenia and Hungary. This was the birthplace of both the Yugoslav leader Tito and Croatian president Franjo Tuđman, who was born in the village of Veliko Trgovišće in 1922. The people of the Zagorje, especially around Krapina, speak a dialect of Croatian known as *kajkavski*.

VELIKI TABOR AND THE STORY OF VERONIKA

A local legend in Desinić tells of Veronika, a beautiful girl who fell in love with Friedrich, the handsome son of Count Herman of Celje, owner of the castle at Veliki Tabor. The count disapproved of the relationship, so the young lovers escaped to Slovenia, where they married in secret. When the count found out, he sent his soldiers to arrest the couple and had his son imprisoned in a tower. An even worse fate awaited Veronika; she was drowned and her body walled into the castle. During restoration work at Veliki Tabor in 1982, the skull of a young woman was found, so perhaps the legend is true after all.

THE SIGHTS

ISTRIA

The Istrian peninsula shows its Italian roots—
most towns have Croatian and Italian names.
This is Croatia's larder, producing cheese,
ham, wine, olives, asparagus and the famous
truffles. Resorts such as Rovinj and Poreč buzz
in summer, while inland is a quieter Istria of
vineyards, oak woods and medieval hilltop towns.

MAJOR SIGHTS

Looking up to the fortified hill town of Buzet

Buje, a large hill town on the site of a Roman settlement, is surrounded by important wine-making villages

BALE (VALLE)

� 294 A5 🛈 Trg Palih Boraca 3, tel 052 824270; Jun–end Sep Mon–Sat 8–8 🚌 From Pula and Rovinj
www.bale-valle.hr

Bale is a typical compact Istrian hilltop town lying on the road from Pula to Rovinj. It was built just inland from the sea on the site of an Illyrian and Roman fort, Castrum Vallis, though its history goes back much farther than that. Recent underwater excavations have discovered dinosaur fossils off the nearby coast; there are plans to build a museum of dinosaurs, but in the meantime the bones are on display inside the town hall (tel 052 824303; weekday mornings in summer). Facing the town hall across the square is the 15th-century Venetian Gothic palace of the Soardo-Bembo family, who were the lords of Bale during the period of Venetian rule. Beneath the tower, with its sundial and winged lion of St. Mark, an archway leads into the walled town. It takes less than five minutes to make a complete circuit of Castel, the main street of the old town, which is little more than a cobbled lane spanned by arches.

BRIJUNI (BRIONI)

See pages 86–87.

BUJE (BUIE)

� 294 A4 🛈 Istarska 2, tel 052 772122; Jun–end Sep Mon–Sat 8–8; Oct–end May Mon–Fri 8–3 🚌 From Pula, Poreč and Rovinj
www.tzg-buje.hr

The largest of Istria's hill towns occupies a strategic position, 5km (3 miles) from the Slovenian border on the old trade route from Pula to Trieste. In medieval times it was known as 'the watchtower of Istria' and it is easy to see why when you stand on the terrace beside Trg Slobode, with views over the countryside and the Italian Alps visible across the sea. At the top of the main street is the Etnografski Muzej (Trg Slobode 4, tel 052 773075; Jun–end Sep Tue–Sun 9–12, 6–8), with rooms full of knick-knacks in the style of a rural Istrian home. From here a short climb leads to the church of Sveti Servula (St. Servolo), built on the site of a Roman temple within the medieval town walls. Note the Venetian winged lion on the bell tower, and the scallop-shell niche above the portal. Buje is also the capital of an important wine-growing area, with much of the best Istrian wine being produced in the nearby villages of Brtonigla and Momjan.

BUZET (PINGUENTE)

🔷 294 B4 🛈 Trg Fontana 7, tel 052 662343; Jun–end Sep Mon–Fri 8–3, Sat 9–2; Oct–end May Mon-Fri 8–3 🚌 From Pula
www.buzet.hr

High on a bluff above the River Mirna, Buzet seems almost to grow out of the rock. From the heart of the modern town on Trg Fontana, a long staircase leads to the old town, entered through the 16th-century Vela Vrata (Large Gate) and still partly enclosed by its medieval walls. With its narrow streets, Venetian palaces and attractive baroque fountain, the old town makes an enjoyable place to stroll. The former Bigatto palace houses the Zavičajni Muzej (Trg Rašporskih Kapetana 1, tel 052 662792; Mon–Fri 12.30–3.30), a regional museum of archaeology, ethnology and crafts. From the walls behind the church of Sveti Juraj (St. George), there are views over the Čićarija mountains, which divide Istria from the rest of Croatia. **Don't miss** The Subotina festival is usually held on the first Saturday in September (▷ 185).

Brijuni (Brioni)

These luxuriant islands off the west coast of Istria have been a playground for the rich and famous for more than 2,000 years.

Passengers on an excursion boat (above)

A photograph of Tito and Castro in the Tito Museum (above left). The ruins of the Byzantine fortress on Veli Brijun (above right)

RATINGS

Good for kids	●●●○
Photo stops	●●●●
Walkability	●●●○

BASICS

✚ 294 A5

ℹ Nacionalni Park Brijuni, Brijunska 10, Fažana, tel 052 525888

🎫 Jul–end Aug: adult 180kn, child (4–14) 90kn; Jun and Sep: adult 170kn, child 85kn; Apr, May and Oct: adult 140kn, child 70kn; Nov–end Mar: adult 100kn, child 50kn

www.brijuni.hr
Comprehensive site in Croatian and English with information on history, wildlife and activities.

SEEING BRIJUNI

Of 14 islands in the Brijuni archipelago, only the two largest, Veli Brijun and Mali Brijun, can be visited. They lie off the west coast of Istria, 3km (2 miles) from the port of Fažana. The best way of visiting is on one of the official Brijuni National Park boat trips which operate several times daily in summer and once or twice a week in winter. Included in the price is a three-hour guided tour of Veli Brijun by miniature safari train, with visits to the safari park, museums and Roman villa. It is best to book several days in advance. In summer, the national park also offers trips to Mali Brijun, including a visit to a fort. Tour operators on the dock at Fažana advertise boat trips to the islands, but most of these cruise around Veli Brijun rather than going ashore.

HIGHLIGHTS

TITO NA BRIJUNIMA (TITO ON BRIJUNI)

This fascinating photographic exhibition recalls the time from 1947 to 1979 when Tito used the Brijuni islands as his summer retreat, entertaining visitors at the Bijela Vila (White House). More than 60 heads of state visited Brijuni, including Emperor Haile Selassie of Ethiopia, Queen Elizabeth II of Great Britain and President Fidel Castro of Cuba. In 1956 Tito hosted the founding of the Non-Aligned Movement on Brijuni, accompanied by President Nasser of Egypt and President Nehru of India. As well as statesmen, he enjoyed the company of film stars and there are pictures of Tito relaxing with glamorous actresses Elizabeth Taylor, Gina Lollobrigida and Sophia Loren.

SAFARI PARK

The safari park at the northern tip of Veli Brijun contains animals given to Tito by world leaders, including antelopes, zebras and a pair of Indian elephants donated by Indira Gandhi. Visitors can walk around a small ethno-park featuring rare breeds of farm animals, including the boškarin (long-horned Istrian cattle).

The archipelago (below left). Tour boats visit the islands (below)

OTHER SIGHTS

Also featured on the tour are the remains of a 1st-century Roman villa, a Byzantine *castrum* (fortress) and a 15th-century church. The safari train also crosses the golf course, where you can look out for wild mouflon and deer. Much of the island is covered in forests of laurel and holm oak, and there is a thousand-year-old olive tree in a meadow near the harbour.

BACKGROUND

Dinosaur footprints have been found on Veli Brijun, but the first human inhabitants were wealthy Roman patricians, who built their summer villas here to take advantage of the mild climate. The modern history of Brijuni begins in 1893, when Austrian magnate Paul Kupelweiser (1843–1919) bought the islands with the intention of turning them into a luxury resort. After hiring Nobel prize-winning bacteriologist Robert Koch (1843–1910) to successfully eradicate malaria, he set about building hotels, tennis courts, a golf course and heated seawater pool. For a while Brijuni was the favoured playground of the Austro-Hungarian aristocracy; visitors included Archduke Franz Ferdinand and the author James Joyce. During the Communist era, Tito used the islands as his private retreat. In 1983, Brijuni was declared a national park and it continues to attract the rich and famous; an Italian company has plans to redevelop Veli Brijun as a luxury spa resort, and a polo tournament last staged in the 1930s was reinstated in 2004.

TIPS

● If you want to explore the island of Veli Brijun on your own, you can rent bicycles or electric golf buggies (carts) or even take an expensive ride in Tito's 1953 Cadillac.
● Guests staying at the hotels on Veli Brijun have unlimited crossings to the mainland included in the price, and also receive discounts on golf, tennis and sailing excursions.

Window detail in a narrow street in Grožnjan

An old, deserted house near the town of Grožnjan, which has been revived by an influx of artists

DRAGUĆ (DRAGUCCIO)

🔲 294 B4
www.draguc.com

The picturesque village of Draguć is little more than a single street of houses perched on a cliff. Under Venetian rule, this was a fortified town and some of the houses are built onto the medieval ramparts. From the terrace beside the main square, there are expansive views over central Istria. The 12th-century cemetery church at the entrance to Draguć contains poorly preserved frescoes, and the altar incorporates a Roman tombstone. At the other end of the village, the lovely little chapel of Sveti Roka (St. Roch) has 16th-century frescoes of the Annunciation and the Adoration of the Magi by Master Antonio of Padova. The chapel is usually locked but you can peer through the open window or ask for the key at the bar. If Draguć looks like a film set, that is because it is. During the 1980s, it was known as the Croatian Hollywood and it is currently experiencing a revival. Among movies shot in Draguç are *La Femme Musketeer* (2003) starring Gérard Dépardieu, and *Libertas* (2005), about the life of

Dubrovnik playwright and libertine Marin Držić, in which Draguć plays 16th-century Florence.

GRAČIŠĆE (GALLIGNANA)

🔲 294 B4

Time seems to have stood still in Gračišće, a village of stone lanes and 15th-century houses inscribed with their dates above the doors. On a hilltop on the road from Pazin to Labin, this was once a fortress on the boundary of the Venetian and Habsburg empires. At one time, Gračišće had 15 churches and Venetian Gothic palaces and was the summer residence of the bishops of Pićan. The church of Sveta Marije na Placu (Our Lady on the Square), just inside the town gate, has a beautiful porch and 15th-century frescoes, which can usually be glimpsed through the window grille. Look carefully for the remains of nails hidden between the stones; this was a votive chapel where infertile women would leave gifts and prayers in the hope of being blessed with a child. From the terrace behind the parish church there are views over the Istrian countryside, with Mount Učka looming on the horizon.

GROŽNJAN (GRISIGNANA)

🔲 294 A4 👤 Umberta Gorjana 3, tel 052 776131
www.tz-groznjan.hr

A few decades ago, Grožnjan was crumbling and deserted; now it is a thriving artistic and cultural centre. Surrounded by walls in the 12th century and ruled by Venice for over 400 years, it was part of Italy along with the rest of Istria from 1918 to 1945. When Istria joined Yugoslavia after World War II, Grožnjan was abandoned by its largely Italian population. In 1965 the decaying town was proclaimed a city of artists; in 1969 it hosted the first annual summer school of Jeunesses Musicales Croatia. Now the town has 30 art galleries and studios, a film academy and concert hall and an active Italian association. On summer evenings concerts of jazz and classical music are held in the churches and squares. The best places for atmosphere are from the Venetian loggia, or from the belvedere on the church terrace.
Don't miss The 16th-century chapel of SS Cosmas and Damian was restored in 1989; it has frescoes by Croatian artist Ivan Lovrenčić (1917–2002).

The church tower in Hum, the
smallest town in the world

Looking down to Rabac
harbour from Labin

A fisherman mends his nets
by Limski Kanal

HUM (COLMO)

✠ 294 B4
www.hum.hr

The self-proclaimed smallest town in the world has
fewer than 20 inhabitants
and a handful of stone
houses lining its two narrow streets. What makes
it a town rather than a village is its annual election
for mayor, when the
judges of the parish
gather around a stone
table beneath the munici-
pal loggia, carving notches
in a wooden stick to make
their choice. First men-
tioned in 1102, Hum still
preserves its medieval
town walls, though the
original entrance gate
now contains a pair of
copper doors engraved
with Glagolitic writing and
a calendar of rural activities. This is the last
monument in the Aleja
Glagoljaša (Glagolitic
Alley), a sculpture trail
which follows the road for
7km (4.5 miles) from Roč
to Hum. The sculptures,
by Želimir Janeš
(1916–96), reflect themes
from Croatian and Istrian
history, in particular the
importance of the
Glagolitic script (▷ 19) in
this region. Some of the
monuments are designed
in the shape of Glagolitic
characters; one is a large
stone block depicting the
letters of the Glagolitic,

Cyrillic and Latin alphabets
in juxtaposition.
Don't miss The cemetery
church of Sveti Jeronima
(St. Hieronymus), outside
the town gates, has 12th-
century frescoes and
Glagolitic graffiti.

LABIN (ALBONA)

✠ 294 B4 ℹ Aldo Negri 20,
tel 052 855560; Jun–end Sep
Mon–Sat 8am–9pm, sun 10–1,
6–9; Oct–end May Mon–Fri 9–3
🚌 From Pula and Rijeka
www.istra.com/rabac

Sitting above Rabac
(▷ 91) on Istria's south-
east coast, Labin is
divided into two parts, its
typical medieval hill town
looking down over the
modern district of
Podlabin. Until the mines
closed in 1999 Labin was
Croatia's coal-mining capital; in 1921 striking miners
declared the town an
independent socialist
republic. These days it
has a new lease of life as
an art colony—at least 30
artists and potters have
their studios here, and in
summer the Labin Art
Republic takes over the
streets, with live theatre,
outdoor concerts and
open ateliers. From the
main square, Titov Trg,
with its Venetian loggia,
steps lead up to the town
gate. Beyond the gate is a
delightful ensemble of
Renaissance and baroque

architecture, with the
palaces of the Venetian
nobility painted in bright
orange, lemon and vanilla.
The 18th-century Battiala-
Lazzarini palace houses
the Narodni Muzej (tel
052 852477; Mon–Fri
10–1, 5–7, Sat 10–1 in
summer; Mon–Fri 7–3 in
winter), where the most
unusual exhibit is a reconstructed coal mine; be
prepared to don a hard hat
as you walk through the
underground passages.
Near here is the parish
church of the Blessed
Virgin Mary, with a rose
window and winged lion
of St. Mark on the façade.

LIMSKI KANAL

✠ 294 A4

This flooded karst valley
forms a fjordlike inlet
which flows for 10km
(6 miles) beneath thickly
wooded cliffs. Boat trips
along the gorge are adver-
tised at the harboursides
in Poreč, Vrsar and Rovinj
in summer; it makes a
popular excursion for families staying on the Istrian
coast. The boats usually
stop for lunch at the far
end of the gorge, where
restaurants serve mussels
and oysters from the
fjord; on the way back you
will probably visit the cave
of Romuald, an 11th-cen-
tury hermit who lived in
the cliffs over the gorge.

The red-tiled rooftops of Motovun (above).
Strolling past a truffle and wine shop (left)

MOTOVUN (MONTONA)

Perched atop a hill, surrounded by vineyards, Motovun is the most attractive inland Istrian town.

At 277m (906ft) above the Mirna valley and visible long before you reach it, Motovun is the perfect hilltop town. Like so many towns in Istria, it had a large Italian population—the former Formula One motor-racing champion Mario Andretti was born here in 1940—and was depopulated after World War II. Now tourists crowd its narrow streets in summer and its international film festival has put it firmly on the European cultural map.

THE WAY IN
You can leave your car at the foot of the hill and walk up—a staggering 1,052 steps—or pay a toll in summer to drive up the twisting road to the town. If you do drive you will have to park outside the gates. Walk through the outer gate to arrive at the Venetian loggia. A second gate leads to the square, Trg Andrea Antico, named after a Renaissance composer from Motovun.

WHAT TO SEE
All of the main sights are found on or around the square. Notice the old well, the crenellated bell tower of the parish church, and the sculptural relief of a winged lion, symbol of the Venetian republic, dating from 1322. From here you can make a short promenade around the ramparts, with views all the way.

Don't miss There is a lapidarium inside the outer gate with a Roman sculpture on one side, Venetian lions on the other, and a recent addition—a stone carving of the Motovun Film Festival logo.

RATINGS
Good for food	● ● ● ○
Historic interest	● ● ● ○
Photo stops	● ● ● ●

BASICS
🔲 294 A4
🏠 Trg Andrea Antico 1, tel 052 681642; Jun–end Sep Mon–Sat 8–4
🚌 From Pazin

www.hotel-kastel-motovun.hr
This hotel website also has a wealth of information on Motovun's history, traditions and cuisine.

TIP
● This is a good place to try Istrian truffles, which grow in the nearby oak woods. Restaurants in Motovun specialize in truffle dishes, and shops sell truffles, local wine and *biska* (mistletoe brandy).

A detail on the façade of Pazin's castle

Pleasure craft moored in the pretty and busy harbour of the popular resort of Rabac

NOVIGRAD (CITTANOVA)

✚ 294 A4 ℹ Porporella 1, tel 052 757075; Jun–end Sep daily 8–8; Apr, May daily 8–7; Oct–end Mar, Mon–Fri 8–3, Sat 8–1 🚌 From Poreč and Umag www.istra.com/novigrad

Built on an islet near the mouth of the River Mirna, Novigrad was originally a Greek and then a Roman colony and was joined to the mainland in the 18th century. Its name dates back to the 6th century, when it was called Neopolis (New Town). The main square, Veliki Trg, is dominated by the parish church, dedicated to local 3rd-century martyrs St. Pelagius and St. Maximus. The present church dates mostly from the 18th century, but it retains its 11th-century crypt. The separate bell tower, added in 1883, is modelled on St. Mark's in Venice, though it is topped by a bronze statue of the town's patron, St. Pelagius. Until 1831 Novigrad was the seat of a bishop and people still refer to the church as the cathedral. Parts of the medieval walls remain intact. A delightful promenade starts at the town beach and continues to the inner harbour. It passes a 16th-century Venetian loggia, overlooking the sea.

PAZIN (PISINO)

✚ 294 B4 ℹ Franine i Jurine 14, tel 052 622460; Jun–end Aug Mon–Fri 9–7, Sat–Sun 9–1; Sep Mon–Fri 9–7; Oct–end May Mon–Fri 8–4 🚌 From Poreč, Pula and Rovinj 🚂 From Buzet and Pula www.tzpazin.hr

Pazin was chosen as the capital of Istria in 1945, partly because of its central position and partly because it did not have the Italian associations of larger coastal towns like Pula. The result is that this small provincial town of 10,000 people has an importance far outweighing its size. On the first Tuesday every month it hosts the largest traditional fair in Istria, the Pazinski Samanj, which has been held here since 1574. The town is dominated by its castle, first mentioned in 983 in a deed of gift from Emperor Otto II to the Bishop of Poreč and later used as a prison in the days of the Austro-Hungarian empire. It now houses the Etnografski Muzej Istre (tel 052 622220; mid-Apr to mid-Oct Tue–Sun 10–6; mid-Oct to mid-Apr Tue–Thu 10–3, Fri 12–5, Sat–Sun 11–5; adult 15kn, child 8kn; www.emi.hr), an enjoyable ethnographic museum with displays of folk costumes, musical instruments, household goods and children's toys. The square tower contains documents and maps on the history of the castle as well as instruments of torture in the old dungeon. The castle is on a cliff overlooking Pazin Pit, where the River Pazinčica enters an underground canyon. The hero of Jules Verne's novel *Mathias Sandorf* made a dramatic escape from the castle by throwing himself into the gorge and then swimming along the subterranean river to the sea.

POREČ (PARENZO)

See pages 92–93.

PULA (POLA)

See pages 94–97.

RABAC

✚ 294 B4 ℹ Labin (▷ 89) 🚌 From Labin www.istra.com/rabac

The largest resort on Istria's southeast coast lies 4km (2.5 miles) beneath the hill town of Labin (▷ 89). Although it has seen extensive tourist development and can accommodate up to 10,000 visitors in summer, Rabac still has the feel of a Mediterranean fishing village, with whitewashed houses, pebble beaches and pretty coves.

Poreč (Parenzo)

Although it has become a busy, modern tourist resort, Poreč is at its heart a Roman town. It is worth coming here just to see the 6th-century basilica, richly ornamented with Byzantine mosaics.

Fishing boats moored along the waterfront

Detail of an intricately carved column

The nave of the Basilica of Euphrasius

RATINGS	
Good for kids	● ● ●
Historic interest	● ● ● ●
Walkability	● ● ●

BASICS

✠ 294 A4
🛈 Zagrebačka 9, tel 052 451293; Jun–end Sep daily 8am–9pm; Oct–end May Mon–Sat 8–3
🚌 From Pula and Rovinj

www.istra.com/porec
Official website of Poreč tourist office.

SEEING POREČ

The oldest part of Poreč occupies a narrow peninsula, but it has expanded on all sides and is now swamped by the hotels, campsites and tourist villages of Lanterna and Zelena Laguna. Coastal footpaths, buses, boats and a miniature road train in summer link the resorts to the old town. The old town is small and easily explored on foot. In summer you can catch a ferry from the harbourside promenade to the wooded isle of Sveti Nikola.

HIGHLIGHTS

EUFRAZIJEVA BASILIKA (BASILICA OF EUPHRASIUS)

✉ Eufrazijeva 🕐 Daily 7am–8pm in summer, 10–7 in winter
✋ Free

The one must-see sight in Poreč is this 6th-century church, built by Bishop Euphrasius on the site of a 4th-century oratory. You enter the complex through the colonnaded atrium; to your left is the octagonal baptistry, which gives access to the bell tower (Easter–end Oct 10–6; adult 10kn, child 5kn), which you can climb for views over the town. On the right is the basilica, with mosaics on the façade. A long nave, lined with Greek marble columns, leads to the altar, sheltered beneath a 13th-century ciborium (canopy). Behind here is the sanctuary, completely covered in mosaic and gold leaf. The central panel depicts the Madonna and Child; on her right is St. Maurus, and beyond him, Bishop Euphrasius holding a model of his church. The upper panel depicts Christ with his Apostles. The bishop's palace, off the atrium, contains a museum (tel 052 451711; Easter–end Oct 10–6; adult 10kn, child 5kn), with stone sculptures and remains of the original 4th-century oratory, including a mosaic fish, a secret symbol of the underground church in Roman times.

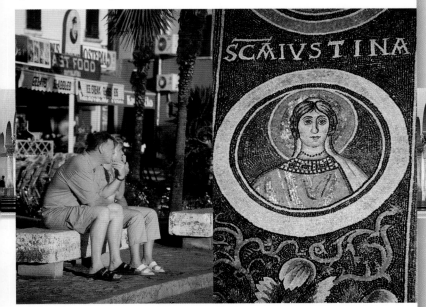

ZAVIČAJNI MUZEJ (REGIONAL MUSEUM)

✉ Dekumanska 9 ☎ 052 431585 ◑ Jun–end Sep Mon–Sat 10–1, 6–9, Sun 10–1; Oct Mon–Sat 10–1; Nov–end May by appointment 🎫 Adult 10kn, child 5kn

Housed in the 17th-century baroque Sinčić palace, the museum contains archaeological and history collections together with 18th-century furniture.

THE ROMAN TOWN

Poreč has retained its original Roman grid plan, with two intersecting streets, Cardo and Decumanus, providing the main routes of the old town. Decumanus ends in Trg Marafor, the ancient Roman forum, where you can see the remains of temples.

BACKGROUND

Poreč was founded as the Roman town of Parentium in the first century BC. Its first bishop was St. Maurus, who was martyred in the 3rd century. In 1267 this was the first town in Istria to be conquered by the Venetians. Tourism began in 1845 with the publication of the first guidebook; the first public beach opened on the island of Sveti Nikola in 1895, and during the 1970s, Poreč was Yugoslavia's biggest resort. In 1997 the Basilica of Euphrasius was designated a UNESCO World Heritage Site.

Byzantine fresco in the Basilica of Euphrasius (above). A couple relaxing by the waterfront (above left)

TIPS

● Look out for classical concerts in the basilica and jazz concerts in the lapidarium of the Regional Museum in summer.
● Mass is held in the basilica at 7.30am and 6pm on weekdays, and at 11am on Sundays.
● If you get too hot after all that sightseeing, take a boat to the island of Sveti Nikola for an afternoon on the beach.

Pula (Pola)

Istria's biggest city has an impressive collection of Roman monuments, including the sixth largest amphitheatre in the world.

The Roman amphitheatre (above left). Negotiating the ruins (above right)

Dramatic arches of the amphitheatre (above left). The Town Hall in Pula's main square (above right)

SEEING PULA

Although Pula is now a sprawling city of 60,000 people, the Roman monuments are concentrated in a small area at its heart. Beginning at the Arena, you can make a brief circuit of the main sights following the streets that wind around the base of a fortified hill. Downhill from the amphitheatre, Ulica Kandlerova leads to the Forum, from where Via Sergia continues to the Arch of Sergi; turn left beyond the arch to return to the Arena via Giardini and the Archaeological Museum. The big hotels and beaches are 5km (3 miles) south, on the Punta Verudela peninsula and around Pješčana Uvala.

HIGHLIGHTS

ARENA

✉ Ulica Flavijevska ☎ 052 219028 🕐 May–end Sep daily 8am–9pm; Oct–end Apr daily 8.30–4.30 🖐 Adult 20kn, child 10kn 📖 30kn 🎧 Audioguide 30kn (May–Sep only) 🎫 👫
Built on a natural slope beside the harbour, the well-preserved Roman amphitheatre has two rows of arches on its seaward side, a single row on the landward side, and tiered stone seats climbing to a grassy hillock. Begun in the reign of Emperor Augustus, it was completed in the 1st century AD and once held more than 20,000 spectators for gladiatorial contests. Today it is a popular concert venue: artists who have played here include Sting, Jose Carreras and Luciano Pavarotti. Beyond the impressive scale of the building itself, there is not much for visitors to see, though you

RATINGS	
Historic interest	●●●●●
Photo stops	●●●
Walkability	●●●

BASICS

✚ 294 A5
🛈 Forum 3, tel 052 219197; Jun–end Sep daily 8am–midnight; Oct–end May 9–4
🚌 From Poreč, Rijeka and Rovinj

www.pulainfo.hr
Official website of Pula tourist office.

www.mdc.hr/pula
The Archaeological Museum maintains all of the Roman monuments in Pula, and its website has detailed information on each sight.

The impressive Roman amphitheatre (opposite)

POVIJESNI MUZEJ ISTRE (ISTRIAN HISTORY MUSEUM)

✉ Kaštel ☎ 052 211566
🕐 May–early Sep daily
8am–9pm; Oct–end Apr
Mon–Fri 9–5 ✋ Adult 10kn,
child 5kn 🚻

Housed in a star-shaped Venetian fortress at the top of the town, this museum contains naval uniforms and medals from the Austro-Hungarian empire and displays on Pula's shipbuilding history. Of greater interest are the views from the grassy ramparts and 19th-century round tower. To get there, climb the steps from Via Sergia and enter across the drawbridge beside a row of cannon.

THE SIGHTS

RIMSKI MOZAIK (ROMAN MOSAIC)

Behind a car park just off the Forum is a perfectly preserved 2nd-century mosaic, discovered as a result of bomb damage in World War II. It probably occupied the floor of a wealthy patrician's home, and features fish, birds and flowers and the legend of the punishment of Dirce, with the twins Amphion and Zethus seen tying their stepmother to the horns of a bull.

KATEDRALA (CATHEDRAL)

Close to the Forum in a small square, Pula's cathedral has a 17th-century façade tacked onto an early Christian basilica, built on the site of a Roman temple with a Roman sarcophagus for an altar. The free-standing bell tower was added in the 17th century using stone from the arena.

are free to wander around and clamber onto the seats. The underground gallery, where wild beasts were kept before fights, houses an exhibition on Roman Istria, with olive presses and amphorae. The gift shop sells models of the Arena as well as replica Roman items.

FORUM

The old Roman forum is still Pula's central square, with open-air cafés, the tourist office and town hall. The Temple of Augustus, built between 2BC and AD14, has steps leading up to a porch supported by six Corinthian columns. Under Venetian rule, it was used as a church and a grain store, but it now houses a lapidarium of Roman sculpture (May–end Sep, daily 9–8). The temple was destroyed by an Allied bomb during World War II and rebuilt in 1947. The arcaded building next door is the Renaissance town hall, which incorporates parts of the Roman Temple of Diana into its rear façade.

SLAVOLUK SERGIJEVACA (ARCH OF SERGI)

This triumphal arch was erected around 30BC by a wealthy widow to commemorate the role played by her husband and brothers in the Battle of Actium, when a fleet commanded by Octavian (later Emperor Augustus) was victorious over Mark Antony for control of the Roman empire. The arch was previously joined to the Porta Aurea (Golden Gate), part of the Roman walls; when the walls were torn down in the 19th century the arch remained. Inscribed in honour of Lucius Sergius Lepidus, it features reliefs of eagles, sphinxes, dolphins, acanthus leaves and bunches of grapes, along with chariots and the Roman goddess of victory. Just inside the arch is a bronze sculpture, by Mate Čvrljak (born 1934), of the Irish novelist James Joyce

(1882–1941) sitting on a chair outside the Uliks bar. Joyce taught English for a few months in 1904–5 at the Berlitz school on this site.

The Temple of Augustus on Pula's main square; the Roman amphitheatre; looking up at the Arch of Sergi (above, left to right)

ARHEOLOŠKI MUZEJ (ARCHAEOLOGICAL MUSEUM)

✉ Ulica Carrarina 3 ☎ 052 218603 ◷ May–end Sep Mon–Sat 9–8, Sun 10–3; Oct–end Apr Mon–Fri 9–3 💲 Adult 12kn, child 6kn 🏛 🚻

The twin arches of Porta Gemina, a surviving Roman gateway, lead to this museum, which displays artefacts from Roman Pula, including jewellery, coins, mosaics, glassware, pottery, oil lamps, sarcophagi and an extensive open-air lapidarium of sculpture. As well as Roman objects, the museum covers the prehistoric and early medieval periods—look for the pre-Roman tombstone depicting a horseman and goddess of fertility, and the carved stone altars with typically ornate braiding from medieval Croatian churches. Climb the hill behind the museum to see a small semi-circular Roman theatre, built in the 2nd century AD.

BACKGROUND

Pula was built on the site of a Histrian hill fort, conquered by the Romans under Julius Caesar in the first century BC. It reached its peak under Emperor Augustus, when it was a city of 5,000 people, with temples, theatres, monumental walls and gates. Decline set in under Venetian rule, but Pula revived in the 19th century, when it became the chief naval base of the Austro-Hungarian fleet. During the 20th century it expanded due to industry and tourism and it is now the seventh biggest city in Croatia.

TIPS

● Tour boats at the harbour offer cruises to the Brijuni islands (▷ 86–87) in summer.
● The tables outside Cvajner Caffe on the Forum make a great venue for people-watching, but go inside to see the 16th-century frescoes uncovered during restoration of the building.

Rovinj (Rovigno)

With red-roofed houses crowded onto a peninsula, surrounded by
the sea on three sides, Rovinj is as pretty as a picture. This is the
most Italian place in Croatia, with a Mediterranean atmosphere.

*Relaxing in a harbourside
café-bar*

*Detail of the Italianate
fountain in the main square*

*A yacht sailing in the
harbour at Rovinj*

RATINGS

Good for food	● ● ●
Good for kids	● ● ● ●
Photo stops	● ● ● ● ●

BASICS

✚ 294 A4

ℹ Obala Pina Budicina 12,
tel 052 811566; Jun–end Aug
daily 8am–10pm; Sep daily 8–4;
Oct–end May Mon–Fri 8–3,
Sat 8–1

🚌 From Poreč and Pula

www.tzgrovinj.hr
Official pages of the Rovinj
Tourist Board.

www.rovinj.hr
The town council's website has
useful information about Rovinj
in Croatian, Italian and English.

SEEING ROVINJ

The best way of seeing Rovinj is from the sea, by
taking the ferry to the islands of Sveta Katarina or
Crveni Otok in summer. From here, Rovinj appears
as a jumble of brightly coloured houses reflected in
the water, crowned by the tall Venetian bell tower
of St. Euphemia's church. The old town is best
explored on foot. Cars are not allowed in the centre,
so leave your vehicle at the large car park by the
jetty on Obala Parih Boraca. This is a short walk
from the market square, Trg Valdibora, and the
main square, Trg Maršala Tita, from where cobbled
streets lead up into the heart of the old town.

HIGHLIGHTS

MUZEJ GRADA ROVINJA (ROVINJ HERITAGE MUSEUM)

✉ Trg Maršala Tita 11 ☎ 052 816720 🕐 Mid-Jun to mid-Sep
Tue–Sun 9–12, 7–10; mid-Sep to mid-Jun Tue–Sat 9–1 💰 Adult
15kn, child 10kn 📷 🏛
www.muzej-rovinj.com

The town museum occupies a 17th-century palace on
the harbour square, and has collections of archaeology,
maritime history, Old Masters and contemporary art.
Among the works is a Madonna and Child by Venetian
artist Giovanni Bellini (1430–1516). One room is
devoted to the seascapes of Alexandar Kircher
(1867–1939), the official artist of the Austro-Hungarian
Navy. In the summer the museum sponsors the annual
Rovinj Art Colony and an outdoor exhibition on Grisia.

BALBIJEV LUK (BALBI ARCH)

In medieval times, Rovinj was surrounded by walls and gates, demolished when the town expanded under Venetian rule. The main entrance to the old town is through Balbi Arch, a baroque archway erected in 1680 on the site of the outer town gate. Above the arch,

The pretty harbourside promenade (left).
Sunbathing on a beach in Zlatni Rt park, Rovinj (below)

beneath the winged lion of the Venetian republic and the coat of arms of the Balbi family, is the sculpted relief of a turbanned Turk's head. On the other side of the arch is a Venetian—a clear message that the town belonged to Venice and that Turks should keep out.

CRKVA SVETE EUFEMIJE (ST. EUPHEMIA'S CHURCH)

🕓 Apr–end Oct daily 8–6; for services at other times

From the Balbi Arch, the narrow lanes of the old town thread their way up the hill. The main street is Grisia, which has the feel of an open-air art gallery in summer, with artists displaying their work on the steps. Grisia ends at the parish church of St. Euphemia, dedicated to a 3rd-century Christian martyr from Turkey who was thrown to the lions in Constantinople on the orders of Emperor Diocletian. According to legend, the sarcophagus containing her body was washed up in Rovinj in AD800 and she was immediately adopted as the town's patron saint. The tomb lies in an aisle to the right of the altar. Climb the 200 wooden steps of the

TIPS

● Young children will enjoy the Aquarium (▷ 184) and Mini Croatia (▷ 184).
● Watch the sunset from the wine bars along Ulica Svetog Križa, which follows the sea wall uphill from the harbour.
● If you want to swim in the heart of town, head for the popular bathing rocks, beneath the church at the top of Ulica Svetog Križa.

View of the town from the campanile (right).
A narrow, cobbled street lined with shops (far right).
The harbour (below)

KUĆA O BATANI (HOUSE OF BATANI)

✉ Obala Pina Budicina 2
☎ 052 805266 🕒 Jun–end Sep daily 10–3, 5–10; Mar–end May and Oct–end Dec daily 10–1, 3–5; closed Jan, Feb
✋ Adult 10kn, child 5kn
🎫 👫

This interactive museum is dedicated to the *batana*, a flat-bottomed wooden fishing boat unique to Rovinj.

GALERIJA ADRIS

✉ Obala Vladimira Nazora 1
☎ 052 801122 🕒 For exhibitions only

Opened in 2001, this modern art gallery is inside Croatia's largest tobacco factory, which dominates the east side of the harbour. The star attraction is a ceramic mural by Edo Murtić (1921–2005), a leading Croatian expressionist artist who had a studio in nearby Vrsar.

campanile (Apr–end Oct daily 10–4; 10kn) for views over the terracotta roofs and out to sea. Note the copper statue on top of the tower; it depicts St. Euphemia with the wheel on which she was tortured.

ZLATNI RT (GOLDEN CAPE)

This attractive forest park was designed by the industrialist Baron Georg Huetterott (1852–1910) as part of an ambitious plan to develop Rovinj as a tourist resort at the beginning of the 20th century. With shady footpaths leading through cedar, pine and cypress plantations to rock and pebble beaches, it makes a lovely place for a walk (▷ 212–213). You can also explore the park by bicycle in summer. Just inside the entrance to Zlatni Rt, Lone is the popular town beach.

THE ISLANDS

The Rovinj archipelago contains around 20 islands and islets, most of which are uninhabited. In summer you can take a ferry from the harbour at Trg Maršala Tita to two of the larger islands. The nearest is Sveta Katarina,

just 200m (220 yards) offshore with magnificent views towards Rovinj. The biggest island, Crveni Otok (Red Island), is actually two islands linked by a causeway, which leads to a number of remote naturist beaches. Both islands have hotels if you want to enjoy them when the crowds have left, and are justifiably popular with day-trippers. Even if you do not want a whole day on the beach, it is worth visiting for the views alone.

BACKGROUND

Originally a small Roman settlement, Rovinj was ruled by Venice from 1283 to 1797. For most of its history it was actually an island, which only became joined to the mainland when engineers filled in the narrow channel in 1763. Like other towns in Istria, it had a large Italian community, but here the Italian influence lives on. The town council is officially bilingual; there is an Italian-language school and in 2001 Rovinj elected an Italian-speaking mayor, Giovanni Sponza.

Looking across the harbour to the town of Umag

The tower of the church of St. Blaise, Vodnjan

A Limski Kanal tour boat on the jetty at Vrsar

UMAG (UMAGO)

⊞ 294 A4 🔢 Trgovačka 6, tel 052 741363; Jun–end Sep daily 9–9; Oct–end May Mon–Fri 9–4 🚢 From Novigrad and Poreč www.tz-umag.hr

The northernmost town on the Istrian coast is just 40km (25 miles) from the Italian city of Trieste; its easy access from Central Europe makes it a popular summer resort. The big hotels and tourist villages are to the north of town, leaving the historic area largely intact. Among the medieval streets and squares and surviving sections of wall, an old fortress is now the town museum (tel 052 741440; Jun–end Sep Tue–Sun 10–12, 6–9; Oct–end May Tue–Sat 10–12), with displays including amphorae and oil lamps from the Roman colony of Umacus. A coast road leads 8km (5 miles) through the pinewoods to Savudrija, where Croatia's oldest lighthouse, built in 1818, stands on a cape at the country's northwest tip.

VODNJAN (DIGNANO)

⊞ 294 B5 🔢 Narodni Trg 3, tel 052 511700; Mon–Sat 8.30–1.30 🚢 From Pula www.vodnjan.hr

Until the mid-19th century Vodnjan was the largest settlement in southern Istria; these days it is a sleepy provincial town 10km (6 miles) north of Pula. There is still a significant Italian community, some of whom speak the Istriot dialect, which survives only here and in Rovinj. The main square, Narodni Trg, is lined with Gothic and Renaissance palaces, including the Venetian Gothic town hall with its balconies and arcades. From the square, a narrow lane leads to the church of Sveti Blaža (St. Blaise), the largest parish church in Istria, with a 63m (206ft) bell tower. Inside the church the Sacred Art Collection (tel 052 511420; Jun–end Sep Mon–Sat 9–7, Sun 2–7; Oct–end May by appointment; 30kn) contains the remains of three mummified saints, whose desiccated but perfectly preserved bodies were brought here from Venice in 1818. As far as is known, the bodies were not embalmed, and there is no scientific explanation for their preservation. One of the saints is Leon Bembo, a 12th-century Venetian noble and ambassador to Syria whose body has been attributed with miraculous healing powers. Also on display is a casket said to contain the tongue of St. Mary of Egypt, a 6th-century prostitute who converted to Christianity. The mummies are kept behind glass cases and the display is poorly lit, but it is worth a visit for its macabre fascination.

VRSAR (ORSERA)

⊞ 294 A4 🔢 Rade Končara 46, tel 052 441746; Jun–end Sep Mon–Sat 8am–9pm, Sun 9–1, 6–9; Oct–end May Mon–Fri 8–2 🚢 From Poreč and Rovinj www.istra.com/vrsar

Vrsar is a busy tourist resort at the mouth of the Limski Kanal (▷ 89). From a distance it looks like a smaller version of Rovinj, with red-roofed houses crowned by a Venetian campanile; in fact, the bell tower on the parish church dates only from 1991. Vrsar's much-restored 12th-century castle was the summer residence of the bishops of Poreč. Since the 1960s Vrsar has been known as the naturist capital of Croatia, with thousands of nudists flocking to its campsites and beaches. It would be interesting to know what the Venetian playboy Giacomo Casanova (1725–98), whose memoirs record numerous conquests in Orsera, would have made of it.

KVARNER

The islands of Kvarner Bay form a natural bridge between Istria and Dalmatia. Sheltered by the Gorski Kotar, Učka and Velebit mountains, Kvarner has a mild climate which attracts numerous summer visitors, though in winter it is often battered by the strong *bora* wind. At the heart of the region is Rijeka, Croatia's third city and biggest port.

MAJOR SIGHTS

A view over the hilltop village of Beli on Cres (above). Bicyclists slowly wheel through Cres town (left)

CRES

The second largest Adriatic island combines wild beauty with a historic town.

Cres is the largest of the Apsyrtides, a group of islands named after the mythical Greek hero Apsyrtus, killed by his sister Medea. According to legend, his body was chopped in pieces and thrown into the sea, and thus the islands were born. Cres is a long, narrow, mountainous island, 65km (40 miles) in length with a deep lake at the middle. A single main road follows a ridge across the island from Porozina to Osor.

THE NORTH
The northern part is known as Tramuntana, whose main settlement is the ancient hill town of Beli. Here you will find the Caput Insulae eco-centre (▷ 186), with its griffon vulture reserve and waymarked walks (self-guided trails). South of Beli, Cres Town is the diminutive island capital, set in a sheltered bay. A 16th-century Venetian loggia stands guard over the harbour square, where an arch beneath the clock tower leads to the church of Sveta Marije Snježne (St. Mary of the Snows).

MUSEUM TOWN
Osor sits at the southern end of the island, where Cres is divided from Lošinj by a narrow canal, built by the Romans. Once a prosperous cathedral city with a population of 5,000, it is now a museum piece, with churches, monasteries and palaces scattered throughout the tiny village. The main square is on the site of the old Roman forum. The Archaeological Museum (Mon–Fri 10–12, also 7–9pm in summer) in the former town hall has a scale model of Osor plus Roman finds.

BASICS

✚ 294 B5

ℹ Cons 10, Cres Town, tel 051 571535; Jun–end Sep daily 8–8; Oct–end May Mon–Fri 8–1

🚌 From Rijeka

🚢 Car ferry from Brestova to Porozina and Valbiska (Krk) to Merag; catamaran from Rijeka to Cres

www.tzg-cres.hr
Official website of the island tourist board.

TIP

● Take a taxi boat across from Cres to Valun, whose church has the Valun Stone, an 11th-century tablet in Glagolitic and Latin recalling three generations of a family. A minor road from Valun climbs to Lubenice, a village of stone houses on a clifftop, with paths to a remote beach.

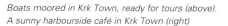

Boats moored in Krk Town, ready for tours (above).
A sunny harbourside café in Krk Town (right)

KRK

**The biggest and most populous of the Kvarner Bay
islands is dominated by its old Roman capital.**

There is intense rivalry between Cres and Krk for the
title of Croatia's largest island, though most experts
agree that Krk just has the edge. What is not in dispute
is that Krk is the most populated and also the most
accessible of the Adriatic islands, linked to the mainland by a toll bridge. Founded as the Roman colony
of Curictum, Krk was the medieval stronghold of the
powerful Frankopan dynasty (▷ 19). Today it is a
lively island, with large resorts at Omišalj, Njivice and
Malinska and one of Croatia's finest beaches at Baška.

POWER BASE
The capital, Krk Town, is buzzing in summer with
tourists from the nearby beaches; in winter it is a dozy
island town, surrounded by the remnants of Roman
walls and a 12th-century Frankopan fortress. Ceramic
plaques to Sveti Kvirina (St. Quirinus), Krk's patron
saint, adorn the gates into the old town, at the heart of
which the church of St. Quirinus shares its onion-dome
campanile with an 11th-century Romanesque cathedral. Nearby, a 15th-century hexagonal tower stands
over the harbour, with a Roman tombstone in its wall.

HOLY ISLAND
Punat, 4km (2.5 miles) east of Krk Town on the bay of
Puntarska Draga, is home to the oldest and one of the
largest marinas in the Adriatic. Taxi boats by the harbour ferry you to Košljun, a wooded isle, home to a
Franciscan monastery since the 15th century, where
you can visit the library and museum of sacred art.

Bicyclists and walkers on the quayside promenade at
Mali Lošinj, the capital of Lošinj

An ornate doorway on the
main square in Lovran

LOŠINJ

🔢 294 C6 ❶ Riva Lošnjskih
Kapetana 29, Mali Lošinj, tel
051 231884; Jun–end Aug
Mon–Sat 8–10, Sun 9–1; 2
Sep–end May Mon–Fri 8–3, Sat
9–1 🚢 From Rijeka and Cres
🚗 Car ferry from Pula and
Zadar to Mali Lošinj in summer;
daily catamaran from Rijeka to
Mali Lošinj
www.tz-malilosinj.hr

Separated from Cres by a
swing bridge across the
Kavuada canal at Osor,
Lošinj is smaller but more
developed than its neigh-
bour. The capital, Mali
Lošinj, is the largest town
on the Adriatic islands.
Ruled by Venice from
1409 to 1797, Mali Lošinj
reached its heyday in the
19th century, when its
tradition of shipbuilding
and seafaring made it the
second biggest port in the
Adriatic. Set in a sheltered
bay lined with pastel-
painted houses, this is
one of Croatia's most
beguiling towns—it has
lanes of handsome villas
and gardens filled with
exotic plants. Paths along
the shore lead to the
beaches and pine woods
at Čikat and Sunčana Uvala
(Sunny Bay). There is also
a seaside promenade to
Veli Lošinj, once the
island's main town, now
a pretty little harbourside
village overlooked by
a Venetian tower and

church. The north of the
island is dominated by
Osoršćica, a mountain
ridge 10km (6 miles) long
with views across Kvarner
Bay from its 588m (1,929ft)
summit, reached by foot-
paths from Nerezine and
Osor. For an easier excursion, take the boat trip
from Mali Lošinj to Susak,
a small traffic-free island.
Susak is best known for
the unusual folk costume
of its women, featuring a
brightly embroidered
mini-skirt over pink tights.
Don't Miss Try to walk
along the 'Lošinj Coast
Path' (▷ 218–219) and
visit the Blue World
dolphin centre (▷ 187).

LOVRAN

🔢 294 B4 ❶ Šetalište
Maršala Tita 63, tel 051 291740;
Jun–end Aug Mon–Sat 8–8,
Sun 8–noon; Sep Mon–Sat 8–3;
Oct–end May Mon–Fri 8–3
🚢 From Opatija and Rijeka
www.tz-lovran.hr

Lovran is named after the
laurel trees which grow in
abundance in the foothills
of Mount Učka. At the
southern end of the
Lungomare promenade, it
is the oldest town on the
Opatija riviera. In the 12th
century it was an impor-
tant maritime trading port,
but all that remains of the
walls that surrounded the
town are a tower and a
drawbridge leading to

Studica gate. The abiding
image of Lovran is of its
neo-Gothic and Viennese
Secession villas, many
designed by Austrian
architect Carl Seidl
(1858–1936) at the turn of
the 20th century, when
Lovran was popular with
the Habsburg aristocracy.

MOŠĆENIČKA DRAGA

🔢 294 B4 ❶ Aleja Slatina,
tel 051 739166; Jun–end Sep
Mon–Sat 8–9; Oct–end May
daily 8–noon 🚢 From Opatija
and Rijeka
www.tz-moscenicka.hr

This attractive old-style
fishing village and low-key
resort is the first place
you come to when you
cross from Istria into
Kvarner along the south-
ern coast. A long pebble
beach leads to the har-
bour, with cafés and
restaurants on a sunny
promenade with views to
Cres and the Velebit mas-
sif. A flight of more than
750 steps climbs to the
medieval town of
Mošćenice, built 173m
(567ft) above the coast
with fine views over
Kvarner Bay; the houses
back onto the old town
walls. There is a small
ethnographic museum
(tel 051 737551; Mar–end
Dec daily from 10am, but
variable), with an ancient
olive oil mill on display.

Formal flower beds in the gardens of Villa Angiolina (above).
Impressive architecture in Opatija (right)

OPATIJA

**This elegant Habsburg resort is experiencing a
second golden age as tourists return to
its villas, parks and promenades.**

Opatija is named after a 15th-century abbey, built on
the site of the chapel of Sveti Jakov (St. James). But
the story of Opatija really begins 400 years later, as the
fashionable winter resort of Viennese high society.

VIENNESE WHIRL

In 1844 Ignacio Scarpa, a wealthy businessman from
Rijeka, bought a holiday home in Opatija and named it
Villa Angiolina after his late wife. He surrounded the
house with lush gardens of palm trees, and invited the
cream of Austro-Hungarian society to stay. This was
the start of Opatija's golden age as the Adriatic playground of the Habsburg aristocracy. Emperors and
royals frequented its *belle époque* villas and hotels;
composers Mahler and Puccini and the playwright
Anton Chekhov all stayed here. Between the world
wars Opatija went into decline, annexed by Italy; only
now is it returning to its former glory as the faded elegance gives way to a new era of high-class tourism.

ON THE PROM

The one thing everyone does in Opatija is to walk the
Lungomare, a seaside promenade which runs north for
4km (2.5 miles) to the fishing village of Volosko and
south for 8km (5 miles) to Lovran (▷ 106). Begun in
1885 and officially named Šetalište Franz Josef I after
the Austrian emperor, this is a delightful walk along a
rocky shoreline, punctuated with gardens, villas and
beaches and lighted by old-fashioned lamps at night.

RATINGS	
Historic interest	● ● ●
Photo stops	● ● ● ●
Walkability	● ● ● ● ●

BASICS

✚ 294 B4
ℹ Ulica Vladimira Nazora 3,
tel 051 271710; Jul–end Aug
daily 8am–9pm; Sep–Oct and
Easter–end Jul daily 8–7;
Oct–Easter Mon–Sat 8–3
🚌 From Pula and Rijeka

www.opatija-tourism.hr
Local tourist office website,
regularly updated with news
of latest events.

TIPS

● Take the bus to
Lovran and walk back
along the Lungomare
coast path.
● Look out for concerts
in Villa Angiolina.
● For a taste of old
Opatija, take tea in the
Hotel Kvarner (▷ 260)
and peer into the ele-
gant Crystal Ballroom.

THE SIGHTS

Rab

The smallest of the major Kvarner islands has sandy beaches
and a well-preserved medieval town.

An aerial view of Rab island and its archipelago (above)

Rab Town (above left). Bell tower in Rab (above right)

Rab's harbour area (above). Towers and rooftops of Rab Town (right)

RATINGS

Good for kids	●●●○
Historic interest	●●●○
Photo stops	●●●●

BASICS

➕ 294 C5

ℹ️ Trg Municipium Arbe, Rab Town, tel 051 771111; Jun–end Aug daily 8am–10pm; Sep daily 8am–9pm; Oct–end May Mon–Fri 8–2

🚌 From Rijeka

⛴ Car ferry from Jablanac to Mišnjak; also from Baška (Krk) to Lopar in summer; passenger ferry from Rijeka to Rab

www.tzg-rab.hr
Tourist board site with information on festivals and events.

SEEING RAB

Rab can be reached throughout the year by the short ferry crossing from Jablanac, some 100km (62 miles) south of Rijeka. In summer there are also car ferries from Baška on the island of Krk. The island is small and easy to get around, with buses linking the main settlements of Rab, Kampor and Lopar. The east coast, facing the mainland and buffeted by the *bora* wind, is rocky and barren, while the west coast has pine woods, sheltered beaches and coves. The greatest attraction is Rab Town, a charming ensemble of churches and medieval lanes squeezed onto a narrow isthmus beside a natural harbour.

HIGHLIGHTS

A WALK AROUND RAB

The oldest part of Rab is intersected by three parallel streets known as Gornja Ulica (Upper Street), Srednja Ulica (Middle Street) and Donja Ulica (Lower Street). To explore Rab in an hour, follow the tourist route around the old town, with informative panels in several languages. Start on Trg Sveti Kristofora, the large open piazza by the harbour, and climb the steps to the 15th-century Gagliardi tower. From here, follow Gornja Ulica to the cathedral. Drop down to the gardens behind the cathedral and return along the waterfront to Trg Muncipium Arbe, the main square. Note the Venetian Gothic Rector's Palace—now the town hall—which has a balcony supported by three stone lions.

THE BELL TOWERS

The most distinctive feature of Rab are its four campaniles standing on Gornja Ulica and silhouetted against the skyline like ships' masts. You can climb the tower of the church of St. John the Evangelist, in the ruins of a 5th-century basilica. It is also possible to climb the Great Bell Tower by the cathedral (May–end Sep daily 10–1, 6–10). For the best view, climb onto the remaining part of the medieval walls.

THE BEACHES

Taxi boats shuttle across the bay in summer to Kandarola, a rocky beach which has been popular with naturists. The best sandy beaches are at Lopar, 15km (9 miles) north of Rab; the biggest is Rajska Plaža (Paradise Beach) by San Marino campsite. For more seclusion, footpaths from Lopar lead to remote bays and Sahara nudist beach.

BACKGROUND

Rab was founded as Arba by Roman emperor Augustus in the 1st century BC. An early bishop was Sveti Marin, a stonemason who later established the Italian republic of San Marino. At one stage a self-governing city state, Rab alternated between Croatian and Venetian rule before coming under the Venetian republic in 1409. The town plan is virtually unchanged since the 12th century, when the cathedral, downgraded to a parish church in 1828, and three of the bell towers were built.

TIPS

● Komrčar park, reached through an archway beneath the medieval walls, is a beautiful 19th-century landscaped park with shady paths and steps leading down to the town beach.

● Look carefully at the fountain on the harbourside square of Trg Sveti Kristofora in Rab Town. The modern sculpture is of Draga, a local shepherdess said to have been turned to stone rather than submit her chastity.

● Take a boat excursion from Lopar in summer to the island of Goli Otok, a notorious prison camp for Soviet sympathisers in Yugoslavia. The guides will show you around the prison buildings and explain its ugly history.

Rijeka

The capital of the Kvarner region is a busy industrial city and shipping port at the mouth of the River Rječina. It is a pleasant place, with a lively café culture and some interesting museums.

Taking a break to catch up on world events

The Korzo, Rijeka's main promenade

The round St. Vitus' Church was built in 1638

RATINGS

Cultural interest	●●●
Historic interest	●●●
Specialist shopping	●●●

BASICS

✚ 294 B4
🛈 Korzo 33, tel 051 335882; mid-Jun to mid-Sep Mon–Sat 8–8, Sun 9–2; mid-Sep to mid-Jun Mon–Fri 8–8, Sat 9–2
🚌 From Opatija, Pula and Zagreb
🚆 From Zagreb

www.tz-rijeka.hr
The tourist board website has lists of accommodation, restaurants, museums and special events.

SEEING RIJEKA

The city centre occupies a compact area behind the Riva, the busy road that runs along the quayside. Korzo is the central promenade, lined with cafés and shops on the site of the old sea walls. From here, the Gradska Vrata (City Gate) leads into the oldest part Rijeka, through a medieval archway topped by a baroque clock tower with busts of Habsburg emperors and a double-headed imperial eagle. To reach the castle and church at Trsat, take bus 1 or 1A from the Riva or climb the pilgrim stairway from Titov Trg, at the confluence of the Rječina and Mrtvi Kanal (Dead Canal).

HIGHLIGHTS

IZLOŽBA GLAGOLJICA (GLAGOLITIC EXHIBITION)

✉ Dolac 1 ☎ 051 336129 ◑ Mon–Fri 8–3 by appointment ▮ 10kn
Housed inside the university library, this fascinating collection of medieval art includes frescoes, manuscripts and stone carvings from Istria and the Kvarner islands, all using the Glagolitic script (▷ 19). Just as interesting as the showpiece exhibits are the examples of Glagolitic in everyday life.

POMORSKI I POVIJESNI MUZEJ (MARITIME AND HISTORY MUSEUM)

✉ Muzejski Trg 1 ☎ 051 213578 ◑ May to mid-Oct Tue–Fri 9–8, Sat 9–1; mid-Oct–end Apr Tue–Fri 9–4, Sat 9–1 ▮ Adult 10kn, child 5kn; www.ppmhp.hr

Rijeka's largest museum, in the former Habsburg governor's palace, has exhibits on seafaring and shipbuilding including maps, charts and model ships, along with costumes and Austro-Hungarian furniture.

CRKVA SVETOG VIDA (ST. VITUS' CHURCH)

⊠ Grivica Trg

Walk through the City Gate and continue uphill past Rijeka's only surviving Roman arch to reach this round church, built in 1638 and dedicated to the city's patron.

A car ferry in Rijeka's port (below left).
Window-shopping in Rijeka (below)

TRSAT CASTLE

⊠ Trsat ☎ 051 217714 🕓 Jun–end Sep daily 9–8; Oct–end May daily 9–5 💷 Free 🚌 Bus 1,1A 🛒 👪

Once the castle of the Frankopans of Krk (▷ 19), this fortress above the Rječina gorge was bought in 1824 by Irish-Austrian general Count Laval Nugent (1777–1862) and restored as a romantic folly. The former dungeons are now an exhibition gallery, along with the Classical-style temple designed as the Nugent family mausoleum and guarded by a bronze basilisk. The nearby church of Our Lady of Trsat is built on the site where angels are said to have delivered the house of the Virgin Mary from Nazareth in 1291. A sculpture of Pope John Paul II stands outside in memory of his visit in 2003. The classic approach to Trsat is via a pilgrim path of more than 500 steps, which begins at a baroque archway on Titov Trg. The stairway was erected by Uskok captain Petar Kružić (▷ 126) in 1531.

BACKGROUND

The earliest inhabitants of Rijeka were a Liburnian hill tribe who settled at Trsat; later the Romans founded Tarsatica on the site of today's city centre. Unlike other Croatian coastal towns, Rijeka remained under Austro-Hungarian control from 1466 to 1918. Occupied by Italy between the world wars, the River Rječina became the border between Italy and Yugoslavia. The late 20th century was a period of industrial decline, but Rijeka is following other Mediterranean port cities turning warehouses and docks into exhibtion and concert venues.

TIPS

● If you are visiting in winter, try to be in Rijeka for the annual Carnival (▷ 189), the biggest and liveliest in Croatia.
● To save the long climb up to Trsat, take the bus instead and walk back down the pilgrim stairway to the city.
● There is free car parking at Trsat and a large pay car park at Delta, beside the River Rječina and a short walk from the sights.
● Look out for the headquarters of the Jadrolinija shipping company in a bright yellow building, dating from 1897, down on the waterfront. The exterior is decorated with statues of ship captains and engineers, while the rear façade on Jadranski Trg has stylised female figures representing the continents.

Landscape reflected in a lake at Risnjak National Park

The view over Senj from Nehaj fortress

Driving along the coastal road between Senj and Zadar

THE SIGHTS

RISNJAK

🚩 294 C3 ✉ Nacionalni Park Risnjak, Crni Lug ☎ 051 836133 💰 Adult 30kn, child 15kn 🚌 Rijeka to Delnice, then Delnice to Crni Lug 🏨 🎎 www.risnjak.hr

Gorski Kotar is a mountainous region of primeval beech forests, limestone peaks and rushing rivers and streams, occupying a large area between Slovenia and Kvarner Bay. Around 64sq km (25sq miles) has been designated the Risnjak National Park, including two of the highest peaks, Veliki Risnjak (1,528m/5,013 ft) and Snježnik (1,506m/4,940 ft). The mountains are only a short distance from the sea, with views of the whole of Kvarner Bay; on clear days you can see the Italian Alps. At the information centre in Crni Lug you can pick up maps of hiking routes to the summits, beneath each of which is a mountain hut for overnight stays. For a less challenging walk, follow the Staza Leska, an educational trail that winds for 4.2km (2.6 miles) through the forest, passing sinkholes, meadows and charcoal kilns. There is a feeding post for deer, with beds of hay that provide winter shelter for dormice, birds and squirrels, keeping them warm and safe from predators such as pine marten. Among the large mammals roaming free in Gorski Kotar are brown bears and lynx. Winters in Gorski Kotar are long and harsh; the high ground is covered by snow for much of the year and even in summer temperatures are much lower than down on the coast.

SENJ

🚩 295 C4 ℹ️ Stara Cesta 2, tel 053 881068; open daily 8–2, 5–8 🚢 From Rab and Rijeka www.senj.hr

This quiet town sits at the foot of a pass in the Velebit mountains; when the *bora* blows through the pass, it becomes the coldest and windiest place on the coast. From 1537 to 1617 this was the stronghold of the Uskoks, legendary warriors who fled the Balkan interior and used Senj as a base from which to attack the Turks with the tacit support of the Austrian rulers. High above the harbour, Nehaj fortress, built by an Uskok captain in 1558, dominates the town. The castle houses a museum about the Uskoks, complete with weapons and costumes (May–end Oct daily 10–6; Jul–Aug, 9–8). Climb the battlements for views over the town.

SJEVERNI VELEBIT (NORTH VELEBIT)

🚩 295 C5 ✉ Nacionalni Park Sjeverni Velebit, Krasno ☎ 053 665380 💰 Adult 30kn, child 15kn ℹ️ Obala Kralja Zvonimira 6, Senj, tel 053 884551 www.np-sjeverni-velebit.hr

The Velebit mountain chain extends for over 100km (62 miles) from Senj to Zadar, rising from the coast like a sheer wall of limestone and shielding Kvarner Bay from the wind, rain and snow which fall on the far side. According to folklore, this is the home of Croatia's good fairy, Vila Velebita. In 1999 the northern end of the range became Croatia's newest national park; it is also much the least visited, attracting fewer than 6,000 visitors per year. The karst uplands make for superb walking, with jagged crags and remarkable caves, in some cases over 1,000m (3,200ft) deep. At a height of 1,480m (4,854ft), Velebitski Botanički Vrt (Velebit Botanical Garden) has rare plants, including mountain violets and the bright yellow *Degenia velebitica*, featured on the 50-lipa coin. The main entrance to the park is via the village of Krasno, on the road from Sveti Juraj to Otočac.

DALMATIA

With pine-scented islands and a sparkling blue sea beneath craggy grey mountains, Dalmatia is Croatia at its most seductive. There are Venetian port towns at Hvar, Korčula and Trogir, islands ranging from brash Brač to remote Lastovo and Vis, and historic cities such as Zadar and Split, both of which retain strong traces of their Roman past.

MAJOR SIGHTS

Brač

Long known for the white limestone that gives its houses an extra layer of polish, this busy holiday island attracts the summer crowds who flock to Croatia's most famous beach.

Coastal views from the road between Bol and Murvica

An artist prepares to paint a harbour scene

A thriving marina at Bol harbour on Brač

RATINGS

Good for kids	●●●○
Outdoor pursuits	●●●○
Photo stops	●●●○

BASICS

✚ 297 F8

🛈 Porat Bolskih Pomoraca, Bol; tel 021 635638; Jun–end Sep daily 8.30am–10pm; Oct–end May Mon–Fri 8.30–3

⛴ Car ferry from Split to Supetar and Makarska to Sumartin; catamaran from Split and Jelsa (Hvar) to Bol

www.bol.hr
www.supetar.hr
The two main towns each have a separate website, with information about activities on the island.

SEEING BRAČ

The largest island off the Dalmatian coast is also the most accessible, with regular ferries making the crossing from Split to Supetar throughout the year. Buses connect Supetar with the resort of Bol on the south coast, and there is also a direct catamaran service from Split to Bol. Although there is a good network of local buses, getting around Brač is easiest if you have your own transport. A rough track at the centre of the island leads to Vidova Gora, at 778m (2,552ft) the highest peak in the Adriatic.

HIGHLIGHTS

ZLATNI RAT (GOLDEN CAPE)

This beautiful beach is the best-known feature of Brač and has become an iconic image of Croatia. Set on a shingle spit extending some 300m (985ft) into the sea, its shape changes constantly with the wind and tides. The water is shallow, making it safe for children, and there are shady pine woods at the centre. Get there by following the 2km (1.2-mile) promenade from the harbour at Bol.

ZMAJEVA ŠPILJA (DRAGON'S CAVE)

☎ 091 514 9787 (guide Zoran Kojdić) 🎫 50kn per person
This remarkable cave in the hills above Murvica, 4km (2.5 miles) west of Zlatni Rat, has dragons and mythical creatures carved into the rock. The climb up here is steep and not always clearly marked, so it is better to

go with the guide, who has a key to the cave. Book by telephone one day in advance.

BRAČKI MUZEJ (MUSEUM OF BRAČ)

✉ Škrip ☎ 021 630033 🕐 Easter–30 Sep daily 8–8; 1 Oct–Easter Mon–Sat 8–2 ♿ Adult 10kn, child 5kn
The village of Škrip is the oldest settlement on the

Sunbathing on Zlatni Rat beach near Bol (below)

island, with a 4th-century chapel and 16th-century castle. The fortified tower houses a small museum of local finds, including a Roman relief of Hercules. The nearby church of Sveta Helena is dedicated to St. Helen, the mother of Roman emperor Constantine the Great. Local legend suggests that she was born in Škrip.

SUPETAR

✚ 297 F8 ℹ Porat 1 (by the harbour), tel 021 630551; Jun–end Sep daily 8am–10pm; Oct–end May Mon–Sat 8–2
The biggest town on Brač is named after the 6th-century basilica of Sveti Petar (St. Peter), mosaic fragments of which can be seen in the floor outside the parish church. On a cape beside the harbour, the town cemetery contains numerous memorials by local sculptor Ivan Rendić (1849-1932).

BACKGROUND

Glistening white houses and churches give a clue to the status of Brač as the source of the limestone used in buildings from Diocletian's palace in Split to the White House in Washington DC. Limestone has been quarried here since Roman times, when the wealthy patricians of Salona and Split had their summer villas on the island. Under Venetian rule the capital was at Nerežišća, moving to Supetar in 1815. Tourism began in the 1920s with the building of the first hotels and today Brač is once again a busy summer resort, popular with the people of Split and beyond.

TIPS

● To explore the island in more detail, follow the drive, ▷ 220–221.
● A steep path leads from Bol to the summit of Vidova Gora. The restaurant at the summit is open in summer.
● If the main beach at Zlatni Rat gets too crowded, try one of the quieter rocky coves further on.
● Take a boat trip in summer from Bol to Blaca, where you can hike up to a dramatic 16th-century hermitage, built into the cliff.
● Milna is a pretty harbourside fishing port around 20km (12.5 miles) southwest of Supetar.

Hvar

The sunniest island in the Adriatic is covered with lavender fields whose scent drifts on the breeze. The capital is Croatia's glitziest resort, the playground of the rich and fashionable.

Boats moored in Hvar marina

A souvenir shop in Hvar

Cafés on the quayside waiting for customers

BASICS

✠ 297 G8

🛈 Trg Svetog Stjepana, Hvar Town, tel 021 741059; Jun–end Sep daily 8am–10pm; Oct–end May Mon–Fri 8–2, Sat 9–12

🚢 Car ferry from Split to Stari Grad and Drvenik to Sućuraj; passenger ferry from Split to Hvar Town; catamaran from Split and Bol (Brač) to Jelsa; catamaran from Split and Korčula to Hvar Town

www.tzhvar.hr
Well-designed site with up-to-date event listings and details of all the main towns and sights.

Detail of the façade of the cathedral (opposite)

SEEING HVAR

Hvar is a long, thin island, stretching for 80km (50 miles) along a limestone ridge from Sućuraj to Hvar Town. The most frequent ferry crossing is from Drvenik on the Makarska riviera to Sućuraj, though you are then left with a long drive across the island. There are also car ferries from Split to Stari Grad, and a passenger ferry to Hvar Town. This makes a lovely way to arrive on the island, with the view of Hvar Town from the sea. The best times to visit are in June, when the lavender is in full bloom, or in August to soak up the atmosphere of Croatia's answer to St. Tropez. Despite the year-round mild climate, Hvar virtually goes to sleep in winter, when most hotels, restaurants and museums are closed.

HIGHLIGHTS

TRG SVETOG STJEPANA, HVAR TOWN

Hvar Town is set in a sheltered bay below a Venetian castle. From the ferry dock, a promenade lined with palm trees leads to the main square. This flagstoned piazza is the largest in Dalmatia, with a 16th-century well at the centre and handsome Gothic buildings on three sides; the fourth side gives straight onto the inner harbour. On one side is the former Venetian governor's mansion, now Hotel Palace, with a clock tower and loggia bearing reliefs of the winged lion of St. Mark. Across the square is the Venetian arsenal and theatre (▷ 118). The landward end is dominated by the 16th-century cathedral, its campanile

MORE TO SEE

FORTICA (FORTRESS)

☎ 021 742620 ⊙ Summer daily 8am–midday; winter 9–7 🖐 Adult 15kn, child 10kn

Climb the steps from Trg Svetog Stjepana to the 16th-century fortress above Hvar Town. There is a small museum and you can visit the underground dungeons, but the main reason for coming is the view over the town, with the Pakleni Islands glistening offshore and Vis on the horizon.

MUZEJ HANIBAL LUČIĆ

✉ Groda, Hvar Town ☎ 021 741052 ⊙ May–end Oct daily 10–12, 5–7 🖐 Adult 15kn, child 10kn

The Benedictine convent in the former house of playwright Hanibal Lučić has a small museum of sacred art, and also sells lace made by the nuns.

JELSA

➕ 297 G8 ℹ Mala Banda, tel 021 761017; Jun–end Sep daily 8am–11pm; Oct–end May Mon–Fri 8–2 🚌 From Hvar

This lively harbourside town faces Brač on the north coast, with regular taxi-boats making the excursion to Zlatni Rat (▷ 114) in summer. Look for the octagonal Crkva Sveti Ivana (Church of St. John) in a square behind the harbour. A Latin inscription on the lintel of a 1561 house in the same square declares *Dominus Chustodiat Introitum Tum et Exitum* (God protect your entrance and exit). A footpath leads for 5km (3 miles) through pine woods to Vrboska, with beaches and a 16th-century crenellated church overlooking the bay.

employing the typical Venetian device of having one arched window on the first floor, two on the second and so on. The bronze doors were sculpted by Kuzma Kovačić (born 1952), a local artist who also designed Croatia's coins. The attached bishop's palace contains a small museum of religious art (summer, Mon–Sat 10–12, 5–7; winter by appointment).

FRANJEVAČKI SAMOSTAN (FRANCISCAN MONASTERY)

☎ 021 741193 ⊙ May–end Oct Mon–Sat 10–12, 5–7 🖐 Adult 15kn, child 10kn

The main square and the 16th-century cathedral

A stone carving on the cathedral façade

A short stroll from the ferry dock at Hvar Town overlooking a pebble cove, the monastery has a lovely 15th-century cloister where concerts are held on some summer evenings.

HVARSKO PUČKO KAZALIŠTE (HVAR COMMUNITY THEATRE)

✉ Trg Svetog Stjepana, Hvar ☎ 021 741009 ⊙ Closed for renovation at time of writing 🖐 15kn

The top floor of the Venetian arsenal houses one of Europe's oldest public theatres, which opened in 1612 and is still in use today. The interior is richly decorated in red velvet, with ceiling frescoes added in the early 19th century. In the lobby, look for the figurehead of a *zvir* (dragon), from the prow of a Venetian galleon which was built in Hvar and saw service at the Battle of Lepanto in 1571. In summer look out for performances of plays by Hanibal Lučić (1485–1553), the leading Croatian Renaissance dramatist, who was born in Hvar.

PAKLENI OTOCI (PAKLENI ISLANDS)

🚤 From Hvar Town

Although there are pebble beaches to the west of Hvar Town, most people take a taxi-boat to this chain of wooded islands just offshore. In winter the islands are uninhabited, but in summer they make a popular retreat, with yachts in the harbours and fish restaurants springing up beside remote beaches and coves. The best beach is at Palmižana, on the biggest island, Sveti Kliment; naturists head for the isle of Jerolim.

THE SIGHTS

STARI GRAD

✚ 297 F8 ℹ Nova Riva 2, tel 021 765763; Jun–end Sep daily 8am–10pm; Oct–end May 8–2 🚌 From Hvar

Hvar's second town is built on the site of the original Greek settlement of Pharos, hence its name Stari Grad (Old Town). The ruins of Pharos can still be seen behind the 12th-century church of St. John. The main sight, set back from the harbour, is Tvrdalj Petra Hektorovića (Jun–end Sep daily 10–1, 5–8), the fortified summer palace and gardens of the poet Petar Hektorović (1487–1572). His best-known work, *Ribanje i Ribarsko Prigovaranje (Fishing and Conversations with Fishermen)*, describing a three-day fishing trip to Brač and Šolta in the company of two fishermen, is a classic of Croatian folk literature.

BACKGROUND

Hvar was founded by Greek settlers from Vis in the 4th century BC, who established a colony at Stari Grad. Its original name of Pharos possibly derives from their home island of Paros, or perhaps from the Greek word for a lighthouse. The Venetians moved the capital to Hvar Town after they conquered the island in the 13th century. Destroyed by Turkish raiders in 1571, Hvar was rebuilt in the Venetian Gothic style. In 1868 the Hvar Hygienic Society promoted Hvar as a health resort because of its 2,700 hours of sunshine a year. The climate is so reliable that hotels offer free board in the event of fog, snow or sub-zero temperatures—something that happened in 2005 for the first time in ten years.

A panoramic view of Hvar and its harbour (above)

TIPS

● Cars are not allowed in the centre of Hvar, so leave your car in the large car park (parking lot) on the edge of town (5kn/hour, 50kn/day) from where it is a short walk to the main square.
● If the crowds in Hvar Town get too much, escape to the unspoiled beaches of the south coast between Sveta Nedjelja and Zavala. Between the two is Ivan Dolac, a hilltop village overlooking the coast, which produces one of Croatia's best red wines.

Korčula

This island of vineyards, olive groves and oak forests is best known for its capital of the same name, a perfectly preserved gem of a Venetian walled town.

The town with its wonderful views of sea and mountains

Vineyards near Smokvica, known for good white wines

West Harbour (above). A beach sign (right)

RATINGS

Cultural interest	● ● ●
Good for wine	● ● ● ●
Historic interest	● ● ● ●

BASICS

✚ 297 G9

ℹ Obala Franje Tuđmana, Korčula Town, tel 020 715701; Jun–end Sep daily 8–3, 4–10, Sun 8–1; Oct–end May Mon–Sat 8–3

🚌 From Dubrovnik

⛴ Car ferry from Split to Vela Luka and Orebić to Dominče; car ferry from Drvenik to Dominče in summer; passenger ferry from Orebić to Korčula Town; catamaran from Split and Hvar to Korčula Town; catamaran from Split to Vela Luka

www.korculainfo.com
Privately run site with lots of information on the island, including ferry and bus timetables and frequent news updates.

SEEING KORČULA

Ferries to Korčula arrive at Vela Luka and Korčula Town, linked by a road which runs for 45km (28 miles) across the island. The easiest approach from Split is to take a ferry to Vela Luka; from Dubrovnik and the south, drive across the Pelješac peninsula for the short crossing from Orebić. The ferry harbour for Korčula is actually 2km (1.2 miles) south of town at Dominče, though passenger boats and some car ferries arrive right on the dockside in Korčula Town. Of the two main towns, Vela Luka is the larger but almost everything of interest is in Korčula Town. Elsewhere, you will find the wine towns of Blato and Smokvica, pine and oak forests, sand and pebble beaches, offshore islands and hidden bays.

HIGHLIGHTS

KORČULA TOWN

The old town of Korčula is like an open-air museum, with churches, palaces, steep alleys and flagstoned piazzas crammed onto a tiny peninsula, partly surrounded by 13th-century walls, bastions and towers. A promenade follows the course of the old walls, offering fine views across the channel to the Pelješac mountains, just 2km (1.2 miles) away. Inside the walls, notice the herring-bone pattern of the grid plan, ingeniously designed to allow sea breezes and views to penetrate the narrow streets while shielding the houses from the effects of strong winds in winter.

GALERIJA IKONA (ICON GALLERY)

✉ Trg Svih Svetih, Korčula Town ☎ 020 711306
🕐 Jul–end Aug daily 9–1, 5–7; May–end Jun and Sep 9–1
✋ Adult 10kn, child 5kn

This small museum contains a fascinating collection of Greek Orthodox icons, taken from Crete during a war between Venetian and Turkish troops. A covered bridge leads into the church of Svih Svetih (All Saints), with a beautiful 18th-century Pietà carved out of walnut wood.

VELA LUKA

ℹ Ulica 41, tel 020 813619; Jun–end Sep Mon–Fri 8am–9pm, Sat–Sun 8–12; Oct–end May Mon–Fri 8–3
🚌 From Korčula
www.tzvelaluka.hr

Korčula's biggest town is set around a long natural harbour, with several good beaches on nearby islands and bays. In a hill above the town, Vela Spila (Jun–end Sep daily 9–12, 5–8) is an enormous cave which was inhabited in the Stone Age. Concerts are held in the cave entrance in summer. Finds from the site are displayed at the Centar Za Kulturu (Jun–end Sep Mon–Sat 9–1, 8–11; Oct–end May Mon–Fri 9–1), in a 19th-century school building beside the church. The museum also contains a collection of wooden ships and an art gallery featuring two sculptures by Henry Moore, donated to Vela Luka after a high tide hit the town in 1978.

KOPNENA VRATA (LAND GATE)

A broad flight of steps leads up from Trg Kralja Tomislava to this archway, erected in 1391 as the main entrance to the old town. The arch is crowned by the 15th-century Revelin Tower, whose outer wall features a relief of the winged lion of Venice and a plaque marking the 1,000th anniversary of the coronation of Tomislav, the first Croatian king. The tower now

houses an exhibition on the *moreška* sword dance (▷ 191) and you can climb onto the roof for views over the town (Jul–end Aug 9–9, Easter–Jun and Sep–Oct 9–1, 4–8).

KATEDRALA SVETOG MARKA (ST. MARK'S CATHEDRAL)

Korčula's Gothic-Renaissance cathedral stands on the main square of the old town, with a rose window looking down on the square and a portal flanked by sculptures of Adam and Eve and topped by a statue of St. Mark. Inside the church, look out for the altarpiece by Tintoretto (1518–94) beneath a 15th-century marble ciborium (canopy) by local stonemason Marko Andrijić. The bishop's palace beside the cathedral houses a Treasury of religious art, pottery and coins (Jul–end Aug 9–9, May–Jun and Sep–Oct 9–1, 4–8. Closed rest of the year except for pre-booked groups).

GRADSKI MUZEJ (TOWN MUSEUM)

✉ Trg Svetog Marka ☎ 020 711420 🕐 Jul–end Aug daily 9–9; Apr–end Jun, Sep–end Oct Mon–Sat 9–1; Oct–end Mar Mon–Fri 9–1 ✋ Adult 10kn, child 5kn

This museum occupies a 16th-century Renaissance palace opposite the cathedral and contains archaeological finds and displays on Korčula's shipbuilding history. In the atrium is a replica 3rd-century BC stone tablet from Lumbarda, granting rights to Greek settlers to live inside the walled town and cultivate land outside. The original is kept in the Archaeological Museum in Zagreb (▷ 50). Another 16th-century palace on the same square is being converted to house a gallery of sculptures by local artist Frano Krsinić (1897–1982).

KUĆA MARKA POLA (MARCO POLO'S HOUSE)

✉ Ulica Depolo ☎ 020 715400 ⊘ Jul–end Aug daily 9–9; Apr–Jun and Sep–Oct 9–1, 4–8 🎫 Adult 10kn, child 5kn
The traveller and writer Marco Polo (1254–1324) is

believed to have been born in Korčula and the island claims him as its favourite son, although there is no firm evidence for the claim. He was captured in a naval battle off Lumbarda in 1298 while commanding a Venetian war galley against the Genoese fleet. Jailed in Genoa, he began dictating his memoirs of life at the imperial court in China, which became the best-known work of travel literature of all time. The historic home of the Depolo family was bought by Korčula Town Council in 2004 with the aim of opening it as a Marco Polo Museum; at present, only the tower is open. There are maps, manuscripts and the Depolo coat of arms on display, and you can climb the wooden steps to the belvedere for views over the old town. There are also ambitious plans to build a replica of Marco Polo's galleon to put on permanent display in the harbour.

BACKGROUND

Although humans have been living on Korčula for at least 10,000 years, its recorded history begins with the arrival of Greek settlers from Vis, who named the island Korkyra Melaina (Black Corfu) because of its dark forests. Under the Venetian republic, which ruled Korčula for 700 years, the island was known for its shipbuilders and stonemasons; its fleet rivalled that of Dubrovnik and stone from Vrnik was used in buildings from Venice to Constantinople. The present layout of Korčula Town dates from the 13th to 15th centuries, when it was one of the finest cities in the Adriatic.

BEACHES AND ISLANDS

Taxi boats from Korčula Town in summer will take you to Lumbarda, with its sandy Prižna beach. Or, take a boat to the isle of Badija, with its 14th-century monastery. There are good beaches on the Pelješac peninsula at Orebić.

St. Mark's Cathedral (far left). A cove (left). Korčula (above)

TIPS

● Cars are not allowed in the old town in Korčula and there is limited parking by the harbour, so leave your car at one of the car parks outside the town and walk in.
● Although the museums in Korčula Town are closed in winter, visits can be arranged through the tourist office.
● Try to catch a performance of the *moreška* sword dance (▷ 191); it is performed regularly on summer evenings at a stage by the Revelin Tower.
● There are some excellent white wines produced on the island, notably Grk from Lumbarda and Pošip from Čara and Smokvica.

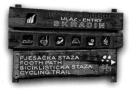

Krka

The stunning Krka river valley with its dramatic canyons and cascades rivals Plitvice Lakes for its beauty, and is much more accessible for visitors to the Dalmatian coast.

An aerial view of Skradin in the national park

Visitors on a small tour boat at Roški Slap

Stunning view of the lakes (above). Skradinski Buk waterfalls (right)

SEEING KRKA

The two main entrances to Krka National Park are at Skradin and Lozovac, both reached by regular buses from Šibenik. From Skradin, boats depart on the hour in summer along a wooded gorge to the foot of the Skradinski Buk waterfalls. From Lozovac, a shuttle bus takes you to the top of the falls, where you can buy tickets for the boat trips upstream to Visovac and Roški Slap. Between November and February, when the shuttle buses and boats do not operate, it is possible to drive to Skradinski Buk from Skradin or Lozovac. In summer you should allow a full day for visiting the park; in winter most people will be content with the two-hour circuit on foot around the falls.

HIGHLIGHTS

SKRADINSKI BUK

Of seven sets of waterfalls, Skradinski Buk is the most spectacular, descending 45m (147ft) in a series of 17 cascades and ending in a clear pool where people swim in summer. The average flow over the falls is around 50 cubic metres (1,765 cubic feet) per second, rising to 350 cubic metres (12,360 cubic feet) after rain. An easy network of footpaths and bridges leads around the falls, taking between one and two hours to complete. The best viewpoints are from the wooden footbridge at the base of the falls, and the Imperial Belvedere halfway up, built in 1875 for the visit of Austrian emperor Franz Josef I.

TIPS

● The entry fee includes shuttle buses and boats from Skradin and Lozovac in summer, but does not include the boat trips to Visovac and Roški Slap.

VISOVAC

From a jetty near the Lozovac entrance to Skradinski Buk, boats make the two-hour return journey (adult 70kn, child 40kn) to this Franciscan monastery on an island in the river at the point where it widens into a lake. The church was founded by Augustinian monks in the 14th century, though only the original cloisters remain. The monks here show visitors around the museum, which includes a 15th-century illustrated Croatian version of *Aesop's Fables*.

ROŠKI SLAP

A four-hour boat trip (adult 100kn, child 60kn) continues along the Krka canyon to the waterfalls at Roški Slap, where several old watermills, some still in use, line the banks. From here you can take a further trip (adult 70kn, child 40kn) along the quieter northern part of the river, to the Serbian Orthodox Krka monastery and the medieval Croatian fortress of Nečven.

BACKGROUND

The River Krka rises near Knin and flows for 72km (45 miles) to its mouth at Šibenik via the estuary at Skradin. Along the way it carves out a series of limestone gorges, forming travertine lakes and streams similar to those at Plitvice (▷ 70–73). Much of this area was declared a national park in 1985. Wildlife includes lizards, snakes and turtles, and flowers such as Adriatic violet and campanula (bell-flower).

● Boats to Visovac and Roški Slap depart from a jetty near the top of Skradinski Buk. At busy times it is worth buying your boat tickets early in the day, before walking around the falls. Tickets are sold at a kiosk beside the arrival point of the shuttle buses from Lozovac.

● There are cafés and souvenir shops at Skradinski Buk and Roški Slap. Kristijan, in a stone mill by the jetty at Roški Slap, serves delicious bread, ham and cheese.

● Take a swimsuit for swimming in the pool at the foot of the falls.

● Be warned that you should always stick to the marked footpaths if you go walking in the wilder northern sections of the park, as there may still be unexploded landmines in this area.

The fortress of Klis towers over the town. The position of Klis on the borders of past empires ensured its survival

Passengers enjoying a boat tour in Southern Dalmatia

THE SIGHTS

KLIS

➕ 297 F7 ℹ️ Megdan 57, tel 021 240578; Jun–end Sep daily 8–3; Oct–end May Tue–Sun 10–4 🚌 From Split

Lying on a strategically important pass between the Kozjak and Mosor mountains, Klis has for centuries played a key role on the borders of the Venetian, Habsburg and Ottoman empires. The town is dominated by its Tvrđava fortress (Jun–end Sep Tue–Sun 9–7; Oct–end May Tue–Sun 10–4), which stands on a rocky bluff overlooking the coast. Built on the site of an Illyrian hill fort, this was the bulwark of the medieval Croatian kings. In the 16th century, the castle was taken over by the legendary Uskok warriors under their commander Petar Kružić, whose capture and execution by Turkish troops in 1537 forced the Uskoks to flee to Senj (▷ 112). After 111 years of Ottoman rule the fortress fell to Venice and later to the Austrian empire. Most of what you see today dates from the Venetian and Austrian eras, including the remains of the 17th-century church of St. Vitus, built over a Turkish mosque. Climb the ramparts for views of Split, just 10km (6 miles) away.

KNIN

➕ 296 F6 ℹ️ Ulica Tuđmana 24, tel 022 664822; Mon–Fri 8–3 🚌 From Šibenik

The small town of Knin played a big part in Croatian history as the seat of the 10th-century kings and later the headquarters of the self-declared Republic of the Serbian Krajina (1990–5). At the start of the Homeland War the population of Knin was 90 per cent Serbian and it made an obvious base for the rebellion, allowing the Serbs to control road and rail links between Zagreb and Dalmatia. The capture of Knin by Croatian forces in August 1995 marked the effective end of the war; President Tuđman arrived the next day to hoist the Croatian flag on the castle. Standing on the Sveti Spas hill, the Tvrđava (Mar–end Oct daily 7–7; Nov–end Feb 7–3) was once the biggest fortress in Dalmatia and its fortunes mirror the region's history, changing hands between the Ottoman, Venetian and Austrian empires. A huge Croatian tricolour flies from the ramparts and it has become something of a nationalist shrine for Homeland War veterans.

KORČULA

See pages 120–123.

KORNATI OTOCI (KORNATI ISLANDS)

➕ 295 D7 ℹ️ Nacionalni Park Kornati, Ulica Butina 2, Murter, tel 022 435740; daily 7–3 in summer; Mon–Fri 7–3 in winter 🚌 From Šibenik to Murter ⛴️ Organized excursions from Biograd-na-Moru, Murter, Šibenik and Zadar in summer ✋ National park entry fee: adult 50kn, child (7–14) 25kn if bought in advance; adult 80kn, child 40kn from mobile boat wardens within the park www.kornati.hr

In this archipelago of 89 islands between Zadar and Šibenik the white rocky islands have a stark, ethereal beauty not seen elsewhere in the Adriatic. The easiest way to visit is on a day-trip from Murter, where boatmen by the quayside advertise tours in summer (250kn including lunch and park entry). There are also organized excursions from Zadar and other coastal towns. Better still, take your own yacht, as the islands are a paradise for sailors. Swimming and snorkelling are allowed within the park but you need a permit for fishing, and diving must be within an organized group. If you want to stay longer, travel agents in Murter offer stays in old fishermen's cottages, with well-water and your own fishing boat.

Folk dancers wearing traditional costumes

Beautiful beaches along the Makarska Riviera

Nin's calm atmosphere hides an important past

KRKA

See pages 124–125.

LASTOVO

🔶 297 G9 🛈 Lastovo Town, tel 020 801018 🚢 Car ferry and catamaran from Split, Hvar and Vela Luka (Korčula) to Ubli
www.lastovo.tz.net

The remote island of Lastovo is one of the last untouched paradises in the Mediterranean. Closed to foreigners from 1976 to 1989 when it was used as a Yugoslav naval base, a visit here feels like a step back in time. A single paved road runs across the island, from the ferry port at Ubli to the main settlement at Lastovo Town and the beautiful Skrivena Luka (Hidden Bay), guarded by Struga lighthouse. The population of 800 lives by subsistence farming and fishing, working the fields by hand and producing their own wine and olive oil. In recent years tourism has started to make an impact, with fish *konobas* springing up at remote beaches and coves to cater for visiting sailors in summer. There are plans to designate the entire Lastovo archipelago a nature park, with the aim of encouraging tourism but at the same time protecting its unique environment and beauty.

MAKARSKA

🔶 297 G8 🛈 Obala Kralja Tomislava 16, tel 021 612002; 16 Jun–15 Sep Mon–Sat 8–8, Sun 8–12, 5–8; 16 Sep–15 Jun Mon–Sat 8–2 🚢 From Dubrovnik and Split
www.makarska-info.hr

The Makarska Riviera is the name for a string of popular beach resorts that stretches for 60km (37 miles) from Brela to Gradac. The most attractive resorts are at either end, with long pebble beaches shaded by pine trees and the dark grey Biokovo massif looming overhead. At the heart of the riviera, Makarska is a lively harbourside town set in a horseshoe bay protected by wooded peninsulas on both sides. Stroll around the palm-lined promenade to the town museum, Gradski Muzej Makarska (daily 8–noon), in a baroque palace on the waterfront, with displays of Bronze Age pottery, Dalmatian folk costumes and early tourist postcards.
Don't miss The Malakološki Muzej (Mollusc Museum) has an extraordinary collection of seashells in an annex to the Franciscan monastery (May–end Oct daily 10–noon), painstakingly put together by Brother Jure Radić (1920–90).

NIN

🔶 295 D6 🛈 Trg Braće Radića, tel 023 265247; Jun–end Aug daily 8am–9pm; Sep and May–Jun 9–8; Oct–end Apr 8–3 Mon–Fri 8–2, Sat 8–1 🚢 From Zadar
www.nin.hr

Nin has been called the cradle of Croatia. Between the 9th and 12th centuries, during the golden age of Croatian independence, this small island village was the ecclesiastical and royal capital of the country. Cross the stone bridge to enter through the 15th-century Donja Vrata (Lower Gate). From here, a single street runs through the town, ending at the Arheološki Muzej (daily Jun–end-Aug 9am–10pm; Sep–end May Mon–Sat 9–noon), behind which stand the remains of a 1st-century Roman temple. Not far from here is Nin's most famous sight, the beautiful white-washed 9th-century Crkva Svetog Križa (Church of the Holy Cross).
Don't miss The 11th-century Romanesque church of St. Nicholas stands on a hillock just outside Nin on the road to Zadar. According to tradition, this was where the medieval Croatian kings rode on horseback to take an oath after their coronation.

THE SIGHTS

The port and craggy mountains at Omiš

The fortress on the barren island of Pag—grazed of all vegetation by sheep

OMIŠ

🕀 297 G8 🛈 Trg Kneza Miroslava, tel 021 86135; Jun–end Sep daily 8–8; Oct–end May Mon–Fri 8–3 🚌 From Dubrovnik, Makarska and Split www.tz-omis.hr

Omiš is situated where the River Cetina flows into the sea, 105km (66 miles) after beginning its journey at an underground spring in the small village of Cetina. From April to October this is Croatia's top rafting destination, as day-trippers flock here to ride the rapids of the dramatic Cetina gorge. Most people pass straight through Omiš on the road from Dubrovnik to Split, but it repays an hour or two of gentle strolling through the cobbled lanes of the old town and up to the Mirabela castle, whose tower you can climb in summer. There is also a long town beach, Gradska Plaža, with a mix of fine pebbles and sand.

OTAVICE

🕀 296 F7 ☎ 022 872630 🕐 Jun–end Sep Tue–Sun 8–12, 5–8; Oct–end May Tue–Sun 10–2 💶 Adult 10kn, child 5kn www.mdc.hr/mestrovic

The pig-farming village of Otavice, 10km (6 miles) east of Drniš, was the childhood home of the sculptor Ivan Meštrović (▷ 21), who chose it as the setting for his family mausoleum in the crypt of the Crkva Presvetog Otkupitelja (Church of the Holy Redeemer). Built of local limestone to a Meštrović design between 1926 and 1931, the church stands at the top of a long flight of steps overlooking the village. The interior is decorated with reliefs by Meštrović including the four evangelists and *Crucified Forever*. From 1991 to 1995 the church was occupied by Serbian soldiers who scrawled graffiti on the walls, desecrated the tombs and laid landmines in the nearby fields. Most of the resulting damage has now been repaired, but the bronze doors bearing portraits of Meštrović, his parents, wives and children were taken away and have not been returned.

PAG

🕀 295 C6 🛈 Ulica Od Špitala 2, Pag Town, tel 023 611301; Mar–14 May and 15 Oct–15 Dec daily 8–noon; 15 May–14 Jun and 15 Sep–14 Oct 8–noon, 4–9; 15 Jun–4 Sep 8–7 🚌 From Zadar 🚢 Car ferry from Prizna to Žigljen; catamaran from Rijeka and Rab to Novalja www.pag-tourism.hr

Arriving on Pag from the mainland—either across the bridge from Dalmatia or by ferry from the Kvarner coast—it seems surprising that it supports any life. Croatia's fifth largest island resembles an arid desert or moon-scape, with all vegetation stripped bare by the sheep, who outnumber the human inhabitants by at least two to one. The main road from Pag Town to Novalja is lined with rocky slopes, dry-stone walls and sheep grazing on the salt marshes. Roadside stalls advertise *paški sir*, a mature sheep's cheese similar to Parmesan and flavoured with salt, herbs and olive oil. Pag's other claim to fame is *paški čipka* (Pag lace), which has been made here for centuries. Buy it from old women in the streets and squares of Pag Town, or visit the small museum attached to the lace-making school. Pag Town was rebuilt from scratch in the 15th century by Renaissance architect Juraj Dalmatinac, giving the old walled town a harmonious feel. The rose window on the façade of the parish church was designed to reflect the intricate patterns of Pag lace.

One surprising fact about Pag is that it has

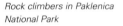

Rock climbers in Paklenica National Park

The reed beds of Vransko Jezero

Primošten is near to some small coves and beaches

the longest coastline of any Croatian island, with numerous pebble beaches and bays. Zrće beach, near Novalja, is Croatia's answer to Ibiza, with open-air clubs scattered around a wide arc of white pebbles and views of the Velebit mountains across the lagoon. Pag has become the summer haunt of Zagreb's clubbers and Zrće is very busy on warm summer nights.

PAKLENICA

✚ 295 D6 ❶ Nacionalni Park Paklenica, Ulica Tuđmana 14A, Starigrad Paklenica, tel 023 369202 ☎ Park entrance: 023 369803 🎟 Adult 30kn, child (7–18) 20kn; three-day ticket and climbing permit, 60kn; cave 10kn; bunkers 5kn
🚌 From Zadar
www.paklenica.hr

Established in 1949, Paklenica National Park covers an area of 96sq km (38sq miles) at the southern end of the Velebit range. The lower slopes are forested with beech and black pine, while above are jagged limestone peaks. The park offers some of Croatia's best and most accessible mountain hiking and climbing. The most popular walk is along the Velika Paklenica canyon; from here, paths lead off to the summit of Anića Kuk

(712m/2,335ft) and the Manita Peć cave, with its stalactites, stalagmites and columns (guided tours only; Jul, Aug daily 10–1; ask at entrance for other times). Serious hikers can climb Vaganski vrh (1,757m/ 5,766ft) for magnificent views over the islands and coast. The underground bunkers in Velika Paklenica, secretly built during the Tito years, are closed until 2009 for renovations.

PAKOŠTANE

✚ 295 D7 ❶ Trg Kraljice Jelene 78, tel 023 381892
🚌 From Šibenik and Zadar
www.pakostane.hr

Pakoštane is a small beach resort 24km (15 miles) south of Zadar, on the shores of Vransko Jezero, Croatia's largest natural lake. A 30km (18-mile) cycle trail circles the lake, whose reed beds attract birds, including a rare colony of purple herons. Just up the coast, Biograd-na-Moru ('white town on sea') was a royal seat where Hungarian monarchs were crowned kings of Croatia; today it is a relaxed holiday resort, deserted in winter but lively in summer, with boats leaving for the peaceful island of Pašman and for cruises to the Kornati Islands (▷ 126).

PRIMOŠTEN

✚ 296 E7 ❶ Trg Biskupa Arnerića 2, tel 022 571111; May–end Sep daily 8am–10pm
🚌 From Šibenik
www.summernet.hr/primosten

The old coast road from Šibenik to Trogir passes small beaches and coves with a relaxed holiday atmosphere. Around 20km (12 miles) south of Šibenik, Primošten is on an island that was joined to the mainland in the 15th century. It was founded by Bosnian refugees fleeing the Ottoman Turks and was fortified by the Venetians, who built town walls. From a distance, it resembles a miniature version of Rovinj (▷ 98–101), with a church tower above the rooftops and houses tumbling down the hills to a crystal-clear sea. Walk through an archway to enter the old town and climb the steps to the white stone church of Sveti Juraj (St. George), with views of nearby islands from the terrace. There are good pebble beaches nearby as well as a large marina at Kremik. The vineyards around Primošten produce Babić, a full-bodied red wine.

To the south, Rogoznica is a busy summer resort on an island with a causeway to the mainland.

THE SIGHTS

The ruins of Salona's Roman amphitheatre

Old women discussing everyday matters in Sinj

The Franciscan monastery in Sinj

SALONA

✚ 297 F7 ✉ Put Starina, Solin
☎ 021 212900 🕐 May–end Sep daily 9–7; Oct–end Apr Mon–Fri 9–3 👆 Adult 20kn, child 10kn 🚌 From Split
📷 50kn 🚌 🅿 🏢 🛈
www.mdc.hr/split-arheoloski

Built at the mouth of the Jadro river delta, the ancient city of Salona was the capital of the Roman province of Dalmatia, with a population of up to 60,000 people. This is undoubtedly Croatia's most evocative archaeological site, with ruined basilicas, temples, cemeteries, theatres and baths standing amid fields on the edge of the modern town of Solin, within sight of Split. Salona flourished between the 2nd century BC and 7th century AD, when its inhabitants fled to Split after the arrival of the Croats. The Roman emperor Diocletian was probably born here; so too was Domnius, the first Bishop of Salona who was executed in AD304 in the amphitheatre during Diocletian's purge of Christians. His tomb is at Manastirine, just inside the entrance gate. Nearby Tusculum museum was built in 1898, incorporating Roman statuary in its walls; it now has an exhibition on the history of the site. From here, you can wander around the ruins of ancient Salona, tracing sections of Roman wall, exploring the amphitheatre and looking out for chariot tracks in the stones. It is fascinating to imagine a time when this was a thriving metropolis and Split was no more than a fishing village.

ŠIBENIK

See page 131.

SINJ

✚ 297 F7 🛈 Ulica Vrlička 41, tel 021 826352; Jul–end Aug daily 8–8; May–end Jun & Sep–end Oct Mon–Fri 8–3, Sat 8–1; Nov–end Apr Mon–Fri 8–3
🚌 From Split
www.tsinjz.hr

Set in the broad Cetina valley 34km (21 miles) inland from Split, Sinj is a potent mix of Catholicism, Croatian nationalism and military history which reaches its peak each August at the Sinjska Alka (▷ 194), a jousting tournament with riders in 18th-century costume. The festival is held to celebrate a famous victory in 1715, when a force of 60,000 Turkish soldiers attempting to storm the fortress were defeated by just 700 locals, with the help of a miracle-working 16th-century portrait of the Sinjska Gospa (Our Lady of Sinj). During the previous Turkish occupation, from 1513 to 1687, the painting was removed to Bosnia for safekeeping, where it was found to perform miracles. Topped with a golden crown, it is kept inside the parish church on the main square; the legend is repeated on the church's bronze doors, which depict the Virgin repelling the Turkish attack.

ŠOLTA

✚ 296 F8 🛈 Grohote, tel 021 654151; Mon–Fri 8–4 ⛴ Car ferry and catamaran from Split to Rogač; catamaran from Split to Stomorska
www.solta.hr

Although it can be reached from Split in less than an hour, Šolta is the forgotten island of Central Dalmatia, attracting none of the summer crowds of neighbouring Brač and Hvar. Experience the relaxed atmosphere on this largely rural island of olives, figs and vines, with pebble beaches on the north coast and steep cliffs in the south. Ferries arrive at Rogač, the harbour for the main town of Grohote, though most people head west to Maslinica, a small village of fishermen's cottages around a sheltered bay, or east to Stomorska, a low-rise beach resort.

*St. James's Cathedral in Šibenik (above and right) combines
different architectural styles brillantly*

ŠIBENIK

**This busy port at the mouth of the River Krka has a
triumph of Gothic and Renaissance architecture.**

Unlike other Dalmatian coastal towns, Šibenik was not
occupied by the Romans but founded by Croatian settlers in 1066. The heart of the city is a labyrinth of
narrow streets linking Trg Republike Hrvatske, the
cathedral square, with Poljana, a large open piazza on
the site of the original town gate.

THE CATHEDRAL
The highlight of Šibenik is Katedrala Svetog Jakova (St.
James's Cathedral)—a fusion of Renaissance and
Gothic styles. It is considered the masterpiece of Juraj
Dalmatinac (c1400–73), a Venetian architect from
Zadar, whose statue by Ivan Meštrović stands on the
square. After his death, the work was continued by
Nikola Firentinac (c1440–1505). The basic structure is a
three-aisled basilica in the shape of a Latin cross, but
the beauty is in the detail. The main portal depicts the
Last Judgment, while the side door is flanked by a pair
of stone lions and statues of Adam and Eve with hands
on their hearts. Don't miss the frieze around the outside of the apse; the 71 carved stone faces are thought
to represent 15th-century Šibenik society.

THE FORTRESS
The Venetian fort Kaštel Svetog Mihovil (St. Michael's
Castle) stands above the town. Climb the steps from
the cathedral square or follow the signs from Ulica
Zagrebačka to reach the castle. It is under restoration
but you can walk around the ramparts for good views
of the cathedral's unusual barrel-vaulted roof.

RATINGS
Architectural interest	●●●○
Good for kids	●●●○
Walkability	●●●○

BASICS

🔲 296 E7

🛈 Obala Franje Tuđmana 5, tel
022 214411; Jul–end Aug daily
8am–10pm; May–Jun and Oct
8am–9pm; Nov–end Apr Mon–
Fri 8–3 🚌 From Split and Zadar

www.sibenik-tourism.hr
Multilingual site of the Šibenik
Tourist Board: details of accom-
modation, festivals and events.

TIPS

● If arriving by car, park
on the Riva (10kn/hr) or
follow signs to the free
car park by the port.
● For an easy circuit of
the old town, walk along
the waterfront prome-
nade to the cathedral,
then return along Ulica
Kralja Tomislava and
Ulica Zagrebačka.
● Children will enjoy
Bunari (▷ 192), a multi-
media exhibition in the
old wells.

Split

Croatia's second city is a bustling port city, with ferries coming and going in the harbour and travellers passing through on their way to the Dalmatian islands.

Relaxing in a café on the Riva

The Croatian National Theatre building in Split

Detail of the façade of the Cathedral of St. Dominus

SEEING SPLIT

The best way to arrive in Split is by sea, with the southern façade of Diocletian's palace at the heart of the city, seen on the waterfront against a backdrop of high-rise apartment blocks and distant mountains. A short stroll from the ferry dock leads to the Riva, a busy harbourside promenade with palm trees and terrace cafés. From here, you enter Diocletian's palace through the Mjedena Vrata (Bronze Gate), which gives access to the underground galleries and central court. The main sights lie within the palace walls, though the city market is just outside the eastern Srebrena Vrata (Silver Gate) and the old town extends west through the Željezna Vrata (Iron Gate) to the shopping streets between Narodni Trg and Trg Republike. Beyond here, a pair of interesting museums is found at the foot of Marjan, the green hill overlooking the city.

HIGHLIGHTS

DIOKLECIJANOVA PALAČA (DIOCLETIAN'S PALACE)

Designed as part imperial villa, part fortified garrison town, this is not a palace in the conventional sense; it is part of the fabric of the city. There is no need to buy a ticket and instead of staring at Roman remains in respectful silence, you are just as likely to find yourself sitting on an ancient tombstone to eat your picnic. The original street plan largely survives, with its north–south and east–west axes, Cardo and Decumanus, meeting at

RATINGS	
Cultural interest	● ● ● ●
Historic interest	● ● ● ●
Specialist shopping	● ● ●

BASICS

✚ 297 F7

ℹ Peristil, tel 021 345606; Jun–end Sep Mon–Sat 8–8, Sun 9–1; Oct–end May Mon–Fri 9–4, Sat 9–1

🚌 From Dubrovnik, Šibenik, Zadar and Zagreb; local bus 37 from Trogir

🚉 From Zagreb

⛴ Ferry connections with Dubrovnik, Rijeka, Zadar, Brač, Hvar, Korčula, Lastovo, Šolta and Vis

www.visitsplit.com
Snazzy tourist board website in Croatian and English, with city maps and details of upcoming events .

Peristyle Court, Diocletian's Palace (opposite)

TIPS

● Guests staying for three nights receive a free Split Card, which gives free or discounted admission at museums and reductions on car rental, theatres and excursions. The card is also on sale at the tourist office (35kn for 72 hours).

● Stari Pazar (Old Bazaar), outside the eastern gate of Diocletian's palace, is one of the best open-air markets in Croatia, with farmers selling eggs, cheese, sausages, bacon, bread, vegetables, olives and dried fruit.

● The city beach is at Bačvice, a crescent bay just beyond the ferry dock. There is also good bathing in summer from the rocky coves at the foot of the Marjan peninsula.

● To visit the Meštrović Gallery and Museum of Croatian Archaeological Monuments, consider taking bus 12 from Trg Republike and returning along the seafront path.

Diocletian's Palace and the Riva (above right)

The Town Hall (above far right)

Traditional loaves (opposite)

the central Peristil courtyard. From here, steps lead up to the vestibule, a domed chamber now open to the sky. The rest of the palace has been dismantled over the centuries, with columns and arches recycled in other buildings, though parts of the old Roman walls survive, pierced by gates on their north, south, east and west sides. For a sense of the original palace layout, visit the Podrum or underground chambers (Jun–end Aug Mon–Sat 9–9, Sun 9–6; Sep and May Mon–Sat 9–8, Sun 9–6; Oct–end Apr Mon–Fri 8–3; adult 12kn, child 6kn), a former dungeon beneath the imperial quarters whose floor plan reflects the outline

of the rooms above. Among the items discovered here is a marble dining table used by Diocletian.

KATEDRALA SVETI DUJE (CATHEDRAL OF ST. DOMNIUS)
✉ Peristil ✪ Apr–end Sep daily 8–8; Oct–end Mar 8–12, 4–7 ✋ 5kn

The octagonal mausoleum designed by Diocletian as his resting place is guarded by a black granite Egyptian sphinx from 1500BC. Originally this was one of a dozen sphinxes in the peristyle court; the rest were destroyed by angry Christians after Diocletian's death. Ironically for an emperor renowned for his persecution of Christians, his mausoleum has become a cathedral, dedicated to one of his victims, the first Bishop of Salona. Note the elaborately sculpted altars to Domnius and Anastasius, another Christian martyr. Diocletian's tomb has long since disappeared, perhaps recycled in the stone pulpit, though traces of the emperor remain; portraits of him and his wife can be seen in the dome, together with scenes of chariot races and hunting. You can climb the adjoining bell tower (Apr–end Sep daily 8–8; Oct–end Mar 9–12, 4–7) for views over the port.

JUPITEROV HRAM (TEMPLE OF JUPITER)
✉ Kraj Svetog Ivana ✪ Apr–end Sep daily 8–8; Oct–end Mar 9–12, 4–7; ask at cathedral at other times ✋ 5kn

A narrow passage opposite the cathedral steps leads to the Roman Temple of Jupiter, now the cathedral baptistry, with images of the gods Jupiter and Hercules above the portal. The highlight is the 11th-century baptismal font, richly carved with the geometric braiding which was a feature of medieval

Croatian art. The font also contains the earliest known portrait of a Croatian king, thought to be Petar Krešimir IV, seated on a throne with his crown and orb, with a citizen prostrated at his feet.

MUZEJ GRADA SPLITA (CITY MUSEUM)

✉ Papalićeva 1 ☎ 021 344917 🕐 Jun–end Sep Tue–Fri 9–9, Sat–Sun 10–1; Oct–end May Tue–Fri 10–5, Sat–Sun 10–12
✋ Adult 10kn, child 5kn 📖 75kn
www.mgst.net
Housed in a Gothic mansion within the walls of Diocletian's palace, this museum began in the 16th century when the owner, Dmine Papalić, collected monuments from Roman Salona (▷ 130) and exhibited them in his courtyard. The museum provides a quick journey through the history of Split, from Roman coins bearing Diocletian's portrait to medieval manuscripts.

ZLATNA VRATA (GOLDEN GATE)

The main entrance to Diocletian's palace was through the monumental north gate, which stood at the start of the road to Salona. Outside the gate, a large bronze statue of Grgur Ninski (Gregory of Nin) by Ivan Meštrović recalls a 10th-century bishop who campaigned for the use of the Slavic script instead of Latin in Croatian churches. The statue was placed in the peristyle in 1929 to mark the thousandth anniversary of the Synod of Split at which Gregory challenged the Pope, but moved here during World War II under Italian occupation. There are copies in Varaždin (▷ 76–79) and Nin (▷ 127) but this is the original. If you are superstitious, touch the bishop's left toe, which has been worn to a bright gold sheen by generations of people.

MORE TO SEE

ETNOGRAFSKI MUZEJ (ETHNOGRAPHIC MUSEUM)

✉ Ulica Severova 1 ☎ 021 344164 🕐 Jun Mon–Fri 9–2, 5–8, Sat 9–1; Jul–end Sep Mon–Fri 9–9, Sat 9–1, Sun 10–1; 15 Sep–end May Mon–Fri 9–2, Sat 9–1
✋ Adult 10kn, child 5kn
www.et-mu-st.com
First opened in 1910 as a temporary exhibition of handicrafts, this museum has recently moved to a new home near the vestibule of Diocletian's palace. It features traditional Dalmatian folk costumes, including fur hats, boots and military uniforms worn by riders at the Sinjska Alka (▷ 194).

MARJAN

The green hill overlooking Split on its western side has shady paths, medieval hermitage chapels and views over the offshore islands (▷ 224–225).

ARHEOLOŠKI MUZEJ (ARCHAEOLOGICAL MUSEUM)

✉ Ulica Zrinsko-Frankopanska 25 ☎ 021 318720 🕐 Jun–end Sep Tue–Sun 9–2, 4–8; Oct–end May Tue–Fri 9–2, Sat–Sun 9–1 💳 Adult 20kn, child 10kn
www.mdc.hr/split-arheoloski

Diocletian's Palace (above). The fish market (right)

Founded in 1820, Croatia's oldest museum displays Greek and Roman objects from across Dalmatia. Items from Salona include a 2nd-century mosaic of Apollo, marble statues of the gods Bacchus, Diana and Venus, and everyday items such as jewellery, pottery, coins and dice. The courtyard gallery has more examples of Roman art, with mosaics and sarcophagi featuring vivid scenes of chariot races and wild boar hunts.

MUZEJ HRVATSKIH ARHEOLOŠKIH SPOMENIKA (MUSEUM OF CROATIAN ARCHAEOLOGICAL MONUMENTS)

✉ Šetalište Ivana Meštrovića 18 ☎ 021 358420 🕐 Mon–Fri 10–1, 5–8, Sat 10–1 💳 Adult 10kn, child 5kn 🚌 12
www.mhas-split.hr
This is one museum in Split where you will not find any Roman objects. In fact, it is the only museum in Croatia dedicated solely to the medieval Croatian state, which ruled from the 9th to 11th centuries. Considering the emotional attachment to Croatia's only previous period of independence, it is surprising that its history tends to be overlooked between the Roman and Venetian eras. Most of the exhibits are taken from medieval churches; they include several fine examples of

delicately carved stonework, adorned with plaiting and Celtic-style geometric motifs typical of this period.

GALERIJA IVANA MEŠTROVIĆA

✉ Šetalište Ivana Meštrovića 46 ☎ 021 340800 ⏲ 15 May–end Sep Tue–Sun 9–9; Oct–14 May Tue–Sat 9–4, Sun 10–3 💰 Adult 20kn, child 10kn 🚌 12
www.mdc.hr/mestrovic

The sculptor Ivan Meštrović (▷ 21) grew up in Dalmatia and planned to retire to this villa overlooking the coast, though in fact he only spent two years here after its completion in 1939 before moving to the USA.

Sarcophagus detail in the Archaeological Museum; the bell tower, Cathedral of St. Dominus; a sphinx, Peristyle Court; café life (below, left to right)

A sculpture at the Meštrović Gallery (bottom)

The house and gardens contain a collection of his work, from female nudes and religious studies to a touching bronze portrait of his mother from 1909. Look out too for monumental wooden sculptures of Adam and Eve (1941) and a rare Meštrović painting of the Last Supper (1945), as well as a portrait of a young Meštrović by the Cavtat artist Vlaho Bukovac (1855–1922). The ticket is also valid for the Kaštelet, a fortified 16th-century residence bought by Meštrović as a home for his *Life of Christ* cycle, a series of wood carvings completed between 1916 and 1950 and displayed in the simple, whitewashed Crkva Svetog Križa (Holy Cross Chapel), built for this purpose. From the Crucifixion produced during World War I to the Nativity and Last Supper completed in the USA, they represent a lifetime's work and are perhaps Meštrović's greatest achievement.

BACKGROUND

The history of Split begins in AD295, when the Roman emperor Gaius Aurelius Valerius Diocletianus (*c*245–312), commonly known as Diocletian, ordered the building of a seafront palace near his childhood home. Born in Salona, the son of slaves, he rose through the army to become ruler of the Roman empire and is chiefly known for his vicious persecution and execution of Christians. In AD305 he became the first Roman emperor voluntarily to abdicate and retired to his palace at Split. In the 7th century refugees from Salona settled in the palace and it has been the core of the city ever since. During the 19th and 20th centuries Split experienced massive growth as an industrial port city and its population now exceeds 200,000.

Palm trees lend a tropical feel to the quayside promenade in the town of Trogir

BASICS

✚ 296 F8

ℹ Trg Ivana Pavla II, tel 021 881412; Jun–end Aug daily 8am–9pm; Apr–end May, Sep–end Oct Mon–Fri 8–5, Sat 8–12; Nov–end Mar Mon–Fri 8–2

🚌 From Šibenik and Split

www.trogir-online.com
Local tourism portal in English with links to hotels and private accommodation, as well as information on sights.

TIPS

● Make Trogir a base for visiting Split—the hotels are cheaper, the atmosphere is relaxed, and local bus 37 runs between Trogir and Split throughout the day.
● Make a complete circuit of the island on foot, following the old town walls. You could end the day with a drink on the Riva—its terrace bars are great spots for people-watching.

TROGIR

This lovely Venetian island town is delightful to explore, with Renaissance palaces and hidden courtyards in its narrow, cobbled streets.

Founded in the 3rd century BC by Greek settlers from Vis, Trogir is set on a small island, linked to the mainland and the larger island of Čiovo by a pair of bridges. You could easily visit as a day-trip from Split, but it is better to spend the night here, enjoying the atmosphere of one of Croatia's most beguiling small towns.

ROMANESQUE MASTERPIECE

The classic entrance to Trogir is via the 17th-century Kopnena Vrata (Land Gate), crowned by a statue of St. John of Trogir, a 12th-century bishop. This leads into a maze of medieval lanes, converging on Trg Ivana Pavla II, the main square. On one side is the Venetian loggia; on the other is the cathedral. The west door, carved in 1240 by stone-mason Radovan, is a triumph of Romanesque art, with exquisite details from rural life among the angels, saints and biblical scenes. The interior is almost equally impressive, especially the chapel of St. John of Trogir by the Florentine architect Nikola Firentinac (c1440–1505). You can climb the bell tower in summer (mid-Jun to mid-Sep daily 9–12, 4–7).

ON THE WATERFRONT

Gradska, the main street of the old town, ends at the Gradska Vrata (Town Gate), beside the only surviving section of 15th-century walls. From here, you can walk along the Riva, a harbourside promenade culminating in Kula Kamerlengo (Jun–end Sep daily 9–8), a Venetian fortress with fine views from the battlements.

The Franciscan monastery beside the harbour in the sheltered bay of Vis

RATINGS				
Good for food	●	●	●	●	●
Good for wine	●	●	●	●
Photo stops	●	●	●	●

VIS

This remote Adriatic outpost is attracting growing numbers of visitors, discovering the charm of one of Croatia's most captivating islands.

Isolated from the outside world as a Yugoslav military base until 1989, Vis remains an unspoiled island of vineyards and fishing bays with a pretty harbourside town at either end. Tourists have discovered Vis, and it now rivals Hvar as a fashionable destination for sailors. The islanders who left during the Tito years are returning and there is a new-found feeling of prosperity.

ISLAND CAPITAL

Vis Town is set in a sheltered bay, watched over by a Franciscan monastery. It was founded as the Greek colony of Issa in the 4th century BC; the ruins of an Greek cemetery stand behind the tennis courts, not far from a Roman bathhouse with mosaic dolphins set into the floor. An Austrian battery by the harbour houses a branch of the Archaeological Museum in Split (Jul–end Aug Tue–Sat 10–1, 5–9, Sun 10–1), whose star exhibit is a bronze head of Greek goddess Aphrodite.

THE BRITISH CONNECTION

British soldiers were stationed in Vis during both the Napoleonic wars and World War II, when Tito briefly ran the Partisan operation from a cave in Mount Hum. A path above the harbour leads to the abandoned George III fortress, with a carved Union Jack (British flag) over the door. There is a small English cemetery on the other side of the bay, with a memorial to the 'comrades of Tito's liberation war'. Vis even has its own cricket club, begun by winemaker Oliver Roki.

BASICS

🔲 296 F9

ℹ️ Šetalište Stare Isse, Vis Town (opposite the ferry dock), tel 021 717017; Jul–end Aug Mon–Sat 8.30–8.30, Sun 9–noon; Jun, Sep Mon–Sat 9–1, 5–8; Oct–end May Mon–Fri 8–2

🛳️ Car ferry and catamaran from Split to Vis

www.tz-vis.hr
Official website of the Vis tourist board.

TIPS

● Try the local wines— white Vugava and red Viški Plavac.
● Take the bus from Vis Town to Komiža, where boats depart in summer for the Modra Špilja (Blue Grotto) on Biševo, seen at its best at noon.
● Walk or drive to the summit of Mount Hum, the highest point on Vis, passing the cave which served as Tito's wartime hideout.

Zadar

●

Roman, Byzantine and Venetian rulers have all left their mark on Zadar, a vibrant modern city and the ancient capital of Dalmatia.

Pretty houses line the waterfront of the new town

The Land Gate is a Venetian triumphal arch

A brightly painted bridge on the coast road near Zadar

RATINGS			
Café life	● ● ● ●		
Historic interest	● ● ● ●		
Walkability	● ● ● ●		

BASICS

✚ 295 D6
ℹ️ Ilije Smiljanica 5, tel 023 316166; Jun–end Sep daily 8am–midnight; Oct–end May Mon–Fri 8–8, Sat–Sun 9–1
🚌 From Šibenik and Split
⛴ From Dubrovnik, Pula, Rijeka and Split

www.zadar.hr
Website of the Zadar county tourist board, with information on the city and its surroundings.

SEEING ZADAR

The oldest part of the city is on a peninsula with the sea on three sides. On the northern side is the ferry port, along with some medieval walls and harbour gates. The southern side of the peninsula is open to the sea, with views from the waterfront promenade to the island of Ugljan. You enter the old town across the footbridge to the north, or through the Kopnena Vrata (Land Gate), a 16th-century Venetian triumphal arch. The old town is closed to traffic and is easily explored on foot. From Narodni Trg, the old town's main square, Široka Ulica, also known as Kalelarga, leads to the Roman forum.

HIGHLIGHTS

FORUM

The forum has been at the heart of city life for more than 2,000 years. All that remains are a few columns and chunks of stone, but it is easy to imagine Roman colonnades and temples on this site. At the centre is St. Donat's Church, a Byzantine round church built by a 9th-century Irish bishop using stone from the forum. The church is no longer used for worship but is open for visits (Apr–end Oct daily 9–8) and concerts are held here on summer evenings.

ARHEOLOŠKI MUZEJ (ARCHAEOLOGICAL MUSEUM)

✉ Forum ☎ 023 250516 🕐 Mon–Sat 9–1, 5–7
🎫 Adult 10kn, child 5kn

Housed in a modern concrete building on the Forum, this is one of Croatia's oldest museums. The top floor is devoted to the prehistoric Liburnian culture, the first floor features Roman exhibits while the ground floor has stone carvings and funeral goods from medieval Croatia.

ZLATO I SREBRA ZADRA (GOLD AND SILVER OF ZADAR)

✉ Forum ☎ 023 250496 ⏲ Mon–Sat 10–1, 5–7, Sun 10–1
✋ Adult 20kn, child 10kn

A view of the old town and port area; St. Donat's Church and the Forum; a friendly stall holder in Zadar (below, left to right)

This stunning exhibition in the convent of St. Mary's Church features the work of medieval goldsmiths. The jewel-encrusted gold and silver reliquaries are said to contain the bones of saints. A separate wing contains the reconstructed chapel of Sveta Nediljica, with 11th-century carvings of biblical scenes adorned with medieval Croatian braiding.

MORSKE ORGULJE (SEA ORGAN)

Zadar's latest attraction was built in 2005 at the end of the Riva promenade. The unique sea organ is 70m (230ft) long and consists of a series of steps descending into the sea, with underwater pipes creating a symphony of nature according to the actions of the waves. Just the place to watch one of Zadar's famous sunsets, described by film director Alfred Hitchcock (1899–1980) as the most beautiful in the world.

BACKGROUND

Zadar was first occupied by the Romans during the 1st century BC and became capital of the Byzantine province of Dalmatia in the 7th century AD. Much later, it became the Venetian capital of Dalmatia and a key trading port in the eastern Adriatic. From 1920 to 1944 the city was under Italian rule. During World War II the old town was largely destroyed by Allied bombing with the result that the city today is a diverse mix of architectural styles. Zadar came under attack again in 1991, when the surrounding villages were occupied by forces of the Republic of the Serbian Krajina.

TIPS

● Climb the 170 steps inside the bell tower of the cathedral (daily in summer, occasional weekends in winter; 10kn) for views over the city and port.
● Have a drink in the restored Venetian arsenal (▷ 245).
● The city beach is at Kolovare, within walking distance of the old town; leave via the Land Gate, walk around the Foša (inner harbour) and continue along the coastal path.
● Ferries leave from Zadar for the peaceful islands of Ugljan, Pašman and Dugi Otok.
● Most hotels are at Borik, 5km (3 miles) from the old town. You can get there by bus or by walking along the shore and taking a rowing-boat taxi from the northern breakwater to the ferry port.

DUBROVNIK AND BEYOND

Christened the 'pearl of the Adriatic' by poet Lord
Byron and 'paradise on earth' by playwright
George Bernard Shaw, Dubrovnik is the perfect
Mediterranean walled city. Heavily damaged
during the Homeland War, Dubrovnik has been
triumphantly restored as a model of Croatian
tourism and has recovered all of its old confidence.

THE SIGHTS

Dubrovnik

Stradun; other offices at Gruž and Lapad ☎ 020 321561 🕓 Daily 8–8
www.tzdubrovnik.hr • Website of the Dubrovnik city tourist board.
www.visitdubrovnik.hr • Website of Dubrovnik-Neretva county,
with information on the city and surrounding areas.

HOW TO GET THERE

✈ Čilipi airport, 20km (12 miles) south of city, with regular shuttle buses to Pile Gate

🚌 The bus station is at Gruž harbour, 4km (2.5 miles) west of the old town; bus 1A,1B to Pile Gate

⛴ Car ferry from Rijeka, Zadar, Split, Hvar and Korčula to Gruž; taxi boats from Cavtat to Old Port in summer

Taking a stroll through Dubrovnik (below). View over the walled city (bottom)

THE SIGHTS

SEEING DUBROVNIK

Dubrovnik is a historic city, shipping port and modern holiday resort rolled into one. The main sights are located within Stari Grad (Old Town), a rocky outcrop enclosed by medieval walls which form an elevated promenade around the city. Inside the walls traffic is banned so walking is the only option. The classic approach is through Vrata od Pile (Pile Gate), conveniently reached by local bus from the bus station and Gruž harbour. From here, Stradun, the main street of the old town, leads to the Gradska Luka (Old Port), where boats depart for Lokrum and Cavtat in summer. Steep and narrow lanes to either side of Stradun climb up to the atmospheric districts beneath the walls. At the opposite end from Pile, Vrata od Ploča (Ploče Gate) leads to the city beach and some of the smartest hotels. Most hotels are situated on the Lapad and Babin Kuk peninsulas, 5km (3 miles) west of the old

DON'T MISS

ELAFITSKI OTOCI (ELAFITI ISLANDS)
Take the boat from Dubrovnik to these peaceful car-free islands (▷ 156)
GRADSKE ZIDINE
A walk around the walls is the perfect introduction to the city (▷ 148–149)
STRADUN
A symphony in stone, best seen from one of the pavement (sidewalk) cafés (▷ 152–153)

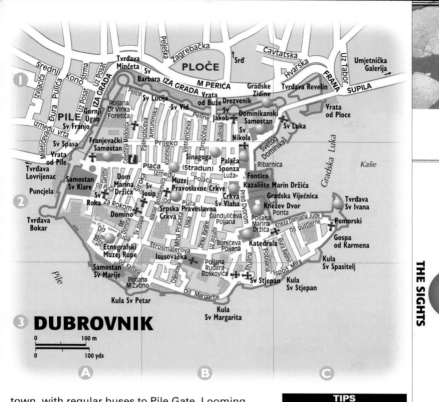

Tvrđava Minčeta
PLOČE
↑Srđ
Cavtatska
Umjetnička Galerija
Srednji
Kono
Strma
Peljeŝka
Zagrebačka
Hvarska
Uz Tabor
FRANA
SUPILA

Izvlačka
Bura
Pulća
Uz Pošat
Uz Pošat
IZA GRADA
Sv Barbara
IZA GRADA
M PERIĆA
Vrata
od Buže
Gradske
Zidine
Tvrđava Revelin

PILE
Gornji
Ugao
Sv Franjo
Između vrta
Peline
Poljana
Dr Vinka
Foretića
Sv Lucija
Sv Vid
Antuninska
Sv Jakob
Drezvenik
Dominikanski
Samostan
Sv Nikola
Vrata
od Ploče

Miletičeva
Vrata
od Pile
Sv Spasa
Franjevački
Samostan
Prijeko
Sinagoga
Palača
Sponza
Svetog
Dominika
Sv Luka

Tvrđava
Lovrijenac
Puncjela
Samostan
Sv Klare
Dom
Marina
Držića
Plača
(Stradun)
Luža
Ribarnica
Kaše
Gradska Luka

Tvrđava
Bokar
Sv
Roka
Za Rokom
Domino
Muzej
Pravoslavne Crkve
Sv Josip
Srpska Pravoslavna
Crkva
Fontico
Kazalište Marin Držića
Gradska Vijećnica
Knežev Dvor
Ponta
Tvrđava
Sv Ivana

Pile
Etnografski
Muzej Rupe
Isusovačka
Gundulićeva
Poljana
Sv Vlaha
Pred Dvorom
Poljana
Marina
Držića
Kneza Damiana Jude
Od pustijerne
Pomorski
Gospa
od Karmena

Samostan
Sv Marije
Poljana
M Zvono
Poljana
Rudera
Boskovica
Bunićeva
Poljana
Katedrala
Sv Stjepan
Kula
Sv Stjepan
Kula
Sv Spasitelj

Kula Sv Petar
Kula
Sv Margarita

DUBROVNIK

0 ——— 100 m
0 ——— 100 yds

A   B   C

town, with regular buses to Pile Gate. Looming over the city is Mount Srđ, which has a snaking path that leads to the summit.

This chapter also includes places of interest within easy reach of Dubrovnik for day trips by bus, boat, car or organized tours.

BACKGROUND

Dubrovnik was founded as the town of Ragusium by refugees from Roman Epidaurum (Cavtat) in the 7th century AD. The Venetians took over the city in 1202, introducing the system of government by nobility which was to be a hallmark of medieval Ragusa (▷ 18). From 1358 to 1808 this was a wealthy mercantile city state to rival Venice, nominally governed by a rector and paying tribute to Hungarian and Turkish rulers in exchange for its freedom. An earthquake in 1667 destroyed half of the city and left over 4,000 people dead. Occupied by Napoleon's troops in 1808, Ragusa later came under Austro-Hungarian and Yugoslav rule, officially adopting its Slavic name of Dubrovnik in 1918. During the siege of Dubrovnik (▷ 23) in 1991–2 the airport and port were destroyed and the majority of houses in the old town were shelled by the Yugoslav army. Dubrovnik today has risen from the ashes and is once again a self-confident, cultured city with a great sense of pride in its much-cherished motto, Libertas (Freedom).

TIPS

● Pick up a copy of the monthly Dubrovnik guide from tourist offices, with bus maps, ferry timetables, and listings of concerts and events.

● Book accommodation well in advance for the Dubrovnik Summer Festival (▷ 198), when the entire city is turned into an open-air stage.

● Between November and February hotel guests receive a Dubrovnik Winter Card, giving discounts at museums and restaurants and free entry to special concerts.

● Buy bus tickets from news kiosks in advance—fares cost more on the bus and the drivers do not give change.

St. Blaise portrayed in stone, Dubrovnik

A view of the red rooftops of Dubrovnik and the tower of the 15th-century Dominican Monastery

CRKVA SVETOG VLAHA (CHURCH OF ST. BLAISE)

✚ 145 B2 ✉ Luža ☎ 020 323462 🕐 Daily 8–8 💲 Free

Dubrovnik's favourite church is dedicated to Sveti Vlaho (St. Blaise), the city's protector and patron saint. Wherever you go in Dubrovnik you will come across statues of St. Blaise. Not much is known about this 3rd-century Armenian bishop, who was martyred by the Romans because of his Christianity and is said to have been flayed to death with an iron comb. Several centuries later, according to tradition, he appeared in a dream to a priest in Dubrovnik warning of a Venetian attack. The invasion was repelled and the city adopted St. Blaise as its patron. The current baroque church was completed in 1715, replacing an earlier church destroyed by fire. Miraculously, the only object to survive was a 15th-century silver statue of St. Blaise holding a model of pre-earthquake Dubrovnik, which is kept in a niche above the altar. The church is the focal point for the annual festival of St. Blaise (▷ 198), when the faithful line up to have their throats blessed by a priest placing a candle around their neck. The reason for this custom is that St. Blaise is also the patron saint of throat ailments.

DOMINIKANSKI SAMOSTAN (DOMINICAN MONASTERY)

✚ 145 B1 ✉ Ulica Svetog Dominika 4 ☎ 020 321423 🕐 Daily 9–6 💲 Adult 15kn, child 7kn

The Dominican order of friars were given land inside Ploče Gate in the 14th century, on condition that they helped to protect the city as the Franciscans did at Pile Gate. The 15th-century monastery complex largely survived the Great Earthquake and today includes a church, cloisters and museum. The tranquil cloisters of orange and lemon trees make a delightfully shady retreat from the city streets in summer. The church is dominated by a large gilded crucifix by 14th-century artist Paolo Veneziano, and also contains works by leading 20th-century Croatian artists, including a portrait of St. Dominic by Vlaho Bukovac and a sculpture of the Virgin and Child by Ivan Meštrović (▷ 21). Highlights of the museum are an 11th-century Bible and an altarpiece by Titian depicting Mary Magdalene and St. Blaise.

Don't miss A Gothic staircase leads up to the monastery with a walled-in balustrade designed to prevent views of women's ankles as they climbed the steps to the church.

ETNOGRAFSKI MUZEJ RUPE (ETHNOGRAPHIC MUSEUM)

✚ 145 A2 ✉ Od Rupa 3 ☎ 020 323018 🕐 Jun–end Sep daily 9–6; Oct–end May daily 9–2 💲 Adult 35kn, child 15kn 🏛 👥

This 16th-century granary is the only survivor of the grain stores built to preserve food for the citizens of Ragusa in the event of a siege. The grain was stored in deep circular wells hewn out of the rock, which still make a dramatic sight. Note the Roman numerals carved into the wall, recording the capacity of each pit. On the top two floors, where the grain was dried, there is now a diverting exhibition of rural costumes and crafts, including the richly embroidered waistcoats and skirts of the Konavle villagers, dyed red Easter eggs and 19th-century jewel-encrusted Turkish daggers and pistols.

Detail of the window of the Franciscan Monastery (above).
Visitors congregating outside the church (right)

FRANJEVAČKI SAMOSTAN (FRANCISCAN MONASTERY)

The cloisters of this 14th-century church shelter an interesting museum and a historic pharmacy.

In the 14th century Franciscan monks were given permission to build their church inside the city walls and granted a plot close to Pile Gate. The original church was gutted by fire following the Great Earthquake and all that remains is the Gothic Pieta over the south door. To visit the cloisters and museum enter via the narrow passage beside the neighbouring church of Sveti Spas.

PEACEFUL RETREAT
With their twin columns, gardens of palm trees and bougainvillea, a fountain at the centre and views of the bell tower, the Franciscan cloisters are a beautiful place to visit. A stone tablet records that they were built by Mihoje Brajkov of Montenegro, who died of plague in 1348. Among the capitals, carved with images of humans, animals and plants, look for the man with a swollen cheek, believed to be a self-portrait of Brajkov suffering from toothache. Just off the cloisters is the pharmacy, which has been in operation since 1317.

THE MUSEUM
The museum contains a reproduction of the old monastic pharmacy. Other exhibits include a 15th-century portrait of St. Blaise. The monastery suffered serious damage during the siege of Dubrovnik, receiving over 50 direct hits despite being used by the Red Cross. As a powerful memorial, two shells which fell on 'Black Friday' (6 December 1991) are on display.

RATINGS

Cultural interest	●●●
Historic interest	●●●●
Photo stops	●●●●

BASICS

✚ 145 A2
✉ Stradun 2
☎ 020 321410
🕐 Daily 9–6
🎫 Church: free. Museum and cloisters: Adult 20kn, child 10kn

www.malabraca.hr
Excellent site in Croatian, English, French, German and Italian with photos, history of the monastery and a full account of the damage in the Homeland War.

TIPS

● The pharmacy (Mon–Sat 9–6) sells herbal remedies and lotions, made from recipes dating back to its opening in 1317.
● Look out for candlelit concerts and recitals of chamber music in the lovely Gothic chapel of Sveti Spas (Holy Saviour).

Gradske Zidine

The walkway around the ramparts offers unrivalled views over Dubrovnik and is a must for first-time visitors to the city.

The city fortifications, built on a steep cliffside

An information plaque at the Pile Gate

Visitors exploring Dubrovnik's city walls (above and above right)

SEEING GRADSKE ZIDINE (CITY WALLS)

A full circuit of the walls is around 2km (1.2 miles) and takes about an hour, excluding rest and photo stops. The best place to begin is just inside Pile Gate, a staircase giving access to the walls. Other entry points are inside Ploče Gate on Ulica Svetog Dominika, and near the entrance to Tvrđava Sveti Ivana (▷ 154). Between these two is a section of free access around the Old Port, so keep your ticket to show at checkpoints. Starting from Pile Gate, a clockwise circuit climbs to Minčeta Tower, continuing to the Old Port and returning along the cliffs. Generally speaking, the views over the old town are better from the landward side, while the seaward side offers scenic views across the water to Lokrum. The audio tour, starting at Pile Gate, assumes you are walking in an anticlockwise direction.

HIGHLIGHTS

VRATA OD PILE (PILE GATE)

The historic entrance to the city is protected by a draw-bridge and fortified double gate. The outer portal, added in 1537, is topped by the city's oldest statue of St. Blaise. Below the statue are three carved heads, thought to represent a monk and two nuns discovered in a sexual act. Inside the gate, a map records the locations of the shells which fell on the old town during the siege of 1991–2. The original gateway, with a figure of St. Blaise by Ivan Meštrović (▷ 21), leads to Stradun and the entrance to the city walls on your left.

TVRĐAVA MINČETA

This crenellated round tower was designed by Michelozzo Michelozzi (1396–1472), chief architect to the Medici family of Florence, and completed by Juraj Dalmatinac, architect of Šibenik Cathedral. The rooftop has great views across the old town and out to sea.

TVRĐAVA SVETI IVANA (ST. JOHN'S FORT)

See page 154.

TVRĐAVA LOVRIJENAC (ST. LAWRENCE'S FORT)

🕐 Apr–end Oct, daily 8–6.30 🖐 Adult 20kn, child 10kn if visited separately

The ticket to the walls also gives access to this sturdy stone fortress, built on a rocky promontory outside Pile Gate. Note the inscription above the entrance: *Non bene pro toto libertas venditur auro* (freedom must not be sold for all the gold in the world), a motto of the Ragusan republic. The sunsets from the roof terrace are magnificent, and there are performances of Shakespeare here during the Summer Festival (▷ 198).

BACKGROUND

The walls that you see today date from the 15th century, when Ragusa felt threatened by the rise of the Ottoman Turks. Up to 25m (82ft) high and 12m (40ft) wide in places, with over 20 bastions and towers, they protected Ragusa's freedom for centuries and were never breached until Napoleon's troops entered the city in 1806. Each of the gates and bastions is guarded by an effigy of St. Blaise.

CHANGING OF THE GUARD

During the summer months costumed guards in the military uniform of the Ragusan republic stand outside Pile and Ploče gates, as they did in medieval times. A ceremonial Changing of the Guard takes place each day between May and October from 10am to noon and 8–10pm at the entrances to the walled town.

The historic Pile Gate, Dubrovnik (above left)

THE SIGHTS

The baroque dome of the Cathedral, Dubrovnik

The Renaissance portico of the Palača Sponza in Dubrovnik, home to the Ragusa state archives

KATEDRALA (CATHEDRAL)

✚ 145 B2 ✉ Pred Dvorom
☎ 020 323459 🕐 Jun–end Sep Mon–Sat 8–8, Sun 11–8; Oct–end May Mon–Sat 8–5.30, Sun 11–5.30. Treasury: open winter hours all year round 🖐 Treasury: Adult 10kn, child 5kn

Legend states that Dubrovnik's first cathedral was built by English king Richard the Lionheart (1157–99) in thanks for being rescued from a shipwreck at Lokrum on his return from the Crusades. Whatever the truth, the cathedral was destroyed in the Great Earthquake and the current baroque church dates from 1713. With its clean white walls and arches, the cathedral has a pleasing simplicity in contrast to so many overblown Croatian Catholic churches. The main attraction is the bizarre Riznica (Treasury), situated behind the altar and containing numerous examples of the gold and silver filigree work of Ragusa's medieval craftsmen. Many of the exhibits are reliquaries for the body parts of saints, giving the treasury the feel of a macabre medieval morgue. Pride of place goes to the relics of St. Blaise, acquired from Constantinople after he became Dubrovnik's patron saint in the 10th century. They include an 11th-century skull cap in the form of a Byzantine crown, and bejewelled and filigreed reliquaries containing the saint's arms, feet and throat. During the festival of St. Blaise (▷ 198), the relics are taken out of the cathedral and paraded around the city, with the faithful reaching out to touch them.

KNEŽEV DVOR

See page 151.

MUZEJ PRAVOSLAVNE CRKVE (ORTHODOX CHURCH MUSEUM)

✚ 145 B2 ✉ Od Puča 8
☎ 020 323283 🕐 Mon–Sat 9–2 🖐 Adult 10kn, child 5kn

The Ragusan republic had a reputation for religious diversity which continues to this day: in addition to numerous Catholic churches there are Baptist and Orthodox churches, a synagogue and a mosque within the city walls. The Serbian Orthodox church of the Annunciation, completed in 1877, is the focus for Dubrovnik's Serb community. Rich in icons, incense and candle wax, it is typically Byzantine in style. A few doors along, climb the stairs of an ordinary-looking house and ring the doorbell to enter the Orthodox museum, which features icons from the 15th to 19th centuries and dark portraits of local Serbs by Cavtat artist Vlaho Bukovac (1855–1922).

PALAČA SPONZA

✚ 145 B2 ✉ Luža ☎ 020 321032 🕐 Daily 8–3 🖐 Free

This elegant 16th-century palace, with its Venetian Gothic windows and Renaissance portico, was one of the few buildings to survive the Great Earthquake of 1667 and was once used as Ragusa's customs house and mint. A Latin inscription in the courtyard cautions traders against cheating, warning that 'the scales we use to weigh your goods are used by God to weigh us'. During the Communist era, the palace became the Museum of the Socialist Revolution, but it now houses the Ragusa state archives and is used as a gallery hosting temporary exhibitions.
Don't miss The Memorial Room to the Defenders of Dubrovnik is a moving tribute to the victims of the 1991–2 siege, with photos of the dead and images of Stradun in flames.

Dubrovnik's Knežev Dvor, once the seat of government, is dramatically lit up at night

KNEŽEV DVOR (RECTOR'S PALACE)

The historic heart of Dubrovnik government is now a museum recalling Ragusa's golden age.

The city state of Ragusa was ruled by a rector, elected by all adult male nobles with a mandate of just one month. Throughout his term of office he was confined to the palace, forbidden to see his family and only allowed to leave on official state business. The rector's palace was not only the seat of government, it was also a courtroom, prison and gunpowder store. Begun by Neapolitan architect Onofrio della Cava in 1435, it survives as a reminder of Dubrovnik's golden age.

THE GROUND FLOOR

You enter the palace through the loggia, with columns carved from Korčula marble and a long stone bench. The main doorway leads to the atrium; at the centre is a bust of Miho Pracat (1528–1607), a wealthy shipowner from Lopud who left his fortune to the Ragusan republic—he is the only commoner ever to be honoured in this way. The former courtroom and prison cells house exhibitions of coins, weapons and Ragusan portraits.

THE STATE APARTMENTS

A ceremonial staircase, used once a month for the inauguration of a new rector, leads to the state rooms on the upper floor. The salons have been re-created with aristocratic furniture, and the rector's study contains the original keys to the city gates. The Latin inscription above the door to the Great Council chambers reminds the rector of his duty: *Obliti privatorum publica curate* (Forget private concerns, think of the public good).

RATINGS	
Cultural interest	● ● ●
Historic interest	● ● ● ●
Photo stops	● ● ●

BASICS

- 145 B2
- ✉ Pred Dvorom 3
- ☎ 020 321422
- ⏰ May–end Oct daily 9–6; Nov–end Apr Mon–Sat 9–2
- 🎟 Adult 35kn, child 17kn

www.mdc.hr/dubrovnik
The website of Dubrovnik city museums has information on the Ethnographic Museum and Maritime Museum as well as the Rector's Palace.

TIPS

● Go to a concert here if you can as the acoustics are superb. The Dubrovnik Symphony Orchestra gives recitals throughout the year and the atrium is used for concerts during the Summer Festival.
● Gradska Kavana, next door to the palace, is Dubrovnik's finest old coffee house.

Stradun

●

The central thoroughfare of the old town is the beating heart of Dubrovnik, thronging with visitors day and night.

The tall clock tower dominates Stradun

A narrow café-lined street, Dubrovnik

Stradun street scenes, Dubrovnik (above and above right)

RATINGS

Photo stops	●●●●○
Specialist shopping	●●●○○
Walkability	●●●●○

BASICS

✚ 145 B2

ℹ Stradun, tel 020 321561; Jul–end Aug daily 8–10; Sep–end Jun 8–8

www.zod.hr
The Institute for the Restoration of Dubrovnik has its offices just off Stradun and this site gives information about its latest projects and exhibitions.

SEEING STRADUN

Stradun, also known as Placa, runs for 300m (0.5km) in an ever widening straight line from Pile Gate to Luža square. With its souvenir shops and pavement (sidewalk) cafés, this is a popular meeting point and the venue for the evening *korzo* (promenade). A walk along Stradun is an essential Dubrovnik experience and the limestone paving has been polished smooth by centuries of passing feet. Stradun is especially atmospheric at night, when street lamps bathe the stone in a golden glow.

HIGHLIGHTS

VELIKA ONOFRIJEVA FONTANA (ONOFRIO'S LARGE FOUNTAIN)

The large domed fountain inside Pile Gate was built by Neapolitan engineer Onofrio della Cava in 1444 as part of a complex system of plumbing which provided Ragusa's first water supply. Severely damaged in the Great Earthquake and again in 1991–2, the fountain has been restored and continues to supply fresh water to the city. Cool water spouts from the gargoyles and thirsty travellers can usually be found filling up their bottles in summer. There is also a smaller fountain by Onofrio della Cava beneath the clock tower in Luža.

LUŽA

The broad square where Stradun meets the Old Port has St. Blaise's Church (▷ 146) on one side and Palača Sponza (▷ 150) on the other. At the centre is Orlandov

Stup (Orlando Column), with a figure of a knight at its base, erected in 1418 and believed to represent the French epic hero Roland, who legend says defended Dubrovnik against the Moors. Under the Ragusan

republic new laws were proclaimed from the column, criminals were executed here and Orlando's forearm was used as an official unit of measurement. The nearby clock tower dates from the 15th century; look out for the 'little green men' Maro and Baro, bronze figures who strike the hour by hitting the bell with their hammers. The originals are kept in the Sponza Palace.

BACKGROUND

Stradun was originally a narrow channel separating the Roman island of Ragusium from the Slavic settlement of Dubrovnik at the foot of Mount Srž; it was only when the channel was silted up during the 12th century that the two sides came together to form a single city. The flagstones were laid down in the 15th century and Stradun has been the city's main promenade ever since. With the exception of Palača Sponza (▷ 150), the grand Gothic and Renaissance palaces which once lined the street were destroyed in the Great Earthquake. Rebuilding from scratch after the earthquake, Roman architect Giulio Cerruti created a street of identical three-storey stone houses, with arched doorways and windows at street level. The arches designed to accommodate shop window displays perform the same function today, and the only advertising allowed is the name of the shop painted onto the old-fashioned lanterns which hang outside. During the siege of 1991–2 Stradun suffered 45 direct hits from mortar shells and was for a time deserted.

TIPS

● North of Stradun, narrow alleys and steep steps lined with potted plants lead uphill through the atmospheric districts beneath the city walls. Halfway up and parallel to Stradun, Prijeko is an attractive street with restaurant tables on the pavement (sidewalk) in summer.
● Apart from a couple of good bookstores, the shops on Stradun mostly sell souvenirs, so for specialist shopping you are better off heading for the parallel street of Od Puča (▷ 196).

THE SIGHTS

MORE TO SEE

CRKVA SVETOG VLAHA (CHURCH OF ST. BLAISE)
See page 146.

FRANJEVAČKI SAMOSTAN (FRANCISCAN MONASTERY)
See page 147.

PALAČA SPONZA
See page 150.

SINAGOGA (SYNAGOGUE)
See page 154.

WAR PHOTO
✉ Ulica Antuninska 6 ☎ 020 322166 🕐 Jun–end Sep daily 9–9; May, Oct Tue–Sat 10–4, Sun 10–2 💰 Adult 30kn, child free www.warphotoltd.com
This thought-provoking gallery just off Stradun has exhibitions of war photography from the conflicts in the Balkans and around the world.

The clock tower on Stradun, Dubrovnik (above left)

A sign showing the opening hours for the Jewish Museum, housed in the 15th-century Synagogue in Dubrovnik

The entrance to the Synagogue on Ulica Žudioska

SINAGOGA (SYNAGOGUE)

✚ 145 B2 ⊠ Ulica Žudioska 3 ☎ 020 321028 🕐 Jun–end Sep daily 10–8; Oct–end May Mon–Fri 10–3 👋 Adult 10kn, child 10kn

Dubrovnik's small synagogue is the oldest Sephardic synagogue in the world and the second oldest surviving synagogue in Europe, after Prague. It was founded in the 15th century by Jews expelled from Spain, and was situated on the main street of the Jewish ghetto, whose gates were locked each night. It was reconsecrated in 1997 after years of Communist neglect and war damage. Brass lamps hang from the ceiling and wooden lattice screens hide an area previously reserved for women. A museum contains religious artefacts and records of the early Jewish community; more recent items include a list of Holocaust victims.

SRĐ

✚ Off map 145 B1

The limestone bulk of Mount Srđ keeps a watchful eye over Dubrovnik, sheltering the city from the wind and rain which fall on the far side. Until 1991 you could take a cable-car to the summit,

but it was destroyed during the war and the only way up now is on foot. Leave the old town by Buža gate near the highest point of the walls and follow the road uphill. Climb the steps on Ulica Od Srđa to reach the Adriatic highway, then turn left and look for the path on your right. The climb to the summit takes about an hour—take plenty of water as there is little shade, and stick to the path in case of unexploded mines. The old French fort at the summit is in ruins, but the views over Dubrovnik are superb. The tall white cross is illuminated at night.

STRADUN

See pages 152–153.

TVRĐAVA SVETI IVANA (ST. JOHN'S FORT)

✚ 145 C2 ⊠ Kneza Damjana Jude

This sturdy 16th-century fortress stands guard over the Old Port, facing across the harbour to Revelin fort on the far side. The upper floors now house a maritime museum, Pomorski Muzej (Jun–end Sep daily 9–6; Oct–end May Mon–Sat 9–2; adult 35kn, child 17kn), with maps and charts, and displays on

Dubrovnik's nautical history. The ground floor makes an unusual setting for Dubrovnik's aquarium (▷ 198).

UMJETNIČKA GALERIJA (MODERN ART MUSEUM)

✚ Off map 145 C1 ⊠ Put Frana Supila 23 ☎ 020 426590 🕐 Tue–Sun 10–8 👋 Adult 30kn, child free

Dubrovnik's modern art museum occupies an elegant Renaissance villa in Ploče, outside the eastern walls. Leave the old town via Ploče Gate and cross the drawbridge to Revelin fort, then continue uphill past the Lazareti (a former quarantine hospital) and Banje beach to reach the museum. Look out for portraits by Cavtat painter Vlaho Bukovac (1855–1922) and an abstract *Crveni Otok* (Red Island) by Dubrovnik artist Ivo Dulčić (1916–75), who also designed the stained glass windows in St. Blaise's Church. Climb the stairs from the courtyard to the sculpture terrace, with works by Ivan Meštrović (▷ 21) and views over the Old Port. The ticket includes entry to the Ronald Brown Memorial House (daily 10–8), which is opposite the main door to the cathedral.

Fishing boats moored at the jetty in Cavtat (above).
Relaxing at a quayside café (right)

CAVTAT

Croatia's southernmost town is an attractive summer resort, with a lively harbourside promenade.

Lying 16km (10 miles) south of Dubrovnik close to Čilipi airport, Cavtat makes a good base for combining a beach holiday with excursions to the city. A palm-lined promenade looks out over a pretty bay, and seafront paths follow the shore to pine woods and beaches on the forested Rat and Sustjepan peninsulas. Boards by the harbour advertise boat trips to the off-shore island of Supetar, and taxi-boats make the 45-minute journey to Dubrovnik throughout the day.

GREEKS AND ROMANS

Cavtat was founded as the Greek colony of Epidaurum in the 3rd century BC, a thousand years before refugees from Epidaurum founded Dubrovnik. The original Greek and Roman settlement was situated on the Rat promontory, where today you will find the cemetery. Climb the path from the Franciscan church at the north end of the harbour to reach the summit, where tombstones are laid out in a peaceful garden overlooking the sea. The white marble mausoleum at the centre was built by Ivan Meštrović (▷ 21) for the wealthy Račić family.

LOCAL PAINTER

Cavtat was the birthplace of one of Croatia's finest artists, Vlaho Bukovac (1855–1922). He is best known for his realistic and charming portraits, though he also dabbled with Impressionism. His 19th-century home and garden, set just back from the harbour, are now a gallery dedicated to his work. You can see more paintings by Bukovac in the museum in the Rector's Palace.

BASICS

✛ 296 J9
🛈 Tiha 3, tel 020 478025;
Jun–end Sep Mon–Sat
8am–8pm, Sun 8–12; Oct–end
May Mon–Fri 8–3
🚌 10 from Dubrovnik
⛴ From Dubrovnik

www.tzcavtat-konavle.hr
Official website of the Cavtat-Konavle county.

TIPS

● Cavtat is the main town of Konavle, a fertile and narrow strip of land between the mountains of Bosnia and the Bay of Kotor. Local tour operators offer jeep safaris and bike rides across Konavle.
● The nearby village of Čilipi has folklore performances on the church square on Sunday mornings in summer.

Beautiful flowers in bloom on Šipan island (above).
A sheltered bay on the island of Lopud (left)

BASICS

✚ 296 J9
🛈 On the harbour at Lopud, tel 020 759086; May to mid-Oct Sat–Thu 8–1, 5–7; there is also an office by the harbour at Šipanska Luka in summer
🚢 From Dubrovnik

www.visitdubrovnik.hr
The website of the Dubrovnik-Neretva county has information on the islands.

TIPS

● The islands virtually shut down between November and April, so make sure you bring your own food and drink.
● The sandy beach at Šunj is one of the finest in Croatia and has a beach bar in summer.
● Look out for the summer houses of the Ragusan nobility on the waterfront at Lopud.

ELAFITSKI OTOCI (ELAFITI ISLANDS)

Enjoy the relaxed pace of life on these traffic-free isles, a short ferry ride from the bustle of the city.

When the people of Dubrovnik need to escape, they head for the Elafiti Islands. Of 13 isles in the archipelago only three are inhabited, with a combined population of under a thousand. There are no cars on Koločep and Lopud and only a handful on Šipan, so the islands are perfect for walking. Three ferries a day make the journey from Dubrovnik; in summer there are additional fast shuttle boats from the Old Port and Cavtat, making it possible to visit all three islands in a day.

KOLOČEP AND LOPUD

The ferry arrives first at Koločep, the smallest inhabited island, which is covered in dense pine forest, vineyards, orchards and olive groves. A walled lane connects the twin settlements of Gornje and Donje Čelo, with their sand and pebble beaches. The ferry docks next at Lopud, whose only village is set around a sheltered bay beneath a fortified 15th-century Franciscan monastery. A footpath behind the harbour climbs to a 10th-century church and ruined castle at the summit of the island, offering views as far as Dubrovnik. From here you can continue to the sandy beach at Šunj.

ŠIPAN

The largest island, Šipan, is also the least visited. Ferries dock at the two main towns of Suđurađ and Šipanska Luka, each based around a pretty harbour. A minibus connects the two, or you can walk the 7km (4.5 miles), passing the church of Sveti Duh (Holy Spirit).

Bathing in the pools of the Dead Sea on Lokrum island

LOKRUM

The nearest island to Dubrovnik is a tranquil and beautiful place of dense woods, gardens, and coves.

As you walk around the city walls in Dubrovnik, your eyes are drawn to the offshore island of Lokrum, a green pearl rising out of a shimmering blue sea. The island has long been famed for its almost mythical beauty; in summer it makes a pleasant retreat from the hot and crowded city. Boats depart regularly from the Old Port in Dubrovnik, taking just 15 minutes to reach Lokrum. The price of the boat ticket includes entry to the Lokrum nature reserve.

SHADY WALKS

As you step ashore at the harbour, you see the old forest ranger's cottage, abandoned since its shelling in 1991. A map details the network of footpaths around the island, beginning with a walk along the northern shore. It takes around two hours to make a complete circuit of the island, including the climb to Fort Royal, a ruined French fort, whose rooftop offers panoramic views of Dubrovnik. From here, a processional route lined with cypress trees leads to the botanical garden.

SUN AND SEA

A short path from the harbour leads to an 11th-century Benedictine monastery, abandoned in the 19th century and later used as a summer villa by Archduke Maximilian von Habsburg, brother of the Austrian emperor. Nearby is the Mrtvo More (Dead Sea), a natural saltwater swimming pool fed by the sea. If you just want to swim and sunbathe, follow the crowds to the FKK (nudist) beach, which has views as far as Cavtat (▷ 155).

RATINGS

Good for kids	●●●○
Photo stops	●●●○
Walkability	●●●●○

BASICS

✚ 296 J9
☎ 020 427242
🕐 Apr–end Oct and at weekends in winter: boats depart Old Port every half hour from 9am–6pm, weather permitting
🖐 Adult 35kn, child 15kn
🚻 ▢

www.lokrum.hr
The history, legends and sights of Lokrum in Croatian and English.

TIPS

● Smoking is not permitted on the island because of the risk of fire.
● Make sure you check the time of the last boat back to Dubrovnik—usually 7pm.
● There is a snack bar near the harbour and a restaurant in the monastery cloisters in summer, but it is a good idea to take food and water to the island just in case.

Mljet

This island of legendary beauty is a place of green forests and turquoise lakes, set within a protected national park.

The pretty waterside Hotel Odisej

A view of the picturesque village of Korita

Enjoying the sunset from a taverna

RATINGS	
Outdoor pursuits	● ● ● ●
Photo stops	● ● ● ●
Walkability	● ● ● ●

BASICS

✚ 297 H9

ℹ Nacionalni Park Mljet, Pristanište 2, tel 020 744041

✋ National park entry fee: Apr–end Oct 90kn, including minibus from Polače and boat trip to St. Mary's island; Nov–end Mar 30kn; child under 6 free

🚢 Car ferry from Dubrovnik and Prapratno to Sobra; car ferry from Trstenik (Pelješac) to Polače in summer; catamaran from Dubrovnik to Sobra and Polače

❓ Details of *Nona Ana* sailing schedules from Atlantagent, tel 020 313355

www.np-mljet.hr
The website of the Mljet National Park has background information on history, mythology and wildlife in Croatian and English.

SEEING MLJET

Mljet is the eighth largest island in Croatia. The main sights are at its western end, which has been designated a national park. It is possible to spend days here walking, cycling, sailing and swimming in crystal-clear waters. Tour operators in Dubrovnik and on the Dalmatian coast offer day trips to Mljet in summer, including the national park entry fee and the boat trip to St. Mary's island. Alternatively, the *Nona Ana* catamaran leaves Gruž harbour in Dubrovnik each morning, taking around an hour to reach Mljet. From June to the end of September it departs at 9am, with tickets (120kn return) going on sale at the quayside at 8am. It then sails to Polače within the national park, giving you plenty of time to explore before the return voyage at 6.20pm. From October to May the boat leaves Dubrovnik at 10am, sailing to the main port of Sobra and continuing to Polače three times a week, though the early return to Dubrovnik gives you little time on the island. On arriving in Polače, buy a national park ticket from the harbourside kiosk before walking or taking the free minibus to the shores of Veliko Jezero. For more information on getting to Mljet, ▷ left.

HIGHLIGHTS
POLAČE

This pretty harbour village within the national park is many people's first view of Mljet. Behind the port are the remains of a 4th-century Roman villa; from here, paths lead to the lakeshore at Pristanište and the abandoned hilltop village of Goveđari.

VELIKO JEZERO AND MALO JEZERO (BIG AND SMALL LAKES)

These two saltwater lakes are fed by the sea through the narrow Solinski channel. A footpath leads around

the shore of both lakes, though it is no longer possible to make a complete circuit as the bridge spanning the seaward end of Veliko Jezero was destroyed in 1960. The two lakes meet at Stari Most (Old Bridge), where you can rent bicycles, rowing boats and canoes in summer. A pleasant cycle path around Veliko Jezero passes St. Mary's island, with fine views of the monastery before you reach the open sea.

OTOK SVETA MARIJA (ST. MARY'S ISLAND)

This monastery on an islet on a lake on an island is one of the most photographed images of Croatia. Used as a hotel in the Communist era, it has now been returned to the church and is currently being restored. Between April and the end of October shuttle boats ferry you across from Pristanište or Stari Most. You can explore the 12th-century cloisters, have lunch in the café, and stroll around the island, looking out for votive shrines built by shipwrecked sailors.

BACKGROUND

According to legend, Mljet was the home of the beautiful nymph Calypso, who seduced the Greek hero Odysseus and kept him in her cave on the south coast for seven years after he was ship-wrecked on the island. The story is told by Homer in his epic poem *Odyssey*, and adds to the mythical appeal of the island. Hotel Odisej at Pomena, Mljet's only hotel, can organize boat trips into the cave where Calypso is said to have enchanted Odysseus.

TIPS

● If you are visiting Mljet in autumn, winter or spring, go on a Sunday. Between October and May, the *Nona Ana* sails from Dubrovnik at 10am and returns from Polače at 5pm on Sundays, giving you enough time to explore the national park. The boat trips to St. Mary's island do not operate in winter, but you can still walk around the lakes.

● There are restaurants at Polače and Pomena, and summer restaurants on St. Mary's island and on the shores of Veliko Jezero.

● For a gentle hike, a footpath from Polače and Veliko Jezero climbs to Montokuc, at 253m (830ft) the highest summit in the national park.

● If you are staying longer, rent a car or bike to explore the rest of the island, including the beautiful sandy beach at Saplunara, on Mljet's southeastern tip.

● Smoking is only allowed at designated places within the national park because of the risk of forest fires.

THE SIGHTS

A stunning aerial view of Mljet (above left)

A view of Korčula, as seen from Pelješac

Statue in the grotto at Trsteno Arboretum

THE SIGHTS

PELJEŠAC

🗺 297 H9 ⓘ Trg Mumbeli, Orebić, tel 020 713718; Jun–end Sep daily 8am–9pm; Oct–end May Mon–Fri 8–1
🚌 From Dubrovnik and Korčula
⛴ From Korčula

This long, mountainous peninsula is virtually an island, joined to the mainland by a slender isthmus at Ston and separated from Korčula by a narrow channel at Orebić. The twin towns of Ston and Mali Ston, guarding the entrance to Pelješac, were second only to Dubrovnik in the days of the Ragusan republic, protected by a complex system of 14th-century fortifications that can still be climbed today. Mali Ston is famed for its oysters and mussels, which you can try at the waterfront restaurants. A single road runs for 90km (56 miles) across Pelješac, passing idyllic bays and offering magnificent views to the islands of Korčula, Lastovo and Mljet. Highlights include the vineyards at Potomje, source of Croatia's finest red wine, Dingač (▷ 233), and the laid-back beach resort of Orebić.

PREVLAKA

🗺 296 K10 ☎ 020 791555
🕐 Hours vary throughout the year 💲 Adult 15kn, child free including unlimited rides on sightseeing train 🚌 From Dubrovnik and Cavtat to Molunat 🍴 🛍 🅿 🏧 🚻
www.prevlaka.hr

At the southern tip of Croatia, facing Montenegro across the water, the rugged Prevlaka peninsula dips its toes into the Bay of Kotor. Acquired by the Ragusan republic from Bosnian rulers in 1441, this lonely spit of land has long had strategic significance. The Austrians built a fort here in the 19th century, which survives at the very edge of the peninsula, and there was a military base here in Yugoslav times. In 1991–2 Prevlaka was occupied by the Yugoslav army during the assault on Dubrovnik. After being guarded by UN peacekeepers for 10 years, it was returned to Croatia in 2001. The far end of Oštro cape is now an adrenaline and nature park, with activities ranging from kayaking and bicycle trails to a climbing wall, children's farm and sightseeing tour by miniature train. You can wander around the old fort and the labyrinth of underground tunnels, or relax on the beach. Just up the coast, the fishing village of Molunat has become a pleasantly low-key resort, with campsites, private accommodation and clear waters.

TRSTENO

🗺 296 J9
Trsteno Arboretum
✉ Trsteno ☎ 020 751019
🕐 Jun–end Sep daily 7–7; Oct–end May daily 8–5
💲 Adult 20kn, child 10kn
🚌 From Dubrovnik 🚻

In the heyday of the Ragusan republic the ruling class built their summer houses on the coast, where they gathered to discuss politics and state affairs. The botanic garden at Trsteno, 18km (11 miles) north of Dubrovnik, was originally part of a Renaissance villa belonging to wealthy patrician Ivan Gučetić. The small village of Trsteno was known for its sailors, and sea captains brought back cuttings and seeds from their travels to create a rich garden of exotic species. The gardens were nationalized in 1948 and turned into an arboretum. With shady avenues of pine trees and the scent of pomegranate, orange and lemon, the garden makes a lovely place to stroll. A path leads to the harbour, with views of the Elafiti islands. **Don't miss** There is a romantic 18th-century water garden and grotto.

This chapter gives information on things to do in Croatia other than sightseeing. It is divided into six regions, which are shown on the map on the inside front cover. Entries in the Zagreb and Dubrovnik and Beyond sections are listed by theme. Within the other regions, entries are listed alphabetically by town or area. Festivals and Events are listed chronologically at the end of each region.

What to Do

SHOPPING

Shopping in Croatia has come a long way since the days of state-run Yugoslav department stores with empty shelves. Young people are becoming increasingly fashion-conscious and cities like Zagreb and Split have boutiques offering the latest trends. Souvenir shops in the coastal resorts sell everything from mass-produced costume dolls to individually designed arts and crafts. For local colour, pay a visit to one of the farmers' markets which take place each morning in all the main towns.

PRACTICALITIES

● Most shops open Monday to Friday 8–8, and Saturday 8–2. Smaller shops may close for a siesta during the afternoon. Many shops on the coast keep longer hours in summer, opening from 8am to 10pm daily. Markets are busiest on weekdays between 8 and noon.

● Credit and debit cards are increasingly accepted for payment, though some smaller shops accept cash only.

● Goods are generally fixed price and bargaining is not acceptable, though you may be able to haggle at markets and open-air stalls.

● Foreign visitors can reclaim up to 17 per cent VAT (sales tax) on transactions over 500kn at shops displaying the Tax Free Shopping logo. Ask for a tax refund form PDV-P and get it filled in and stamped at the time of purchase. You must leave the country within three months and present the receipt, tax refund form and unwrapped goods at the border for authorization of your refund.

WHAT TO BUY
Arts and Crafts

Artists sell their paintings at open-air street stalls in summer, and studios and galleries in Dubrovnik and the Istrian towns of Grožnjan, Labin, Poreč and Rovinj. Much of it consists of standard tourist landscapes, but

---

CHAIN STORES

Most shopping in Croatia is done at small, individual stores. However, the following retail chains have branches in the bigger cities.

NAME	DESCRIPTION	NUMBER OF SHOPS	LOCATIONS IN CROATIA
Algoritam	Bookstore with foreign-language books and magazines	7	Zagreb, Dubrovnik, Osijek, Pula, Split, Varaždin
Aquarius	The biggest producer and retailer of music CDs in Croatia	5	Zagreb, Dubrovnik, Poreč, Rijeka, Šibenik
Croata	Silk ties, scarves and accessories	9	Zagreb, Cavtat, Dubrovnik, Osijek, Rijeka, Split, Varaždin
Heruc Galeria	Stylish men's and women's fashions at reasonable prices	10	Zagreb, Opatija, Pula, Rijeka, Zadar
Kraš	Chocolate, sweets and confectionery	23	Zagreb, Dubrovnik, Karlovac, Krapina, Opatija, Osijek, Rijeka, Rovinj, Slavonski Brod, Split, Varaždin
Zigante Tartufi	Istrian truffles, wine and truffle-based products	6	Buje, Buzet, Grožnjan, Livade, Motovun, Pula

look carefully and you will discover some work of real quality. The village of Hlebine (▷ 62), near Koprivnica, has painters and sculptors specialising in naïve art. Popular handicrafts include embroidery, ceramics, woodwork, stonework, model boats and intricate lacework from the island of Pag. In Istria and Dalmatia, they sell miniature stone houses which are typical of the region, while a reproduction of the Vučedol Dove makes a powerful souvenir of Vukovar. One item that is unique to Croatia is the *morčić*, an enamel figure of a turbanned Moor attached to earrings and gold jewellery. Its origins as a good-luck charm worn by the citizens of Rijeka are said to date back to the Ottoman empire.

Cosmetics

The pure air and water of the Adriatic coast create the perfect climate for the wild flowers and herbs that grow on Croatia's islands. They include rosemary, sage, thyme, mint and wild tangerines but best known is Hvra lavender. Some are made into natural cosmetics and toiletries. You can buy them in Zagreb or at open-air markets on Hvar and the Dalmatian islands in summer.

Cravats and Ties

Few people realize that the necktie, the uniform of businessmen, has its origins in Croatia. The red silk scarves worn by Croatian officers during the Thirty Years War (1618–48) attracted the attention of the French and were soon adopted in fashionable Parisian society, where the custom of dressing with a necktie became known as *à la croate*, later adapted to *cravate*. Silk scarves, cravats and ties are still manufactured in Croatia by the Croata company, many adorned with typical Croatian designs such as medieval braiding or the red and white checkerboard of the Croatian flag.

Food, Wine and Spirits

Foodstuffs to take home include Pag cheese, Dalmatian ham, fig jam, Samobor mustard, lavender honey, Istrian truffles and olive oil. Check the customs regulations of your home country as there may be restrictions on some food items. Croatia produces a wide variety of wines and spirits (▷ 233) which make delicious souvenirs. It is

Locally made spirits make a good souvenir or gift

best to buy from the vineyard or a market, where you can usually taste before you buy.

Music

Bookstores and record shops sell CDs of folk music, including the *tamburica* (mandolin) music of Slavonia and *klapa* (male voice choirs) from Dalmatia. For traditional Croatian folk music, the best groups to listen to are the Lado and Linđo ensembles.

CONTACT NUMBER AND WEBSITE

01 235 9333
www.algoritam.hr

01 304 0700
www.aquarius-records.com

01 481 4600
www.croata.hr

01 365 0888
www.herucgaleria.hr

01 239 6111
www.kras.hr

052 777409
www.zigantetartufi.com

ENTERTAINMENT

Croatia has a rich tradition of performance arts, from classical music and opera in grand Habsburg-era theatres to the many open-air festivals which take place across the country. Cities such as Zagreb and Dubrovnik have an active cultural scene throughout the year, while smaller towns on the islands and coast come alive for a few weeks each summer.

WHAT TO DO

PRACTICALITIES
● Tourist offices and travel agents are good sources of information about local events. You can find out what's on by looking in newspapers or checking out the billboards you can find

Concerts take place outdoors and in traditional venues

in most towns. *Zagreb In Your Pocket* magazine is published every two months with full listings of concerts and theatre performances. Tourist boards in Zagreb and Dubrovnik also publish monthly events guides.
● It is generally best to book at least a day or two in advance, though it is usually possible to buy tickets just before the performance. The easiest way to book in advance is to go to the

theatre box office. Some venues, including the Croatian National Theatre (www.hnk.hr), take online and phone bookings. Most seats are in the *parter* (stalls) or *balkon* (balcony), but if you want a special experience, choose a reasonably priced seat in a *loža* (box).
● There is no strict dress code, but most people dress up for the theatre or opera and you would look out of place in a T-shirt, shorts or jeans. However, for outdoor events in summer, casual clothing is acceptable.

THEATRE, OPERA AND BALLET
The most prestigious venue is the Croatian National Theatre, which has branches in Zagreb, Split, Rijeka, Osijek and Varaždin. Most of these are based in magnificent Austro-Hungarian opera houses that are worth visiting for the buildings alone. Plays are performed in Croatian, but opera is sung in the original language. The National Theatre in Zagreb is also home to the National Ballet and

National Opera. Other good venues are the Marin Držić Theatre in Dubrovnik and the community theatre at Hvar (closed for renovation).

MUSIC
Performances of classical music take place throughout the year at the Croatian National Theatre and Vatroslav Lisinski concert hall in Zagreb. The Dubrovnik Symphony Orchestra has year-round events. For many, the most memorable musical experiences are the open-air concerts that take place in summer at venues such as the Roman arena at Pula, Trsat castle at Rijeka and the island of Lokrum. The biggest event is the Dubrovnik Summer Festival (▷ 198).

CINEMA
The latest international movies are shown in the original language with Croatian subtitles. Widescreen multiplexes such as Broadway Tkalča and Cinestar in Zagreb are just like those in any other big city. Almost every town has at least one cinema.

NIGHTLIFE

Nightlife for most Croatians means sitting out of doors on a summer evening sharing a drink with friends. Few people can afford the cost of clubbing, so café terraces and ice-cream parlours make the perfect venues for drinking, chatting and flirting beneath the stars.

BARS

There can be few greater pleasures in Croatia than sitting at a harbourside bar sipping chilled wine or beer on a balmy night. From Istria to Dalmatia, if you want to find the best bars, just head for the Riva or waterfront promenade to be found in all coastal and island towns. The in-crowd congregates at chic cocktail bars like Valentino in Rovinj and Carpe Diem in Hvar, but thousands of ordinary bars and pubs offer outdoor seating and sea views. The most popular spots in Zagreb are in the traffic-free streets around Trg Bana Jelačića: Tkalčićeva, Bogovićeva and Trg Petra Preradovića.

CLUBS

As the only big city in Croatia, Zagreb is the centre of the club scene, though Osijek, Rijeka and Zadar are catching up fast. The biggest club in Zagreb is Aquarius, which plays electronic music on the shores of Lake Jarun. There are others on the banks of the River Sava. For the lowdown on the hottest clubs in Zagreb, check

out the latest edition of *Zagreb In Your Pocket*. During the warm summer months, the club scene shifts to Pag, with open-air nightclubs spread around the wide arc of Zrće beach.

LIVE MUSIC

Keep an eye out for posters advertising live music, especially in summer when many coastal towns host open-air performances of pop, jazz and traditional folk music. Live music can also be heard in pubs, bars and jazz clubs in the bigger cities. Two of the best are the BP Club in Zagreb, owned by vibra-phoneplayer Boško Petrović, and the legendary Troubadour in Dubrovnik, where former Eurovision Song contestant Marko Brešković plays his double-bass some nights.

GAY AND LESBIAN SCENE

Although same-sex relationships have been legal since 1977, attitudes to gay and lesbian people have been slow to change in Croatia and it is still very unusual to see overt displays of

homosexuality in public. It is only in Zagreb that there are gay clubs and bars, though resorts such as Hvar, Rovinj and Dubrovnik are generally gay-friendly. The website http://travel.gay.hr has information in English on the gay and

Enjoying an evening meal in Rovinj's old town

lesbian scene in Croatia, including gay-friendly clubs, bars and beaches. In Zagreb, Queer Zagreb (www.queerzagreb.org) is an annual festival of gay culture. The same organization hosts film nights at the Tuškanac cinema on the third Friday and Saturday each month. The Pride march (www.zagreb-pride.net) is at the end of June and has been held in Zagreb each year since 2002.

SPORTS AND ACTIVITIES

Croatia's mountains, rivers, lakes and sea are a paradise for outdoor sports enthusiasts. Walking, cycling and fishing are all popular, while extreme sports such as climbing and rafting attract adventurous visitors. The crystal-clear Adriatic waters provide perfect conditions for sailing, diving and swimming. Croatians are passionate about spectator sport, and the country has enjoyed huge success in soccer, handball and tennis.

WHAT TO DO

BASKETBALL
There are top teams in Split and Zadar but the biggest basketball team is Cibona of Zagreb. The season is September to April and matches are held at the Dražen Petrović stadium.

BICYCLING
Bicycle trails have been established in Istria, Kvarner, Dalmatia and Zagreb. In summer it is possible to rent bicycles in most coastal resorts. For information, ▷ 43.

CANOEING, KAYAK-ING AND RAFTING
Extreme sports enthusiasts can get their thrills on Croatia's rivers, enjoying canoeing, kayaking and rafting between April and October. Canoeing takes place on the River Dobra near Karlovac and the River Neretva north of Dubrovnik. The top rafting destination is the River Cetina near Omiš, though there is also good rafting on the River Korana and River Una. Sea-kayaking is on offer at Dubrovnik and the Elafiti Islands. It is important to book with

a reputable operator and to check that full safety equipment, including helmets and lifejackets, is provided. Huck Finn Adventure Travel (tel 01 618 3333, www.huck-finn.hr) offer canoeing, kayaking and rafting in Dalmatia and the Plitvice Lakes National Park.

DIVING
The clear Adriatic waters provide excellent conditions for scuba-diving, with underwater cliffs, caves, reefs and shipwrecks to explore. All divers must buy an official diving card issued by the Croatian Diving Federation, which costs 100kn for a year. Diving is not permitted in the Brijuni and Krka national parks, and is only allowed in the Kornati Islands and Mljet in organized groups. Diving centres in Istria, Kvarner and Dalmatia offer lessons and equipment; for a full list go to www.diving.hr

FISHING
Croatia's rivers, lakes and sea are teeming with fish. Freshwater

fish include trout, perch, pike, carp and catfish, while sea fishermen can catch grouper, bass and bream. To fish in Croatia you need a licence, available from harbourmasters and travel

Hikers on a mountain track in Paklenica National Park

agencies. Tour operators on the coast have deep-sea fishing trips.

GOLF
Golf has been slow to develop in Croatia, and until recently there was only one 9-hole course, on Brijuni. There are now courses at Zagreb and Krašić, with others under construction at Zaprešić, Motovun and Dubrovnik. New courses are planned in Istria, Dalmatia and Hvar.

HANDBALL
Croatia won Olympic gold medals in 1996 and 2004. Sixteen teams play in the national league and the season is from September to May.

HIKING AND CLIMBING
There is good walking in the mountains and national parks, especially the Gorski Kotar and Velebit ranges. Conditions in the mountains can change quickly even in summer, so take warm and waterproof clothing as well as food, water, map, compass and a phone. Paths, mountain huts and refuges are managed by the Croatian Mountaineering Association (tel 01 482 4142, www.plsavez.hr). Footpaths are marked with a white dot inside a red circle. Serious hikers should get hold of *Walking in Croatia* by Rudolf Abraham (Cicerone Press), while *Landscapes of Croatia* by Sandra Bardwell (Sunflower Books) is more suitable for families, with a wide range of graded walks. Rock-climbers can tackle the challenging faces of the North Velebit and Paklenica national parks.

SAILING
You can charter your own motorboat or yacht to explore the Croatian islands, but novices must take a skippered boat. Most marinas offer boat charter and some run learn-to-sail courses. The biggest operator of marinas is ACI Club (tel 051 271288, www.aci-club.hr). Useful websites for yacht charter are www.charter.hr and www.ayc.hr, while complete sailing holidays can be booked through Sail Croatia (www.sailcroatia.net) and Sailing Holidays (www.sailingholidays.com).

SKIING
Croatia has a small number of ski slopes. The most accessible is Sljeme, at the summit of Medvednica in Zagreb while Bejelolasica is the highest and biggest ski resort in Croatia. There is skiing and ski-jumping at Delnice, and skiing with a view of the sea at Platak near Rijeka.

SOCCER
Soccer is Croatia's most popular spectator sport. There is fierce rivalry between the two biggest teams, Dinamo Zagreb and Hajduk Split. Most matches take place at weekends between August and May, with a two-month break between December and February. It is generally easy to buy tickets on the gate. The national team play at Dinamo's Maksimir stadium.

SWIMMING
The Adriatic is enticing for bathers, but most beaches have either pebbles or rocks, while private hotel beaches are often concrete bathing platforms above the water. Take plastic sandals or waterproof shoes to protect your feet. Most large hotels have outdoor pools open in summer, and there are public swimming pools in most seaside towns.

Many Croatians are passionate about soccer

TENNIS
Tennis is growing in popularity, thanks to the success of players like Goran Ivanišević, Mario Ančić and Ivan Ljubičić. Many hotels and campsites have courts with equipment for hire, and there are public courts in most towns.

WINDSURFING
Boards and equipment can be rented at sailing schools and windsurf centres on the coast.

WHAT TO DO

HEALTH AND BEAUTY

Health tourism has a long tradition in Croatia, going back to the days of the Austro-Hungarian empire, when the cream of Viennese high society would take the waters in Croatia's thermal spas. In recent years there has been a revival of interest in health and beauty treatments, and many hotels now offer state-of-the-art spa and wellness facilities.

SPA RESORTS

Croatia has a number of traditional spa resorts, based on thermal springs whose curative waters are rich in sulphur, magnesium, calcium and other minerals. They include Istarske Toplice in Istria, Varaždinske Toplice near Varaždin, and Krapinske Toplice, Stubičke Toplice and Tuheljske Toplice in the Zagorje. Many date back to the 18th and 19th centuries. Although most have been modernized, they retain an old-fashioned sanatorium feel and most visitors come for the medicinal benefits rather than relaxation. Hotels in Opatija offer spa treatments, and there is a thalassotherapy centre (tel 051 202600, www.thalassotherapia-opatija.hr) with heated seawater pools.

HOTELS

Many top hotels offer spa and wellness centres with Turkish baths, saunas, beauty treatments and massage. The Energy Clinic (www.energyclinic.com) uses treatments based on traditional Chinese medicines, natural remedies and aromatherapy. It has various branches including at the Hotel Westin in Zagreb.

FOR CHILDREN

Croatia is a very welcoming country for families with children. Although there are few attractions aimed specifically at children, they are welcome almost everywhere and given a lot of attention. Most large hotels and campsites have children's pools and playgrounds, and activities such as mini-golf and table-tennis. Many also run children's clubs in summer, with organized sports and entertainment. Children love splashing about in the water, whether it is playing on the beach or taking a ride in a pedal-boat or canoe. There are few sandy beaches, so a pair of plastic sandals will help to protect children's feet.

ATTRACTIONS

The biggest attraction for children is probably the Adriatic, which provides hours of water-based fun. Boat trips are always popular, whether it is taking a ferry to one of the islands or a pirate cruise on the Limski Kanal. Inland, the Plitvice Lakes and Krka national parks also offer boat trips, though smaller children might find the walking difficult. Children usually love animals and there are zoos at Zagreb and Osijek, a brown bear sanctuary in the Velebit mountains, a vulture reserve on Cres, a dolphin research centre at Veli Lošinj, a safari park on Brijuni and aquariums at Poreč, Pula, Rovinj, Rijeka and Dubrovnik. With a bit of imagination, many sights can be turned into children's attractions, as they play gladiators in the arena at Pula or climb over the ramparts of Dubrovnik's walls.

FESTIVALS AND EVENTS

Hardly a day goes by in Croatia without a traditional festival taking place. Every town and village has its own saint's day, celebrated with music, dancing, fireworks and religious processions. Most festivals are Catholic in origin but also include elements of pagan ritual and a large dose of Croatian patriotism, particularly those held to commemorate a historic victory over the Turks. On top of this are the numerous summer festivals, with open-air concerts and folk performances taking place along the Adriatic coast. Full details of all these events can be found on the following pages.

RELIGIOUS FESTIVALS

The biggest religious festival is the feast of St. Blaise in Dubrovnik at the beginning of February. Large crowds gather at pilgrimage sites such as Marija Bistrica and Trsat on holy days in the Catholic calendar, particularly Assumption (15 Aug) and the Birth of the Virgin (8 Sep). Across Croatia, local saint's days are a good excuse for a party even in the smallest towns and villages. Local tourist offices will have details.

CARNIVAL

The pre-Lenten Carnival in February is traditionally a time for Catholics to abandon their inhibitions before the fasting and denial of Lent. The biggest celebrations are Rijeka, which has balls and parades to rival Venice. Carnival parades also take place in Dubrovnik, Samobor and on the Dalmatian island of Lastovo.

FOLK FESTIVALS

The region of Slavonia has a rich folk heritage which is celebrated at several traditional festivals each summer. Highlights include the Brodsko Kolo at Slavonski Brod in June and Đakovački Vezovi at Đakovo in July. The biggest folk festival is the International Folklore Festival held in Zagreb in July. Harvest festivals such as the wine fair in Ilok are accompanied by Slavonian folk music and dancers in traditional costume performing the *kolo* (circle dance).

TRADITIONAL FESTIVALS

Some of Croatia's festivals have their origins in the historic battles between the Venetian, Austrian and Turkish empires. The best-known example is Sinjska Alka, held in the Dalmatian town of Sinj in August, which features jousting competitions and riders in 18th-century cavalry uniform. A similar event is held in the Istrian town of Barban. In Rab there are annual re-enactments of medieval tournaments by costumed knights fighting with crossbows.

CULTURAL FESTIVALS

The festival calendar in summer is filled with outdoor music and arts festivals taking place in atmospheric venues across the country. The biggest event is the Dubrovnik Summer Festival, which lasts for six weeks in July and August. Similar events take place in Split, Zadar and other coastal towns. In Pula, concerts are held in the Roman arena, while in Zagreb there are promenade concerts in the bandstand of Zrinjevac park. Another annual event is the summer school of Jeunesses Musicales Croatia in the Istrian hill town of Grožnjan.

ZAGREB

Zagreb is not just the political capital of Croatia, it is also the centre of shopping, entertainment and nightlife. Shoppers have everything from department stores and malls to markets and small, specialist shops. The main shopping street is Ilica, which runs west from Trg Bana Jelačića. This is where you will find boutiques selling the latest fashions in clothes and shoes, but for a quirkier selection of art galleries and individual shops, head for Radićeva and Tkalčićeva, which lead north off the main square. The latter is also the focus of Zagreb nightlife, popular with young promenaders who sit outside its bars on summer evenings. Café and bar life also rules on the streets around Bogovićeva, whose trendy lounge bars attract Zagreb's nouveau riche. Although Zagreb is a grown-up city, there is plenty to keep children amused, from rides on its trams, funicular and cable-car to the enjoyable Technical Museum and outings to Maksimir zoo and park.

KEY TO SYMBOLS

- 🏬 Shopping
- 🎭 Entertainment
- 🍸 Nightlife
- ⚽ Sports
- ✪ Activities
- ♡ Health and Beauty
- ✪ For Children

🏬 SHOPPING

BOOKS AND MUSIC

ALGORITAM
Gajeva 1, Zagreb
Tel 01 488 1555
www.algoritam.hr
This bookstore beneath Hotel Dubrovnik is the best place for foreign-language books and magazines. It has books about Croatia, including history, fiction, travel guides and maps.
🕐 Mon–Fri 8.30am–9pm, Sat 8.30–3 🚋 Tram 1, 6, 11, 12, 13, 14, 17 to Trg Bana Jelačića

AQUARIUS
Varšavska 13, Zagreb
Tel 01 492 0380
www.aquarius-records.com
A branch of Croatia's leading music store selling CDs, from international pop releases to Croatian folk, jazz and classical music.
🕐 Mon–Fri 8–8, Sat 8–3 🚋 Tram 1, 6, 11, 12, 13, 14, 17 to Trg Bana Jelačića

PROFIL MEGASTORE
Bogovićeva 7, Zagreb
Tel 01 487 7300
www.profil.hr
Three floors full of books, films, music and computer games are on sale at this multimedia megastore. It also has a gift shop and internet café.
🕐 Mon–Sat 9am–10pm 🚋 Tram 1, 6, 11, 12, 13, 14, 17 to Trg Bana Jelačića

DEPARTMENT STORES AND SHOPPING MALLS

CENTAR KAPTOL
Nova Ves 17, Zagreb
Tel 01 486 0241
www.centarkaptol.hr

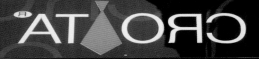

This US-style shopping mall has trendy bars and boutiques, a cinema and a branch of British chain Marks and Spencer. There are entrances on the road above the cathedral and on Medvedgradska, a continuation of Tkalčićeva.
⚙ Most shops open Mon–Sat 9am–9pm 🚋 Tram 1, 6, 11, 12, 13, 14, 17 to Trg Bana Jelačića

NAMA
Ilica 4, Zagreb
Tel 01 455 2233
www.nama.hr
The large domed building on the corner of Ilica and Trg Bana Jelačića was built in 1880 and was the leading state-owned department store in Yugoslavia. It now looks dated but is worth a visit for its history alone.
⚙ Mon–Fri 8–8, Sat 8–2 🚋 Tram 1, 6, 11, 12, 13, 17 to Trg Bana Jelačića

FASHIONS AND ACCESSORIES

CROATA
Prolaz Oktogon, Ilica 5, Zagreb
Tel 01 481 2726
www.croata.hr
The main branch of Croata is situated in the Oktogon passage, a lovely Viennese shopping arcade built in 1899. It sells silk ties, scarves and other accessories. There is another branch near the cathedral at Kaptol 13.
⚙ Mon–Fri 8–8, Sat 8–3 🚋 Tram 1, 6, 11, 12, 13, 14, 17 to Trg Bana Jelačića

ETNO-BUTIK MARA
Ilica 49, Zagreb
Tel 01 480 6511
This tiny boutique is on the first floor of the Croatian Chamber of Trade, a historic trades hall on Ilica. The owner makes and sells her own clothing, bags and gifts, made from natural materials embroidered with Croatian designs and motifs.
⚙ Mon–Fri 12–8, Sat 10–2 🚋 Tram 1, 6, 11, 12, 13, 14, 17 to Trg Bana Jelačića

GHARANI ŠTROK
Dežmanov Prolaz 5, Zagreb
Tel 01 484 6152
www.gharanistrok.co.uk
Founded by Croatian designer Vanya Štrok and Iranian Nargess Gharani, this store has dressed some of the world's most famous women, including Nicole

Colourful cravats and neckties on display

Kidman, Madonna and Kylie Minogue. In 2005 the company launched its first shop in Zagreb, offering quality ready-to-wear, sexy clothes for women.
⚙ Mon–Fri 9–8, Sat 9–2 🚋 Tram 1, 6, 11 to Frankopanska

HERUC GALERIA
Ilica 26, Zagreb
Tel 01 483 3569
www.herucgaleria.hr
This chain, with branches across Croatia, offers Italian and Croatian fashions at sensible prices for both men and women.

⚙ Mon–Fri 8–8, Sat 8–3 🚋 Tram 1, 6, 11, 12, 13, 14, 17 to Trg Bana Jelačića

IMAGE HADDAD
Ilica 6, Zagreb (also at Ilica 21)
Tel 01 483 1035
www.image-haddad.com
This is the flagship store of Croatian designer Zrinka Haddad, whose boutiques throughout the country offer affordable, stylish clothes for women, characterized by their elegant lines and feminine design.
⚙ Mon–Fri 8–8, Sat 8–3 🚋 Tram 1, 6, 11, 12, 13, 14, 17 to Trg Bana Jelačića

VALENTINO MODA
Jurišićeva 1, Zagreb
Tel 01 481 3401
www.valentino-moda.hr
If you need to buy a gift for a soccer fan, this shop, on the corner of the main square, sells the official Croatian national football shirts as well as club scarves and caps.
⚙ Mon–Fri 9–8, Sat 9–3 🚋 Tram 1, 6, 11, 12, 13, 14, 17 to Trg Bana Jelačića

FOOD

BAKINA KUĆA
Strossmayerova Trg 7, Zagreb
Tel 01 485 2525
www.bakina-kuca.hr
This little cellar sells products from across Croatia, including truffles, olive oil, honey, wine, liqueurs and natural cosmetics.
⚙ Mon–Sat 9am–9pm 🚋 Tram 6, 13 to Zrinjevac

KRAŠ
Trg Bana Jelačića 12, Zagreb
Tel 01 481 0443
www.kras.hr
Kraš chocolates and confectionery are popular all over Croatia, with 11 branches in

Zagreb alone. This shop sells all the favourites, from hand-made chocolates to gift packs for adults and children.

🕐 Mon–Sat 7am–8pm 🚋 Tram 1, 6, 11, 12, 13, 14, 17 to Trg Bana Jelačića

NATURA CROATICA
Preradovićeva 8, Zagreb
Tel 01 485 5076
www.naturacroatica.com

It is hard to resist this tempting delicatessen, which sells only Croatian products made from natural ingredients. Among the items on sale are candied fruits, Istrian truffles, olive oil, wild boar salami, pepper biscuits, herbal brandy, liqueurs and aromatic wines. There is another shop near the cathedral at Pod Zidom 5.

🕐 Mon–Fri 9–9, Sat 10–4 🚋 Tram 6, 13 to Zrinjevac

PRŠUT GALERIJA
Vlaška 7, Zagreb
Tel 01 481 6129

This small deli near the cathedral specializes in Dalmatian and Istrian ham—anything from a sandwich to an entire leg of *pršut* (cured ham). It also sells Pag sheep's cheese, olive oil, wines and brandies.

🕐 Mon–Fri 8–8, Sat 8–2 🚋 Tram 1, 6, 11, 12, 13, 14, 17 to Trg Bana Jelačića

GIFTS AND SOUVENIRS
ARKADIJA
Radićeva 35, Zagreb
Tel 01 492 0704

This gallery specializes in miniature hand-made models of Croatian houses and famous buildings. It also sells masks, toy soldiers, Glagolitic stone crosses and ceremonial swords.

🕐 Mon–Sat 9–8, Sun 10–5 🚋 Tram 1, 6, 11, 12, 13, 14, 17 to Trg Bana Jelačića

AROMATICA
Vlaška 7, Zagreb
Tel 01 481 1584
www.aromatica.hr

Aromatica sells natural cosmetics and toiletries made from Adriatic plants and herbs, including a range of aromatic massage oils and shampoos. You can make your own selection and have it individually wrapped in an attractive gift box.

A farm cheese stall at Dolac market in Zagreb

🕐 Mon–Fri 8–8, Sat 8–3 🚋 Tram 1, 6, 11, 12, 13, 14, 17 to Trg Bana Jelačića

JEWELLERY
LAZER ROK
Tkalčićeva 53, Zagreb
Tel 01 481 4030

Jeweller Lazer Lumezi has attracted a cult following in Zagreb for his unusual designs. This is jewellery meets cutting-edge art, and you can see it in action at the open-plan studio.

🕐 Mon–Fri 9–8, Sat 9–3 🚋 Tram 1, 6, 11, 12, 13, 14, 17 to Trg Bana Jelačića

ZLATARNA KRIŽEK
Prolaz Oktogon, Ilica 5, Zagreb
Tel 01 492 1931
www.zlatarna-krizek.hr

In the Oktogon passage near Croata, Križek is the official seller of *morčić* jewellery, which originated in Rijeka and features an enamel figure of a Moor's head. It comes in the shape of earrings, brooches, necklaces and chains.

🕐 Mon–Fri 9–1, 4–8, Sat 9–2 🚋 Tram 1, 6, 11, 12, 13, 14, 17 to Trg Bana Jelačića

MARKETS
DOLAC
Dolac, Zagreb
Tel 01 481 4400

Zagreb's vivid central market is held on a raised terrace above the main square, where farmers sell fruit, vegetables and cheese. There are indoor halls for meat, fish and dairy products.

🕐 Mon–Sat 6–2, Sun 6am–12pm 🚋 Tram 1, 6, 11, 12, 13, 14, 17 to Trg Bana Jelačića

HRELIĆ
Sajam Jakuševec, Novi Zagreb
Tel 01 660 9900

This vast, sprawling flea market takes place every Sunday morning on the south bank of the River Sava in Novi Zagreb. Hawkers sell everything from car parts to second-hand furniture and posters of nationalist heroes. This is a great place to soak up some Croatian atmosphere, but it is not a standard tourist experience, so take care of all your possessions. An antiques market is also held on Sunday mornings at Britanski Trg.

🕐 Sun 7–3 🚌 Bus 295 from behind the railway station

WINE

ILOČKI PODRUMI
Kaptol 12, Zagreb
Tel 01 481 4593
www.ilocki-podrumi.hr
This small shop, hidden away in a car park near the cathedral, sells white wines from the Slavonian town of Ilok, which was devastated during the Homeland War but is now producing quality wines once again.
🕐 Mon–Sat 8–8 🚊 Tram 1, 6, 11, 12, 13, 14, 17 to Trg Bana Jelačića

VINARIJA
Kaptol 14, Zagreb
Tel 01 481 4675
This wonderfully atmospheric cellar sells Zagreb County wine straight from the barrel. Old men gather here to drink Graševina by the glass, or you can get your own plastic bottle filled for 20kn per litre.
🕐 Mon–Fri 8–2, 4–7, Sat 8–2, Sun 9–1 🚊 Tram 1, 6, 11, 12, 13, 14, 17 to Trg Bana Jelačića

VINOTEKA BORNSTEIN
Kaptol 19, Zagreb
Tel 01 481 2361
www.bornstein.hr
Bornstein has an extensive cellar of Croatian and foreign wines, together with olive oil and cheese. It also sells wooden gift boxes that can be filled with Croatian wines, spirits and liqueurs.
🕐 Mon–Fri 9–7, Sat 9–2 🚊 Tram 1, 6, 11, 12, 13, 14, 17 to Trg Bana Jelačića

ŽITNJAK
Ulica Nikole Tesle 7, Zagreb
Tel 01 487 2576
www.zitnjak.hr
This ordinary-looking grocery store, on a corner near the main square, has a surprisingly well-stocked cellar, including wines from Zagreb, Slavonia, Istria and Dalmatia.
🕐 Mon–Fri 7am–9pm, Sat 8–1 🚊 Tram 1, 6, 11, 12, 13, 14, 17 to Trg Bana Jelačića

🎭 ENTERTAINMENT

CINEMAS

BROADWAY 5 TKALČA
Nova Ves 17, Zagreb
Tel 01 466 7686
www.broadway-kina.com
This multiplex inside the Centar Kaptol shopping mall has five screens and comfortable seats. It shows the latest international films

Outdoor café seating on Trg Bana Jelačića in Zagreb

in their original language with subtitles in Croatian. The Candy Bar sells snacks.
🕐 Daily 12–11 💰 20–30kn 🚻 🛈
🚊 Tram 1, 6, 11, 12, 13, 14, 17 to Trg Bana Jelačića

CINESTAR
Branimirova 29, Zagreb
Tel 01 468 6600
www.blitz-cinestar.hr
This 13-screen cinema is situated inside the Branimir shopping centre near the railway station.
🕐 Box office open Mon–Fri 12–9, Sat–Sun 10–9 💰 20–30kn 🚻 🛈
🚊 Tram 2, 6, 8 to Branimirova

CLASSICAL MUSIC

HRVATSKI GLAZBENI ZAVOD
Gundulićeva 6, Zagreb
Tel 01 483 0822
The Croatian Music Institute was founded in 1827 and is one of the oldest cultural institutions in Zagreb. Its concert hall near Trg Bana Jelačića hosts recitals of chamber music and occasional performances by a big band jazz orchestra.
🕐 Box office open Mon–Fri 11–1 and one hour before performance 💰 Varies 🚻 🛈 🚊 Tram 1, 6, 11 to Frankopanska

KONCERTNA DVORANA VATROSLAV LISINSKI
Trg Stjepana Radića 4, Zagreb
Tel 01 612 1167
www.lisinski.hr
Zagreb's main concert hall, built in 1973, was named after Vatroslav Lisinski (1819–54), composer of the first Croatian opera. It is home to the Zagreb Philharmonic Orchestra and also hosts visiting orchestras from abroad.
🕐 Box office open Mon–Fri 9–8, Sat 9–2, and one hour before performance 💰 Varies 🚻 🛈 🚊 Tram 3, 5, 13 to Lisinski

THEATRES

HRVATSKO NARODNO KAZALIŠTE (CROATIAN NATIONAL THEATRE)
Trg Maršala Tita 15, Zagreb
Tel 01 482 8532
www.hnk.hr
The company is housed in an ostentatious Habsburg-era opera house on Trg Maršala Tita. This is the home of classical drama in Zagreb, and also home to the National Ballet and National Opera. The season usually runs from October to June.

🎫 Box office open Mon–Fri 10–2 and 90 minutes before performance 🎭 Drama 35–100kn, ballet and opera 70–200kn ♿ 🚊 Tram 12, 13, 14, 17 to Trg Maršala Tita

KAŽALISTE KOMEDIJA
Kaptol 9, Zagreb
Tel 01 481 3200
www.komedija.hr
Opened in 1950, this small theatre near the cathedral hosts operettas, musicals and dramatic performances in Croatian. The box office is in Oktogon passage, Ilica 5 (tel 01 481 2657).
🎫 Box office open Mon–Fri 8–5.30, Sat 8–1; at theatre one hour before performance 🎭 Drama 30–50kn, musicals 40–100kn ♿ 🚊 Tram 1, 6, 11, 12, 13, 14, 17 to Trg Bana Jelačića

🍸 NIGHTLIFE

BARS AND PUBS
THE MOVIE PUB
Savska Cesta 141, Zagreb
Tel 01 605 5045
www.the-movie-pub.com
This popular bar on the outskirts of Zagreb has been decked out like an English-style pub with the addition of Hollywood film memorabilia and photos of movie stars. There is live music most nights, and karaoke on Wednesday and Thursday.
🎫 Mon–Wed 7am–2am, Thu–Sat 7am–4am, Sun 9am–2am 🚊 Tram 4, 5, 14, 17 to Prisavlje

ŠKOLA
Bogovićeva 7, Zagreb
Tel 01 482 8196
www.skolaloungebar.com
Everything is white except the plants at this ultra-trendy lounge bar, above a bookshop and the terrace bars of Bogovićeva. The restaurant serves Japanese-inspired cuisine and the bar

offers expensive cocktails such as champagne with gold flakes.
🎫 Mon–Sat 10am–1am, Sun 11am–1am 🚊 Tram 1, 6, 11, 12, 13, 14, 17 to Trg Bana Jelačića

CLUBS
AQUARIUS
Aleja Matije Ljubeka, Zagreb
Tel 01 364 0231
www.aquarius.hr
Aquarius was the founding father of the Zagreb club scene when it opened beside Lake Jarun in 1992. It plays electronic and hip-hop music to more than 2,000

Café terraces are busy on sunny days and at night

people spread over two dance floors, five bars and a large summer terrace. Big-name Croatian pop acts appear live here in summer. Aquarius also runs a beach club on the island of Pag.
🎫 Tue–Sun 10pm–5am 🎭 Varies 🚊 Tram 5, 17 to Jarun

GLOB@L CLUB
Pavla Hatza 14, Zagreb
Tel 01 481 4878
www.globalclubzg.hr
Glob@l Club is the hangout of Zagreb's gay and lesbian community, but a spirit of tolerance means that

anyone is welcome. It has three bars, a dance floor, VIP lounge, and video room.
🎫 Daily 8/10pm–4am 🎭 Free some nights, 15–20kn on Sat–Sun 🚊 Tram 2, 4, 6, 9, 13 to station

LIVE MUSIC
BP CLUB
Ulica Nikole Tesle 7, Zagreb
Tel 01 481 4444
www.bpclub.hr
This intimate jazz club near Trg Bana Jelačića is owned by Croatian jazz legend Boško Petrović, who still plays here some nights. There is live jazz and blues most evenings.
🎫 Daily 5pm–1am, music from 10pm 🎭 20–30kn 🚊 Tram 1, 6, 11, 12, 13, 14, 17 to Trg Bana Jelačića

SAX
Palmotićeva 22, Zagreb
Tel 01 487 2836
www.sax-zg.hr
This busy central basement club has live music every night, ranging from jazz and blues to rock and pop. It closes for a summer break in July and August.
🎫 Daily 9am–4am, music from 10pm 🎭 Varies 🚊 Tram 1, 6, 11, 12, 13, 14, 17 to Trg Bana Jelačića

🏀 SPORTS AND ACTIVITIES

BASKETBALL
CIBONA
Savska 30, Zagreb
Tel 01 484 3333
www.cibona.com
Croatia's top basketball team plays at the Dražen Petrović stadium, named after a famous former player (▷ 15). Euroleague matches take place between September and April. The best mid-price tickets are in the red and blue sections to either side of the court.

Call or check press for match times 🎫 20–300kn 🚊 Tram 3, 4, 9, 12, 13, 14, 17 to Tehnički Muzej or Studenstski Centar

GOLF

GOLF & COUNTRY CLUB ZAGREB
Jadranska Avenija 6, Zagreb
Tel 01 653 1177
www.gcczagreb.hr
This short nine-hole (par 30) course opened in 2004 on the Sava river embankment in Novi Zagreb. There is also a golf academy and driving range. There are plans to build a full 18-hole championship course here.
🕐 All year 🎫 Adult 150kn, child 75kn 🍴 ♿ 🚗 Cross the River Sava, take the highway to Karlovac and turn right after first gas station

SKIING

SLJEME
Sljeme, Zagreb
Tel 01 467 3006
www.sljeme-skijanje.com
Olympic medallists Janica and Ivica Kostelić learned to ski on the ski slopes of Medvednica. In winter you can ski without leaving the city, with pistes ranging from white (easy) to red (challenging). There is also a snowboard park, and sledging (sledding) for children. Skis and boots can be hired. In January, Sljeme plays host to the FIS World Cup Snow Queen trophy.
🕐 Dec–Mar, daily 9–4 🎫 Ski pass 70kn per day, 50kn per half-day
🚊 Tram 8, 14 to Mihaljevac then 15 to Dolje followed by cable-car

SOCCER

DINAMO ZAGREB
Maksimirska Cesta 128, Zagreb
Tel 01 232 3234
www.nk-dinamo.hr
Dinamo are the biggest club in Croatia and were league

champions in 2006. They play at the Maksimir stadium, which seats 40,000 spectators and is also used by the Croatian national team. The domestic season runs from August to May, with a winter break between December and February. Tickets are cheap and usually available on the gate, except for matches against arch-rivals Hajduk Split.
🕐 Call or check press for match times 🎫 From 30kn 🚊 Tram 11, 12 to Bukovačka

Golf is an increasingly popular sport in Croatia

WATERSPORTS

JARUN
Jarun, Zagreb
Tel 01 303 1888
www.jarun.hr
On this artificial lake you can swim from beaches, canoe, kayak, sail or windsurf, or take a scuba-diving course. There are jogging and cycle paths, lakeside walks, bicycle rental, minigolf, table-tennis, volleyball, basketball and handball courts, plus bars, cafés.
🕐 All year 🎫 Varies according to activity 🚊 Tram 5, 17 to Jarun

❂ FOR CHILDREN

MAKSIMIRSKI PERIVOJ
Maksimirska Cesta, Zagreb
Tel 01 232 0460
www.park-maksimir.hr
Maksimir Park (▷ 56) is a paradise for children, with playgrounds, swings and open spaces to explore as well as the city's zoo (▷ below). Or children can let off steam at central parks. The best are Ribnjak and Zrinjevac.
🕐 Open during daylight hours 🚊 Tram 11, 12 to Bukovačka

TEHNIČKI MUZEJ (TECHNICAL MUSEUM)
Savska 18, Zagreb
Tel 01 484 4050
www.mdc.hr/tehnicki
This enjoyable science museum has planetarium shows and an underground tour of a reconstructed mine. Kids will enjoy the transport gallery, with cars, planes and trains. There are free tram rides at 9.30am on Sundays.
🕐 Tue–Fri 9–5, Sat–Sun 9–1; mine tours Tue–Fri 3, Sat–Sun 11; planetarium Tue–Fri 4, Sat–Sun 12
🎫 Adult 15kn, child 10kn; planetarium 15kn 🚊 Tram 3, 4, 9, 12, 13, 14, 17 to Tehnički Muzej or Studenstski Centar

ZOO ZAGREB
Maksimirski Perivoj, Zagreb
Tel 01 230 2198
www.zoo.hr
The city zoo, on an island in Maksimir Park, has native animals including brown bears and wolves as well as other species ranging from elephants to lions, tigers, leopards, chimpanzees, crocodiles and penguins.
🕐 May–end Sep daily 9–8; Oct–end Apr daily 9–4 🎫 Adult 20kn, child 10kn; adult 10kn on Mon 🚊 Tram 11, 12 to Bukovačka

FESTIVALS AND EVENTS

APRIL

BIENNALE OF NEW MUSIC
Croatian Composers Society,
Berislavićeva 9, Zagreb
Tel 01 487 2370
www.biennale-zagreb.hr
Held only on odd-
numbered years (eg 2007
and 2009), this biennial
festival showcases con-
temporary classical music
from Croatia and abroad.

QUEER ZAGREB
www.queerzagreb.org
This annual festival is five
days of cinema, theatre,
music and dance on gay
and lesbian themes at
venues across the city.

APRIL/MAY

ST MARK'S FESTIVAL
Trg Svetog Marka 5, Zagreb
Tel 01 481 4052
www.festivalsvmarka.hr
Chamber, orchestral and
sacred music at St. Mark's
church and venues such as
the Croatian Music Institute.

MAY–SEPTEMBER

PROMENADE CONCERTS
Trg Nikole Šubića Zrinskog, Zagreb
Big bands, children's
choirs and chamber
orchestras play at the
bandstand in Zrinjevac
park on Saturday
mornings from Easter to
the end of September.
◉ Sat 11–1 ▣ Tram 6, 13 to
Zrinjevac

JULY

ZAGREB BAROQUE FESTIVAL
Zagreb Concert Management,
Kneza Mislava 18, Zagreb
Tel 01 450 1200
www.zabaf.hr

Recitals of baroque music
take place throughout the
month at venues in the
upper town, including
the cathedral and
St. Catherine's church.

INTERNATIONAL FOLKLORE FESTIVAL
Zagreb Concert Management,
Kneza Mislava 18, Zagreb
Tel 01 450 1200
www.msf.hr
Founded in 1966, this
festival has Croatian and
international folk groups
performing on an outdoor

*Many Croatian festivals
celebrate classical music*

stage in Trg Bana Jelačića,
along with dance work-
shops, world music and
a concert at Vatroslav
Lisinski concert hall.

JULY AND AUGUST

ZAGREB SUMMER EVENINGS
Zagreb Concert Management,
Kneza Mislava 18, Zagreb
Tel 01 450 1200
www.kdz.hr
Classical and chamber
music concerts take
place in the cathedral
and Gornji Grad.

AUGUST AND SEPTEMBER

INTERNATIONAL PUPPET THEATRE FESTIVAL
Božidara Magovca 17, Travno,
Zagreb
Tel 01 660 1626
www.mcuk.hr
Puppet theatre has a
long tradition in
southeast Europe and
this festival features a
week of performances
in the Komedija theatre
and venues across
the city.

OCTOBER

ZAGREB FILM FESTIVAL
Savska 25, Zagreb
Tel 01 459 3692
www.zagrebfilmfestival.com
The annual film festival
at the Student Centre
showcases feature
films, short films and
documentaries, with
an emphasis on a
different country
each year.
▣ Tram 3, 4, 13, 14, 17 to
Studenstski Centar

DECEMBER

ADVENT IN THE HEART OF ZAGREB
Trg Bana Jelačića
Throughout the month
of December Trg Bana
Jelačića is turned into
a winter playground,
with Christmas markets,
stalls selling hot dogs
and mulled wine, and
evening concerts
held on an open-air
stage. There are also
special events for
children, including
miniature train rides
with Santa.
◉ 5–22 Dec

INLAND CROATIA

Activities in inland Croatia range from drinking in bars to gentle country walks and boat trips on rivers and lakes. Nightlife is thin on the ground here, except in Osijek with its large student population. There are branches of the Croatian National Theatre in Osijek and Varaždin, the latter of which is the principal venue for the wonderful Varaždin Baroque Evenings each autumn. Children might enjoy the castles of the Zagorje region and the scenery of the Plitvice Lakes, as well as the naive art galleries of Hlebine and the open-air museum village at Kumrovec. The traditional festivals of Slavonia are well worth a visit, from famous events like the Brodsko Kolo at Slavonski Brod to village feasts held to mark the local saint's day.

KEY TO SYMBOLS

- ⊕ **Shopping**
- ⊕ **Entertainment**
- ⊗ **Nightlife**
- ⊗ **Sports**
- ⊕ **Activities**
- ♡ **Health and Beauty**
- ⊛ **For Children**

ILOK

⊕ ILOČKI PODRUMI
Franje Tuđmana 72, Ilok
Tel 032 590003
www.ilocki-podrumi.hr
The wine cellars of Ilok produce first-class Slavonian white wines, including Graševina, Traminac and Chardonnay. Ask about a visit to the Stari Podrumi, the atmospheric old wine cellars inside the castle, which were looted by Serbian troops during the war but are now open for tours.
⊙ Mon–Fri 8–8, Sat 8–2

KRAŠIĆ

⊗ GOLF & COUNTRY CLUB DOLINA KARDINALA
Krašić
Tel 01 370 1134
www.croatia-golf.hr
The 'Valley of the Cardinals' was the first 18-hole golf course in Croatia when it opened in 1998. Designed by British architect Howard Swan, it also includes a driving range, a golf academy and a 9-hole par 3 family course.
⊙ All year 🏌 18 holes 300kn, 9 holes 200kn, family course 100kn
🚌 Just off the road from Krašić to Ozalj

OSIJEK

⊕ PIERRE CARDIN
Kapucinska 25, Osijek
Tel 031 205252
www.herucgaleria.hr
The Osijek branch of this popular clothing chain, originally opened in 1889, sells men's and women's fashions on a pedestrian shopping street facing the cathedral. The nearby underground shopping mall was built as part of the post-war reconstruction of Osijek.
⊙ Mon–Fri 8–8, Sat 8–2

🅗 HRVATSKO NARODNO KAŽALIŠTE (CROATIAN NATIONAL THEATRE)

Županijska 9, Osijek
Tel 031 220700
www.hnk-osijek.htnet.hr
Housed in a magnificent Austro-Hungarian casino from 1866 and restored after the Homeland War, the Croatian National Theatre is the city's venue for serious drama and opera.
🕐 Box office open Mon–Fri 9–1, Sat 9–12, and one hour before performance 🎫 30–100kn 🎭 🚫

🅗 KINO EUROPA

Šetalište Petar Preradovića 2, Osijek
Tel 031 205484
This Cubist-style modernist cinema has been showing films since 1939. Shows are usually evenings only, but check the posters outside the cinema for times.
🕐 Varies 🎫 20kn 🚫

🅗 KINO URANIA

Šetalište Vjekoslava Hengla 1, Osijek
Tel 031 211560
This, the oldest movie house in Osijek was built in 1912 in Viennese Secession style on the corner of a pretty park. It is worth going in here just to admire the art deco lobby.
🕐 Varies 🎫 20kn 🚫

🅥 POSH CLUB

Kuhačeva 10, Osijek
Tel 031 215020
Tvrđa has a growing number of atmospheric cafés, bars and eateries. This trendy café/bar in the main square is mainly frequented by local students. Other popular places with students and others include Papa Joe, Carpe Diem, Q Club and the Irish-themed St. Patrick's Pub.

🕐 Sun–Thu 9am–midnight, Fri–Sat 9am–3am

☺ COPACABANA

Tvrđavica, Osijek
Tel 031 285000
Cool down in summer by crossing the footbridge to this sports and recreation centre on the north bank of the River Drava, optimistically named after the famous Rio beach. There are open-air pools, a sandy riverside beach, waterslides, beach volleyball and a restaurant.
🕐 Jun–end Sep

A bright sign outside Plitvice National Park

☺ OSIJEK ZOO

Sjevernodravska Obala 1, Osijek
Tel 031 285234
Osijek's zoo was closed during the war but has reopened on the north bank of the River Drava. The elephants have not returned but you can see lions, tigers, wolves, monkeys, crocodiles, snakes and birds. There are pony rides for children in summer. Get there by walking west along the north bank of the river, or by ferry from the heart of the city.

🕐 May–end Sep daily 8–8; Oct–end Apr daily 9–5 🎫 Adult 10kn, child 5kn 🚻 7 🚌 Cross the bridge towards Bilje and turn left along the north bank, following signs to the zoo

PLITVIČKA JEZERA

☺ HUCK FINN ADVENTURE TRAVEL

Vukovarska 271, Zagreb
Tel 01 618 3333
www.huck-finn.hr
This company specializes in canoeing, kayaking, rafting, walking, bicycling and swimming in the Plitvice Lakes National Park, with itineraries ranging from half a day to a week and accommodation in village houses by the River Korana.
🕐 All year 🎫 Varies

SAMOBOR

⊕ OBITELJ FILIPEC

Stražnička 1A, Samobor
Tel 01 336 4835
The Filipec family produce *bermet*, an aromatic vermouth flavoured with carob and herbs, and sweet, spicy Samobor mustard. Both specialities of Samobor date back to the occupation by Napoleon's French troops in 1808. You can buy them at the small shop in an alley off the main square; if the shop is closed, just ring the bell.

☺ ŽUMBERAČKO EKO SELO

Kravlak 13, Koretići
Tel 01 338 7472
www.eko-selo.hr
Deep in the forests of the Žumberak Nature Park, this eco-lodge and ranch offers horse and pony rides, quad-biking, rustic food and accommodation in alpine huts.
🕐 All year

SLAVONSKI BROD

🌐 ZDJELAREVIĆ

Vinogradska 102, Brodski Stupnik
Tel 035 427775
www.zdjelarevic.hr
This family-run winery was established in 1991, at a time when everyone else was fleeing war-torn Slavonia. The cellars beneath the hotel stock white wines from the vineyards, including Chardonnay, Manzoni and Rizling.
🕐 Ask at hotel 🚗 Take the road from Slavonski Brod to Nova Gradiska and turn right after 7km (4 miles) in Brodski Stupnik

VARAŽDIN

🌐 EKSKLUZIVA

Franjevački Trg 1, Varaždin
Tel 042 313364
This small craft shop is found in the Centar Mrazović arcade, facing the town hall on the south side of Trg Kralja Tomislava. It sells hand-made ceramics and pictures of local scenes.
🕐 Mon–Sat 10–8

🎭 HRVATSKO NARODNO KAZALIŠTE (CROATIAN NATIONAL THEATRE)

Ulica A. Cesarca 1, Varaždin
Tel 042 214688
www.hnkvz.hr
Designed by Viennese architect Hermann Helmer in 1873, this grand old theatre hosts classic drama and operatic performances, as well as recitals during the Varaždin Baroque Evenings festival.
🕐 Box office open Mon–Sat 10–12, 6–7.30, and one hour before performance 🎟 20–80kn 🚻 🚫

🍷 KAVANA KORZO

Trg Kralja Tomislava 2
Tel 042 320914
The old-style Viennese coffee house on the main square is the best place for a drink in Varaždin. The opulent interior features dark wood, mirrors, chandeliers and red velvet benches, while the terrace makes the perfect spot to observe the evening *korzo* (promenade).
🕐 Daily 8am–11pm

A wine barrel advertising a hotel in the Zagorje region

✪ AQUACITY

Međimurska 26, Varaždin
Tel 042 350555
www.aquacity.hr
An artificial lake in a former gravel pit has become Varaždin's city beach, crowded with locals on hot summer days. As well as bathing, other attractions include tennis and beach volleyball courts.
🕐 Jun–end Sep 🚗 3km (2 miles) from Varaždin on the road to Koprivnica

VUKOVAR

🌐 GALERIJA NAVIS

Strossmayerova 5, Vukovar
Tel 032 442632
Vukovar may seem a surprising place for a souvenir shop, but miniature reproductions of the Vučedol Dove (▷ 50) have become a powerful symbol of peace since the war. This shop also sells models of the shell-scarred Vukovar water tower, plus books and videos about the war.
🕐 Mon–Fri 8–8, Sat 8–3

ZAGORJE

🌐 ZOZOLLY

Nova Cesta 13, Marija Bistrica
Tel 049 469070
Shops and open-air stalls around the main square of Marija Bistrica sell candles and other religious souvenirs to pilgrims, especially on feast days. Zozolly is one of the oldest candle-makers in the town, and also makes local specialities such as pepper biscuits and *licitarsko srce* (gingerbread hearts).
🕐 Mon–Sat 8–8

✪ TRAKOŠĆAN

Children are always fascinated by castles and Trakošćan (▷ 80) is no exception with its fairy-tale appearance reflected in the lake. In summer there is a pleasant lakeside terrace café where you can rent pedal boats and rowing-boats for trips on the water.

FESTIVALS AND EVENTS

WHAT TO DO

FEBRUARY
CARNIVAL
Samobor
Tel 01 332 5136
www.fasnik.com
For two weeks in February Samobor hosts some wild Carnival celebrations, with traditions dating back to 1827. They include masked dances, fancy dress balls and parades of Carnival floats on the final weekend. It all culminates with a bonfire and firework display.
⚅ Dates vary according to Easter

MAY
FESTIVAL TAMBURAŠKE GLAZBE (FESTIVAL OF TAMBURICA MUSIC)
Osijek
Tel 031 283253
The *tamburica* (mandolin) was introduced to Croatia by the Ottoman Turks and has become an authentic expression of Slavonian folk music. This week-long festival has *tamburica* concerts in Osijek and Vukovar.
⚅ Late May

JUNE
BRODSKO KOLO
Slavonski Brod
Tel 035 445801
www.fa-broda.hr
The oldest folk festival in Croatia attracts musicians and dancers from across Croatia. It lasts two weeks, but the central Sunday has parades of wedding carriages and horse-riding and a beauty contest with girls wearing traditional costume.
⚅ Mid-Jun

INTERNATIONAL FIREWORK FESTIVAL
Samobor
Tel 01 336 0044
www.vatromet.com
Music and pyrotechnics take place on an open-air stage at the football stadium in Samobor over four days in June.
⚅ Mid-Jun

JUNE/JULY
ĐAKOVAČKI VEKOVI (ĐAKOVO EMBROIDERY)
Đakovo
Tel 031 812319
www.tz-djakovo.hr
A large festival of Slavonian folk culture. Much of the action takes place in Strossmayer Park, but there are also organ concerts in the cathedral.
⚅ Late Jun and early Jul

OSJEČKO LJETO KULTURE (OSIJEK SUMMER OF CULTURE)
Osijek
Tel 031 229229
www.tzosijek.hr
Like most towns in Croatia, Osijek puts on a summer festival, with open-air drama and concerts of classical and jazz music.
⚅ Late Jun to late Jul

AUGUST AND SEPTEMBER
ASSUMPTION AND BIRTH OF THE VIRGIN
Marija Bistrica
Tel 049 468380
www.marija-bistrica.hr
Crowds of pilgrims descend on Marija Bistrica for the feasts of the Assumption (15 Aug) and Birth of the Virgin (8 Sep). Open-air masses are held in the arena behind the church.
⚅ 15 Aug, 8 Sep

SEPTEMBER
ŠPANCIRFEST
Varaždin
Tel 042 210987
www.spancirfest.com
For ten days each year, the streets and squares of Varaždin come alive with musicians, acrobats, mime artists, jugglers, traditional craftsmen and elegant lords and ladies in baroque costume as part of the annual 'street promenaders' festival. It also includes pop and world music concerts on outdoor stages across the city.
⚅ Early Sep

ILOČKA BERBA GROŽDA (ILOK GRAPE FAIR)
Ilok
Tel 032 590020
The annual grape fair in Ilok is a major harvest festival. Dancers in folk costume perform the *kolo* (circle dance) while everyone else drinks wine and throws bunches of grapes into the air.
⚅ Second or third Sat in Sep

SEPTEMBER/OCTOBER
VARAŽDINSKE BAROKNE VEČERI (VARAŽDIN BAROQUE EVENINGS)
Varaždin
Tel 042 212907
www.vbv.hr
One of Croatia's major cultural festivals, featuring two weeks of baroque music recitals.
⚅ Late Sep to early Oct

ISTRIA

It may have historic sights like the Byzantine mosaics at Poreč and the Roman arena at Pula, but for most visitors to Istria, the sea is the main attraction. Daytime activities revolve around the beach, with options such as windsurfing and diving for the more active. Most large hotels and campsites have sports and leisure facilities ranging from swimming pools and tennis courts to beach volleyball and mini-golf. Children are well catered for, with aquariums in Poreč, Pula and Rovinj and the Mini Croatia park. Evening entertainment generally consists of relaxing at a seafront bar, and the harboursides at coastal resorts such as Novigrad, Poreč and Rovinj are buzzing on summer nights. Most towns in Istria put on a summer festival, with concerts taking place in magical settings from the hill town of Grožnjan to the arena at Pula. Away from the coast, you can shop for truffles, wine and brandy at towns like Buzet and Motovun, or at monthly agricultural fairs.

KEY TO SYMBOLS

- 🅑 Shopping
- 🅑 Entertainment
- 🅥 Nightlife
- 🅚 Sports
- 🅧 Activities
- 🅞 Health and Beauty
- 🅧 For Children

BRIJUNI

🅑 ULYSSES THEATRE
Mali Brijun
Tel 052 525581
www.ulysses.hr
This Zagreb-based theatre company puts on performances of Shakespeare and other classics, as well as contemporary drama, at the old Austrian fort on Mali Brijun in July and August. Tickets are available in advance from the national park office in Fažana, or from 4pm until the departure of the boat.
🅦 150kn 🚢 From Fažana

🅚 BRIJUNI GOLF
Veli Brijun
Tel 052 525888
www.brijuni.hr
Play golf in beautiful surroundings on this unique island course, with deer strolling about the fairways and putting greens covered in sand. Built in 1922, this was for many years the only golf course in Croatia and was at one stage exclusively reserved for Tito and his guests. It has been expanded to 18 holes. Book through the national park office in Fažana and take the boat transfer to Brijuni.
🅞 All year 🅦 200kn, boat transfer 15kn 🚢 21 from Pula to Fažana 🚢 From Fažana

BUJE

🅑 ZIGANTE TARTUFI
Trg J.B.Tita 12, Buje
Tel 052 772125
www.zigantetartufi.com
The Zigante Tartufi truffle shops were opened by local farmer Giancarlo Zigante

after he earned a place in the Guinness Book of World Records by finding the world's biggest ever white truffle, weighing a massive 1.31kg (2.8lb), near Buje in 1999. During the autumn harvest from October to December, fresh white truffles can sell for over €3,000 per kg but more affordable products include minced black truffles and *tartufata* (truffle paste). Other Zigante Tartufi shops are in Buzet (▷ below), Grožnjan, Livade, Motovun and Pula.

🕐 Daily 9–9 (to 8 in winter)

BUZET

🌐 ZIGANTE TARTUFI
Trg Fontana, Buzet
Tel 052 663340
www.zigantetartufi.com
The hill town of Buzet is known as the city of truffles, and this shop sells the full range of products, together with Istrian wines, spirits and olive oil.

🕐 Daily 9–9 (to 8 in winter)

GROŽNJAN

🌐 GALERIJA JEDAN PLUS
Vicenta iz Kastva 3
Tel 052 776354
One of many galleries in this hilltop village, Mirjana Rajkovic is a potter specializing in hand-formed fruit, decorated with a variety of coloured glazes.

🕐 Jul–Aug daily 10–9; May–Jul & Sep to mid-Oct 10–1, 4–8. Call for winter opening times

MOTOVUN

🌐 EVA
Prolaz Veli Jože 4, Motovun
Tel 052 681915
This small shop on the way up to the town gate sells local food and drink, including bottles of *biska*

(mistletoe brandy) and *medenica* (honey brandy) in gift boxes.

🕐 Mon–Sat 8–8, Sun 8–12

❶ ACTIVA TRAVEL
Scalierova 1, Pula
Tel 052 215497
www.activa-istra.com
This company can organize truffle-hunting expeditions in the woods around Motovun between October and December for up to four people, with a guide and dogs. The price includes a farmhouse dinner.

🕐 Oct–Dec 💶 From €45 per person

A line of posters advertising boat tour companies

NOVIGRAD

❼ VITRIOL
Ribarnička 6, Novigrad
Tel 052 758270
This trendy terrace bar is the best place to watch the sun go down over the sea, with a cool beer or a glass of the house cocktail.

🕐 Daily 8am–midnight

POREČ

🌐 PER BACCO
Trg Slobode 10, Poreč
Tel 052 451600
This delicatessen has an extensive selection of

Istrian wines, spirits, liqueurs, olive oil, truffles, honey and preserves, all tastefully displayed and reasonably priced.

🕐 Mon–Fri 8–7, Sat 9–6, Sun 10–2

🌐 VINOTEKA ARMAN
Ulica Marta, Poreč
Tel 052 446229
New-wave Istrian wine-maker Marijan Arman has opened a shop in Poreã to showcase his award-winning Malvazija, Teran, Chardonnay and Cabernet Sauvignon.

🕐 Mon–Sat 10–5

❼ TORRE ROTONDA
Narodni Trg, Poreč
Tel 098 255731
This 15th-century Venetian round tower houses a pleasant summer café, with stone walls and a rooftop terrace that is an enjoyable place for a sunset drink.

🕐 Apr–end Oct daily 10am–1am

❶ RONILAČKI CENTAR PLAVA LAGUNA
Plava Laguna, Poreč
Tel 098 367619
www.plava-laguna-diving.hr
This diving centre can offer everything from shore diving and night diving from a wooden boat to longer trips to explore underwater caves and the wreck of the British Royal Navy warship *Coriolanus*, which sank near Poreč in 1945.

🕐 Apr–end Oct 🚗 3km (2 miles) south of Poreč

❶ JAMA BAREDINE
Nova Vas, Poreč
Tel 052 421333
www.baredine.com
Children and adults can explore the Baredine Cave on a 40-minute tour, seeing stalactites, stalagmites and

subterranean chambers. Teenagers and older children can try their hand at rope climbing or join a five-hour Speleo Adventure tour with a caving guide.

🅖 Jul, Aug daily 9.30–6; May, Jun, Sep, daily 10–5; Apr and 1–15 Oct daily 10–4 🎟 Adult 50kn, child 25kn 🚌 7km (4.5 miles) from Poreč on the road to Višnjan

PULA

🍷 CVAJNER CAFFE
Forum 2, Pula
Tel 052 216502
Soak up the atmosphere at the best people-watching spot in Pula, with outdoor tables on the old Roman forum. Be sure to go inside, though, to see the modern art and the frescoes uncovered during the restoration.

🅖 Daily 8am–11pm

🍷 MMC LUKA
Istarska 30, Pula
Tel 052 224316
www.mmcluka.hr
This multimedia outlet near the Roman arena is an art gallery, internet café and trendy bar in one. It hosts exhibitions of contemporary art and acts as an unofficial meeting place during the annual film festival.

🅖 Mon–Fri 8am–midnight, Sat 8–3

🍷 ULIKS
Trg Portarata 1, Pula
Tel 052 219158
The bar beside the Roman Arch of Sergi has become a shrine to Irish author James Joyce (1882–1941), who taught at the Berlitz school on this site in 1904–05. A bronze sculpture of Joyce sits outside. The terrace tables are snapped up quickly, so go inside to enjoy the dark wood, marble counters, stained

glass and cabinet of Joyce memorabilia. You can pick up a leaflet about Joyce's Pula links at the entrance.

🅖 Daily 7am–11pm

☸ WINDSURFING CENTAR PREMANTURA
Premantura, Pula
Tel 091 512 3646
www.windsurfing.hr
The best windsurfing in Istria is at Premantura, at the far southern tip of the peninsula beside Cape Kamenjak nature reserve. Spring and autumn are the best times for experienced

Taking to the waters for a tour on a sunny day

surfers, while the calm winds of July and August are ideal for beginners. This friendly centre offers multi-lingual courses for adults and children, together with rental of equipment.

🅖 Apr–end Oct 🚌 26 from Pula 🚌 At Stupice campsite, 12km (7.5 miles) south of Pula

☸ AQUARIUM PULA
Fort Verudela, Pula
Tel 052 381402
www.aquariumpula-istra.hr
Housed in an old Austro-Hungarian fort on Punta Verudela, a wooded

peninsula surrounded by shingle beaches and hotels, Pula's aquarium makes an enjoyable day out with children. The ground floor is devoted to Adriatic marine life, the first floor has old fishing tools and underwater photography, while a tunnel leads to the moat, now a pond containing fish from Croatia's rivers and lakes. The aquarium can also organize three-hour fishing expeditions.

🅖 Apr–end Oct daily 9–9; Nov–end Mar Sat–Sun 11–5 🎟 Adult 20kn, child (7–18) 15kn, child (3–7) 10kn 🍴 🚌 2A, 3A from Pula

ROVINJ

🏛 AROMATICA
Via Carera 33, Rovinj
Tel 052 812850
www.aromatica.hr
This natural cosmetics shop distils the colours and scents of the Adriatic into an attractive range of products, including herbal soaps, dried flowers and massage oils.

🅖 Mon–Sat 9–1, 3.30–7.30

🏛 BACCUS
Via Carera 5, Rovinj
Tel 052 812154
Baccus doubles as a wine shop and wine bar with outdoor seating and harbour views. It sells a good range of Istrian wine, spirits, truffles and olive oils of consistently high quality.

🅖 Summer daily 8am–1am, winter daily 8am–10pm

🏛 ZELENA TRŽNICA (GREEN MARKET)
Trg Valdibora, Rovinj
The open-air market in Rovinj is particularly attractive, with fresh produce laid out on stalls behind the

harbour square. Farmers sell home-made wine, liqueur and herb brandy, together with peppers and dried figs. You could make up a picnic here out of bread, tomatoes and local cheese. The nearby fish market sells freshly caught fish and seafood.
🕓 Daily 7–2

🍴 LA PUNTULEINA
Ulica Svetog Križa 38, Rovinj
Tel 052 813186
This chic restaurant (▷ 240) is also a wine bar with the best sunset views in town, from terraces above the bathing rocks on the cliffs beneath the church.
🕓 Apr–end Oct daily 6pm–2am

🍴 VALENTINO
Ulica Svetog Križa 28, Rovinj
Tel 052 830683
This cool cocktail bar is great for an evening drink, sitting on silk cushions on the rocks by candlelight with your feet almost dangling in the water as you watch the sun go down.
🕓 Apr–end Oct daily 6pm–3am

🍴 ZANZI BAR
Obala Pina Budicina, Rovinj
Tel 052 813206
A busy harbourside bar with wicker chairs on a covered terrace, plus DJs and occasional live music.
🕓 Apr–end Oct daily 9am–1am

⚙ DIVING CENTAR PETRA
Matije Vlačića 22, Rovinj
Tel 052 812880
www.divingpetra.hr
This diving outlet is open all year and offers courses for beginners. For more experienced divers it can organize dives to the *Baron Gautsch*, an Austrian navy steamship which sank after hitting a

mine in 1914. It is known as the *Titanic* of the Adriatic.
🕓 All year

⚙ LIMSKI KANAL
Boatmen by the harbour and Delfin jetty advertise cruises through the Lim Fjord (▷ 89) in summer, including trips on a mock 'pirate ship' with alcohol and soft drinks. The full-day excursions include a barbecue fish picnic or lunch at one of the restaurants in the fjord.
🕓 Apr–end Oct 🎫 Adult 100kn, child 50kn

A pretty restaurant terrace in Rovinj's old town

⚙ ZLATNI RT
Vetura Rent A Car, Ulica Vladimira Nazora, Rovinj
Tel 052 815209
You can rent bicycles to explore Zlatni Rt forest park (▷ 100) from this agency at the Delfin jetty. In summer you can rent bicycles from stalls by the harbour and at the entrance to the park.
🕓 All year 🎫 20kn per hour, 50kn per half day, 80kn per day

⚙ AQUARIUM
Obala Giordano Paliage 5, Rovinj
Tel 052 804712

Rovinj's aquarium is housed in a 19th-century building officially known as the Ruđer Bošković Institute Centre for Marine Research. Its old-fashioned approach will appeal to small children, who can enjoy staring at tanks of starfish, scorpion fish, lobsters and other marine life.
🕓 Apr–end Oct daily 9–9 🎫 Adult 20kn, child 10kn

⚙ MINI CROATIA
Rovinj
Tel 091 206 8885
This theme park has scaled-down miniature models of Croatia's monuments, buildings and landscapes.
🕓 Apr–end Oct daily 9–8 🎫 Adult 25kn, child under 10 free 🚗 Just outside Rovinj on the road to Pazin

UMAG

⚙ ATP CROATIA OPEN
International Tennis Centre, Umag
Tel 052 741704
www.croatiaopen.hr
The leading professional men's tennis tournament in Croatia is held in Umag at the end of July.
🕓 Late July

ISTRIAN FAIRS
There is a tradition of rural fairs in the towns of inland Istria. Originally livestock markets, today they attract a mixed crowd of locals and foreigners with food stalls, folk dancing and craft displays. Market day is a chance to experience true Istrian atmosphere. Markets take place once a month on the following days:
Vodnjan—first Saturday
Pazin—first Tuesday
Žminj—second Wednesday
Motovun—third Monday
Buzet—third Thursday
Višnjan—last Thursday

WHAT TO DO

FESTIVALS AND EVENTS

MAY

Z ARMONIK U ROČ (ROČ ACCORDION FESTIVAL)
Roč
Tel 098 329833
The medieval village of Roč, near Hum, hosts traditional musicians who play the *trieština* (Istrian accordion) at an open-air stage on the square.
◎ Second weekend in May

JUNE–SEPTEMBER

GROŽNJAN MUSICAL SUMMER
Grožnjan
Tel 01 611 1604
www.hgm.hr
The beautiful hill town of Grožnjan comes alive each summer with the international summer school of Jeunesses Musicales Croatia, with workshops and concerts of chamber music, jazz and brass and recitals on harp, piano and violin.
◎ Jun–end Sep

JULY

PULA FILM FESTIVAL
Pula
Tel 052 393321
www.pulafilmfestival.hr
Not quite what it once was, the Pula Film Festival is still a prestigious event, with nightly film shows in the Roman arena and directors competing for the Golden Arena award.
◎ Mid- to late Jul

MOTOVUN FILM FESTIVAL
Motovun
Tel 01 374 0699
www.motovunfilmfestival.com
One of the liveliest events in the Croatian cultural calendar, this features more than 80 independent films from Croatia and abroad, with open-air screenings on the town's main square.
◎ Late Jul

JULY AND AUGUST

HISTRIA FESTIVAL
Kandlerova 14, Pula
Tel 052 522720
www.histriafestival.com
Opera, ballet and music are performed in the spectacular setting of the Roman arena. Performers have included Sting, José Carreras, Luciano Pavarotti and the Bolshoi Ballet.
◎ Jul, Aug

NOVIGRAD CULTURAL SUMMER
Novigrad
Tel 052 758011
www.laguna-novigrad.hr
Two months of outdoor concerts and events, including fishermen's nights, folk singers and classical music in the parish church, culminating with the festivities of town patron St. Pelagius over the final weekend in August.
◎ Jul, Aug

KONCERTI U EUFRAZIJANI
Poreč
Tel 052 431595
www.concertsinbazilika.com
Classical, chamber music, choral and orchestral concerts are held in the lovely setting of the Basilica of Euphrasius at Poreč. The same organization puts on jazz concerts on Wednesday evenings throughout July and August in the courtyard of the Regional Museum.
◎ Fri evenings in Jul and Aug

JULY–SEPTEMBER

ROVINJ SUMMER FESTIVAL
Rovinj
Tel 052 811566
www.tzgrovinj.hr
Concerts of early music, piano recitals and string quartets take place in St. Euphemia's church and the cloisters of the Franciscan monastery in Rovinj.
◎ Mid-Jul to early Sep

AUGUST

TRKA NA PRSTENAC (TILTING AT THE RING)
Barban
Tel 052 372113
This traditional festival dating back to the 17th century was revived in 1976. It features horsemen in medieval costume attempting to spear a metal ring with a lance while riding at full gallop.
◎ Mid-Aug

SEPTEMBER

SUBOTINA
Buzet
Tel 052 662343
A giant truffle omelette, cooked using 10kg (22lb) of truffles and more than 2,000 eggs, is served up on the main square on Saturday evening as the centrepiece of a weekend of festivities including folk dance and craft fairs.
◎ Second weekend in Sep

WHAT TO DO

KVARNER

WHAT TO DO

Rijeka is the biggest city in the Kvarner region and the focus of shopping, entertainment and nightlife. This once thriving port is enjoying a new lease of life, turning its industrial heritage to its advantage as former docks and warehouses are reborn as arts centres, nightclubs and bars. Most of the action takes place on the Korzo, the pedestrian shopping street at the heart of the city, and the nearby waterfront Riva. Elsewhere there are plenty of outdoor activities to enjoy, from sailing around the islands to hiking and skiing in the mountains of Gorski Kotar. Children can have fun looking out for dolphins off the coasts of Cres and Lošinj, or admiring the cute bear cubs at Kuterevo. Huge crowds come onto the streets for Rijeka's winter Carnival, while towns such as Opatija, Rab and Krk put on festivals of music on summer evenings.

KEY TO SYMBOLS

- 🛍 Shopping
- 🎭 Entertainment
- 🍸 Nightlife
- 🏃 Sports
- ⭐ Activities
- ♥ Health and Beauty
- ✹ For Children

CRES

✹ EKO-CENTAR CAPUT INSULAE
Beli, Cres
Tel 051 840525
www.caput-insulae.com
Housed in an old school in the remote hamlet of Beli, this eco-centre includes a hospital for griffon vultures who have been injured or fallen into the sea while learning to fly. There are exhibitions on the ecology of Cres and an enjoyable sculpture trail (▷ 216–217).
🕐 16 Jan–14 Dec daily 9–8
💶 Adult 25kn, child 10kn, family 60kn

GORSKI KOTAR

⭐ BJELOLASICA
Vrelo, Jasenak
Tel 01 617 7707
www.bjelolasica.hr
The Croatian Olympic Centre at Bjelolasica is where the country's élite athletes train throughout the year. In winter it is home to Croatia's biggest ski resort. Ski rental is available and there is a ski and snowboard school.
🕐 Jan, Feb daily 9–4 🎿 Ski pass 80kn per day, 60kn per half-day
🚗 27km (17 miles) west of Ogulin; take A1 motorway to Split and follow signs from Ogulin exit

⭐ PLATAK
Platak
Tel 051 230904
www.platak.com
On winter weekends, the people of Rijeka head for Platak to go skiing on the slopes of Radesevo mountain with a view of the sea. As well as ski slopes, attractions include a snow park for boarders, night skiing and cross-country pistes.

🔆 Jan, Feb daily 9–4 ⛷ Ski pass 80kn per day, 60kn per half-day 🚗 30km (19 miles) from Rijeka; take A6 motorway to Zagreb and follow signs from Čavle exit

KRK

⊕ KATUNAR

Vrbnik, Krk
Tel 051 857393
www.katunar.com
This family-run winery at the entrance to Vrbnik sells the well-known Žlahtina white wine from Krk, and also makes an unusual sparkling wine, Porin. Call in advance to arrange a visit to the winery and a tasting of wine, cheese and ham.
🔆 Daily 8–4

✪ MARINA PUNAT

Punat, Krk
Tel 051 654111
www.marina-punat.hr
Croatia's oldest marina, opened in 1965, is also one of the largest, with mooring for 900 boats. As well as yacht and motorboat charter, it offers a sailing school and can arrange diving lessons with a local club.
🔆 All year

LOŠINJ

✪ BLUE WORLD

Veli Lošinj
Tel 051 604666
www.blue-world.org
This marine education facility is run by the Adriatic Dolphin Project, which monitors the bottlenose dolphin population off Cres and Lošinj. The multimedia visitor centre includes a film about the dolphins, as well as educational games and activities for younger children. Local tour companies offer boat trips to see dolphins in summer, but Blue World does not take part.

🔆 Jun & Sep daily 9–1, 6–8; Jul & Aug daily 9–1, 6–10; May & Oct Mon–Fri 9–4, Sat 9–2; Nov–Apr Mon–Fri 10–1 💶 Adult 10kn, child (6–10) 7kn

OPATIJA

⊕ VIVAT I PARTNERI

Šetalište Maršala Tita 129, Opatija
Tel 051 272553
www.vivatipartneri.hr
This smart wine shop sells a selection of Croatian and foreign wines and liqueurs, together with quality local products such as truffles, olive oil and preserves.
🔆 Mon–Fri 9–8, Sat 9–2

Young Croatians taking a stroll in Rijeka

♡ THALASSO WELLNESS CENTAR OPATIJA

Šetalište Maršala Tita 188, Opatija
Tel 051 202600
www.thalassoterapia-opatija.hr
Thalassotherapy uses seawater for healing and relaxation. This state-of-the-art facility, opened in 2005, has heated seawater pools, Finnish and Turkish saunas and a variety of beauty, wellness and massage packages.
🔆 All year

RAB

⊕ NATURA RAB

Barbat, Rab
Tel 051 721927
www.natura-rab.hr
Ecological products including honey, fig brandy, beeswax candles and lavender oil are sold by a family of beekeepers from a stone cottage at Barbat. In summer the same family opens another shop on the main square of the old town.
🔆 Ring bell 🚗 On the main road from Rab to the ferry port at Mišnjak

RIJEKA

⊕ FRAJONA

Riva 16, Rijeka
Tel 051 321333
This wine shop on the ground floor of the Jadrolinija shipping company sells award-winning wines from the island of Krk, with the chance to taste before you buy.
🔆 Mon–Sat 8am–9pm

⊕ KRAŠ

Korzo, Rijeka
Tel 051 214362
www.kras.hr
The people of Rijeka must have a sweet tooth as there are two shops on the Korzo selling this well-known Croatian confectionary brand. Look out for Kraš 1911, a range of chocolates using original recipes.
🔆 Mon–Fri 7am–8pm, Sat 7–2

⊕ MALA GALERIJA

Užarska 25, Rijeka
Tel 051 335403
www.mala-galerija.hr
The narrow street of Užarska was once lined with artisans making the *morčić* jewellery for which Rijeka is renowned. You can buy *morčić* souvenirs at this arty gallery, along

with figures of local folk heroine Karolina, who protected Rijeka from British troops during the Napoleonic wars.

🕐 Mon–Fri 8.30–2, 4-8, Sat 8.30–2

🍷 VINOTEKA BLATO
Demetrova 14a, Rijeka
Tel 051 213924

You can buy wine from the barrel at this atmospheric old bodega, which opened in 1902. It is found behind Rijeka's city market, which is crowded on weekday mornings with fruit, flowers and vegetables sold from outdoor tables and meat, fish and dairy produce inside wonderful art nouveau market halls.

🕐 Mon–Sat 8–2, Sun 8–12

🎭 HRVATSKO NARODNO KAZALIŠTE (CROATIAN NATIONAL THEATRE)
Uljarska 1, Rijeka
Tel 051 355900
www.hnk-zajc.hr

Designed in 1885 by Viennese architects Hermann Helmer and Ferdinand Fellner, who also designed the Croatian National Theatre in Zagreb, this is the city's home of Croatian and Italian drama, opera, ballet and classical music. A statue of composer Ivan Zajc (1832–1914) stands at the centre of the park in front of the theatre.

🕐 Box office open Mon–Sat 9.30–12.30 and one hour before performance 🎫 30–150kn 🔲 🚻

🍸 CAPITANO
Adamićeva 3, Rijeka
Tel 051 213399

The name of this pub is a nod to Rijeka's seafaring history, with dark wood and mirrors adding to the nautical effect. During the day it serves simple meals like pasta and salads, but at night it becomes a fashionable joint, with chairs on the harbour-facing terrace and DJs at weekends.

🕐 Daily 7am–4am

🍸 HEMINGWAY
Korzo 28, Rijeka
Tel 051 272887
www.hemingway.hr

Part of a chain of cocktail bars across Croatia, Hemingway occupies the ground floor of a grand Austro-Hungarian building on the Korzo and doubles as

Walkers on the Leska Trail in Risnjak National Park

a coffee house by day and trendy lounge bar at night, with a piano, art gallery, comfortable sofas and crystal chandeliers.

🕐 Daily 7am–5am

🍸 KAROLINA
Gat Karoline Riječke, Rijeka
Tel 051 330909

This stunning glass building on the quayside, with a terrace right by the sea, has become the hottest nightspot in town, serving cool cocktails. The walls are hung with pictures of heroine Karolina of Rijeka.

🕐 Sun–Thu 6am–midnight, Fri 6am–2am, Sat 6am–4am

☕ MALI CAFÉ
Korzo 18a, Rijeka
Tel 051 335606

This terrace café on the Korzo makes a good place for a daytime coffee or late-night drink while watching the passing fashion parade.

🕐 Daily 7am–midnight

🏛 PRIRODOSLOVNI MUZEJ (NATURAL HISTORY MUSEUM)
Lorenzov Prolaz 1, Rijeka
Tel 051 553669
www.prirodoslovni.com

This museum on the edge of Vladimira Nazora Park makes a good choice for a rainy day. There is an aquarium where you can get up close to Adriatic species, and collections of rocks, fossils, reptiles, mammals and birds. A botanical garden of native plants was opened in 2005.

🕐 Mon–Sat 9–7, Sun 9–3 💰 Adult 10kn, child 5kn

VELEBIT

🐻 REFUGIUM URSORUM
Kuterevo
Tel 053 799222
www.kuterevo-medvjedi.hr

Most children adore furry creatures, and they don't come more adorable than the bear cubs at this refuge in the mountains, which was founded to look after young bears orphaned as a result of hunting. There is an eco-trail around the village and you can see the bears at four feeding times a day. The centre is open all year but the bears hibernate in winter.

🕐 Daily 9–6 💰 Adult 20kn, child 10kn

FESTIVALS AND EVENTS

JANUARY AND FEBRUARY

CARNIVAL
Rijeka
Tel 051 315710
www.ri-karneval.com.hr
Rio comes to Rijeka for six weeks as the city hosts some of Europe's wildest Carnival festivities. As this is a pre-Lenten event, the dates vary according to Easter, but it always starts with the raising of the Carnival flag on Trsat, the election of a Carnival queen and handing the city keys to the Master of Festivities. The first big parade features the *zvončari*, dancers dressed in animal skins and masks who ring bells to frighten away the evil spirits of winter as they did in pagan times. For the next few weeks, the city is one big festival, with theatre performances, concerts, and a grand masked ball in the former governor's palace. A children's Carnival parade takes place a week before the main international Carnival parade, which threads its way along the Korzo on the Sunday before Shrove Tuesday. What began in 1982 with a handful of revellers now has 10,000 participants from 12 countries and more than 100 floats. At the end of the parade, an effigy of Carnival is ritually burned in the harbour. The festival ends on Ash Wednesday with the lowering of the Carnival flag to mark the start of Lent.
🕙 Dates vary according to Easter

APRIL

KRIŽEVO
Rab
Tel 051 771111
www.tzg-rab.hr
A votive feast day for the islanders of Rab, marked by religious processions that culminate in Mass at the cathedral.
🕙 Last Sun in Apr

JUNE–SEPTEMBER

OPATIJA SUMMER FESTIVAL
Opatija
Tel 051 271377
www.festivalopatija.hr
Performances of music, theatre and folk dance take place at an open-air theatre throughout the summer. The festival includes Liburnia Jazz, three days of jazz concerts on the outdoor stage and at Villa Angiolina.
🕙 Jun–end Sep

RAPSKE GLAZBENE VEČERI (RAB MUSICAL EVENINGS)
Rab
Tel 051 771111
www.tzg-rab.hr
Classical and chamber music concerts are held in Rab's churches.
🕙 Thu evenings Jun–end Sep

JULY

RAPSKA FJERA
Rab
Tel 051 771111
www.tzg-rab.hr
Three days of festivities for the feast of Rab's patron, St. Christopher, include a medieval craft fair in the streets of the old town. On the evening of 27 July there is a re-enactment of a medieval tournament in which costumed knights fight each other with crossbows. Similar events take place on 9 May, 25 June and 15 August each year.
🕙 25–27 Jul

JULY AND AUGUST

LUBENIČKE GLAZBENE VEČERI (LUBENICE MUSICAL EVENINGS)
Lubenice, Cres
Tel 051 571535
www.tzg-cres.hr
Open-air classical music concerts are held in a magical clifftop setting, on the main square of the usually deserted hilltop hamlet of Lebenice.
🕙 Fri evenings Jul, Aug

OSORSKE GLAZBENE VEČERI (OSOR MUSICAL EVENINGS)
Osor, Cres
Tel 051 237110
This festival is mostly devoted to Croatian composers, with soloists and ensembles performing delightful chamber music in the old cathedral and on the town square.
🕙 Jul, Aug

KRK SUMMER FESTIVAL
Krk
Tel 051 221359
www.krk.hr
Classical music, jazz, opera, ballet and drama are staged in the cathedral and Frankopan castle and at the Franciscan monastery on the islet of Košljun.
🕙 Mid-Jul to mid-Aug

WHAT TO DO

DALMATIA

Whatever your tastes, there is always something to do in Dalmatia. The major cities of Split and Zadar are lively throughout the year, with a full range of shopping, entertainment and nightlife. During the summer months the action moves to the islands, from the open-air nightclubs of Pag to the beaches of Brač and the fashionable bars of Hvar Town. Active types can go island-hopping by yacht, learn to dive or windsurf, or head inland to go rafting on the River Cetina or hiking and climbing in Paklenica National Park. If you prefer to watch sports rather than taking part, a soccer match among Hajduk Split's fanatical supporters is a memorable experience, as is the bizarre sight of cricket at the Sir William Hoste club on Vis. Summer evenings on the coast are mostly spent relaxing at waterside bars, but there is also the usual mix of cultural festivals and events, including performances from the celebrated sword dancers of Korčula.

KEY TO SYMBOLS

- 🌐 Shopping
- 🎭 Entertainment
- 🍸 Nightlife
- 🏃 Sports
- ✪ Activities
- ♡ Health and Beauty
- ✱ For Children

BRAČ

✪ BIG BLUE SPORT
Podan Glavice 2, Bol
Tel 021 635614
www.big-blue-sport.hr
Bol is a major base for watersports and this company near a beach offers windsurfing courses for all ages, rental of equipment, plus mountain bike excursions, scuba-diving courses and sea-kayaking.
🔵 Apr–end Oct

✪ YELLOW CAT
Bol
Tel 098 288581
www.zutimacak.hr/kite
If you fancy trying your hand at kite-surfing, this outlet on the beach between Bol and Zlatni Rt offers five-day courses.
🔵 Apr–end Oct 💰 €290

✪ ZMAJEVA ŠPILJA (DRAGON'S CAVE)
Murvica, Bol
Tel 091 514 9787
The best way to visit this remarkable cave (▷ 114–115) is with a guide, who can show you the way and has a key to the cave. The walk up here is steep and rocky in places, so take plenty of water and wear good shoes.
🔵 Book by telephone one day in advance 💰 50kn per person

✪ NATURE PARK SUTIVAN
Sutivan
Tel 098 133 7345
Set among pine woods on the north-west coast of Brač, this enjoyable park has a small zoo of farm

animals and birds, including ostriches, peacocks, turkeys, donkeys, sheep and goats.
🕐 May–end Jun & Sep–end Oct 10–8; Jul–Aug daily 10am–midnight 🎟 Free 🍴 🚌 3km (2 miles) outside Sutivan on the road to Milna

HVAR

🎭 HVARSKO PUČKO KAZALIŠTE (HVAR COMMUNITY THEATRE)
Trg Svetog Stjepana, Hvar
Tel 021 741009
This beautiful old Venetian theatre (▷ 118) closed for restoration in 2006 and is planned to reopen by 2008. It stages Croatian drama.
🕐 Call for details

⭐ CARPE DIEM
Riva, Hvar
Tel 021 717234
www.carpe-diem-hvar.com
Carpe Diem has spawned a chain of bars across Croatia, but this cocktail bar and harbourside terrace is the original. In July and August the rich and beautiful step straight off their yachts and you need a reservation. At other times anyone is welcome but you may feel out of place if you are not dressed fashionably. There are resident DJs and music nights.
🕐 Jun–end Sep 9am–3am

KORČULA

🍷 VINARIJA TORRETA
Smokvica 165
Tel 020 832100
The Baničević family have a small wine museum at their vineyards in Smokvica. Tours and tastings of Pošip and Rukatac wines are on offer, and you can buy local brandy and olive oil.
🕐 Call for details 🚌 On main road across the island from Korčula to Vela Luka

🎭 MOREŠKA SWORD DANCE
Tickets from Marko Polo Tours, Biline 5, Korčula
Tel 020 715400
www.korcula.com
The *moreška* dancers of Korčula perform a ritual that began in the 16th century under Venetian rule. Dressed in black and red, to the accompaniment of brass bands and clashing swords, rival armies battle over the love of a maiden. The dance is a feature of all the main festivals on Korčula and is performed

Visitors on the road to Dragon's Cave on Brač

twice a week in summer on an open-air stage outside the city walls.
🕐 Jun–end Sep Mon and Thu at 9pm 🎟 100kn

⭐ MM-SUB
Lumbarda
Tel 020 712288
www.mm-sub.hr
This scuba-diving base in the village of Lumbarda runs diving courses for beginners and can also offer organized dives through caves, underwater cliffs and shipwrecks.
🕐 Apr–end Sep

OMIŠ

⭐ SLAP
Poljički Trg, Omiš
Tel 021 757336
www.hrslap.hr
This company offers half-day rafting trips through the River Cetina gorge, with all safety equipment provided. The trip starts at Slime waterfall near Kučiće, but a transfer from Omiš is included in the price.
🕐 Apr–end Oct daily at 9.30 and 2.30 🎟 Adult 160kn, child 80kn

PAG

🛒 PAŠKA SIRANA
Trg Kralja Krešimira IV, Pag
Tel 023 612717
www.paskasirana.com
The island of Pag is famous for its hard, salty sheep's cheese, which at its best is similar to Parmesan. You can buy it from markets and farm shops all over the island, but for a reliable selection of local cheeses, visit this shop on the main square of the old town.
🕐 Mon–Fri 8–8, Sat 8–2

⭐ AQUARIUS/ KALYPSO/PAPAYA
Plaža Zrće, Novalja
On hot summer nights Zrće beach is crowded with clubbers. The club scene on Pag started with Kalypso in the 1980s and now there are three open-air beach clubs scattered around an arc of white pebbles. The Zagreb club Aquarius even opens a branch here in summer. All the clubs are open day and night so you can drift from one to the other. During the day, there are sports competitions, waterslides and beach parties; at night there are DJs, live bands and breakfast at 5am.
🕐 Jun–end Aug 24 hours a day

ŠIBENIK

⊕ ŠIBENSKO KAZALIŠTE
Ulica Kralja Zvonimira 1, Šibenik
Tel 022 213123
This gorgeous theatre was started in 1864 by Trogir architect Josip Slade, with a Renaissance exterior, baroque interior and magnificent frescoed ceiling. In 1991 it took a direct hit from a grenade and was closed for 10 years but is now showing plays once again.
🕲 Check posters for details

⊗ BUNARI—SECRETS OF ŠIBENIK
Trg Republike Hrvatske, Šibenik
Tel 098 265924
This unusual attraction, in the vaults of the 15th-century wells, uses interactive multimedia to explore the city's history through themes such as seafaring and food. Children can race to build an ancient fort, or help Šibenik's patron St. Michael in his battle against the dragon. It is down steps opposite the cathedral.
🕲 Daily 9–1, 4–11 🎫 Adult 30kn, child 20kn 🅿

SPLIT

⊕ KARLA
Dioklecijanova 1, Split
Tel 021 486803
www.karla.hr
This funky boutique in the corner of the Peristyle sells stylish and expensive shoes and boots for women There are six branches in the city.
🕲 Mon–Fri 8–8, Sat 9–2

⊕ STARI PAZAR
Stari Pazar, Split
The central market, known as the 'old bazaar', is on the eastern edge of Diocletian's Palace outside the Silver Gate. This is where the Dalmatian countryside

comes to town, as farmers set up stalls selling eggs, cheese, sausages, bacon, bread, vegetables and wine.
🕲 Daily 7–2

⊕ HRVATSKO NARODNO KAZALIŠTE (CROATIAN NATIONAL THEATRE)
Trg Gaje Bulata 1, Split
Tel 021 344999 or 021 363014 (box office)
www.hnk-split.hr
The Croatian National Theatre is the city's main venue for drama, ballet and opera, with a season from October to June. It is also

Style on the street and in store windows in Split

the main organizer of the Split Summer Festival (▷ 194).
🕲 Box office open Mon–Sat 9–1, 4–8 and one hour before performance 🎫 30–150kn 🅿 🚫

⊗ HAJDUK SPLIT
Mediteranskih Igara 2, Split
Tel 021 381235 or 060 470470
www.hnkhajduk.hr
Founded in 1911, this soccer club has a passionate following across Dalmatia. A match at the Poljud stadium is an unforgettable experience, with fireworks, banners and colourful

entertainment. The stadium seats 35,000 spectators and is sometimes used by the Croatian national team. The season runs from August to May, with a break between December and February. Tickets are cheap and usually available on the gate.
🕲 Call or check press for match times 🎫 From 30kn 🅿 17

⊗ PRIRODOSLOVNI MUZEJ (NATURAL HISTORY MUSEUM)
Poljana Kneza Trpimira 3, Split
Tel 021 322988
The museum is down an alley off a square near the city market. It has displays of coral and shells from the Adriatic and Indian Ocean.
🕲 Mon–Fri 10–5, Sat 9–1 🎫 Adult 8kn, child 4kn

TROGIR

⊕ GENA
Ribarska 6, Trogir
Tel 021 884329
www.gena-trogir.com
If you have always wanted an elegant hand-made gentlemen's suit, then visit tailor Boris Burić Gena in his atelier on the top floor of a Renaissance palace. His formal evening suits are in the style of the 19th century, complete with black silk collars and white bow-ties. Opera singer Luciano Pavarotti is a client.
🕲 Call in advance

VIS

⊗ ISSA DIVING CENTER
Komiža, Vis
Tel 021 713651
www.scubadiving.hr
The waters around Vis are among the clearest in the Adriatic, providing excellent conditions for scuba-diving. This dive school based at Hotel Biševo runs courses

for all levels and can also arrange diving expeditions to the Modra Špilja (Blue Cave) on Biševo or to see a US B17 bomber from World War II under the water.
🕓 Apr–end Nov

❻ VIS CRICKET CLUB
Contact: Oliver Roki
Tel 021 714004
The Sir William Hoste Cricket Club was founded in 2002 to restore the tradition of cricket on Vis, which began when British troops were stationed here during the Napoleonic wars. Its name comes from a British naval commander of the time. Matches take place in April and May against teams from Zagreb and Split. The club plays on an artificial pitch but there are plans to build a grass pitch.
🕓 Call for details

ZADAR

⊕ BIBICH
Široka Ulica, Zadar
Tel 023 329260
This small delicatessen and wine shop, in a corner of the Forum, sells gourmet wines, honey and olive oil.
🕓 Mon–Sat 9–1, 5–9

⊕ MARASKA
Ulica Mate Karamana 3, Zadar
Tel 023 208808
www.maraska.hr
Zadar's most famous product is Maraschino cherry liqueur, produced at the landmark Maraska factory on the waterfront. This small shop in the old town sells Maraschino made according to a 16th-century recipe, as well as other liqueurs based on walnuts, pears and aromatic herbs.
🕓 Mon–Sat 8–8

⊕ STUDIO LIK
Don Ive Prodana 7, Zadar
Tel 023 317766
Hand-made lace from Pag, embroidered textiles from Dalmatia and traditional sheepskin slippers are sold at this folksy souvenir shop.
🕓 Mon–Sat 9–2, 5–9

❼ HRVATSKA KAZALIŠNA KUĆA
Široka Ulica 8, Zadar
Tel 023 314586
www.hkk-zadar.hr
Founded in 1945, the Croatian Theatre House is Zadar's biggest cultural

An attractive narrow street in the town of Trogir

institution, hosting a repertoire of classical music and drama all year and organizing the annual Zadar Summer Theatre festival.
🕓 Box office open Mon–Fri 11–1, 6–8, Sat 11–1, and one hour before performance 🎫 Varies 🎫 🚫

❼ ARSENAL
Trg Tri Bunara 1, Zadar
Tel 023 253833
www.arsenalzadar.com
Opened in 2005 in the cathedral-like space of the 18th-century Venetian arsenal, this is a café, nightspot, bar, restaurant, art gallery

and shopping arcade rolled into one. By day, you can relax on sofas or sip coffee beneath extraordinary Venetian architecture. At night, it turns into a trendy lounge bar, with DJs and live music ranging from Irish folk to modern jazz.
🕓 Daily 7am–3am; live music Sun–Thu from 8pm, Fri–Sat from 10.30pm

❼ FORUM
Široka Ulica, Zadar
Tel 023 250537
If your idea of nightlife is a café terrace rather than a cocktail bar, you won't do better than this café on the Forum, with outdoor tables beneath St. Donat's church bell-tower. It serves good coffee and cakes, and on sunny days it is the busiest meeting place in town.
🕓 Daily 7.30am–1am

❼ THE GARDEN
Liburnska Obala 6, Zadar
Tel 023 364739
www.thegardenzadar.com
Opened in 2005 by British music producer Nick Colgan and James Brown, the drummer with reggae group UB40, The Garden has become the coolest place to be seen in Zadar. High up on the city walls with a beautiful garden terrace, it is open 'whenever the sun is shining or the stars are twinkling'. During the day people chill out on white sofas; after dark, there are DJs and visiting musicians. You can arrive in style—a rowing boat taxi will take you across the water from the jetty by the Maraska factory. The service runs until midnight in summer and costs just 3kn.
🕓 May–end Sep 10am–1am

FESTIVALS AND EVENTS

FEBRUARY

POKLAD

Lastovo
Tel 020 801018
www.lastovo-tz.net/poklad.html
An unusual Carnival celebration takes place on Lastovo, when Poklad, a straw figure, is paraded through town and tied to a rope with fireworks attached to his boots. The ritual burning of Poklad starts a day of festivities marking the end of winter.
🎭 Shrove Tuesday

JUNE–SEPTEMBER

HVAR SUMMER FESTIVAL

Hvar
Tel 021 741788
www.tzhvar.hr
Concerts of classical music, jazz and Dalmatian folk singing are held in the cloisters of the Franciscan monastery, and plays are staged in the old theatre throughout the summer months on Hvar.
🎭 Jun–end Sep

FESTIVAL DALMATINSKIH KLAPA

Omiš
Tel 021 861015
www.fdk.hr
The biggest festival of Dalmatian klapa (traditional a cappella singing) takes place in Omiš each July, with open-air concerts on the square in front of the parish church.
🎭 Three weeks in Jul

SVETI TODOR

Korčula
Tel 020 715701
Korcula's biggest festival, for the feast of St. Theodor,

features a performance of the moreška sword dance. There are also regular moreška shows in summer on a stage near the Revelin tower and weekly performances of the kumpanija sword dance in Vela Luka.
🎭 29 Jul

SPLIT SUMMER FESTIVAL

Split
Tel 021 363014
www.splitsko-ljeto.hr
This festival has been going for more than 50 years and comprises four weeks of music, ballet and drama in spectacular settings including the underground chambers of Diocletian's Palace and Ivan Meštrović's Holy Cross Chapel. A highlight each year is the open-air opera performance in the Peristyle of Diocletian's Palace. Tickets are available in advance from the tourist office and Croatian National Theatre.
🎭 Mid-Jul to mid-Aug

TROGIR SUMMER FESTIVAL

Trogir
Tel 021 881412
Concerts of classical, jazz and Dalmatian folk music are held in venues including the cathedral, Kamerlengo fortress and outdoor stages.
🎭 Jul, Aug

ST. DONAT'S MUSICAL EVENINGS

Zadar
Tel 023 300430
www.donat-festival.com

This long-running festival features recitals of early music and orchestral concerts in churches. The main venue is the beautiful setting of St. Donat's Church, but other events take place in the cathedral and Roman Forum. Tickets are available in advance from the Croatian Theatre House.
🎭 Jul, Aug

SINJSKA ALKA

Sinj
Tel 021 821542
www.alka.hr
Dalmatia's most traditional festival takes place in the inland town of Sinj to commemorate a victory over Turkish troops in 1715. The climax is a jousting contest on the Sunday, with brass bands and galloping riders in 18th-century costume attempting to spear a metal ring suspended on a rope. The winner is crowned with the Croatian tricolour by the Duke of Sinjska Alka. Tickets are sold for the main event, but you can watch two days of rehearsals for free.
🎭 First Sun in Aug

MARCO POLO RE-ENACTMENT

Korčula
Tel 020 715701
A re-enactment of the naval battle of 1298 between the Venetian and Genoese fleets in which Marco Polo was captured takes place on the anniversary of the battle each year.
🎭 Early Sep

DUBROVNIK AND BEYOND

There is so much life on the streets of Dubrovnik that there is little need for organized entertainment. Most visitors spend much of their time sitting at pavement cafés on Stradun, soaking up the atmosphere and the views along one of the most beautiful streets in the world. Nevertheless, Dubrovnik does have a thriving cultural scene, which reaches its peak during the six weeks of the Summer Festival. Throughout the summer months, there are open-air performances of folk dance and music, both in Dubrovnik and nearby Čilipi. If you need to escape from the city, tour agencies offer activities ranging from canoeing and rafting on the River Neretva to sea-kayaking off the Elafiti Islands. Alternatively you could just chill out on Banje, the popular city beach, or take a boat to Lopud or Lokrum. If you are visiting Dubrovnik in winter don't miss the chance to be there during the feast of St. Blaise, when the whole city comes out onto the streets for two days of marching bands, explosions and religious processions.

KEY TO SYMBOLS

- 🌐 **Shopping**
- 🎭 **Entertainment**
- 🍸 **Nightlife**
- ⚽ **Sports**
- ✪ **Activities**
- ♡ **Health and Beauty**
- ✿ **For Children**

🌐 SHOPPING

BOOKS

ALGEBRA
Stradun 9, Dubrovnik
Tel 020 323217
This bookshop on Stradun has an interesting selection of English-language books

on Croatian history, war, Dubrovnik legends and cuisine. It also sells model ships, dolls in folk costume and statues of St. Blaise.
🕐 Daily 8.30–8

ALGORITAM
Stradun 8, Dubrovnik
Tel 020 322044
www.algoritam.hr
This branch of Croatia's biggest bookstore sells a wide range of English-language titles, including guidebooks and maps to Dubrovnik and Croatia.
🕐 Jun–end Sep Mon–Sat 9am–11pm, Sun 10–1, 6–10;

Oct–end May Mon–Fri 9–8.30, Sat 9–3

FOOD AND DRINK

DUBROVAČKA KUĆA
Ulica Svetog Dominika 4, Dubrovnik
Tel 020 322092
This attractive gallery on the square opposite the Dominican Monastery sells Dalmatian wines and liqueurs, candied fruits from the Elafiti Islands, aromatic oils, natural cosmetics and work by local artists. On the same square is a small unnamed workshop selling stone and marble sculptures of St. Blaise.

⚫ Jun–end Sep daily 9am–11pm;
Oct–end May Mon–Sat 9–8

FRANJA

Od Puča 9, Dubrovnik
Tel 020 324818
This upmarket delicatessen
on the main shopping street
of the old town sells a wide
variety of Croatian wines
and spirits plus olive oil,
Pag cheese, gingerbread,
honey, truffles, chocolates
and coffee as well as
attractively presented gift
baskets of lavender oils
and soaps.
⚫ Daily 8am–9pm

INDIJAN

Potomje, Pelješac
Tel 020 742235
This family-run winery in
the village of Potomje has a
giant wine-barrel in the
garden where you can help
yourself, fill up your plastic
bottles and leave your
money in the cash box. Ring
on the doorbell to buy
bottled wines and home-
made spirits made out of
walnuts, blueberries
and figs.
⚫ Ring bell

MATUŠKO

Potomje, Pelješac
Tel 020 742393
One of the better producers
of Pelješac wine sells direct
from the cellar and you
can taste before you buy.
Products range from
inexpensive Rukatac and
Pošip whites to a vintage
organic Dingač red.
⚫ Ring bell

MILIČIĆ

Ulica Od Sigurate 2, Dubrovnik
Tel 020 321777
This wine shop on a corner
of Stradun offers you the
chance to taste Miličić

wines from the Pelješac
peninsula. It also sells various
fruit brandies and liqueurs.
⚫ Jun–end Sep daily 9am–10pm;
Oct–end May Mon–Sat 9–12, 5–8,
Sun 9–1

VINARIJA DINGAČ

Potomje, Pelješac
Tel 020 742010
The most famous name
in Croatian wine has a
modern winery in Potomje
and a showroom offering
sales and tastings of
Dingač, Postup and Plavac
Mali wines.
⚫ Hours vary

*A typical souvenir shop on
Stradun in Dubrovnik*

JEWELLERY AND GIFTS

LINDA

Od Puča 18, Dubrovnik
Tel 020 324082
A small stretch of Od Puča
is lined with jewellery
shops selling the gold
and silver filigree work
that has been produced in
Dubrovnik since medieval
times. This one also has
chunky silver necklaces and
Ottoman-inspired pieces.
⚫ Daily 9.30–1, 4–7

RONCHI

Ulica Lučarica 2, Dubrovnik
Tel 020 323699
This traditional hat shop
was founded by Euphilius
Ronchi from Milan in 1858
and is still in the same
family. Today his great-
granddaughter Marina
Grabovac Ronchi continues
to make both men's and
women's hats, using the
same antique tools and
blocks that have survived
for over a century.
⚫ Mon–Fri 9–12, 5–7, Sat 9–12

TEDI

Od Puča 20, Dubrovnik
Tel 020 323273
Pavle Čivljak crafts hand-
made silver and filigree
jewellery with precious
stones, as well as unusual
sculptures of volcanic lava.
⚫ Mon–Sat 9am–midnight, Sun
9am–10pm

🎭 ENTERTAINMENT

KAZALIŠTE MARINA DRŽIĆA

Pred Dvorom 3, Dubrovnik
Tel 021 321006
www.kazaliste-dubrovnik.hr
This lovely 19th-century
theatre is named after
Renaissance playwright
Marin Držić (1508–67), a
libertine and author of
bawdy comedies about
upper-class Ragusan life.
It mostly performs serious
Croatian drama, with
occasional shows in English
by visiting companies.
⚫ Box office open Mon–Sat
10–12.30, 6–9 and one hour before
performance 🎫 Varies 🔄 🔄

LINDO

Tel 020 324023
This well-known folklore
ensemble performs
Croatian songs and dances

twice a week in summer on an outdoor stage at Lazareti, the former quarantine hospital outside Ploče Gate. It also puts on regular concerts during the Dubrovnik Summer Festival.

🎫 Jun–end Sep Mon, Fri 9.30pm
🎟 80kn

FOLK MUSIC

Look out for free displays of folk music and dance in Dubrovnik and nearby towns throughout the summer. Between May and October concerts take place on Sunday mornings at 11am outside St. Blaise's Church, with performances ranging from majorettes to traditional sword dancers from Korčula. The other popular event is the Sunday morning folk dance display in the church square at Čilipi, with dancers in traditional Dalmatian costume.

🌙 NIGHTLIFE

BUŽA
Access from Ulica Od Margarite, Dubrovnik
No tel
Pass through a hole in the city wall beneath a wooden sign saying 'Cold Drinks', walk down the steps and you come to this atmospheric bar, perched on the rocks in a cliff face with views across the water to Lokrum. It is easy to spend hours here, relaxing to mellow music and occasionally diving into the sea. It only serves cold drinks (beer, wine and soft drinks in plastic cups) but you will not get a better view anywhere.

🎫 Hours vary depending on the weather

KARAKA
Gradska Luka, Dubrovnik
Tel 020 358108
www.karaka.info
This fine replica of a 16th-century Dubrovnik merchant galleon, built out of oak and pine, can accommodate 200 passengers. In winter it is moored in Gruž harbour but in summer it moves to the Old Port, where it is open every night as a bar unless it is operating pirate and sunset cruises.

🎫 Jun–end Sep daily 8pm–midnight

A poster for a candlelit classical music concert

LABIRINT
Ulica Svetog Dominika 2, Dubrovnik
Tel 020 322222
www.labirint-dubrovnik.com
What looks like a stone cave built into the city walls turns out to be a terrace restaurant and nightclub overlooking the Old Port, where you can dine by candlelight, climb the steps to a rooftop fortress and then dance the night away.

🎫 Restaurant daily 12–12, nightclub daily 10pm–5am

TROUBADOUR
Bunićeva Poljana 2, Dubrovnik
Tel 020 323476
Almost everyone in Dubrovnik ends up at the Troubadour, whose friendly owner Marko Brešković, a member of the Dubrovački Trubaduri who represented Yugoslavia in the 1968 Eurovision Song Contest, can be seen playing his double-bass most nights. There is live jazz every night from 10pm in summer, spilling out of doors with wicker chairs on the square. In winter the bar has a more intimate atmosphere as visitors and locals gather around the piano. Drinks are not cheap but you are paying for the atmosphere.

🎫 May–end Oct daily 9am–3am; Nov–end Apr daily 5–11

🏃 SPORTS AND 🎯 ACTIVITIES

ADRIATIC KAYAK TOURS
Zrinsko Frankopanska 6, Dubrovnik
Tel 020 312770
www.adriatickayaktours.com
This American-owned company offers half-day tours of Lokrum and full-day visits to the Elafiti Islands by kayak. The tours are suitable for beginners as instruction and safety equipment are provided. Accompanied children are welcome.

🎫 May–end Oct

BEACHES

The nearest beach to the old town is Banje, just outside Ploče Gate, where you can swim or sunbathe with a fabulous view of the Old Port. In summer Banje is crowded with locals who hang out both day and night at the fashionable East-West beach club.

There are pebble beaches on the Lapad peninsula and a nudist beach at Lokrum, but for a real sandy beach, take the ferry to Lopud (▷ 156) and walk across the island to Šunj.

🟠 FOR CHILDREN

AKVARIJ (AQUARIUM)

Tvrđava Sveti Ivana, Dubrovnik
Tel 020 323978

Housed in the ground floor of St. John's fort (▷ 154) with seawater tanks built into the city walls, this enjoyable aquarium features Adriatic sea creatures such as starfish, grouper and loggerhead turtles.

🕐 May–end Oct daily 9–9; Nov–end Apr Mon–Sat 9–1 💰 Adult 25kn, child 15kn

---

FESTIVALS AND EVENTS

FEBRUARY

FESTA SVETOGA VLAHA (FEAST OF ST. BLAISE)

Dubrovnik

The feast day of Dubrovnik's patron saint brings the whole city out onto the streets for two days in the middle of winter. The festival begins on the afternoon of 2 February, when the bishop releases white doves into the air as a symbol of Dubrovnik's freedom and the flag of St. Blaise is raised outside St. Blaise's Church. At the same time the *trumbunjeri* (musketeers), dressed in scarlet berets and red cloaks, fire their guns in the Old Port to signal the start of the festivities. Throughout this day and the next the faithful queue at St. Blaise's Church for the *grličanje* (blessing of the throat) ceremony, in which a priest holds a twisted candle around each person's neck while reciting a prayer for protection from 'ailments of the throat and other evils'. Early on 3 February the people of the surrounding villages gather at the city gates, dressed in traditional embroidered costume and carrying banners. Led by the *festanjuli*, the feast hosts elected annually from among the local sea captains and craftsmen, they process down Stradun to the accompaniment of marching bands and gunpowder explosions from the *trumbunjeri*. After an open-air Mass outside the cathedral, the bishop leads a procession along Stradun carrying the holy relics of St. Blaise,

The Dubrovnik Summer Festival features live music

including the casket said to contain his skull. The festival ends with the lowering of the flag and the singing of the hymn of St. Blaise, followed by the national anthem as the Croatian tricolour is raised in its place.

🕐 2–3 Feb

JULY AND AUGUST

DUBROVNIK SUMMER FESTIVAL

Dubrovnik
Tel 020 326100
www.dubrovnik-festival.hr

The biggest and most prestigious cultural event in Croatia takes place in Dubrovnik each summer, with more than 80 performances of music, drama and folk dance at venues including the cathedral, Rector's Palace, Sponza Palace and the island of Lokrum. It begins on 10 July, with fireworks and the raising of the Libertas flag on Luža square to the recital of *Ode to Liberty*, a celebration of Dubrovnik's freedom by Ragusa's greatest Renaissance poet Ivan Gundulić (1589–1638). For the next six weeks, the city turns itself into an open-air stage. Past performers have included the Vienna Philharmonic Orchestra, jazz musician Dizzy Gillespie, and British flautist Sir James Galway. A highlight of the festival is the performance of Shakespeare's *Hamlet* at Lovrijenac fort. Tickets for events can be bought at the festival office on Stradun or the kiosk outside Pile Gate.

🕐 10 Jul–25 Aug

WHAT TO DO

This chapter describes five driving tours and eight walks that explore Croatia's varied scenery. The location of each walk and tour is marked on the map on page 200, where you will also find a key to the individual maps. For both walks and tours it is advisable to buy a detailed map of the area before you set out.

Out and About

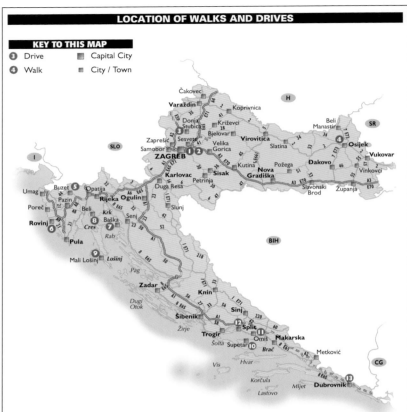

❸ Drive ▪ Capital City
❹ Walk ▪ City / Town

KEY TO ROUTE MAPS IN THIS CHAPTER

★ Start point
— Route
▪▪ Alternative route
▶ Route direction

⑥ Featured sight along route
● Place of interest in Sights section
☀ Viewpoint
621
▲ Height in metres

*Rooftops in Dubrovnik (above).
The Makarska riviera below
Mount Biokovo (above right)*

WALKS AND DRIVES

1. **Walk** Old Zagreb (▷ 201–203)
2. **Walk** Zagreb's Green Horseshoe (▷ 204–205)
3. **Drive** Through the Zagorje (▷ 206–207)
4. **Walk** Along the River at Osijek (▷ 208–209)
5. **Drive** Hill Towns of Istria (▷ 210–211)
6. **Walk** The Golden Cape at Rovinj (▷ 212–213)
7. **Drive** Around Krk Island (▷ 214–215)
8. **Walk** Vultures on Cres (▷ 216–217)
9. **Walk** Lošinj Coast Path (▷ 218–219)
10. **Drive** Off the Beaten Track in Brač (▷ 220–221)
11. **Drive** Around Mount Biokovo (▷ 222–223)
12. **Walk** On Split's Green Hill (▷ 224–225)
13. **Walk** In and Out of Dubrovnik (▷ 226–227)

OUT AND ABOUT

OLD ZAGREB

This short walk explores the upper town of Gornji Grad, historically divided
between Gradec (the citizens' district) and Kaptol (the ecclesiastical
capital). With several interesting museums and churches en route,
it can easily be extended to last all day.

THE WALK
Distance: 3km (2 miles)
Allow: 1–2 hours plus visits
Start/end: Trg Bana Jelačića
🕇 48 C2

HOW TO GET THERE

Trams 1, 6, 11, 12, 13, 14 and 17
all stop at Trg Bana Jelačića.

★ Start the walk at Trg
Bana Jelačića (▷ 59),
Zagreb's central square.
With the statue of Josip
Jelačić behind you, begin
by heading down Ulica
Ljudevita Gaja (Gajeva) on
the southern side of the
square. Turn right into
Bogovićeva, a busy
shopping street with café
tables out on the pave-
ment. The street ends in
Trg Petra Preradovića.

❶ Trg Petra Preradovića
is named after the
poet Petar Preradović
(1818–72), whose statue
stands on the square.
Most locals refer to it as
Cvjetni Trg (Flower
Square) because of the
florists who sell here.
On the right-hand corner
with Bogovićeva,
Oktagon is the finest of
Zagreb's Viennese-style
shopping arcades,
erected in 1899, with a
stained-glass dome.

Cross Trg Petra
Preradovića diagonally
to your right, passing the
Orthodox church of the
Transfiguration to arrive
on Ilica. Turn left and then
immediately right into

Detail of a building, Gornji Grad

Ulica Tomića (Tomićeva).
From here you can take
the funicular railway or
walk up the steps to
Gornji Grad.

❷ The *Uspinjača* (funic-
ular) is popularly known
as the old lady of Zagreb.
First opened in 1890, it
is sometimes said to be
the shortest public
transport journey in the
world, travelling 66m at
a gradient of 1:2 in
around 55 seconds.

Emerging from the funicu-
lar station opposite Kula
Lotrščak (▷ 52), you
arrive on Strossmayerovo
Šetalište.

❸ This shady prome-
nade occupies the site of
the former defensive
wall of Gradec, and
offers fine views. A
short diversion to the
right brings you to a
sculpture depicting the
Croatian writer Antun

Gustav Matoš (1873–
1914) sitting on a bench.

Turn back to walk along
Strossmayerovo Šetalište.
Continue past the funicu-
lar station and take the
Grič alley to your right to
arrive on Markovićev Trg.
From here, turn left along
Ulica Matoševa.

❹ This pretty street is
lined with 18th- and
19th-century houses,
including the baroque
mansion housing the
Hrvatski Povijesni Muzej
(**Croatian History
Museum**; ▷ 53–54).

At the end of Ulica
Matoševa, turn left then
right onto Ulica Demetrova,
passing the Hrvatski
Prirodoslovni Muzej
(Croatian Natural History
Museum; ▷ 54). Stay on
this road as it bends to the
right towards the Muzej
Grada Zagreba (Zagreb
City Museum; ▷ 57). At
the end of the road, turn
right onto Ulica Opatička.

❺ This short stretch of
Ulica Opatička boasts
two very handsome
buildings. Narodni Dom
(National Hall) is a neo-
classical mansion, built
in the 1830s and used
variously as a museum,
reading room, casino
and ballroom. The
nearby Zlatni Dvorana
(Golden Palace) is
notable for its wrought-
iron gates, designed by

OUT AND ABOUT

the architect Hermann Bollé and topped by the coats of arms of Croatia, Dalmatia and Slavonia. Now home to the Croatian History Institute, the walls are decorated with scenes from Croatian history.

Take the next right along Ulica 29 Listopad 1918 to arrive on Markov Trg (St. Mark's Square).

❻ St. Mark's Square (▷ 53) is the focal point

to stand on this site. The monastery buildings now house Klovićevi Dvori, a gallery hosting modern art exhibitions.

Turn right on Ulica Kamenita to pass through the Kamenita Vrata (▷ 55). Beyond the gate, turn right by a statue of St. George and the Dragon onto Ulica Radićeva. Walk down this steep, cobbled shopping street and turn left onto Krvavi Most.

was the city's artisan quarter, and many of the townhouses and work-shops from then, with their pastel façades, are now art galleries and terrace bars. A short way up on the left, look out for a bronze statue of a woman holding an umbrella. This is Marija Jurić Zagorka (1873–1957), Croatia's first female journalist and the author of novels including *Grička Vještica* (The Witch from Grič).

of Gradec and the heart of Croatian political life. The Sabor (Parliament) is on one side and the Banski Dvor (the former Governor's palace, now the seat of the Croatian government) on the other. Walk around St. Mark's church to admire the roof tiles from the far side of the square.

Keep straight ahead towards Kula Lotrščak and turn left on Katarinin Trg with the church of Sveta Katarina (St. Catherine) ahead of you. Bear left in front of the church to arrive on Jezuitski Trg.

❼ Jezuitski Trg takes its name from the Jesuit monastery which used

❽ Krvavi Most (Bloody Bridge) stands on the site of the historic boundary between Gradec and Kaptol, which were separated by the Medveščak stream. Its name reflects cen-turies of confrontation between the two districts.

At the end of Krvavi Most, turn left onto Ulica Tkalčić (Tkalčićeva).

❾ Tkalčićeva is Zagreb's most popular promenade, where the young and beautiful strut on summer nights. It was built on the site of a dried-up river bed where the Medveščak stream once flowed. In the 19th century, this

Continue along Tkalčićeva until you see the Oliver Twist pub on your right. Beside the pub is a surviv-ing section of the city wall which once enclosed Kaptol. Walk through a gap in the wall and up the steps to a small park.

❿ Opatovina park is named after a Cistercian abbey which once stood nearby. Across the park is the church of Sveti Frane (St. Francis of Assisi), with stained-glass windows by Ivo Dulčić (1916–75).

Walk past the church and turn right along Kaptol, passing the Komedija the-atre and the cathedral on your return to the start.

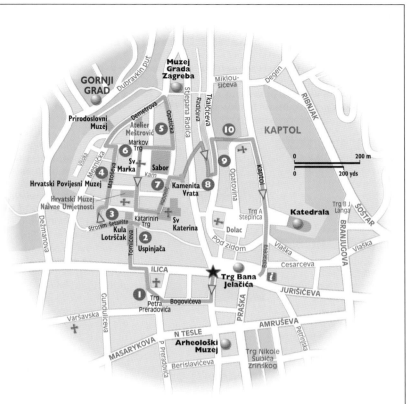

GORNJI GRAD

Muzej Grada Zagreba

Prirodoslovni Muzej

Atelier Meštrović **5**

Markov Trg **6**

Sv Marka

Sabor

Hrvatski Povijesni Muzej **4**

Kamenita Vrata **8**

7

9

10

KAPTOL

Hrvatski Muzej Naïvne Umjetnosti

Kula Lotrščak **3**

Šetalište Strossm

Katarinin Trg

Sv Katerina

Uspinjača **2**

Dolac

Katedrala

ILICA

★ Trg Bana Jelačića

1 Trg Petra Preradovića

Bogovićeva

JURIŠIĆEVA

AMRUŠEVA

Arheološki Muzej

0 — 200 m
0 — 200 yds

The funicular and Kula Lotrščak (Burglars' Tower); detail of a window with shutters; a wall sign on Ulica Kaptol (opposite, left to right). Kula Lotrščak in Gornji Grad (left)

WHERE TO EAT
Ivica i Marica (▷ 235)
Kaptolska Klet (▷ 234)
Mangiare (▷ 235)

PLACES TO VISIT
Atelier Meštrović (▷ 54)
Hrvatski Muzej Naivne Umjetnosti (▷ 55)
Hrvatski Povijesni Muzej (▷ 53–54)
Hrvatski Prirodoslovni Muzej (▷ 54)
Katedrala (▷ 51)
Kula Lotrščak (▷ 52)
Muzej Grada Zagreba (▷ 57)

ZAGREB'S GREEN HORSESHOE

Donji Grad (Lower Town) is the setting for this relaxing walk, which follows a series of parks, avenues and squares laid out in a horseshoe shape by Milan Lenuci (1849–1924) in the late 19th century. Along the way, you pass the grand cultural institutions of Habsburg-era Zagreb and several works by the sculptor Ivan Meštrović.

THE WALK

Distance: 2km (1.2 miles)
Allow: 1 hour
Start: Trg Maršala Tita
✚ 48 B3
End: Trg Bana Jelačića
✚ 48 C2

HOW TO GET THERE

Trams 12, 13, 14 and 17 all stop at Trg Maršala Tita. Alternatively, it is a short walk from Trg Bana Jelačića.

★ Trg Maršala Tita, named after the Yugoslav leader Tito, is surrounded by impressive Austro-Hungarian buildings. On the north side is the rectorate of Zagreb University. At the foot of the steps leading up to the building is one of Meštrović's most famous works, a bronze statue of a seated woman known as *History of the Croats* (1932). Facing the university is the imposing Hrvatsko Narodno Kazalište (▷ 51). Another sculpture by Meštrović, the mildly erotic *Zdenac Života* (Well of Life), is in front of the theatre.

Begin by the sculpture and walk around the theatre with the Muzej Za Umjetnost i Obrt (▷ 58) to your right. Keep going south across a succession of green squares. Walk across Mažuranićev Trg with the Etnografski Muzej (▷ 51) on your right and cross the road to reach Marulićev Trg.

Enjoying a view of the lake in the Botanical Gardens

❶ Marulićev Trg is named after Marko Marulić (1450–1524), from Split who is known as the father of Croatian literature. His portrait is featured on the 500 kuna banknote. A statue of him by Meštrović sits at the heart of the square. Ahead is the former University Library, now housing the State Archive. Designed by Rudolf Lubinsky in 1912, this is considered Zagreb's finest Viennese Secession-style building. Walk to the front for a closer look at the façade. A statue of archaeologist Frane Bulić stands outside.

Facing you across the street is the Botanički Vrt (Botanical Garden). Cross the road to enter the gardens, then stroll through the park before leaving via the gate at the far end.

❷ This English-style landscape garden, with ponds, paths, bridges and arboretums, was founded in 1889 and contains over 10,000 species of plants from around the world. From November to March, when the gardens are usually closed, walk along Vodnikova.

Follow Mihanovićeva past the headquarters of Hrvatske Željeznice (Croatian Railways) on the left and the Regent Esplanade hotel (▷ 253) on the right, then take the steps down into Trg Ante Starčevića, an attractive park with flowerbeds, lawns and a fountain.

❸ On your right is the main train station, built in 1892 and at one time a major stop on the Orient Express. Across from the station is a statue of Tomislav, the first Croatian king (925–28), on horseback and wielding a sword. The statue, by Robert Mihanović, was placed here in 1947. Behind the statue, the lawns of Trg Kralja Tomislava stretch to the yellow Umjetnički Paviljon (Art Pavilion), which was built for the Millennium Exhibition in Budapest in 1896 before being dismantled and moved to Zagreb. Art exhibitions are still held

OUT AND ABOUT

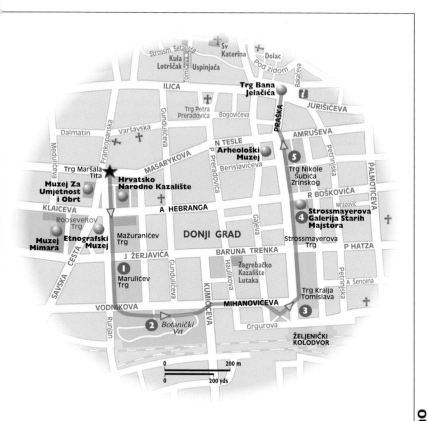

here and it also houses a famous restaurant, Paviljon (▷ 235).

Walk around the Art Pavilion and cross the main road to reach Strossmayerova Trg.

4 Strossmayerova Trg is named after Josip Strossmayer (1815–1905), the Bishop of Đakovo and an early campaigner for Croat-Serb unity. A statue of Strossmayer stands in the square, behind the Croatian Academy of Arts and Sciences. The building contains the Strossmayerova Galerija Starih Majstora (▷ 58) and the original Bašćanska Ploča (Baška Stone) from Krk, one of

the earliest examples of the Glagolitic script in Croatia.

Cross Ulica A Hebranga to arrive on Trg Nikole Šubića Zrinskog, known as Zrinjevac.

5 Founded as a cattle fair in 1826, Zrinjevac is Zagreb's favourite park, with fountains, tree-lined avenues and a bandstand. The benches around the park are popular trysting spots for courting couples. On the west side of the square is the Arheološki Muzej (▷ 50).

From the northwest corner of the square, a short walk along Ulica Praška leads to Trg Bana Jelačića.

WHERE TO EAT

Paviljon (▷ 235)

PLACES TO VISIT

Arheološki Muzej (▷ 50)

Botanički Vrt
Tel 01 484 4002
🕓 Jun–Sep Mon–Tue 9–2.30, Wed–Sun 9–7; Apr–May & Oct Mon–Tue 9–2.30, Wed–Sun 9–6
💲 Free

Etnografski Muzej (▷ 51)
Muzej Mimara (▷ 58)
Muzej Za Umjetnost i Obrt (▷ 58)
Strossmayerova Galerija Starih Majstora (▷ 58)

THROUGH THE ZAGORJE

The Zagorje region north of Zagreb is Croatia's little Switzerland, an enchanting land of alpine meadows, vineyards, castles and forested hills. This circuit of the region takes in all of the main sights and passes through some delightful rural scenery along the way.

THE DRIVE

Distance: 160km (100 miles)

Allow: 3-4 hours

Start/end: Donja Stubica

✚ 290 E2

★ Donja Stubica is on the main road from Marija Bistrica to Stubičke Toplice. Beside the parish church is an attractive park, with a bridge-spanned brook. The nearby spa town of Stubičke Toplice is in the foothills of Medvednica (▷ 56). A road from here leads to the summit of Sljeme and over the mountain to Zagreb.

Leave Donja Stubica in the direction of Stubičke Toplice. Reaching the town, follow the road round to the right and climb towards Oroslavje. Take the second exit at the roundabout (sign-posted Zabok and Kumrovec) and stay on this road as it passes beneath the Zagreb–Krapina highway, passing through a green valley before climbing to the village of Klanjec with views to your left.

❶ Klanjec sits on the east bank of the River Sutla, which forms a natural border between Croatia and Slovenia. The village was the birthplace of Antun Augustinčić (1900–79), who was a pupil of Ivan Meštrović. Augustinčić became the official

Our Lady of the Snows church, Marija Bistrica

Yugoslav state artist and his sculpture *Peace* stands outside the United Nations headquarters in New York. His works are displayed in a gallery and sculpture park off Klanjec's main square. Also here is a memorial to Antun Mihanović (1796–1861), author of the Croatian national anthem, *Lijepa Naša Domovino* (Our Beautiful Homeland).

Stay on this road as it drops down to the Sutla valley, running beside the river on its way to Kumrovec (▷ 65). Beyond Kumrovec, take the right fork just before the Slovenian border and keep on this minor road as it climbs to the hilltop village of Zagorska Sela, dominated by the mustard-coloured church of Sveta Katarina (St. Catherine). After passing

through Plavić, turn right in Miljana and continue until you see the castle of Veliki Tabor high on a hill to your left.

❷ Veliki Tabor (▷ 82) is worth a visit for the views across the Zagorje to all sides.

Continue to Desinić and turn left to Pregrada. Arriving in Pregrada, turn right towards Zagreb and stay on this road for 4km (2.5 miles) before taking a left turn towards Krapina beside Dvorac Bezanec hotel. The road rises and falls through the vineyards before snaking down the hillside to Krapina (▷ 80–83).

❸ A short detour to your left leads to the Museum of Evolution.

Cross the railway line and turn right, skirting the centre and following signs to Maribor (Slovenia). When you see the church ahead of you, turn right to climb to the highway and bridge above the town. Turn right here and stay on the main road, passing through tunnels (a new motorway is due to open by 2007). When you reach the Slovenian border, fork right onto a forest road which leads to Trakošćan.

❹ Trakošćan (▷ 80) has a museum and lake-side walks.

Turn right at Trakošćan and follow the Bednja valley to Lepoglava.

5 Lepoglava is notable for its fortress-like Pauline monastery, founded in 1400. The monks established Croatia's first grammar school in 1503. From 1854 to 2001 the monastery was a notorious prison, whose inmates included Tito and the future Croatian president Franjo Tuđman. In 2001 the monastery was returned to the church.

Turn right at the junction on the outskirts of Lepoglava and stay on this road as it criss-crosses the railway line

for the next 5km (3 miles), then turn left, following signs for Zlatar and Marija Bistrica. Pass through Zlatar and continue to Zlatar Bistrica. Arriving in Marija Bistrica (▷ 83), keep straight ahead to visit the town or fork right and turn right again to return to Donja Stubica.

WHERE TO EAT
Grešna Gorica (▷ 237)

PLACES TO VISIT

Galerija Augustinčić, Klanjec
Tel 049 550343
🕐 Apr–end Sep,daily 9–5; Oct–end Mar Tue–Sun 9–3
💰 Adult 20kn, child 10kn
www.mdc.hr/augustincic

Marija Bistrica (▷ 83)
Muzej Krapinskog Pračovjeka, Krapina (▷ 82)
Staro Selo, Kumrovec (▷ 65)
Trakošćan (▷ 80)
Veliki Tabor (▷ 82)

Religious items in Our lady of the Snows church (left)

ALONG THE RIVER AT OSIJEK

This walk links the 18th-century fortress at Tvrđa with the heart of modern Osijek in Gornji Grad. You walk one way along Europska Avenija, a grand boulevard lined with parks and art nouveau townhouses, then return along a pleasant riverside promenade.

THE WALK

Distance: 5km (3 miles)
Allow: 2 hours
Start/end: Trg Svetog Trojstva

HOW TO GET THERE

The Tvrđa district is situated 2km (1.2 miles) east of the centre. Tram No. 1 runs from Trg Ante Starčevića in front of the cathedral with a stop on Europska Avenija near Tvrđa.

★ Trg Svetog Trojstva (Holy Trinity Square) is the main square of Tvrđa. Originally known as Weinplatz because of the wine market that was held here, it has had many changes of name, reflecting the political upheavals of the last 200 years. It has variously been named after the Austrian emperor Franz Josef I, the Serbian Karađorđe dynasty and Tito's Partisan liberation movement. The column at the middle was erected in 1730 by the widow of a plague victim as a plea to God to deliver the people of Osijek from an epidemic that was sweeping the town. Among the fine Austro-Hungarian buildings surrounding the square is the former City Guard in the northwest corner, with its distinctive clock tower and ground-floor arcades.
 Begin by taking the street alongside the City Guard, which leads to the church of Sveti Mihovil (St. Michael).

The baroque bell tower of St. Michael's church in Osijek

❶ The parish church of St. Michael, with its twin onion-domed spires and restored yellow façade, stands out among the war-damaged buildings of Tvrđa. It was begun in 1704 on the site of the old Turkish mosque, though the present church dates from 1725.

Follow the road to the left in front of the church, and turn right on Kuhačeva to emerge by a park.

❷ Perivoj Kralja Tomislava (King Tomislav Park) was laid out in the 18th century. On your left, notice a small section of Turkish wall, the only remains of the Ottoman fortifications that once encircled Tvrđa.

Walk across the park to arrive on Europska Avenija and continue along the pavement. At the junction with Ulica Kardinala Alozija Stepinca, cross to the other side of the road to admire the triangular 1912 Post Office building.

❸ The next stretch of Europska Avenija is lined with fine houses built in the Viennese Secession style, an Austrian equivalent of art nouveau, in the first years of the 20th century for wealthy German, Austrian and Hungarian industrialists. Look out for details such as sculpted angels on the pastel-coloured, stuccoed façades.

Continue along the southern side of Europska Avenija, passing the Galerija Likovnih Umjetnosti (▷ 69). Cross back to the northern side at the next junction with Ulica Stjepana Radića (Radićeva).

❹ Kino Urania, on the right, is a Viennese Secession-style cinema, opened in 1912 and still in use. In front of the cinema, a pair of stone sphinxes marks the entrance to Šetalište Petar Preradovića, a small park promenade lined with busts of local notables. The park ends at another cinema, Kino Europa, in a 1939 modernist building.

Keep straight ahead on the pedestrian shopping street Kapucinska to arrive at Trg Ante Starčevića, the large open square in front of the parish church.

5 The enormous Gothic red-brick church of Sv Petra i Pavla (Ss Peter and Paul) is universally referred to as the cathedral, though in fact it does not have cathedral status.

Turn right here and walk down to the Zimska Luka (winter harbour). When you reach the river, turn right and follow the riverside promenade past Hotel Osijek until you come to a footbridge across the Drava.

6 This elegant suspension bridge, built in 1980, managed to survive the 1991–5 war. Its total span is 210m (690ft) and the pylons have a height of 30m (100ft). The bridge was built to connect the city centre with the Copacabana summer recreation area on the north bank. On both sides of the river are promenades.

From here you have a choice. For a short walk, keep straight ahead along the south bank and take the footpath to your right at the end of the park to return to Tvrđa. For a longer walk, cross the footbridge and follow the Drava's north bank, passing Copacabana beach club with views of Tvrđa across the river. Climb the steps to the road bridge, walk across, and descend the steps to the south bank and take the riverside path to enter Tvrđa via Vodena Vrata (Water Gate), the only surviving gateway to the fortress.

WHERE TO EAT
Mirna Luka (▷ 236–237)

PLACES TO VISIT
Galerija Likovnih Umjetnosti (▷ 69)
Muzej Slavonije (▷ 68–69)

Mirna Luka floating restaurant, Osijek (above)

The fountain and plague monument in the Tvrđa district of Osijek (left)

OUT AND ABOUT

HILL TOWNS OF ISTRIA

Take a day out from the coast to explore the Istrian interior, with its vineyards, olive groves, oak woods and medieval hilltop towns. This gentle circuit forms a figure-of-eight around Motovun, so it is easy to divide it into two shorter loops.

THE DRIVE

Distance: 112km (70 miles)
Allow: 2.5 hours
Start/end: Buzet
✠ 294 B4

★ Buzet (▷ 85), perched on a hill above the River Mirna, is still partly surrounded by its medieval walls. Most residents live in the modern district of Fontana.

Begin by the roundabout in Trg Fontana, at the foot of the old town. With Hotel Fontana to your right, follow the road out of town and turn right towards Buje. Stay on this wide road as it winds its way through the Mirna valley, bypassing the spa town of Istarske Toplice. After 12km (7.5 miles) you get your first glimpse of Motovun on its hill. Continue for another 4km (2.5 miles) to a crossroads. For the shorter drive, turn left here.

❶ The oak forests around the Mirna valley are where Istria's truffles are found. The village of Livade, 1km (0.5 miles) to the right, is home to the celebrated Zigante Tartufi restaurant (▷ 240).

For the longer drive, turn right at the crossroads, pass through Livade and stay on this road as it climbs high above the valley with dizzying views as you ascend to Oprtalj.

A medieval cart track, now lined with trees

❷ Oprtalj (Portole), first mentioned in 1102, was built on the ruins of a prehistoric fort. This small town occupies a spectacular position, with views over the vineyards from the terrace and the rampart walk. The chapels at either end of the town are decorated with frescoes, sadly in a poor state of repair. The 17th-century loggia contains a lapidarium of ancient sculpture, including a winged lion of St. Mark.

Drive through Oprtalj and continue for 1km, then turn left in Sveta Lucija and follow this minor road all the way to Buje.

❸ Buje (▷ 85) is Istria's largest hill town with a strategic position. Under Venetian rule, it was known as 'the watchtower of Istria'.

On the outskirts of Buje, turn left and left again to arrive at a crossroads. Turn right here if you want to visit the town; otherwise turn left and stay on this road for 7km (4.5 miles) to Grožnjan.

❹ Grožnjan (▷ 88) is a lovely hilltop town with cobbled streets and artists' studios.

Leaving Grožnjan, continue for 5km (3 miles) on a dirt track that drops back down to the main road. At the end of the track, turn left and shortly afterwards turn left again to return to the Motovun crossroads. Now turn right across the bridge over the Mirna. The road climbs in a series of bends to reach the car park at the foot of Motovun (▷ 90).

❺ Leave your car here and climb to Motovun, or pay a toll in summer to drive up the hill.

Stay on this road as it crosses typical Istrian countryside, keeping straight on at a roundabout in the direction of Pazin. About 12km (7.5 miles) out of Motovun, you skirt a crest and see the village of Beram below, with the slopes of Mount Učka rising in the distance. Reaching a main road, turn left towards Pazin to arrive at Beram.

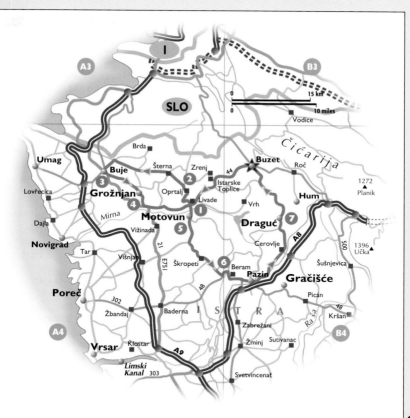

6 Beram is known for its macabre frescoes, a 15th-century Dance of the Dead with skeletons, musicians and medieval court jesters. The frescoes are on the walls of the chapel of the Virgin Mary on Škriline, around 1km outside the village.

The road now continues to Pazin (▷ 91). Keep straight ahead at a roundabout and turn left at a junction to drive through the town. Leaving Pazin, keep left, following signs to Buzet to emerge on a straight road with Mount Učka looming up ahead of you. After 8km (5 miles) you reach Cerovlje. Turn left immediately before the railway tracks and turn left again, signposted

Buzet and Draguć. The road climbs to Kovačići, where a magnificent vista opens up, across the vineyards to Draguć with the whole of central Istria spread out beneath you. After another 2km (1.2 miles) you reach Draguć.

7 Draguć (▷ 88) is an attractive village, dramatically perched on a cliff. Walk to the far end of the village to see the frescoes in the tiny chapel of St. Roch.

Stay on this road as it rises and falls through a succession of rural villages, with views of the Čićarija mountain ridge to the right and glimpses of Lake Butoniga to your left on the way back to Buzet.

A rock statue in front of the fortified hill town of Buzet

WHERE TO EAT
Barbacan (▷ 240)
Zigante Tartufi (▷ 240)

PLACE TO VISIT

The chapel at Beram is usually kept locked. To see the frescoes, contact the keyholders (tel 052 622088 or 052 622444).

THE GOLDEN CAPE AT ROVINJ

This short, easy walk explores Zlatni Rt forest park, where shady paths lead along the shore to rock and pebble beaches. To make a day of it, take a picnic and swimsuit, or rent bicycles to explore the park in depth.

THE WALK

Distance: 3km (2 miles)

Allow: 1 hour

Start/end: Zlatni Rt forest park (Park Šume Zlatni Rt), Rovinj

✚ 294 A4

HOW TO GET THERE

From the centre of Rovinj, follow the seafront path past the Delfin jetty and marina and continue walking along the shore. The entrance to Zlatni Rt is found beyond Uvala Lone, a small cove at the back of Hotel Eden.

Walking along a footpath in the Zlatni Rt forest park

★ Zlatni Rt (Golden Cape) forest park was laid out by Baron Georg Huetterott (1852–1910) after he purchased the peninsula and the nearby islands in 1890. A successful industrialist from Trieste, he was knighted by the Austrian emperor Franz Josef I in 1898. He planted the cape with trees such as holm oak, cedar, cypress and Aleppo pine, and created paths and walkways for his visitors to enjoy. Huetterott had ambitious plans for this area. In a booklet published in 1908, he sang the praises of the Istrian coastline, which he called the Costa del Sole (Sunny Coast) and outlined his vision of a spa resort to match Brijuni (▷ 86–87) and Opatija (▷ 107). He set up a company to build hotels and villas on Zlatni Rt, but his death in 1910 meant that the plans

were never carried out. Since 1948, the cape has been owned by the state as a protected nature reserve.

Walk through the entrance gates and keep to the right on a path which follows the shore. In summer, this area is crowded with visitors sunbathing on the popular Lone beach. Reaching the end of a long, flat section, the path divides at a point where you have a fine view of Rovinj straight ahead. The right fork leads to a small beach and jetty; instead, keep left to climb to the top of a hill.

❶ This is Zlatni Rt (Golden Cape), also known in Italian as Punta Montauro. The cliffs to your left, part of a former Venetian stone quarry, are used for free climbing.

Walk over the hill and back down towards the sea, with views of Crveni Otok (Red Island) through the trees. The landscape becomes greener, with stone pine, tamarisk and cypress trees around a pretty garden. At a junction of paths beside a summer café, turn right to keep to the coast.

❷ The path now rounds Punta Corrente, the Italian name for all of Zlatni Rt. Just across the water, Crveni Otok (Red Island) was the summer home of Georg Huetterott, where his guests included Habsburg princes and princesses and the Austrian archduke Franz Ferdinand. The castle which he built on the site of an old monastery is now part of the Hotel Istra. The restaurant at Punta Corrente is housed in the old stone stables, formerly used by Georg Huetterott for his horses while he visited the island.

Stay on the seaside path beyond Punta Corrente as it passes a series of rocky coves. The beaches here are much less crowded than those nearer Rovinj and they tend to attract nudists. Reaching a viewpoint with a bench beneath the trees looking out to Crveni Otok, the path divides once again, with

OUT AND ABOUT

the right fork continuing along the shore to Škaraba Bay. Turn left here to leave the sea behind and follow the path uphill to reach a large meadow. Walk around the meadow, turn right at a junction of paths, then right again on a wide track through the forest to return to the park entrance.

❸ Shortly before leaving the park, you pass a small pink-painted cottage on your right. This is the Huetterott memorial room, opened in 2003 in the old forest ranger's house. There is memorabilia relating to Georg Huetterott.

From the entrance gates, it is an easy walk back to Rovinj.

WHERE TO EAT

The restaurant at Punta Corrente is open in summer. Alternatively, buy picnic provisions from the market in Rovinj.

PLACE TO VISIT
Huetterott Memorial Room
🕐 Jun–end Sep daily 9–7
🖐 Free

IN MORE DEPTH

If you want to ride rather than walk, you can rent bicycles from Vetura (tel 052 816012) at the Delfin jetty and bicycle into the forest park from there.

OUT AND ABOUT

Boats moored at Rovinj on the Zlatni Rt park coast (top)

A tranquil forested area in the park (above)

Taking a leisurely stroll along a footpath in the park (right)

AROUND KRK ISLAND

There is more to Croatia's largest island than an old Roman capital and a splendid beach. On this circuit of the island you will explore hilltop towns and villages and visit the site where the famous Baška Stone was discovered.

THE DRIVE

Distance: 77km (48 miles)

Allow: 2 hours

Start/end: Baška

✚ 294 C5

★ Baška is best known for its superb beach, which stretches for nearly 2km (1.2 miles) around the bay. In summer this is a lively holiday resort, but in winter it is almost deserted and the coast is exposed to the biting *bora* wind. Alongside the modern hotels and apartments the old town survives virtually unscathed, with stone houses and narrow lanes set just back from the harbour.

Leave Baška by taking the main road across the island in the direction of Krk Town. After 2km you come to the village of Jurandvor.

❶ Jurandvor is the setting for the early Romanesque church of Sveta Lucije (St. Lucy), where the Bašćanska Ploča (Baška Stone) was discovered in the floor of the church by the local priest in 1851. This limestone tablet, measuring 2m (6.5ft) in length and 1m (3.3ft) in height, contains one of the oldest examples of the Glagolitic script (▷ 19), dating from the 11th century and recording a donation of land from King Zvonimir to the parish. This is the earliest recorded mention of

The Cathedral of the Assumption of Mary, Krk

a Croatian king and the first known use of the word Croatian. The original stone is kept in the lobby of the Strossmayerova Galerija (▷ 58) in Zagreb, but a reproduction is on display inside the church.

Continue along the main road through the village of Draga Bašćanska before climbing through a part rocky, part forested landscape. Eventually you crest a summit with panoramic views of Krk and Cres spread out beneath you and the Gorski Kotar mountain range visible on the horizon. Shortly afterwards, there is a magnificent view of the monastery

islet of Košljun (▷ 105) to your left, set in a sheltered bay. Turn right at the next junction, signposted Šilo and Vrbnik, and follow this road as it drops gently towards the coast before reaching the vineyards which signal the entrance to the wine town of Vrbnik.

❷ Vrbnik stands on a cliff, 48m (157ft) above the sea. You can park your car outside the centre and stroll through the cobbled streets before taking the steps down to the small harbour. Vrbnik is known throughout Croatia for its dry white Zlahtina wine, which you can buy at the Katunar winery at the entrance to the town (▷ 187).

Leaving Vrbnik, turn right, following signs to Dobrinj. The road soon leaves the vineyards behind and winds uphill through forest to Risika. Reaching a crossroads, turn left through the village of Sveti Vid to arrive at Dobrinj.

❸ Dobrinj is the only town on Krk to be located away from the sea. It is first mentioned in a Glagolitic script dated 1 January 1100. Although it has a population of just over 100, this tiny village is buzzing in summer, with art galleries, concerts

OUT AND ABOUT

and museums of ethnography and sacred art. You can drive as far as the church square to explore the village on foot. From the garden above the square and from the terrace of the bell tower there are wide-ranging views which take in Rijeka, Opatija, Mount Učka and the Gorski Kotar mountains.

The road now crosses the island from east to west, passing over the main road from Krk to Rijeka and dropping down to the coast at Malinska.

❹ Malinska is a busy summer resort, set in a wide bay fringed with pine woods and beaches. The walk around the harbour makes a pleasant stroll, letting you admire the yachts and the chapel of Sveti Nikola (St. Nicholas), built in 2000 on the harbour square with a striking stone-carved altar of Christ and his apostles.

Drive through the centre of Malinska, passing the harbour and climbing out of the village to return to the main road. Follow signs towards Krk until you reach a junction, where you should turn right towards the ferry port at Valbiska. After 8km (5 miles), you come to a crossroads. Turn left here, signposted to Bajčići and Vrh.

❺ A right turn at the crossroads leads to Poljica and one of the most atmospheric restaurants in Croatia, Tri Maruna (▷ 241).

Stay on this minor road for 5km (3 miles) to Vrh. Turn right and then left, following signs to Krk. On the outskirts of Krk (▷ 105), turn right and drive down to the harbour if you want to explore the town, or turn left to return directly to Baška.

(▷ 241).

A spectacular view of the Franciscan monastery on the islet of Košljun (below and bottom)

OUT AND ABOUT

WHERE TO EAT
Nada (tel 051 857065) serves excellent food and wine on a clifftop terrace in Vrbnik, but for good-value home cooking it's hard to beat Tri Maruna at Poljica (▷ 241).

PLACE TO VISIT
Crkva Sveta Lucije, Jurandvor
Tel 051 221018
🕐 Apr–end Oct, daily 9.30–5.30
💰 Adult 15kn, child (10–15) 7kn

VULTURES ON CRES

Keep an eye out for griffon vultures and other birds of prey on a well-marked eco-trail through the landscapes of the Tramuntana region of northern Cres. The path is steep and rocky in places, so you will need good walking shoes.

THE WALK

Distance: 10km (6 miles)
Allow: 3–4 hours
Start/end: Caput Insulae
eco-centre, Beli
✚ 294 B4

HOW TO GET THERE

Follow the signs to Beli and Caput Insulae from the main Porozina to Cres road, 13km (8 miles) north of Cres. The eco-centre is signposted up a hill to your left, just before you enter the village.

★ Caput Insulae eco-centre is housed in a former primary school, built 1929 and closed in 1980 as a result of depopulation. There are two permanent exhibitions, one on the history of Beli and the other on the ecology of Cres and Lošinj. Behind the centre is a sanctuary for injured griffon vultures, including young birds who have fallen into the sea while learning to fly. Around 60 pairs of griffon vultures nest on the nearby cliffs, along with golden eagles, buzzards, peregrines and eagle owls. Before doing the walk, pick up a copy of the excellent book *Tramuntana...through ancient forest...return to yourself* (100kn), which gives background information on fauna, flora, folklore and traditional architecture as well as maps and descriptions of the sculptures on the trail.
   There are several marked trails around Beli

A griffon vulture on Cres

but this follows the trail 'History and Art in Nature', which is waymarked with red and white circles. Walk downhill from the eco-centre and turn left onto a stony path between dry-stone walls.

❶ A stone sculpture beside the path portrays a *crkvica*, a small chapel similar to those once built by shepherds. This is one of 20 sculptures along the trail by the artist Ljubo de Karina, engraved with verses by local poet Andro Vid Mihičić (1896–1992): 'When I arrived in Beli it was dark...gorges and glens full of ghosts, the sea full of stars and the sky full of deep secrets.'

Turn right at a junction, marked by a sculpture of a white stone cross, traditionally placed at a crossroads as a protection from evil fairies known as

kudlaci. Reaching a road, turn left to the village. Almost immediately, follow the red and white waymarks to drop down to your right beside olive grove terraces. Turn right at the foot of the slope to cross a bridge across the Potok stream.

❷ The single-arched bridge dates from Roman times and was probably built in the first century AD. The name Caput Insulae (Latin for 'head of the island') also dates from this time, when Beli was a fortified Roman settlement on the site of a Liburnian hilltop fortress.

Keep to the wide path as it climbs gently above the stream, at first with views of Beli to your left. Eventually you reach the old Roman road. Cross straight over the road and continue to climb through forests of oak, hornbeam and chestnut, with sea views opening up as you ascend. This is the steepest section of the walk. The track becomes less clear as you head into the woods, so use the waymarks as your guide.

❸ Reaching a plateau, you will see the Kirinići meadow to your right. The maze here was constructed out of 3,000 stones and is a larger version of a labyrinth from

OUT AND ABOUT

Chartres cathedral in France. It is dedicated to Vesna, the ancient Slavic goddess of spring.

After passing a ruined cottage, bear right to join a wide track. Stay on this path for about 3km (2 miles) as it passes through oak woods, meadows, sheep pastures and dry-stone walls. When the blue route crosses the path, keep straight ahead, but at the next junction, where the two trails briefly join, turn right. After a few minutes, turn left to leave the blue route and head into the woods (signposted Jama Čampari).

4 The karst scenery of the Tramuntana is riddled with sinkholes, fissures and caves. It is possible to go into the Čampari cave (known locally as Banic cave), which is 101m (331ft) deep, though access is only recommended for experienced potholers (cavers). A rope is provided at the entrance and a torch (flashlight) is essential. Skeletons of brown bears more than 12,000 years old have been discovered in the cave and there is also evidence of prehistoric humans in the form of pottery and the bones of domesticated dogs.

Follow the waymarks as the path drops steeply through the forest before turning right onto a clearly defined track which drops down towards Beli. The village appears beneath you as a jumble of brown and white houses perched on a cliff, over-looking a small harbour.

5 Beli has been inhab-ited for about 4,000 years and probably takes its name from a Celtic god or king. In the Middle Ages, it was an independent commune that paid tribute to the Venetian doge in exchange for its free-dom. At one time, Beli had a population of more than 1,000 but now only about 30 people live in the village.

Stay on this path to return to the eco-centre.

WHERE TO EAT
Pansion Tramuntana (tel 051 840519), beside the eco-centre, offers simple meals and drinks. There are no facilities on the walk so you should take plenty of drinking water with you.

PLACE TO VISIT
Eko-centar Caput Insulae
Tel 051 840525
🕐 16 Jan–14 Dec daily 9–7
💰 Adult 25kn, child 10kn, family 60kn
www.caput-insulae.com

Visitors at the Caput Insulae eco-centre (above)

A sign for the eco-centre (top)

LOŠINJ COAST PATH

The island of Lošinj has an extensive network of footpaths, including this delightful coastal promenade connecting the two main towns. If you are lucky, you may be able to spot dolphins playing in the clear waters just offshore.

THE WALK

Distance: 7km (4.5 miles)
Allow: 2 hours
Start: Mali Lošinj
✚ 294 C6
End: Rovenska

HOW TO GET THERE

Trg Republike Hrvatske is the harbourside square at the heart of Mali Lošinj, a short walk from the bus stop and ferry port.

Boats moored in the harbour at Mali Lošinj

★ With a population of 7,000, Mali Lošinj is the biggest settlement on any of Croatia's Adriatic islands. Set in a sheltered bay surrounded by pastel-coloured houses, the town has a real buzz on summer evenings, when the people come out to stroll around the harbour and the promenade cafés are bursting with life. Mali Lošinj grew prosperous in the 18th century on the shipping trade, with many of its sea captains returning to build grand villas by the sea. The first tourist society was formed here in 1866 and in the late 19th century the town promoted itself as a health resort for the Austro-Hungarian aristocracy.

Start at Trg Republike Hrvatske, the triangular piazza by the harbour, and walk along Riva Lošinjskih Kapetana, the promenade on the northern side of the bay. After passing the tourist office and ferry port, follow the road out of town as it climbs to a busy junction at Kadinj.

Cross the main road carefully and look for the start of the coast path – for most of its route it is an asphalted promenade clinging to the shore. Stay on this path as it makes a circuit of the Bojčić peninsula before arriving at the pretty cove of Sveti Martin.

❶ Sveti Martin is the original nucleus of Mali Lošinj, founded when farmers settled here in the 12th century. The church dates from 1450 and the town cemetery is also situated here.

After visiting the church, leave the coast behind to climb uphill on Ulica Sveti Martin. Reaching the main road, turn left and walk for around 100m (110yd) to arrive at a junction. When you see Veli Lošinj signposted to the left, take the steps down to Valdarke bay to rejoin the coast path.

❷ The path now follows the shore all the way to Veli Lošinj, passing the small cove of Valeškura and continuing as far as Hotel Punta. This is the best section of the route for observing bottlenose dolphins, around 150 of which inhabit the coastal waters around Cres and Lošinj now the Lošinj Dolphin Reserve.

Walk through the grounds of Hotel Punta and follow the path downhill with views over Veli Lošinj.

❸ Veli Lošinj used to be the main town on the island (*veli* means large, *mali* means small) but it has long been eclipsed by its neighbour and now has a population of under a thousand. This is a charming spot, with pastel façades set around a narrow harbour guarded by

OUT AND ABOUT

the 18th-century baroque church of Sveti Antun (St. Antony). The bell-tower is 15th-century Venetian, as is the circular defence tower above the harbour which now houses a museum and art gallery. The star exhibit is a copy of Apoxyomenos, a 4th-century BC lifesize bronze statue of a Greek athlete discovered in the sea at Veli Lošinj in 1999. Also at Veli Lošinj, you can visit the Blue World dolphin research centre (▷ 187) to learn about the lives of these remarkable creatures.

Arriving at the harbour in Veli Lošinj, take the steps down to the waterfront. From here, walk around the bay, climbing to St. Antony's church. Behind the church is the grave-yard, where you can pick up the coast path to Rovenska.

❹ Rovenska is a pretty fishing harbour shel-tered by a breakwater, built to protect the boats from the effects of the harsh *bora* wind. The foundation stone was laid by the Austrian archduke Maximilian in 1856. These days, it is a popular spot for lunch,

and a good place to end your walk, sitting by the harbour eating fresh fish and watching the fisher-men mending their nets and repairing their boats.

You can return to Mali Lošinj the same way, or pick up a taxi or bus from the main road at Veli Lošinj. If you are walking, retrace your route as far as the steps above Valdarke bay, then cross over the main road and take Ulica Braće Vidulića downhill to return to Trg Republike Hrvatske.

The quayside promenade at Mali Lošinj (below)

WHEN TO GO

This walk is pleasant at any time of year, but you stand the best chance of seeing dolphins between October and May as they are driven further out to sea during the summer tourist season by excursion boats and yachts.

WHERE TO EAT

Sirius (tel 051 236399), the fish restaurant by the harbour at Rovenska, is open daily from April to the end of October.

TOURIST INFORMATION

Riva Lošinjskih Kapetana, Mali Lošinj
Tel 051 231884
www.tz-malilosinj.hr

PLACE TO VISIT

Blue World
Tel 051 604666
🕓 May & Oct Mon–Fri 9–4, Sat 9–2; Jun–Sep daily 9–1, 6–8; Jul & Aug daily 9–1, 6–10; Nov–Apr Mon–Fri 10–1
✋ Adult 10kn, child (6–10) 7kn
www.blue-world.org

OFF THE BEATEN TRACK IN BRAČ

See another side to this busy holiday island by renting a car for a circuit of its north and west. Along the way, you will pass beaches, bays, historic towns and villages, and the quarries that are the source of the famous Brač stone.

THE DRIVE

Distance: 68km (42 miles)
Allow: 1.5 hours
Start/end: Supetar
✚ 297 F8

★ Supetar is the largest town on Brač and the administrative centre of the island, having taken over from the Venetian capital Nerežišća in 1815. It takes its name from a 6th-century early Christian basilica of Sveti Petar (St. Peter), though the modern town only developed in the 16th century as the harbour for Nerežišća. With hourly ferries to Split in summer and many people from the mainland having holiday homes here, Supetar feels much bigger than its population of 4,000 would suggest.

Leave Supetar in the direction of Sutivan and follow the coast road, with views across the water to Split. After 7km (4.5 miles) you will see Sutivan on the right, dominated by the onion dome of its church. The road now swings inland, passing between olive groves and dry-stone walls with the island of Šolta to your right. After another 6km (4 miles), you reach Ložišća, dramatically situated at the head of a gorge. Drive carefully through the narrow main street of the village.

❶ Ložišća also has an onion-domed church, designed by Supetar

Detail of a fishing boat tied up at Bol harbour on Brač

artist Ivan Rendić (1849–1932) and typical of Brač. Beyond the church, the main road continues down into the valley to the sheltered harbour at Milna, with stone houses on the Riva promenade. The marina is popular with yachtsmen in summer.

Turn left just beyond the church to climb a hill out of the village.

❷ The road from Ložišća to Nerežišća clings to a narrow ridge with heaps of stones piled up in the fields to either side. Some of these have been fashioned into sheep shelters or stone walls, but most have simply been moved to clear space for agriculture. Between Dračevica and Donji Humac you pass a limestone quarry where marble is still produced.

Continue to a junction with Nerežišća visible on a hill to your right. Keep straight ahead and turn right at the next T-junction, staying on the main road and skirting Nerežišća as the road bends left.

❸ Nerežišća was the island capital during the period of Venetian rule. The former governor's palace stands here, along with a Venetian loggia adorned with the winged lion of St. Mark, symbol of the Venetian republic.

The road now climbs in a dizzying series of bends to arrive at the access road for Vidova Gora.

❹ Vidova Gora (778m/2,552ft) is the highest peak on any of the Croatian islands. An easy detour of 5km (3 miles) on an asphalt road leads to the summit, marked by a white stone cross.

The main road continues across the island to Pražnica. Turn left here, signposted to Pučišća. Stay on this road for 7km (4.5 miles) as it drops down towards the sea before travelling through a fertile valley of vineyards to Pučišća.

❺ The harbourside village of Pučišća is the source of the best Brač

OUT AND ABOUT

stone and was once the chief export port for the marble used in Diocletian's palace in Split. The houses here are even whiter than elsewhere and there are stone sculptures throughout the village. A stone-carving school stands on the bay, facing the Palača Dešković hotel (▷ 212).

Turn left at Pučišća and follow the coast road back to Supetar. The road climbs at first and clings to the cliffs high above the coast before dropping back down to sea level at Postira and Splitska.

6 From Splitska it is possible to make a short detour inland to the village of Škrip, the oldest settlement on the island and home to the Museum of Brač (▷ 115).

Stay on the coast road as it passes pine woods and shingle beaches on its way back to Supetar.

WHERE TO EAT

The restaurant on the summit of Vidova Gora (tel 021 549061) is open between April and October, offering hearty plates of Dalmatian ham and cheese and roast Brač lamb.

The gorgeous Zlatni Rat beach, Brač; Stipančići deserted village; yachts moored off Zlatni Rat beach; bicycling on the road to Dragon's Cave, near Murvica, on Brač (top to bottom)

AROUND MOUNT BIOKOVO

This half-day tour begins on the coast before heading inland to make a circuit of Croatia's third highest mountain. With pebble beaches, rugged limestone peaks and the dramatic Cetina gorge, it makes a good introduction to the varied landscapes of central Dalmatia.

THE DRIVE

Distance: 148km (92 miles)
Allow: 3–4 hours
Start/end: Omiš
✚ 297 G8

★ Omiš is at the mouth of the River Cetina, which rises near the Bosnian border in the foothills of Mount Dinara and carves a steep valley down to the coast before emptying into the sea through the Cetina gorge. In summer there are rafting trips through the gorge (▷ 191) as well as canoe hire and fishing excursions.

From the bridge at the mouth of the Cetina, head south on the Magistrala coastal highway with views of the limestone massif of Mount Biokovo up ahead. Shortly after Pisak, the final town on the Omiš riviera, the road rounds a huge bay and continues on the Makarska riviera to Brela.

❶ Brela is the most attractive of the Makarska riviera resorts. In 2003 the influential American business magazine *Forbes* rated Punta Rata as the most beautiful beach in Europe and one of the top ten beaches in the world.

Turn right off Magistrala to drop down to Brela through the pine woods. Drive through the village and continue on a narrow road beside the beach to

A scenic view of Makarska below Mount Biokovo

the neighbouring resort of Baška Voda, where you turn inland to rejoin the Magistrala. Turn right and drive towards Makarska.

❷ Makarska (▷ 127) is the main town of the Makarska riviera, set around a horseshoe bay at the foot of Mount Biokovo. It is also the departure port for ferries to Sumartin on Brač.

Continue on the coastal highway, bypassing Makarska, or follow signs to explore the town. When you reach the southern outskirts of Makarska, turn left on a road which is signposted to Vrgorac. The road climbs steeply through the village of Gornje Tučepi, offering spectacular views over the islands and coast. After 6km (4 miles) you reach the entrance to Biokovo Nature Park.

❸ The summit of Biokovo at Sveti Jure (1,762m/5,781ft) is the highest point on the Croatian coast. From the park entrance, a road twists for 23km (14 miles) up to the TV tower at the summit. From April to October you pay a fee to visit the park. If you drive to the summit, allow at least an extra hour each way, and do not attempt it in winter or in difficult conditions. On a clear day, you can see Monte Gargano in Italy, more than 200km (125 miles) away.

The road to Vrgorac continues around the edge of the mountain, crossing a stark limestone landscape on its way to Ravča.

❹ From Ravča you can make a detour of 6km (4 miles) each way to the wine town of Vrgorac.

Turn left at Ravča and stay on this road for 48km (30 miles) to arrive at Šestanovac.

❺ The landward-facing slopes of Podbiokovo are much greener than the rugged limestone face of Mount Biokovo as seen from the sea. On this side of the mountain, the greater snow and rainfall produces a gentler landscape, the karst fields interspersed with vineyards,

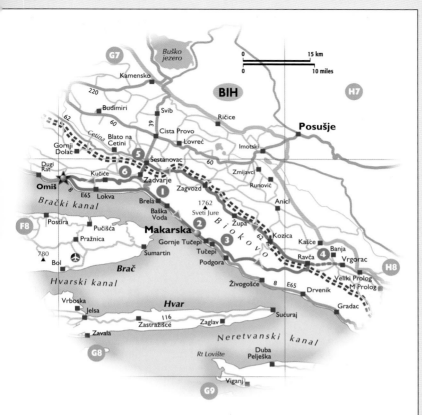

strawberry plantations and rural villages.

Turn left at the crossroads in Šestanovac and drive through Zadvarje. Just beyond the village is a huge crucifix at a viewpoint overlooking the Cetina. Shortly after, take the right fork to drop down to the river beside the Kraljevac hydroelectric plant.

⑥ The nearby waterfall and village of Slime is the start point for rafting trips through the gorge.

Stay on this road as it climbs to Kučiće before returning to the river at Radmanove Mlinice. From here, the road clings to the banks of the river as it carves through a dramatic canyon on its way to Omiš.

The Makarska riviera against the backdrop of Mount Biokovo

WHERE TO EAT
Jeny (tel 021 623704), in the village of Gornje Tučepi, offers creative Dalmatian dishes on a summer terrace high above the sea. Radmanove Mlinice (tel 021 862073), in an old mill beside the river Cetina, serves local trout, frogs and eels as well as roast and grilled meat. Both are open from April to October.

PLACE TO VISIT
Park Prirode Biokovo (Biokovo Nature Park)
Tel 021 625136
🕐 Apr–15 May and Oct daily 8–4; 16 May–end Sep daily 7am–8pm
💰 20kn
www.biokovo.com

ON SPLIT'S GREEN HILL

A walk on the wooded Marjan peninsula offers wonderful views over Split, with the islands of Brač, Hvar and Šolta shimmering offshore. This is where the people of Split come on weekend afternoons to escape the bustle and traffic-filled streets of the city.

THE WALK

Distance: 5.5km (3.5 miles)
Allow: 2 hours
Start/end: Trg Franje Tuđmana, Split

HOW TO GET THERE

Walk west along the waterfront Riva from Diocletian's palace. Trg Franje Tuđmana is the small square with a fountain at the centre, situated at the western end of the Riva beneath the steps leading to Trg Republike.

★ The walk starts at the entrance to the Veli Varoš quarter, once a separate district of artisans and fishermen and still one of the most attractive parts of the city, with its traditional stone houses and cobbled streets.

With the Riva behind you, begin by taking the road to the right of the Franciscan monastery church of Sveti Frane. The street is called Šperun at first but soon narrows and becomes Ulica Senjska. Climb the steps at the top of the lane to arrive at Café Vidilica.

❶ Café Vidilica is a popular meeting-point, particularly on summer evenings when people gather here for drinks on the terrace overlooking the port. A shady garden behind the café contains the remains of a 16th-century Jewish cemetery.

Cross over the parking area, walk through a gate

The distinctive emblem of the Hajduk Split soccer team

and continue to climb. The steps end at a road in front of a small zoo. Turn left here, stay on the road and after 200m (220yd) turn left again on the road to the summit. Look for a footpath beside the road to the left; this soon becomes a long flight of stone steps leading to Telegrin.

❷ Telegrin (178m/584ft) is the highest point on the Marjan peninsula and is marked by the inevitable Croatian flag. From the raised terrace, there are views out to sea and over the port. To one side, there is a bird's-eye view of Poljud stadium, home of soccer giants Hajduk Split, while to the north the views stretch along the coast as far as Trogir. The islands of Brač, Hvar and Šolta are clearly visible, and on fine days you should be able to make out the island of Vis in the distance.

Take the steps down on the far side of the terrace. Keep straight ahead on Marjanski Put and look for a sign on the left pointing to *Špomenik Đirometa*. Take this path as it leads through woods of pine and holm oak, with glimpses of the sea through the trees.

❸ After 350m (385yd) you pass a memorial to Professor Umberto Girometta (1883–1939), a distinguished archaeologist, speleologist and mountaineer.

Continue on this path as it climbs briefly to a summit then drops down to rejoin the road at a junction.

❹ The Marjan peninsula is believed to take its name from a Roman landowner, Marin. It has long been considered a sacred place; during the 15th century, hermits built caves and chapels on its southern slopes.

Turn right at the junction to visit two of these hermitages. Keep to the shore road to arrive first at the 14th-century chapel of Betlem and then the 15th-century chapel of Sveti Jere (St. Hieronymus), with caves built into the cliff face above the church. It is reached by taking a path to the right at a 180-degree bend in

OUT AND ABOUT

the road. Return to the junction and keep straight ahead along Šetalište Alberta Marangunića, on a gravel path which clings to the shore, offering fine views out to sea.

5 Towards the end of the walk, you pass the 13th-century chapel of Sveti Nikole (St. Nicholas), with its separate sloping belfry.

The path now becomes paved and drops steeply back down to Café Vidilica. Take the staircase to the right of the café terrace to reach the waterfront and turn left to return to Trg Franje Tuđmana.

Harbourfront Split (right) and Hajduk Split soccer stadium (below)

WHERE TO EAT

There are no restaurants on Marjan, so save your appetite for a meal at Konoba Hvaranin (▷ 244) or Konoba Varoš, two traditional restaurants in the Veli Varoš quarter near the end of the walk.

PLACE TO VISIT

Split Zoo
Kolombatićevo Šetalište 2
Tel 021 394525
🕐 Daily 8–6 in summer, 8–4 in winter
🎟 Adult 8kn, child 4kn

TOURIST INFORMATION

Peristil
Tel 021 345606
The tourist office on the Riva can issue a map of the city which includes the paths on the Marjan peninsula.

OUT AND ABOUT

IN AND OUT OF DUBROVNIK

Lying outside the city walls in the shadow of Lovrijenac fortress, Pile is the forgotten corner of Dubrovnik. This short walk explores the sights of Pile, including its peaceful park, before passing through Pile Gate to wander the narrow streets of the old town.

THE WALK

Distance: 3km (2 miles)
Allow: 1–2 hours
Start/end: Vrata od Pile (Pile Gate)
✛ 145 A2

HOW TO GET THERE

Pile is the arrival point for buses to the old town from the bus station, Gruž harbour and Lapad peninsula.

★ Pile Gate is the main entrance to the walled city, topped by a statue of Sveti Vlaha (St. Blaise). Most people arrive here by bus and head straight into the old town, but this walk begins by exploring the district of Pile itself.

With Pile Gate behind you, look for the gravel park with a fountain at the centre outside Café Dubravka. Take the steps down from the park to arrive on Ulica Svetog Đurđa, following signs to Lovrijenac. Walk along this street, passing a small church with an upturned boat on the pavement and turn left into Ulica Od Tabakarije to emerge at Orhan (▷ 247), a restaurant overlooking a small beach on the site of Dubrovnik's first harbour.

❶ Tvrđava Lovrijenac (▷ 149) can be visited in summer using the same ticket as for the city walls. The quickest route is to take the steps behind the restaurant; afterwards you can go

down the main path to rejoin the walk.

Continue to the end of Ulica Od Tabakarije, passing the main path to Lovrijenac, then climb the steps to Dubrovnik

Inter-University Centre. Walk up a steep slope and take a sharp left around the building to climb to a gravel car park on a cliff between two coves.

❷ From the car park, you can divert briefly down the hill to Danče. Here you will find the church of Our Lady of Danče and a beautifully kept cemetery and garden, tended by the nuns from the Franciscan convent. The nuns still maintain the tradition of ringing the church bells whenever a ship passes at sea. Beneath the church, the

bathing rocks offer views across the bay to Lapad.

Return to the car park and enter Gradac, the leafy park on your left, with a clifftop promenade and views stretching from Mount Srđ to Lokrum. Take the steps which lead up into the park and continue to climb on a pine-shaded path to the summit. When you see another flight of steps coming up from your left, turn right through a narrow gateway and walk down the steps between stone walls.

❸ On your right is the stately mansion and garden of the Pucić family, now home to the Dubrovnik Symphony Orchestra.

Turn right at the foot of the steps and follow busy Ulica Branitelja Dubrovnika to return to Pile Gate. Now it is time to enter the old town. Cross the moat and drawbridge to pass through the outer gate, then continue beneath a second arch to arrive on Stradun (▷ 152–153) beside the Onofrio fountain. Bear right around the fountain to Ulica Od Puča, the main shopping street of the old town.

❹ The street ends in Poljana Gundulićeva, where a market is held on weekday mornings.

Bear right across the market square and look for a lane in the opposite corner leading to Bunićeva Poljana, a lively café-filled plaza which is animated on summer evenings. Keep left alongside the cathedral and go through the small archway ahead of you to arrive at the old harbour, passing the fish market and Lokanda Peskarija (▷ 247). Keep left to walk around the harbour, then turn left to return to the walled town through Ribarnica gate. Turn right here to climb the steps towards the Dominican monastery (▷ 146). At the top of the steps, turn left through an archway to enter Prijeko along a narrow alley beside the church of Sveti Nikola (St. Nicholas). Walk straight ahead along Prijeko and take the second right up Ulica Žudioska.

❺ Ulica Žudioska was the main street of the 16th-century Jewish ghetto. The synagogue used by Dubrovnik's Jewish community is a few steps downhill to your right.

Turn left at the top of Ulica Žudioska into Peline, the highest street of the old town. Pass the Buža gate and pass beneath the city walls with the Minčeta tower visible up ahead. Turn left down Ulica Kunićeva or any of the steep, narrow lanes of stone steps to return to Stradun and Pile Gate.

A view across the rooftops in Dubrovnik (opposite).
Dubrovnik's busy harbour (left)

WHERE TO EAT
Arsenal (▷ 246)
Kamenice (▷ 246–247)
Lokanda Peskarija (▷ 247)
Orhan (▷ 247)
Rozarij (▷ 247)
Sesame (▷ 247)

PLACE TO VISIT
Tvrđava Lovrijenac (▷ 149)

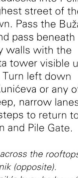

OUT AND ABOUT

ORGANIZED TOURS

Travel agents in the main towns and resorts offer numerous excursions, from fish picnics and boat cruises to bus tours and national parks. The biggest agency is Atlas, which is based in Dubrovnik but has branches across the country. Many of these tours only operate in summer. The price sometimes includes lunch and transfers from your hotel.

ZAGREB

CITY SIGHTSEEING TOURS
Tourist Information Centre, Andrijićeva 12
Tel 01 370 3088
www.event.hr
Walking or bus tours of the capital are led by costumed guides. The two-hour walking tours depart from Trg Bana Jelačića, while the three-hour bus and walking tours leave from Arcotel Allegra near the railway station. Tours take place every day; you need to book at least one day in advance.
🕙 All year; times vary
💶 Walking tours 13kn; bus tours 20kn. Child under 7 free, 7–12 half price. A Zagreb Card gives you a 50 per cent discount.

INLAND CROATIA

PANTURIST
Kapucinska 19, Osijek
Tel 031 214388
www.panturist-plus.hr
This agency offers full-day bus tours of eastern Slavonia, including visits to Đakovo, Vukovar and boat trips in Kopački Rit nature park. Most tours depart from the boat dock at Vukovar.
🕙 Apr–end Oct 💶 €17

ISTRIA

ACTIVA TRAVEL
Scalierova 1, Pula
Tel 052 215497
www.activa-istra.com
This outfit offers bicycle tours along the wine routes of Istria, plus autumn truffle-hunting expeditions.
🕙 All year; truffle-hunting Oct–end Dec 💶 Prices vary

KVARNER

DA RIVA
Šetalište Maršala Tita 170, Opatija
Tel 051 272990
www.da-riva.hr
Trips include bus tours of Istria and Krk, trips to the Brijuni islands and Plitvice Lakes in summer, as well as guided walks in the Gorski Kotar and Učka mountains.
🕙 May–end Oct; a few tours operate throughout the year
💶 From €30

DALMATIA

ATLAS
Nepotova 4, Split
Tel 021 343055
www.atlas.hr
Organised excursions by Atlas include Dubrovnik, Sarajevo, Mostar, Hvar, the Blue Cave on Biševo island and rafting.
🕙 May–end Oct; a few tours operate throughout the year
💶 €26–81

BIOKOVO ACTIVE
Gundulićeva 4, Makarska
Tel 021 679655
www.biokovo.net
This company offers walking and driving tours in the Biokovo Nature Park, from short sunrise walks to strenuous half-day treks.
🕙 Apr–end Nov 💶 30–45kn including meals and drinks

DUBROVNIK AND BEYOND

ADRIATIC LUXURY SERVICES
Ulica Kardinala Stepinca 21
Tel 020 437288
www.als.hr
ALS offers luxury yacht charter as well as a variety of bus tours such as a Pelješac wine tour and a tour of the Konavle villages, with folklore performances and lunch.
🕙 Mar–end Oct 💶 €26–81

ATLAS
Cina Carica 3
Tel 020 442222
www.atlas.hr
Tours on offer from Dubrovnik include Korčula, Mljet, Pelješac vineyards, boat trips on the Neretva river and a day trip to Montenegro.
🕙 May–end Oct; a few tours operate throughout the year
💶 €26–81

OUT AND ABOUT

This chapter lists places to eat and stay, broken down by region, then alphabetically by town or area. Entries in the Zagreb section are listed alphabetically.

Eating and Staying

EATING OUT IN CROATIA

Croatian food is an intriguing blend of Central European and
Mediterranean influences, with the light, Italian-style cuisine of the
coastal regions contrasting with the heavier Balkan fare of the interior.
The range of fresh produce is superb and the modern generation of chefs
is discovering a lighter touch, influenced by the Slow Food movement
from Italy. The best restaurants serve simple, fresh, local food.

Samobar sausage, bread and mustard; a busy market in Zagreb; fresh fish for sale

PRACTICALITIES
● Mealtimes are around 7–10am for breakfast (*doručak*), 12–3pm for lunch (*ručak*) and 7–10pm for dinner (*večera*), but many restaurants stay open throughout the day.
● It is not necessary to make a reservation at the vast majority of restaurants. However, opening times vary throughout the year and many restaurants close their doors or reduce their hours in winter, so it is always a good idea to check before you go. It is also sensible to book in advance if you want to eat out at a popular restaurant in July or August or at weekends.
● Casual dress is acceptable in all but a handful of restaurants, though Croatians do like to look smart and you will look like a tourist if you are dressed in T-shirt and shorts.
● Non-smokers should note that smoking is allowed in almost all restaurants in Croatia.
● Some restaurants accept credit cards but many do not, so it is always best to carry enough cash.

PRICES
● The cost of eating out in Croatia is reasonable by European standards, but much higher on the coast than inland.

● There is usually a small cover charge for bread.
● Fresh fish is sold by weight, which makes it appear very expensive on the menu as it is priced by the kilogram. A portion of around 150–250g (6–10oz) should be sufficient for one person.
● House wine is sold by the litre. It is quite acceptable to ask for a 0.5l or 0.3l carafe, or a glass of 0.2l. More expensive wines are sold by the bottle.
● If you have received good service, round up your bill (check) with a tip of around 10 per cent.

WHAT TO EAT
Breakfast
Hotels offer a buffet of bread, pastries, yogurt, fruit, omelettes and cold meats. Alternatively, head for a café for continental-style croissants or pastries.

Brunch
Many restaurants serve *merenda* or *gableci* between around 10am and 2pm—cheap, filling snacks such as sausages, tripe, goulash and bean stew.

Starters
The most popular cold starters are *pršut* (cured ham), salami and cheese. A cheaper option is soup.

Warm starters
Pasta and risotto dishes are listed as 'warm starters' on the menu, but are usually enough for a main course.

Meat dishes
Croatians love their meat. The most common meats are lamb, pork, chicken and veal, served either roasted, grilled or as a breaded schnitzel. A mixed grill is a popular standby.

such as *ćevapčići*, *pljeskavica* and *ražnjići*. Another popular snack is *burek*, a greasy filled filo pastry.

REGIONAL SPECIALITIES
● Istria is the gourmet capital of Croatia and the home of the Slow Food movement. Look for dishes containing the local truffles.
● Along the Adriatic coast, meat is roasted *ispod peka* (under the bell),

A young woman in a café on the Riva, Split; Pršut (cured ham), cheese, olives and bread

Fish dishes
Fresh fish is served simply grilled, with olive oil and lemon, accompanied by *blitva* (Swiss chard) with potatoes, garlic and olive oil. Other favourites include shrimps, oysters, octopus and fish stew.

Salads and side dishes
These are ordered separately. The most common are green salad, cabbage salad, beetroot salad, mixed salad, boiled potatoes, chips (fries), rice and pasta.

Desserts
The national dessert is pancakes with chocolate, jam, walnuts or cream. The only other choice is usually ice-cream.

Fast food
Street stalls and kiosks sell grilled meats

cooked slowly in a metal dish which is placed in the embers of a fire.
● Dalmatian specialities include *pašticada* (sweet veal casserole), *brodet* (fish stew) and Dalmatian-style steak with garlic and red wine.
● The cooking of inland Croatia is heavy and spicy. Barbecued meat, game dishes and stews predominate in the mountains. Slavonia specializes in Hungarian-style casseroles such as goulash.

VEGETARIANS
Vegetarians are not well catered for in Croatia. There are a handful of vegetarian restaurants in Zagreb and other major cities, but the concept is not readily understood. Vegetarian-sounding dishes may contain bacon, sausage or pork, or be cooked in meat stock.

WHERE TO EAT	
gostionica	rustic-style inn offering cheap, filling local food
kavana	café serving drinks, pastries and snacks
konoba	traditional tavern specialising in local dishes and wine
pekara	bakery selling bread and snacks
pivnica	pub or beer hall, sometimes attached to a brewery, offering beer and simple fare such as sausages and stews
pizzeria	pizzeria serving wood-fired, Italian-style pizza
restoran	formal restaurant with waiter service and a range of Croatian and international dishes
slastičarnica	pastry shop specializing in ice-cream and cakes

EATING

Menus are divided into appetisers or cold starters, warm starters, meat dishes, fish dishes, salads, side dishes and desserts.

Ajvar Spicy aubergine (eggplant) and pepper relish to accompany grilled meats.

Bečki odrezak Wiener schnitzel (veal cutlet in breadcrumbs).

Blitva Swiss chard, usually fried in olive oil with potatoes as the standard accompaniment to fish, especially in Dalmatia.

Brodet Dalmatian-style fish stew.

Burek sa mesom Filo pastry stuffed with minced meat.

Burek sa sirom Filo pastry stuffed with cottage cheese.

Crni rižot Black cuttlefish risotto.

Ćevapčići Minced-meat rissoles or meatballs, grilled and served with raw onions, bread and *ajvar*.

Češnjovke Garlic pork sausage, a speciality of Samobor, served with mustard and sauerkraut.

Čobanac Hot, spicy meat stew from Slavonia.

Dalmatinski pržolica Dalmatian-style rib-eye steak with garlic and red wine.

Fiš paprikaš Spicy, peppery fish stew from Slavonia.

Fuži Istrian-style pasta twirls, served with truffles or goulash.

Grah Bean stew, sometimes with sausage added.

Gregada Hvar-style fish casserole with potatoes and white wine.

Gulaš Goulash (spicy meat casserole), usually served with gnocchi or pasta.

Ispod peka Meat roasted 'under the bell'.

Janjetina na ražnju Spit-roast lamb.

Kiseli kupus Sauerkraut.

Kobasica Sausages.

Kulen Spicy salami from Slavonia, flavoured with paprika.

Maneštra Istrian-style vegetable soup, with bacon or sweetcorn added.

Mješana salata Mixed salad of lettuce, tomatoes, cabbage, carrot and beetroot.

Mješano meso Mixed grill of lamb and pork chops, *ćevapčići* and other grilled meats.

Na buzaru Seafood flash-fried with tomatoes, onions, herbs and wine.

Na žaru Barbecued or grilled.

Njoki Gnocchi (a kind of pasta dumplings).

Palačinke Pancakes, served with chocolate, jam, walnuts or cream.

Pašticada Dalmatian casserole of veal stewed in sweet wine, served with gnocchi.

Paški sir Hard, salty sheep's cheese from Pag.

Pljeskavica Croatian-style burger or minced-meat patty.

Pogača Vis-style pizza or focaccia bread topped with anchovies, tomatoes, vegetables and cheese.

Pomfrit Chips (French fries).

Pršut Cured, air-dried ham from Istria or Dalmatia.

Punjene lignje Stuffed squid.

Punjene paprike Peppers (capsicums) stuffed with minced meat and rice.

Purica z mlincima Roast turkey with thin sheets of Zagorje-style pasta.

Ražnjići Grilled pork kebabs on a skewer.

Riblja juha Fish soup.

Rožata Dubrovnik-style dessert, similar to *crème caramel*.

Salata od hobotnice Octopus salad with potatoes, onions, olive oil and vinegar.

Samoborska kremšnita Flaky custard tart, a speciality of Samobor.

Sarma Cabbage leaves stuffed with minced meat and rice.

Sladoled Ice-cream, sold in a huge variety of flavours.

Štrukli Cottage cheese parcels, a speciality of Zagorje.

Šurlice Pasta tubes from the island of Krk.

Tartufi Istrian truffles.

Zagrebački odrezak Zagreb-style veal steak, stuffed with ham and cheese and fried in breadcrumbs, similar to *cordon bleu*.

Zelena salata Green salad.

EATING

Wine has been produced in Croatia ever since Greek settlers planted the first vineyards on the Dalmatian islands of Korčula, Hvar and Vis. Today, Croatia is attracting a growing reputation for its quality wines.

WHITE WINE

● Malvazija is a straw-coloured dry white wine from Istria, where some of the best wines in Croatia are being produced by a new generation of winemakers such as Marijan Arman, Gianfranco Kozlovic and Ivica Matošević.

● Graševina is a dry white wine from Slavonia. The same region produces classic white wine varieties such as Chardonnay, Rizling (Riesling) and Fume (Sauvignon Blanc).

● Traminac is the local name for Gewürztraminer, a delicate floral white wine produced in the cellars of Ilok.

● White wines on the islands include Žlahtina from Krk, Vugava from Vis, and Grk and Pošip from Korčula.

RED WINE

● Dingač is the finest and most expensive red wine in Croatia. It is produced from Plavac Mali grapes grown on the southern sea-facing slopes of the Pelješac peninsula. Closely related to Californian Zinfandel, Plavac Mali produces a powerful, heavy wine. Cheaper wines labelled Plavac Mali rather than Dingač use the same grapes, but grown on the landward side.

● Other Dalmatian red wines include Postup from Pelješac, Viški Plavac from Vis, Ivan Dolac from Hvar and Babić from Primošten.

● Teran is a light fruity red wine from Istria. In winter it is heated with olive oil, pepper and toast and served as *supa*.

● Portugizac is a red wine from the Samobor region which is drunk immediately after the harvest in autumn, rather like Beaujolais Nouveau.

APERITIFS AND DESSERT WINES

● Bermet is an aromatic vermouth from Samobor, introduced by French troops during the Napoleonic occupation and still produced today.

● Muškat Momjanski is a semi-sweet white wine made from the Muskat grape near Buje in Istria.

● Prošek is a sweet red wine, usually made from the Plavac Mali grape in Dalmatia and best served chilled.

MIXED DRINKS

bambus   red wine and cola
bevanda   red wine and water
gemišt   white wine and sparkling mineral water
miš-maš   red wine and lemonade

BEER

● Most beer produced in Croatia is European lager-type beer. Popular brands include Karlovačko from Karlovac, Ožujsko from Zagreb, Osječko from Osijek, Pan from Koprivnica and Laško, imported from Slovenia.

● Tomislav is a dark beer from the Ožujsko brewery in Zagreb.

● If you prefer draught to bottled beer, ask for *pivo točeno*.

SPIRITS AND LIQUEURS

Croatia produces a vast range of brandies, spirits and liqueurs, using everything from blueberries to figs. At markets you will be greeted by a kaleidoscopic array of bottles, containing home-made brandy or eau-de-vie with the addition of various preserved fruits and herbs. Most of these come under the broad heading of *rakija*, a generic term similar to brandy or Italian grappa. *Rakija* is an essential aspect of Croatian culture and hospitality, and you can expect to be offered a glass at any time of day.

EATING

RAKIJA READER	
biska	mistletoe brandy from Istria
kruškovac	pear brandy
lozovača	grape brandy
maraschino	sour cherry brandy
medenica	honey brandy
orahovica	walnut brandy
pelinkovac	bitter wormwood and herbal liqueur
šljivovica	plum brandy
travarica	herb brandy

ZAGREB

As you would expect from the capital, Zagreb has the full range of dining options, from temples of gastronomy and high-end business and hotel restaurants to cafés, fast-food chains and 24-hour bakeries. Almost every taste is catered for here—ethnic eateries offer Chinese, Indian, Italian and Mexican cuisine, and Zagreb also has some of Croatia's few vegetarian restaurants. For lunch on the run, the grills around Dolac market serve inexpensive and filling snacks.

EATING

BOBAN

Gajeva 9, Zagreb
Tel 01 481 1549
www.boban.hr
This brick-vaulted cellar off the main square attracts a buzzy crowd for its Italian cuisine and faux antique décor. Choose from classics such as tagliatelle with truffles, cream and brandy, or order a 'hunter's platter' of venison salami, ham and smoked cheese to share.
🕓 Daily 10am–midnight
🍴 L 80kn, D 120kn, Wine from 75/110kn
🚋 Tram to Trg Bana Jelačića

K PIVOVARI

Ilica 222, Zagreb
Tel 01 375 1808
www.kpivovari.com
This busy pub is attached to the Ožujsko brewery. In summer, you can enjoy draught beers in the garden; in winter, tuck into plates of sausages, baked potatoes and mixed grills.
🕓 Mon–Sat 10am–midnight, Sun 10–5
🍴 L 70kn, D 100kn, Beer from 10kn
🚋 Tram 2, 6,11 to Slovenska

KAPTOLSKA KLET

Kaptol 5, Zagreb
Tel 01 481 4838
www.kaptolska-klet.hr
Choose from a crowded beer hall with communal wooden tables and a terrace facing the cathedral, or a pretty courtyard restaurant serving a wider variety of Zagreb and Zagorje-style dishes. At lunchtime the pub offers inexpensive, filling fare such as goulash, stuffed peppers, bean stew, sausages and scones with bacon.
🕓 Daily 9am–midnight
🍴 L 50kn, D 110kn, Wine from 80/140kn
🚋 Tram to Trg Bana Jelačića

KEREMPUH

Kaptol 3, Zagreb
Tel 01 481 9000
www.kerempuh.hr
This famous restaurant above Dolac market is popular with Zagreb's professionals, who come here to enjoy good, freshly prepared Croatian cooking. The menu changes daily according to what is in the

IVICA I MARICA

Tkalčićeva 70, Zagreb
Tel 01 482 8999
www.ivicaimarica.com
Vegetarian cooking is raised to an art form at this trendy modern restaurant, which combines Hansel-and-Gretel wooden cottage décor and waiters in folk costume with a *nouvelle cuisine* approach to food. There are some meat and fish dishes but most are meat-free, such as *štrukli* with cheese and spinach, vegetarian goulash and grilled mushrooms. The owners have a cake shop next door.
🕐 Daily 12–11
🍽 L 60kn, D 100kn, Wine from 105kn
🚋 Tram to Trg Bana Jelačića

market, with an emphasis on meat dishes. Arrive early to grab a seat on the terrace. Lunch only.
🕐 Mon–Sat 9–4
🍽 L 80kn, Wine from 70/100kn
🚋 Tram to Trg Bana Jelačića

MANGIARE

Tkalčićeva 29, Zagreb
Tel 01 482 8173
Delicious pizzas are stone-baked in a large brick oven at the entrance to this stylish pizzeria, with tables out of doors on Zagreb's favourite promenade. The chef uses authentic Italian ingredients such as mozzarella, Parmesan, rocket (arugula) and cherry tomatoes, and the menu also includes pasta, salads and Italian desserts.
🕐 Mon–Sat 9am–11pm, Sun 10am–11pm
🍽 L 65kn, D 85kn, Wine from 70/90kn
🚋 Tram to Trg Bana Jelačića

POD GRIČKIM TOPOM

Zakmardijeve Stube 5, Zagreb
Tel 01 483 3607
With a flower-filled terrace overlooking the city, the restaurant is perfect on a summer evening. The menu focuses on steaks and fish, and also includes veal schnitzel stuffed with ham and cheese. Get there by climbing the steps or taking the funicular to Gradec.
🕐 Mon–Sat 11am–midnight, Sun 11–5
🍽 L 100kn, D 150kn, Wine from 70/100kn
🚡 Funicular to Gradec

Boban serves Italian cuisine

RUBELJ

Dolac 2, Zagreb
Tel 01 481 8777
www.rubelj-grill.hr
This flagship of a chain of fast-food restaurants offering *ćevapčići*, sausages and kebabs is on the terrace of Dolac market. It isn't fancy, but the perfectly grilled meat is served with crusty bread and *ajvar* (aubergine/eggplant and pepper relish). Just the place for a filling lunchtime snack.
🕐 Daily 8am–11pm
🍽 L 40kn, D 60kn, Wine from 60/100kn
🚋 Tram to Trg Bana Jelačića

PAVILJON

Trg Kralja Tomislava 22, Zagreb
Tel 01 481 3066
www.restaurant-paviljon.com
Housed in the splendid setting of the 19th-century Art Pavilion, this is one of Zagreb's top restaurants. Chef Stanko Erceg creates modern Croatian classics such as swordfish carpaccio, broccoli and shrimp soup and his signature dish, crispy roast duck with red cabbage and figs. On some nights a grand piano plays. Dress up to come here or you will feel out of place.
🕐 Mon–Sat noon–midnight
🍽 L 150kn, D 250kn, Wine from 75kn
🚋 Tram to Glavni Kolodvor (train station)

STARI FIJAKER

Mesnička 6, Zagreb
Tel 01 483 3829
The pub, one of Zagreb's oldest, has model carriages hanging from the ceiling. The cuisine includes Zagorje-style soup, cottage cheese *štrukli* and pasta with roast duck and turkey.
🕐 Mon–Sat 7am–11pm, Sun 10–10
🍽 L 70kn, D 100kn, Wine from 50/100kn
🚋 Tram to Frankopanska

VALLIS AUREA

Tomićeva 4, Zagreb
Tel 01 483 1305
This snug restaurant offers tasty Slavonia home cooking, served at small wooden tables. The inexpensive daily specials include wine goulash, boiled beef with horseradish and squid.
🕐 Mon–Sat 8am–11pm
🍽 L 50kn, D 75kn, Wine from 50/70kn
🚋 Tram to Trg Bana Jelačića

EATING

INLAND CROATIA

The regions of inland Croatia all have their own culinary styles and special dishes, rooted in centuries of tradition. From Samobor come sausages, accompanied by sauerkraut and local mustard. In Varaždin and the Zagorje, you find *štrukli* (cottage cheese parcels) and *mlinci*, thin sheets of pasta served with roast turkey. The eastern region of Slavonia has its own distinctive cuisine, based on the heavy use of paprika in *kulen* (salami), *čobanac* (meat stew) and *fiš paprikaš* (fish casserole).

PRICES

The prices given are approximate, for a two-course lunch (L) and three-course dinner (D), without drinks. The wine price is for a litre of table wine followed by the least expensive bottle of quality wine. For a key to the symbols, ▷ 2.

JASENOVAC

KOD RIBIĆA

Ulica Vladimira Nazora 24, Jasenovac

Tel 044 672066

If you are heading into the Lonjsko Polje, stop for lunch at this simple fish restaurant. The fish soup is almost a meal in itself, or you can choose from spicy *fiš paprikaš* or fried catfish.

🕐 Mon–Sat 8am–10pm

🍷 L 50kn, D 100kn, Wine from 50/120kn

KARLOVAC

POD STARIMI KROVOVI

Radićeva 8, Karlovac

Tel 047 615420

This traditional restaurant in a baroque house on the main street of the old town is staffed by students from the local catering school. Dishes such as steak with oyster mushroom sauce, cranberry jam and semolina croquettes lean towards the heavy side, but there are lighter choices like grilled trout with Swiss chard and potatoes.

🕐 Mon–Sat 9am–10pm

🍷 L 60kn, D 80kn, Wine from 50/70kn

KOPRIVNICA

PIVNICA KRALUŠ

Zrinski Trg 10, Koprivnica

Tel 048 622302

A wooden carving of beer drinkers in the naïve art style of Hlebine adorns the door of this atmospheric beer cellar on the main square of Koprivnica, with brick arches, flagstoned floors and low benches around a traditional chimney at the centre. It serves hearty pub food such as beer sausages, venison casserole and hard Podravina cheese.

🕐 Daily 8am–11pm

🍷 L 40kn, D 60kn, Wine from 50/80kn

OSIJEK

MIRNA LUKA

Zimski Luka, Osijek

Tel 031 781 8963

It's hard to beat the setting of this fish restaurant, on a barge moored in the winter harbour beneath the glass skyscraper of Hotel Osijek. In summer open-air tables are laid out on the deck,

EATING

PRI STAROJ VURI

Giznik 2, Samobor
Tel 01 336 0548

The name of this restaurant means 'at the old clock' and it is found in an 18th-century yellow-painted house behind the church, decorated with old clocks and Carnival masks. It serves recipes from the 19th century, as well as the more modern *štrukli* soup and Samobor sausages with sauerkraut and mustard. With a free canapé, why not try a glass of *bermet*, local vermouth.

ⓒ Mon–Sat 11–11, Sun 11–6
🍴 L 80kn, D 100kn, Wine from 70/120kn

with views over the River Drava. House specials include fresh grilled fish, fish casserole, seafood risotto, stuffed squid and fried river carp.

ⓒ Daily 11–11
🍴 L 80kn, D 100kn, Wine from 70/100kn

SAMOBOR

SAMOBORSKA PIVNICA

Šmidhenova 3, Samobor
Tel 01 336 1623

Traditional red-and-white embroidered checked tablecloths are matched by the waiters' waistcoats at this folksy beer hall just off the main square. Start with a plate of salami or beef tongue, followed by local sausages with mashed potatoes or a mixed sausage platter for two, best washed down with Ožujsko or Tomislav beer from Zagreb.

ⓒ Mon–Fri 9am–11pm, Sat–Sun 9am–midnight
🍴 L 60kn, D 80kn, Wine from 55/120kn

SLAVONSKI BROD

ZDJELAREVIĆ

Brodski Stupnik
Tel 035 427040
www.zdjelarevic.hr

The restaurant attached to Croatia's first wine hotel (▷ 256) serves excellent dishes to accompany Graševina, Rizling, Chardonnay or Manzoni white wines from the hotel vineyards. Specialities include chicken with wild thyme sauce, beef in Samobor mustard sauce, venison ragout and a 'vineyard plate' of cured meats.

The carved door of Pivnica Kraluš

ⓒ Tue–Sat 11–11, Sun–Mon 12–8
🍴 L 80kn, D 130kn, Wine from 80kn
🚗 Take the road from Slavonski Brod to Nova Gradiska and turn right after 7km (4 miles) in the village of Brodski Stupnik.

VARAŽDIN

GRENADIR

Kranjčevićeva 12, Varaždin
Tel 042 211131

Tuck into hearty Zagorje-style cuisine on a side street near the castle drawbridge, with tables out on the sidewalk in summer. Inexpensive, filling lunchtime specials include Grgur Ninski soup (bread

ZLATNA GUŠKA

Habdelićeva 4, Varaždin
Tel 042 213393

Set in a brick-vaulted cellar beneath a 17th-century palace, the 'Golden Goose' recreates the feel of the Austro-Hungarian empire, with pikestaffs and coats of arms on the walls. Dishes include The Daggers of the Count of Brandenburg (skewers of pork, chicken and beef with strawberries) and Countess Julijana's Flower (pancakes with fruit).

ⓒ Mon–Sat 8am–11pm, Sun 10–10
🍴 L 80kn, D 120kn, Wine from 60/100kn

and potato soup) and Zagorje steak (pork topped with cheese, bacon and onions and served with fried potatoes).

ⓒ Mon–Sat 9am–11pm, Sun 12–10
🍴 L 50kn, D 80kn, Wine from 70/100kn

ZAGORJE

GREŠNA GORICA

Taborgradska 3, Desinić
Tel 049 343001
www.gresna-gorica.com

This farmhouse restaurant with a terrace overlooking Veliki Tabor castle has children's play areas and farm animals to keep little ones amused. It serves good, down-to-earth Zagorje home cooking such as cheese, sausages, veal with mushrooms and venison goulash with dumplings, accompanied by home-made wine.

ⓒ Daily 10–10
🍴 L 70kn, D 90kn, Wine from 50/100kn
🚗 Off the road from Miljana to Desinić

EATING

ISTRIA

Istria is the gourmet capital of Croatia, producing cheese, ham, seafood, vegetables, olive oil and wine as well as wild asparagus, mushrooms and the region's famous truffles. Restaurants like Toklarija, Valsabbion and Zigante have embraced the Slow Food movement from neighbouring Italy, with its emphasis on fresh, locally grown cuisine. These places regularly appear on lists of Croatia's best restaurants, but in Istria good food is a way of life and you will eat well even in the humblest village bar.

EATING

BUJE

POD VOLTOM
Ulica Ante Babića, Buje
Tel 052 772232
This old-fashioned *konoba* is in a narrow alley off the main street. It serves classic Istrian fare such as sheep's cheese, pasta with truffles, scampi *na buzaru* and grilled fish. On warm days, dine on a terrace.
🕑 Daily 10am–11pm
🍴 L 80kn, D 100kn, Wine from 30/90kn

BUZET

STARI OŠTARIJA
Ulica Petra Flega 5, Buzet
Tel 052 694003
The village inn was reopened in 2005 as a classy restaurant offering Istrian specialities such as *maneštra* (vegetable soup), *frittata* (truffle omelette) and steak with truffles. You dine in a stone-walled room jutting out over the cliffs with views over the town below. Bread is served with olive oil from Oprtalj, and the wine list has Istrian wines.
🕑 Wed–Mon 12–11
🍴 L 100kn, D 150kn, Wine from 60/90kn

GRAČIŠĆE

KONOBA MARINO
Gračišće 75
Tel 052 687081
This traditional *konoba* inside the town gate has a

summer terrace and serves delicious inexpensive Istrian cuisine, such as home-made sausages, *fuži* with game and *maneštra* (vegetable soup). If you just want a snack, try a sandwich of crusty bread filled with sheep's cheese or Istrian ham. Wine is Malvazija and Teran from the local vineyards.
🕑 Jul–Aug Thu–Tue 2–11; Sep–Jun Mon–Wed, Fri–Sat 2–10, Sun 2–11
🍴 L 50kn, D 70kn, Wine from 40/50kn

GROŽNJAN

ENOTEKA ZIGANTE
Ulica Gorjana 5, Grožnjan
Tel 052 721998
www.vzigantetartufi.com
This wine bar belonging to the Zigante Tartufi empire (▷ 181–182) has tables under the Venetian loggia in

TOKLARIJA

Sovinjsko Polje, Buzet
Tel 052 663031

In a 14th-century olive mill in the village of Sovinjsko Polje, this has become a pilgrimage for food lovers from Italy, Slovenia and Zagreb. From the designer cutlery and wine glasses to the cosy fireside alcoves, every detail is planned to enhance the Slow Food experience. The eight-course tasting menu might include grilled vegetables, *maneštra* (vegetable soup), cured ham, ravioli, grilled beef and chocolate truffles, with local wines. Reservations are essential.

🕐 Wed–Mon 1pm–10pm
🍴 Five-courses 370kn, eight-courses 550kn, Wine from 50/90kn
🚗 Take the road from Buzet to Motovun and turn left through the village of Sovinjak to reach Sovinjsko Polje.

summer, where you can sip local Malvazija while feasting on Istrian ham, cheese and truffle-based canapés. On cooler days, sit indoors in an old stone house.

🕐 Summer daily 10am–11pm, winter daily 10–8
🍴 Snacks from 20kn

LIMSKI KANAL

FJORD

Sveti Lovreč
Tel 052 448222

This is one of two popular restaurants beside the jetty where the tour boats stop after their journey along the Limski Kanal. It serves fresh oysters and mussels from the fjord, including a feast of mussels for two people to share. Other good options are seafood risotto and plain grilled fish.

🕐 Mar–end Dec daily 12–11
🍴 L 70kn, D 100kn, Wine from 60/100kn

MOTOVUN

POD VOLTOM

Trg Josefa Ressela, Motovun
Tel 052 681923

This brick-vaulted cellar beneath the arches leading up to the main square serves hearty dishes of Istrian home cooking, many using fresh truffles in season. Signature dishes include turkey escalope and veal medallions with truffles, as well as pasta and omelettes.

The Enoteka Zigante restaurant

🕐 Daily 12–11
🍴 L 100kn, D 120kn, Wine from 60/90kn

NOVIGRAD

DAMIR I ORNELA

Ulica Zidine 5, Novigrad
Tel 052 758134

The trendiest spot in town is in a stone cottage in one of the back streets seating just 28 diners, so reservations are essential in summer. Owner-chef Damir Deletić is a Japanese-trained sashimi master, who offers fresh takes on Istrian seafood such as scampi marinated in salt, pepper and olive oil.

HUMSKA KONOBA

Hum 2
Tel 052 660005

A traditional stone cottage at the entrance to Hum hides this rustic *konoba*, offering simple dishes of ham, sheep's cheese and *fuži* with truffles, served on wooden trays. The *maneštra* (vegetable soup) here is a meal itself, with sweetcorn and sausage. Start with a glass of home-made *biska* (mistletoe brandy), or try a jug of *supa*, warm red wine with olive oil, pepper and toast.

🕐 Jun–end Oct daily 11–10; Nov–end May Sat–Sun 11–10
🍴 L 50kn, D 70kn, Wine from 40/90kn

🕐 Tue–Sun 12–3, 6–10 (11 Jul–Aug). Closed 2 weeks Oct
🍴 L 100kn, D 120kn, Wine from 60/100kn

PULA

VALSABBION

Pješčana Uvala, Pula
Tel 052 218033
www.valsabbion.hr

Set in a bay on the outskirts of Pula, Valsabbion has been consistently voted one of the best restaurants in Croatia. The emphasis is on simply prepared, seasonal ingredients such as truffles, asparagus, wild mushrooms and seafood. If you want to sample everything, choose from six-course 'sea' or 'forest' menus or a gourmet tasting menu of ten courses.

🕐 Daily 12–12; closed Jan
🍴 L 300kn, D 350kn, tasting menus 355–435kn, Wine from 135kn
🚗 Take the ring road around Pula and continue south, then turn left, following signs to Pješčana Uvala

EATING

ZIGANTE

Livade 7
Tel 052 664302
www.zigantetartufi.com
The flagship restaurant of truffle king Giancarlo Zigante offers a range of seasonal truffle-tasting menus. Dishes vary but might include octopus carpaccio with black truffles, *fuži* (pasta) with white truffles and pancakes with white chocolate and truffle mousse. Almost all the dishes can be ordered with extra black or white truffles. It is expensive, but worth it for an authentic Istrian treat.

🕐 Daily 12–11 in summer; 11–10 in winter
🍴 L 200kn, D 250kn, tasting menus 380–500kn, Wine from 120kn
🚗 Take the Buzet to Motovun road and turn right at the Motovun crossroads to reach Livade

VELA NERA

Marina Veruda, Pješčana Uvala, Pula
Tel 052 219209
www.velanera.hr
This seafood restaurant overlooking the marina has a lovely boardwalk summer terrace. Specialities include salmon carpaccio in whisky and herbs and risotto Vela Nera, made with scampi, peaches and sparkling wine. Great wine list.

🕐 Daily 12–12
🍴 L 150kn, D 200kn, Wine from 90kn
🚗 Take the ring road around Pula and continue south, then turn left, following the signs to Pješčana Uvala.

ROVINJ

AL GASTALDO

Ulica Iza Kasarne 14, Rovinj
Tel 052 814109
With candles on the tables and wine bottles lining the walls, this stylish trattoria has a cosy, intimate interior and is one of the few places here to stay open all year. It serves Italian fare such as grilled vegetables, carpaccio of beef, ravioli with spinach, sole with almonds and veal cutlet *Milanese*.

🕐 Daily 11–3, 6–11
🍴 L 100kn, D 150kn, Wine from 70/100kn

La Puntuleina on the coast

LA PUNTULEINA

Ulica Svetog Križa 38, Rovinj
Tel 052 813186
Perched at the tip of the old town above the popular bathing rocks, La Puntuleina is both a wine bar and a chic restaurant. Get here early to grab a table on the balcony, which must be the most romantic place in town to watch the sun set over the sea. The food is a mix of Italian and Istrian influences, with an emphasis on seafood and fresh fish, such as grilled sole with truffles. There is also a four-course tasting menu,

BARBACAN

Ulica Barbacan 1, Motovun
Tel 052 681791
Art and food come together at this funky bistro, which serves inventive Istrian truffle dishes in a laid-back ambience of cool jazz, candlelit tables and exposed stone walls. Dishes include bruschetta with black truffles, saffron and truffle risotto, and polenta with truffles and sheep's cheese. It is just outside the outer town gate, in an old stone house with a summer terrace.

🕐 Mid-Mar to end Nov Mon 12.30–3.30, Wed–Sun 12.30–3.30, 6.30–10.30
🍴 L 150kn, D 200kn, Wine from 70kn

each course accompanied by a different Istrian wine.

🕐 Apr–end Nov daily 12–3, 6–11
🍴 L 200kn, D 250kn, tasting menu 350kn, Wine from 100kn

VELI JOŽE

Ulica Svetog Križa 3, Rovinj
Tel 052 816337
With communal wooden benches and shelves cluttered with farm tools and antiques, this waterfront *konoba* is rustic in appearance in contrast to its trendier neighbours. First-class Istrian ingredients create simple tavern classics like *fuži* (noodles) with goulash, grilled vegetables, roast lamb with potatoes and steak with truffles. There are a few outdoor tables by the harbour, but these get snapped up quickly, so be prepared to wait or share.

🕐 Daily 11am–midnight; closed Jan
🍴 L 80kn, D 120kn, Wine from 60/100kn

EATING

KVARNER

The cuisine of the coastal Kvarner region is similar to that of Dalmatia. Fresh fish and seafood feature heavily, together with pasta dishes and meat cooked under a metal lid. The islands have their own specialities, lamb on Cres and *šurlice* on Krk, a kind of pasta usually served with goulash. In the highlands of Gorski Kotar the cooking reflects the harsher climate, with meat and game dishes predominating, along with trout from the River Kupa.

KRK

TRI MARUNA

Poljica, Krk
Tel 051 861156

Behind an unmarked wooden door on the edge of the church square at Poljica it's all stone walls and wooden tables. There is no menu, just whatever the cook suggests—perhaps a choice of *šurlice* with goulash, stuffed cabbage or roast lamb. Bread arrives with a free plate of nibbles such as pork scratchings, liver sausage and onion. The cooking is not sophisticated, but a visit here is a culinary experience.

🕐 Daily 1–10

🍴 L 40kn, D 60kn, Wine from 40kn

🚗 Take the road from Malinska to the ferry port at Valbiska and turn right at a crossroads opposite the road to Bajčići

OPATIJA

LE MANDRAĆ

Obala Frana Supila 10, Volosko
Tel 051 701357

An old fisherman's cottage on the Lungomare promenade houses an avant-garde restaurant whose conservatory and terrace provide harbourside dining all year. The menu is seasonal. The nine-course 'Exploring' menu includes small portions of everything from sashimi, soup and fish tempura to *foie gras* and truffle desserts. Or you can choose owner Deniz Zembo's signature dish— mussels and clams *buzara*, served in a soup with lemon foam and Istrian ham.

🕐 Daily 11–11

🍴 L 150kn, D 200kn, tasting menu 390kn, Wine from 150kn

RIJEKA

BRACERA

Ulica Kružna 12, Rijeka
Tel 051 322498

One of a pair of restaurants on a street off the Korzo Bracera serves delicious pizzas from a clay oven. It also does great crispy salads, which make for a complete and healthy meal. There is a seafaring theme to the décor, with wooden planks, ropes, portholes, model ships, fishing nets on the walls and billowing sails hanging from the ceiling.

🕐 Daily 11–11

🍴 L 50kn, D 80kn, Wine from 50kn

EATING

DALMATIA

The cooking of Dalmatia is Mediterranean, making abundant use of fresh fish and seafood from the Adriatic. Fish is served simply grilled with potatoes and *blitva* (Swiss chard), or cooked in casseroles such as *brodet* or *gregada*, a speciality of Hvar. Pasta and risotto feature widely, a clear sign of Italian influence and a legacy of Venetian rule. More than anywhere else in Croatia, restaurants in Dalmatia are seasonal and many places close down altogether for the winter between November and March.

EATING

BRAČ

BISTRO PALUTE
Porat 4, Supetar
Tel 021 631730
This harbourside restaurant is popular for its well-priced specials of roast veal, suckling pig and Brač lamb. It has tables by the water in summer. There is also a children's menu featuring turkey, steak and fish.
🕒 Daily 10am–11pm
🍷 L 60kn, D 80kn, Wine from 50/100kn

GRADAC

GUSTIRNA
Uz Kuk 6, Gradac
Tel 021 697561
There is only one thing on the menu at this quirky cellar restaurant set back from the seafront promenade: thin, crusty pizza, cooked in a brick oven. Choose from small, medium or family sizes; then sit back to enjoy the musical décor, with antique accordions, fiddles and trumpets on the walls.
🕒 Summer daily 12–11, winter 6–11
🍷 Pizza from 25kn, Wine from 50/70kn

HVAR

BOUNTY
Mandrac, Hvar
Tel 021 742565
In contrast to some of the trendy bistros nearby, this waterfront restaurant serves classic Dalmatian fare such as grilled meat and fish, stuffed squid and *brodet* (fish stew). The tables on the quayside are perfectly placed to soak up the sun while enjoying the view of fishing boats and yachts.
🕒 Daily 11–11
🍷 L 60kn, D 80kn, Wine from 40/80kn

LUCULLUS
Ulica Petra Hektorovića 7, Hvar
Tel 021 742498
Housed in a 16th-century palace just off the main square, Lucullus serves Italian-Mediterranean Slow Food such as *gregada* (fish stew with potatoes and wine), roast lamb, and lobster. Start with Hvar goat's and sheep's milk cheeses.
🕒 Apr–end Oct daily 12–2, 6–11
🍷 L 200kn, D 250kn, Wine from 60/120kn

KONOBA MENEGO

Groda, Hvar
Tel 021 742036
www.menego.hr

Hidden away in an old stone wine-cellar on the steps leading to the castle, this family-run tavern serves *tapas*-style cold dishes accompanied by home-made wine. From Hvar goat's cheese with honey to marinated aubergines (eggplants) and peppers or a selection of cold meats, almost everything is produced on the island. For dessert, try 'drunken figs' stuffed with almonds and soaked in brandy, followed by wild orange liqueur.

🕙 Apr–end Oct daily 12–2, 5–10
🍴 Dishes from 25kn, Wine from 35kn

ZLATNA ŠKOLJKA

Ulica Petra Hektorovića 8, Hvar
Tel 098 168 8797

One of several upscale eateries in Hvar's trendy restaurant quarter, the 'Golden Shell' is credited with introducing the Slow Food revolution to Hvar. Local ingredients are used in unexpected ways, such as gnocchi with octopus, 'drunken' fish in sweet wine, lamb in coconut sauce and rabbit with figs. Reservations are essential in summer.

🕙 Apr–end Oct daily 12–3, 7–12
🍴 L 150kn, D 200kn, Wine from 60/100kn

KORČULA

MASLINA

Lumbarajska Cesta, Korčula
Tel 020 711720

This farmhouse restaurant, on the road to Lumbarda, is one of the few places on the island to stay open all year. Set among olive groves, it offers a simple menu of roast lamb, Dalmatian casseroles and home-made macaroni. The speciality is *pogača maslina*, a pizza-like dish of crusty bread topped with cheese, vegetables and olives.

🕙 Apr–end Oct daily 11am–12am; Nov–end Mar daily 11–3, 5–12
🍴 L 50kn, D 80kn, Wine from 40/60kn
🚗 Leave Korčula in the direction of Lumbarda, and Maslina is on your right

A display of pumpkins

MORSKI KONJIĆ

Šetalište Petra Kanavelića, Korčula
Tel 020 711878

This long terrace restaurant on the promenade around the outer walls is a lovely place to dine on a summer evening, with moonlit views across the water to the Pelješac peninsula. Its name means 'seahorse' and it duly specializes in seafood, from octopus salad to steamed mussels and plain grilled fish, accompanied by local Grk and Pošip wines.

🕙 Apr–end Oct daily 8am–midnight
🍴 L 100kn, D 150kn, Wine from 60/100kn

PALAČA PALADINI

Ulica Petra Hektorovića 4, Hvar
Tel 021 742104

The 16th-century palace overlooking the harbour square was given to the Paladini family as a reward for their service in a sea battle between the Turkish and Venetian fleets. A meal here is a feast for all the senses, as you sit at a candlelit table in a courtyard of lavender and lemon trees, enjoying Luci and Antun Tudor's freshly prepared Dalmatian cooking. The specialities are grilled meat and fish, but there are good vegetarian dishes.

🕙 Apr–end Oct daily 12–3, 6–12
🍴 L 150kn, D 200kn, Wine from 60/100kn

MAKARSKA

RIVA

Obala Kralja Tomislava 6, Makarska
Tel 021 616829

This fish restaurant with a summer courtyard behind the seafront promenade is the best place in town for a formal meal. The emphasis is on traditional seafood dishes, such as prawn cocktail, scampi soup and grilled scorpion fish. More adventurous choices include spaghetti with vodka and caviar, frogfish in vermouth sauce, and beef medallions with cured ham in basil sauce.

🕙 Daily 10am–1am
🍴 L 150kn, D 200kn, Wine from 70/120kn

ADIO MARE

Ulica Svetog Roka 2, Korčula
Tel 020 711253

You may need to wait for a table at this traditional fishermen's tavern, which serves some of the best food in Korčula at an old stone house beneath Marco Polo's tower. Steaks and kebabs are barbecued on an open fire in the corner, or you can have grilled fish, octopus or filling staples like *brodet* (fish soup with polenta) or *pašticada* (veal casserole with plums and sweet red wine). The menu and the décor have hardly changed in 30 years, but Adio Mare has built up a loyal following as a cheerful classic.

🕐 Apr–end Oct daily 6–12
🍽 D 100kn, Wine from 60/100kn

STARI MLIN

Ulica Prvosvibanjska 43, Makarska
Tel 021 611509

Set in an old stone mill with a vine-covered patio and modern art on the walls, this enjoyable bistro offers new variations on Dalmatian seafood dishes, as well as a Thai menu featuring steamed mussels, prawn curry and grilled snapper with orange and chilli. There is a simple children's menu.

🕐 Daily 10–2, 6–12
🍽 L 150kn, D 200kn, Wine from 70/120kn

MURTER

TIC-TAC

Ulica Hrokošina 5, Murter
Tel 022 435230

This trendy bistro in a quiet street behind the harbour offers alternatives to the standard menu of grilled fish available elsewhere.

Among the Mediterranean-inspired dishes are grilled vegetables, octopus sushi, bouillabaisse, oven-baked monkfish and Greek salad.

🕐 Apr–end Oct daily 12–11
🍽 L 120kn, D 170kn, Wine from 45/65kn

OMIŠ

RADMANOVE MLINICE

Radmanove Mlinice, Omiš
Tel 021 862073
www.radmanove-mlinice.hr

Set in an 18th-century stone mill on the banks of the River Cetina, this busy restaurant has a large

Olive oil and fresh olives

riverside garden and play area. Meat and bread are cooked in the traditional style under a metal lid. The menu also features frogs, eels and trout. There are performances of Dalmatian folk dances on Wednesdays at 8pm in July and August.

🕐 Apr–end Oct daily 8am–10pm
🍽 L 100kn, D 120kn, Wine from 60/120kn
🚌 Start in Omiš and follow the Cetina for 6km upstream

SKRADIN

CANTINETTA

Ulica Svirala 7, Skradin
Tel 022 771183

GRADSKA VIJEĆNICA

Trg Republike Hrvatske 3, Šibenik
Tel 022 213605

The highlight here is the setting, on the ground floor of the Venetian Gothic town hall, with tables under the loggia in summer offering views across a piazza to the cathedral. The menu is classic Dalmatian cuisine, including ham, sheep's cheese, octopus salad, steak and turkey in mustard sauce,with walnut pancakes for dessert.

🕐 Daily 8am–11pm
🍽 L 120kn, D 150kn, Wine from 60/100kn

It may look like a private house outside, but Cantinetta serves up excellent Dalmatian cuisine in a bright, arty atmosphere with low lighting, soft music and abstract art on the apricot- and mustard-coloured walls. Steak comes rare, topped with mustard and capers, surrounded by fries, bacon and roast peppers, with a basket of warm bread on the side. In summer you can dine in the garden.

🕐 Daily 12–12
🍽 L 100kn, D 150kn, Wine from 60/100kn

SPLIT

KONOBA HVARANIN

Ulica Ban Mladenova 9, Split
Tel 091 547 7496

With wooden benches, red cushions and checked tablecloths, this cosy *konoba* offers home cooking. They serve Dalmatian-style casseroles such as goulash and *pašticada* with gnocchi, as well as moussaka, boiled lamb, scampi and grilled fish.

EATING

KONOBA ŠKRAPA

Ulica Hrvatskih Mučenika 9, Trogir
Tel 021 885313

Chaotic, friendly and great fun, a meal at Škrapa is an experience. The small stone-walled dining room is cluttered with everything from hanging vines and dried flowers to vegetables in vases of water and wine bottles dripping with candle wax. Waiters bring steaming bowls of vegetable soup and *fažol* (bacon and bean stew), or plates of ham, cheese, sausages and sardines. The wine comes out of a tap in the wall.

🕐 Mon–Sat 11–11, Sun 4–11; closed Sun in winter
🖐 L 50kn, D 70kn, Wine from 60kn

🕐 Daily 11am–midnight
🖐 L 120kn, D 140kn, Wine from 70/120kn

KONOBA VAROŠ

Ulica Ban Mladenova 7, Split
Tel 021 335468

This traditional fishermen's tavern is in the Veli Varoš quarter. Lamb, veal, squid and octopus are roasted under the *peka* (metal lid), and other options include salted sardines, home-made sausages and ostrich steak.

🕐 Daily 9am–midnight
🖐 L 120kn, D 140kn, Wine from 65/120kn

VIS

BAKO

Gundulićeva 1, Komiža
Tel 021 713742
www.konobabako.hr

This charming *konoba* has wine barrels, fishing nets and tables on the terrace beside a pebble beach in the fishing village of Komiža. It serves traditional local dishes, such as octopus in wine, lobster soup and yellowtail fish with capers, laurel, rosemary and olive oil.

🕐 Apr–end Oct daily 11am–2am; Nov–end Mar 5pm–midnight
🖐 D 140kn, Wine from 60/100kn

JASTOŽERA

Gundulićeva 6, Komiža
Tel 021 713859
www.jastozera.com

You need a mortgage to eat here, or at least a private yacht, which is how many of the customers arrive on Vis. Set in an old house on

A sign for Konoba Škrapa

the quay at Komiža, Jastožera serves fresh fish and lobster, along with more affordable choices such as chicken and beef. The tables are set on wooden platforms overlooking the sea.

🕐 May–15 Oct daily 5–12
🖐 D 300kn, Wine from 70/130kn

VILLA KALIOPA

Ulica Vladimira Nazora 32, Vis
Tel 021 711755

There are few more romantic settings for a summer evening than the walled garden of the 16th-century Garibaldi palace, with its fountains, statues and palm

DORUČAK KOD TIHANE

Obala Sveti Jurja 5, Vis
Tel 021 718472
www.restorantihana.com

An art nouveau hotel has been restored as a waterfront fish restaurant, whose name means 'Breakfast at Tiffany's'. On summer nights you can dine on the terrace, with dreamy views across the bay. The emphasis is on fresh fish and seafood, served as paté, shrimp risotto or simply grilled fish, accompanied by the local Vugava wine. Round off your meal with a plate of *hruštule*, traditional biscuits from Vis.

🕐 Apr–end Oct daily 8am–midnight
🖐 L 120kn, D 150kn, Wine from 60/100kn

trees. You dine by candlelight on fabulous fresh fish, with the menu changing according to what is in season. A meal here is an extravagant treat, but it is worth it for a special occasion. Reservations essential.

🕐 Apr–end Oct daily 5–12
🖐 D 300kn, Wine from 70/130kn

ZADAR

ARSENAL

Trg Tri Bunara 1, Zadar
Tel 023 253833
www.arsenalzadar.com

The old Venetian arsenal has become one of Zadar's trendiest meeting places and entertainment venues. If you're tired of Croatian food, choose from international chioces such as soya burger, Caesar salad, or fish and chips. The snack menu includes sandwiches, pizzas, croissants and ice-cream.

🕐 Daily 7am–3am
🖐 L 50kn, D 75kn, Wine from 90/150kn

EATING

DUBROVNIK AND BEYOND

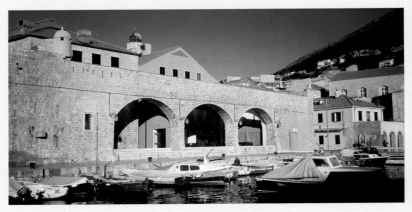

Dubrovnik has a wide range of restaurants which stay open throughout the year. Most offer variations on traditional Dalmatian cuisine, but others specialize in Bosnian, Italian, Chinese, Mexican or Spanish food. Prijeko, parallel to Stradun, is lined with restaurants whose tables spill out onto the street in summer, though many are overpriced tourist traps and it pays to choose carefully. The nearby fishing village of Mali Ston, on the Pelješac peninsula, is known for its oysters and mussels.

PRICES

The prices given are approximate, for a two-course lunch (L) and three-course dinner (D), without drinks. The wine price is for a litre of table wine followed by the least expensive bottle of quality wine. For a key to the symbols, ▷ 2.

CAVTAT

GALIJA
Vuličevićeva 1, Cavtat
Tel 020 478566
www.galija.hr
With tables under the pine trees at the end of the harbourside promenade, this restaurant in an old stone cottage is a delightful place to spend a summer evening. The food is a mix of traditional and modern, including grilled fish, steaks, prawns with honey,

carpaccio of grouper with Parmesan and oven-baked octopus. Reservations are essential in summer.
🕓 Daily 11am–midnight
🍴 L 150kn, D 200kn, Wine 90/120kn

DUBROVNIK

ARSENAL
Gradska Luka, Dubrovnik
Tel 020 321065
The old arsenal of Ragusa is now a popular wine bar and restaurant with shipping ropes, wooden planks and nautical décor. It serves Dalmatian classics like cured ham, Pag cheese and steaks, as well as delicious pastries from Gradskavana. Dine at a window table in the shape of an upturned boat, or on the terrace. The main entrance is by the harbour, or enter via Gradskavana.

🕓 Daily 10am–2am
🍴 L 100kn, D 150kn, Wine from 100/150kn

BUFET ŠKOLA
Antuninska 1, Dubrovnik
Tel 020 321096
If you fancy a snack, this tiny bar in an alley off Stradun serves great sandwiches, with thick crusty bread filled with Dalmatian ham and cheese in olive oil. Other choices are salted sardines and green salad.
🕓 Daily 8am–midnight
🍴 Sandwiches from 18kn, Wine from 60kn

KAMENICE
Gundulićeva Poljana 8, Dubrovnik
Tel 020 323682
This lively café on the market square is popular with locals at lunchtime. Its name means 'oyster' and it makes a great place for a

LOKANDA PESKARIJA

Ribarnica, Dubrovnik
Tel 020 324750

With wooden tables outside the fish market and views over the Old Port, Lokanda makes the perfect setting in which to enjoy simply prepared but delicious seafood dishes. The menu is limited but everything is first-class, from fish paté to seafood risotto and fried sardines to grilled squid. The only accompaniments you need are a crisp green salad and a glass of chilled Pošip white wine from Korčula.
🕐 Daily 8am–midnight
🍴 L 80kn, D 100kn, Wine from 60/90kn

fishy snack of oysters, scampi *na buzaru*, mussel risotto, octopus salad or *girice* (small fried fish).
🕐 Apr–end Oct daily 7am–10pm; Nov–end Mar daily 7am–8pm
🍴 L 65kn, D 90kn, Wine from 70/100kn

ROZARIJ

Zlatarska 4, Dubrovnik
Tel 020 321257

The best of the restaurants off Prijeko is tucked away off a narrow passage between St. Nicholas's church and the Dominican Monastery. With just a handful of tables, it serves good Dalmatian classics like mussels, *brodet* (fish stew) and *crni rižot* (black cuttle-fish risotto).
🕐 Mar–end Nov daily 11am–midnight
🍴 L 100kn, D 120kn, Wine from 60/90kn

SESAME

Ulica Dante Alighierija, Dubrovnik
Tel 020 412910
www.sesame.hr

This bistro outside Pile Gate is popular with artists, musicians and students. It offers a wide menu of Mediterranean cuisine, with lots of vegetarian choices such as courgette (zucchini) carpaccio and asparagus omelette. Specialities are *gregada* (Hvar fish stew with potatoes and white wine) and Porporela-style fish, baked in egg white and sea-salt. There is an extensive wine list.
🕐 Daily 8am–midnight
🍴 L 100kn, D 150kn, Wine from 90kn

A decorative lamp in Dubrovnik

TONI

Ulica Nikole Božidarevića 14, Dubrovnik
Tel 020 323134

If you feel like an Italian meal, it's hard to beat this spaghetteria in the old town, which offers home-made pasta dishes such as spaghetti carbonara and tortellini with walnuts and gorgonzola, along with bruschetta and salads. Get here early if you want one of the two outdoor tables.
🕐 Daily 12–11
🍴 L 60kn, D 80kn, Wine from 70/100kn

ORHAN

Ulica Od Tabakarije 1, Dubrovnik
Tel 020 414183

Hidden away beside a pebble cove outside Pile Gate, Orhan is one of Dubrovnik's best-kept secrets. On summer evenings, you can dine on a covered terrace beside the sea, with views of Fort Lovrijenac on one side and the city walls on the other. Fresh grilled fish is the speciality—the waiter will bring a tray to your table to help you make your choice—but less expensive options include risotto and Dalmatian steak dishes.
🕐 Feb–end Oct daily 11am–midnight
🍴 L 150kn, D 200kn, Wine from 70/130kn

PELJEŠAC
KAPETANOVA KUĆA

Mali Ston
Tel 020 754555
www.ostrea.hr

Gourmets head out to eat fresh oysters at this famous restaurant, whose glass conservatory offers sea views. The waiter brings you a free starter of fish paté while you look at the menu. Oysters are served raw, fried or in soup, or you might prefer beef in oyster sauce. The house special is black risotto, made with cuttlefish, squid and mussels from Ston.
🕐 Daily 9am–10pm
🍴 L 120kn, D 170kn, Wine from 70/110kn
🚗 Take the Magistrala coast road north from Dubrovnik and turn left after around 40km (25 miles) to reach Mali Ston

EATING

STAYING IN CROATIA

Accommodation in Croatia ranges from practical to palatial, from stone cottages and lighthouses to campsites and five-star hotels. Since independence from Yugoslavia, standards have risen and soulless Communist-era hotels have been upgraded or replaced by smaller establishments emphasizing character and service. Hotels in Zagreb and the bigger cities open all year, but on the islands most places close in winter and it can be difficult to find rooms between November and March.

The Palace Hotel, Hvar; a stunning view from the Villa Dubrovnik; the Korana Hotel, Karlovac, in winter

PRACTICALITIES

● The Croatian National Tourist Board publishes an annual hotel directory and guides to camping, marinas and private accommodation. The guides are available free from tourist offices or can be downloaded from www.croatia.hr. You can also use the website to search for accommodation by region.

● It is always a good idea to reserve ahead, particularly between June and September.

● The cost of accommodation varies significantly throughout the year. The most expensive months are July and August, followed by June and September. Mid-season prices usually apply in April, May and October. For hotels that remain open in winter, low season is November to March, with exceptions for busy periods like Christmas and New Year.

● All visitors over 12 must pay a tourist tax which varies according to season, locality and class of accommodation. A typical cost is 5kn per person per day in a mid-range hotel, with children aged 12–18 paying half price.

HOTELS

● Most large hotels on the coast were built during the 1960s and are lacking in architectural character. They are frequently situated out of town, in purpose-built resort areas a few kilometres from the centre. Many were damaged or used to house refugees during the war but these former state-run hotels have now been privatized and upgraded with the help of foreign investment. Most offer comfortable accommodation together with facilities like swimming pools, tennis courts, playgrounds, wellness centres, spas, watersports and private beaches.

● A recent trend has been the opening of small, family-run hotels, often in buildings of historic interest. Many of these are members of the Association of Small and Family Hotels (tel 021 317880, www.omh.hr), which publishes an annual directory of over 70 hotels.

● Hotel prices are usually quoted in euros, though you can pay in either euros or Croatian kuna. Where prices are quoted in euros, they are given in euros in this book. Most hotels accept credit cards but there is often a discount for paying in cash.

● The price of a single room is typically 60–80 per cent of the cost of a double.

● A buffet breakfast is usually included in the price.

STAYING

PRIVATE ACCOMMODATION

● Private accommodation ranges from a spare room with shared bathroom in a family home to self-contained studios and apartments. Although it can be basic, it is usually good value, and staying with a Croatian family gives you a taste of local life.

● The cheapest rooms are available by negotiating with owners who meet buses and ferries arriving in popular resorts. However, you should be aware

● In Zagreb, NEST (tel 01 487 3225, www.nest.hr) offers modern city centre apartments for short-term rentals, with a minimum stay of three nights.

● Apartments in Dubrovnik can be booked through www.dubrovnik-apartments.com and www.dubrovnik-online.com

AGROTOURISM

● Rural tourism is growing in popularity in Croatia, from accommodation on

Exterior of the Kvarner Hotel, Opatija; the outdoor swimming pool at the San Rocco Hotel in Brtonigla

that these rooms may not be officially licensed or inspected and you should ask to see the room before you commit yourself.

● Private rooms (*sobe*) and apartments (*apartmani*) can also be booked through local accommodation agencies, though you will probably pay a small supplement as commission. Agencies can be found in all main towns and resorts, usually close to the bus station, ferry port or tourist office. The accommodation has been licensed and graded according to standards. If you want to book in advance, there is a searchable database of private accommodation at www.croatia.hr

● Prices start from around 100kn per person per night. Breakfast is not included. There is usually a supplement for stays of less than three nights.

SELF-CATERING

● Self-catering properties include everything from stylish city apartments to restored stone cottages. Staying in self-catering accommodation can make a good option for families or larger groups. A number of UK tour operators (▷ 251) offer self-catering villas and cottages, mostly in Istria and Dalmatia, some with private pools.

working farms to upmarket rural hotels. It is particularly developed in Istria and areas of inland Croatia such as Zagorje and the Plitvice Lakes.

● Look out for signs advertising *agro-turizam* or *seoski turizam* (rural tourism).

● In addition to accommodation, many places offer farmhouse cooking using local produce and home-made wine. Some of the best examples are given in the regional listings.

STAYING

The dining room at the Marco Polo Hotel, Gradac

- A directory of rural accommodation in Istria can be found at www.istra.com/agroturizam or www.istra.hr/en/agritourism

YOUTH HOSTELS

- There are youth hostels in Zagreb, Pula, Rijeka, Krk, Zadar and Dubrovnik which are open throughout the year. The youth hostels at Punat (Krk) and Veli Lošinj (Lošinj) are open from May to September only.

- To stay in a youth hostel, you must hold a membership card of an IYHF (International Youth Hostels Federation) affiliated organization. Non-members can join by paying a supplement for the first night's stay and will receive a membership card entitling them to stay at youth hostels in over 100 countries for one year.
- Bookings and information from the Croatian Youth Hostels Association (tel 01 482 9294, www.hfhs.hr).

Regent Esplanade Hotel, Zagreb; a room in the Scaletta Hotel, Pula; a view of the Park Hotel, Lovran

- Some hostels are located in modern settings, while others are in historic buildings or places of interest. The hostel at Rijeka is in a 19th-century villa, the hostel at Krk is in the island's first tourist hotel and the hostel at Pula is on a beach with its own campsite.
- Accommodation is generally in multi-bedded dormitories, though the hostel at Rijeka has double rooms and Zagreb also offers single and double rooms with adjoining bathrooms. Prices range from around 80kn for a bed in a six-bed dorm to 250kn for a double room with private shower. Breakfast is an extra charge.

LIGHTHOUSES AND FISHING COTTAGES

If you really want to get away from it all with a back-to-nature experience, there are two adventurous options.

- Eleven of Croatia's lighthouses have been converted into self-catering apartments for between two and eight people. Three are on the mainland at Umag, Poreč and Makarska, while the others are on islands with varying degrees of remoteness. The most remote is on the tiny island of Palagruža, 70km (44 miles) from Vis. In most cases, there is a resident lighthouse keeper. Prices start from around €150 per person per week. Contact Adriatica (tel 01 241 5611, UK tel 020 7183 0437, www.adriatica.net).
- Travel agents in Murter offer 'Robinson Crusoe' fishermen's cottages for rent on the Kornati Islands in summer. These are old stone cottages, a few metres from the sea, with no electricity and water from a well. Conditions are basic, but you can rent your own fishing boat and supplies are delivered by boat twice a week. If you are seeking solitude in a beautiful setting, this could be the experience of

The Manora Hotel in Lošinj (left)

STAYING

a lifetime. Contact Kornatturist (tel 022 435854, www.kornatturist.hr).

CAMPING AND CARAVANNING

● Camping is the most popular form of tourist accommodation in Croatia, accounting for over a third of all visitors. The majority of campsites are situated on the coast in Istria, Kvarner and Dalmatia. An exception is Camping Korana, in the Plitvice Lakes National Park.

● The Croatian National Tourist Board publishes an annual brochure, the *Top 20 Campsites in Croatia*. In 2006, 15 were in Istria (including five naturist sites), three in Kvarner (on the islands of Cres, Krk and Lošinj) and two in Northern Dalmatia.

● You can make a complete search of campsites by region at www.camping.hr and www.croatia.hr

● Camping outside official campsites and caravan (RV) parks is forbidden.

Wine barrels in a hotel cellar; a balcony at the Marco Polo Hotel, Gradac; a view from the Villa Dubrovnik

● There are over 150 registered campsites, which are graded from two to five stars according to facilities. Some consist mainly of tent pitches, while others are sprawling camping villages with bungalows, chalets, mobile homes and accommodation for over 5,000 people. There are also a large number of mini-camps with up to 30 pitches. Most campsites have hot and cold water, showers and laundry facilities, and most large campsites also have pools, tennis courts, boat and bicycle hire and access to a beach. Around 12 campsites, mainly in Istria, cater exclusively for naturists, while many others have nudist beaches.

● Most campsites are open from May to September, though a small number stay open throughout the year.

MARINAS

● Sailors with their own boat can stay at one of 50 marinas along the Adriatic coast, with a total of over 13,000 berths at sea. The largest operator of marinas is ACI Club (tel 051 271288, www.aci-club.hr), which owns 21 marinas. Many are open throughout the year, with facilities including yacht charter, parking, petrol and repairs, plus showers, shops, restaurants, laundry service, internet access and currency exchange. A few also offer accommodation on land. Smaller marinas are open in summer only. In addition, sailors can moor their boats at some 350 natural harbours along the Adriatic coast and islands.

● You can search for marinas at www.croatia.hr

UK TOUR OPERATORS TO CROATIA		
NAME	**TELEPHONE**	**WEBSITE**
Bond Tours	01372 745300	www.bondtours.com
Bosmere Travel	01473 834094	www.bosmeretravel.co.uk
Cottages to Castles	01622 775217	www.croatia-villas-online.com
Croatian Affair	020 7385 7111	www.croatianaffair.com
Croatian Villas	020 8888 6655	www.croatianvillas.com
Hidden Croatia	0871 208 0075	www.hiddencroatia.com
Holiday Options	0870 420 8386	www.holidayoptions.co.uk
My Croatia	0118 961 1554	www.mycroatia.co.uk
Simply Travel	0870 166 4979	www.simplytravel.co.uk
Vintage Travel	01954 261431	www.vintagetravel.co.uk

STAYING

ZAGREB

Most accommodation in Zagreb is aimed firmly at business travellers. Major international chains like Regent, Sheraton and Westin have large hotels in the city, offering all the facilities and five-star luxury you would expect. Unlike elsewhere in Croatia, rates stay the same throughout the year, though discounted rooms are sometimes available at weekends and prices tend to rise during events like the Zagreb International Trade Fair in September. If you are staying in Zagreb for more than a few days, consider renting an apartment through NEST (tel 01 487 3225, www.nest.hr). Budget options include the central Zagreb Youth Hostel (tel 01 484 1261, www.hfhs.hr), Ravnice Youth Hostel near Maksimir Park (tel 01 233 2325, www.ravnice-youth-hostel.hr) and Hostel V at Remetinec (tel 01 614 0042, www.nazor.hr).

STAYING

ASTORIA

Petrinjska 71, Zagreb
Tel 01 480 8900
www.bestwestern.com
The elegant 1930s lobby, with its dark wood panelling and tiled floor, sets the tone for this discreet and stylish hotel on a quiet street near the railway station. After a recent refurbishment, the Astoria reopened in 2005

as the first Best Western hotel in Croatia.
🛏 From €101
🛌 102 (51 non-smoking)
🆒 🅿
🚋 Tram 2, 4, 6, 9, 13 to railway station

CENTRAL

Branimirova 3, Zagreb
Tel 01 484 1122
www.hotel-central.hr
Directly opposite the railway station, this functional but comfortable hotel provides a convenient mid-price option within walking distance of the centre. If you can, ask for a room on the top floor, with views of the cathedral across the city.

🔵 All year
🛏 720kn
🛌 79
🆒
🚋 Tram 2, 4, 6, 9, 13 to railway station

DUBROVNIK

Gajeva 1, Zagreb
Tel 01 486 3555
www.hotel-dubrovnik.hr
Built in 1929, the Dubrovnik has a prime position in a corner of Trg Bana Jelačića, with some rooms overlooking the square. You enter through a striking glass wing on Gajeva, central to Zagreb's open-air café life. This makes a good choice if you want four-star comforts in the heart of the city.

SPECIAL

ARCOTEL ALLEGRA

Branimirova 29, Zagreb

Tel 01 469 6000

www.arcotel.cc/allegra

Designed by Viennese artist Harald Schreiber, the Allegra is full of bright colours and funky touches like the fish tank in the lobby, and all rooms include DVD players and mobile tables which double up as desks or for breakfast in bed. The buffet breakfast here is one of the best in town, and the restaurant does an excellent all-you-can-eat Sunday brunch. The hotel is part of a modern shopping mall near the railway station, which also includes a cinema.

🍽 From €90

🛏 151 (most non-smoking)

🚭 📺 🅿

🚊 Tram 2, 6, 8 to Branimirova or a short walk from railway station

🔆 All year

🍽 From €140

🛏 266 (some non-smoking)

🚭

🚊 Tram 1, 6, 11, 12, 13, 14, 17 to Trg Bana Jelačića

ILICA

Ilica 102, Zagreb

Tel 01 377 7522

www.hotel-ilica.hr

Although the rooms are on the small side, this friendly hotel, just two tram stops from the main square, offers the best budget option in the city centre. The 12 rooms are divided into singles, doubles and triples, all with private bathrooms. Reserve in advance. No credit cards.

🍽 499kn

🛏 12 (all non-smoking)

🚭 🅿

🚊 Tram 1, 6, 11 to Britanski Trg

JAEGERHORN

Ilica 14, Zagreb

Tel 01 483 3877

www.hotel-pansion-jaegerhorn.hr

The main appeal of this small hotel is its setting, in the attractive Lovački Rog shopping arcade, which dates back to 1827 and is reached through an arch just off the main square. Rooms are simple and functional, and there is a

Exterior of the Palace Hotel

lovely garden restaurant, where you dine by a waterfall at the foot of the steps leading up to Gradec.

🍽 800kn

🛏 13

🚭 🅿

🚊 Tram 1, 6, 11, 12, 13, 14, 17 to Trg Bana Jelačića

MOVIE HOTEL

Savska Cesta 141, Zagreb

Tel 01 600 3600

www.themoviehotel.com

Zagreb's first theme hotel opened in 2006 above The Movie Pub, a popular English-style pub on the

SPECIAL

REGENT ESPLANADE

Mihanovićeva 1, Zagreb

Tel 01 456 6666

www.theregentzagreb.com

The *grande dame* of Zagreb hotels opened in 1925 for train passengers arriving on the Orient Express, and the guest list has included Tito, Orson Welles and Pele. After a complete renovation by Regent Hotels, the Esplanade reopened in 2004 and is once again the classiest address in town. From the moment you step into the art deco marble and walnut lobby, you feel the history and elegance of this place. Rooms are luxuriously decorated with rich fabrics and fresh flowers, together with marble bathrooms and walk-in showers. Modern touches include free wireless internet access throughout the hotel.

🍽 From €150

🛏 209 (some non-smoking)

🚭 📺 🅿

🚊 Tram 2, 4, 6, 9, 13 to railway station

outskirts of town filled with Hollywood memorabilia. Rooms are named after famous film stars, and there are plans to offer DVD players and a selection of movies for guests to watch.

🍽 €82

🛏 20

🚭 🅿

🚊 Tram 4, 5, 14, 17 to Prisavlje

PALACE

Strossmayerova Trg 10, Zagreb

Tel 01 489 9600

www.palace.hr

Built as the Austro-Hungarian Schlessinger

STAYING

Palace in 1891 and converted to a hotel in 1907, the Palace is the oldest hotel in Zagreb and one of the oldest in Central Europe. Recent renovations have introduced modern facilities such as internet access in the rooms, but the hotel still exudes old-world style and art nouveau design. Most of the rooms overlook a pretty series of parks and squares between the railway station and the main square. There is a delightful Viennese-style café on the ground floor, a good place to meet friends over coffee.

From 980kn

123 (some non-smoking)

Tram 6, 13 to Zrinjevac or a short walk from railway station or Trg Bana Jelačića

SLIŠKO

Bunećeva 7, Zagreb
Tel 01 618 4777
www.slisko.hr

This small family-run hotel in a quiet street near the bus station makes a convenient choice for travellers arriving on the airport bus. Rooms are simply furnished but comfortable, and guests have free access to a computer to check their email.

517kn

15

Tram 2, 5, 6, 7, 8 to Autobusni Kolodvor (bus station)

TOMISLAVOV DOM

Sljemenska Cesta 24, Zagreb
Tel 01 456 0400
www.hotel-tomislavovdom.com

This mountain lodge, surrounded by pine woods at a height of 1,000m (3,000ft), allows you to combine a visit to Zagreb with some walking in summer or skiing

in winter. Just beneath the summit of Medvednica a short distance from the ski slopes, it has an indoor pool and excellent spa facilities, including sauna and massage treatments.

From 730kn

42 (some non-smoking)

Indoor

Tram 15 to Dolje followed by cable-car

VILLA TINA

Bukovačka Cesta 213, Zagreb
Tel 01 244 5138

Set in a large house high above Maksimir Park, Villa

The Regent Esplanade (▷ 253)

Tina offers a peaceful retreat from the city, with tasteful modern décor, art and antiques. The hotel also has an indoor pool and fitness centre.

€90

26

Indoor

Bus 203 from Maksimir Park

Take Maksimirska Cesta out of the city and turn left up Bukovačka Cesta just before Maksimir Park

WESTIN ZAGREB

Kršnjavoga 1, Zagreb
Tel 01 489 2000
www.westin.com/zagreb

The former Hotel Opera is a high-rise Zagreb landmark, towering over the city close to the Mimara Museum and Croatian National Theatre. Now owned by the Westin chain, it offers modern five-star luxury and comforts, including the signature Heavenly Bed with its layers of plush white sheets. The top floors have some of the best views in Zagreb.

From €135

378 (some non-smoking)

Indoor

Tram 12, 13, 14, 17 to Hotel Opera

OUTSIDE ZAGREB
GARNY

Mikulčićeva 7a, Velika Gorica
Tel 01 625 3600
www.hotel-garny.hr

Although it is officially in Velika Gorica, this family-run hotel in the vicinity of Zagreb airport makes a good choice for anyone with a flight to catch the next morning. The rooms are tastefully decorated with bright colours, warm furnishings and paintings by Croatian artist Vladimir Zopf. Help-yourself baskets of fruit, biscuits and sweets add a thoughtful touch. If you want to relax before your flight, there is a small pool, sauna, solarium and fitness suite. This is an unexpectedly special place and a world away from the standard image of monotonous airport hotels.

750kn

19

Indoor

Follow the signs off the airport approach road just before you reach the terminal

INLAND CROATIA

Accommodation in inland Croatia is not as plentiful as on the coast, but prices are reasonable and hotels are rarely full even in summer. As in Zagreb, most hotels are open year round and there are few seasonal variations in price, except at the Plitvice Lakes. This region contains some striking examples of small, individual hotels. In Karlovac and Osijek, new hotels are breathing life into cities still recovering from war, while Croatia's first wine hotel in the rural heartland of Slavonia symbolizes the transition from mines into vines. At the other end of the price scale, farmhouses in the Zagorje and Lonjsko Polje have opened their doors to guests, offering home-grown food and a peaceful stay in idyllic surroundings.

PRICES AND SYMBOLS

Prices are for a double room for one night, including breakfast. All hotels listed accept credit cards unless otherwise stated. For a key to the symbols, ▷ 2.

KARLOVAC

KORANA
Perivoj Josipa Vrbanića 8, Karlovac
Tel 047 609090
www.hotelkorana.hr
Set on the edge of a park on the banks of the River Korana, this former sanatorium has re-emerged as one of Croatia's most stylish small hotels. Breakfast is taken on a summer terrace overlooking the river and city beach. The old town is a 10-minute walk away.
🛏 From 850kn
🚪 15 (9 non-smoking)
❄ ⛱ Indoor 🅿

KOPAČKI RIT

GALIĆ
Ritska 1, Bilje
Tel 031 750393
Snježana Galić is one of several hosts offering private rooms in the village of Bilje, near the entrance to Kopački Rit Nature Park. There are two rooms in the main house, with a shared bathroom, and four rooms with private bathrooms in a bungalow in the garden. The hearty Slavonian breakfast will set you up for the day. If this place is full, the tourist office on the main street has details of families offering accommodation.
🛏 328kn
🚪 6
🅿
🏠 Off the main street, near Kod Varge restaurant

OSIJEK

OSIJEK
Šamačka 4, Osijek
Tel 031 230333
www.hotelosijek.hr
This gleaming glass skyscraper beside the River Drava reopened in 2004 and is as a symbol of post-war reconstruction. Rooms are equipped with all modern conveniences, including wireless internet access. The 14th-floor spa has Turkish

SPECIAL IN LONJSKO POLJE

RAVLIĆ

Mužilovčica 72
Tel 044 710151
The guest room of this 200-year-old oak cottage has wooden beds, antique furniture and shutters opening to a view of the River Sava. The Ravlić family welcome visitors seeking a back-to-nature experience. Horse-riding, boating and fishing can be arranged, and meals are served in the garden. Conditions are basic—there is an outdoor shower and toilet—but a stay here is an adventure.

🅒 Closed Nov–end Mar

💷 340kn; breakfast 25kn per person. Discunt for stays of more than three nights

🛏 2

🚗 On the main road through Mužilovčica, between Čigoć and Lonja

baths and Jacuzzis with panoramic views.

💷 From 950kn

🛏 140 (most non-smoking)

🅢 🍴 🅿

PLITVIČKA JEZERA

JEZERO

Plitvička Jezera
Tel 053 751400
www.np-plitvicka-jezera.hr
Of the three hotels within the Plitvice Lakes park, the Jezero, is the largest, with rooms overlooking Lake Kozjak. Its facilities include an indoor pool, tennis courts and gym. Five of the rooms are specially adapted for visitors with disabilities.

💷 From €106 (Jun and Sep); rates vary throughout the year

🛏 229

🏊 Indoor 🍴 🅿

SLAVONSKI BROD

ZDJELAREVIĆ

Vinogradska 102, Brodski Stupnik
Tel 035 427040
www.zdjelarevic.hr
One of the top wineries in Slavonia was extended in 2004 with the opening of Croatia's first wine hotel, surrounded by vineyards in the village of Brodski Stupnik. Rooms are decorated in traditional style, with large hand-made wooden beds. Tours of the vineyards are available, or you can visit the winery, have a tasting in the cellar

Lojzekova Hiža in the snow

and sample the wines in the restaurant (▷ 237).

💷 580kn

🛏 15

🅢 🅿

🚗 Take the road from Slavonski Brod to Nova Gradiska and turn right after 7km (4 miles) in Brodski Stupnik

VARAŽDIN

MALTAR

Ulica Prešernova 1, Varaždin
Tel 042 311100
This friendly family-run pension in the centre is the best place to stay in town. Rooms are small but adequate for a one-night stay.

SPECIAL IN SAMOBOR

LIVADIĆ

Trg Kralja Tomislava 1, Samobor
Tel 01 336 5850
www.hotel-livadic.hr
This family-run hotel In a 19th-century townhouse on the main square of Samobor is one of the most romantic, relaxing and characterful places to stay in Croatia. The spacious rooms have rugs, antiques and parquet floors, while the breakfast room is a riot of luxurious drapes and high-backed chairs. The attached coffee house, Kavana Livadić is the best in town. Parking is available behind the hotel.

💷 465kn

🛏 23

🅢 🅿

💷 380kn

🛏 15

🅿

🚗 In the city centre

ZAGORJE

LOJZEKOVA HIŽA

Gusakovec 116, Marija Bistrica
Tel 049 469325
www.lojzekovahiza.com
One of the earliest examples of rural tourism in the Zagorje is still one of the best, with rooms in the attic of a traditional farmhouse with a stream running through the garden. The owners can arrange carriage rides in the forest, and there is a playground and football pitch. The half-board option includes hearty farmhouse dinners.

💷 240kn

🛏 9

🅿

🚗 Signposted from the road between Marija Bistrica and Donja Stubica

ISTRIA

The west coast of Istria is where package tourism is most developed in Croatia. In summer, the hotels, campsites and beaches of Poreč, Pula, Rovinj, Novigrad, Umag and Vrsar are crowded with visitors from Germany, Austria, Italy and elsewhere. Many of Croatia's biggest campsites are situated here, including Koversada (tel 052 441378, www.maistra.hr), Europe's largest naturist resort. At the same time, Istria has some fine examples of small, boutique hotels. Away from the coast, agrotourism is increasingly popular, from rural hotels like Stancija Negričani to farmhouses offering rustic accommodation and home-cooked food.

BRIJUNI

NEPTUN-ISTRA

Veli Brijun
Tel 052 525807
www.brijuni.hr
This quayside hotel on Veli Brijun offers the chance to stay after the day-trippers have left, and enjoy golf, tennis, cycling and horse-riding. Car parking and boat transfers are included in the price. The national park also rents out seaside villas.

🕐 Closed Jan
🛏 From €101
ⓘ 87
🅿 At Fažana
🚢 National park boat from Fažana

BUZET

FONTANA

Trg Fontana 1, Buzet
Tel 052 662615
On the square near steps leading up to the walled town, the Fontana offers plain, comfortable rooms. It is a good base for a night in inland Istria, with views of the old town and a chance to stock up on goodies from Zigante Tartufi (▷ 182) nearby.
🛏 €60
ⓘ 57
🅿

LABIN

PALAČA LAZZARINI-BATTIALA

Sveti Martin, Nedešćina
Tel 052 856006
www.sv-martin.com
The pink-painted baroque palace of the last Baron Labin, reached via a stone gateway and an avenue of chestnut trees, is now six apartments with kitchens, for two to five people. There is a restaurant in the palace walls, and a wine cellar and *konoba* around the fireplace The palace, on a hillside, has large gardens.
🛏 €45; breakfast 40kn per person
ⓘ 6
🅿
🚗 Take the main road from Labin to Rijeka and turn left at Vinež to reach Sveti Martin

SAN ROCCO

Srednja Ulica 2, Brtonigla
Tel 052 725000
www.san-rocco.hr
A small, friendly, family-run hotel in an old stone townhouse with a poolside terrace overlooking a garden of olive trees with distant sea views. The excellent restaurant specializes in fresh Istrian produce such as ham, cheese, seafood and truffle dishes, accompanied by local wines. Sauna, massage and bicycle rental are available.

From €133
12
Outdoor
On the road from Buje to Novigrad

MOTOVUN

KAŠTEL

Trg Andrea Antico 7, Motovun
Tel 052 681607
www.hotel-kastel-motovun.hr
This stylish hotel on the main square is set in a Renaissance manor house. Its rooms, gardens and terraces offer tranquil views. The restaurant serves classic Istrian truffle dishes.

€76
28

NOVIGRAD

CITTAR

Prolaz Venecija 1, Novigrad
Tel 052 757737
www.cittar.hr
This family-run hotel beside the walls and near the marina was one of the first private hotels in Croatia. Rooms are spacious and tastefully decorated, and the airy breakfast room is a treat. There are tennis

courts, and the marina and beach are a walk away.

€80
14

POREČ

FILIPINI

Filipini, Poreč
Tel 052 463200
www.istra.com/filipini
This small hotel in the woods, surrounded by olive groves and vineyards, with tennis courts and bicycles, makes a good base for an active holiday.

The brightly painted Hotel Kaštel

€56
8

5km (3 miles) outside Poreč on the road to Pazin

ROVINJ

VILLA ANGELO D'ORO

Via Svalba 38-42, Rovinj
Tel 052 840502
www.rovinj.at
This charming hotel is set in a 17th-century bishop's palace in the old town, tastefully decorated with antique furniture and oil paintings. Breakfast is served in summer in a

SCALETTA

Flavijevska 26, Pula
Tel 052 541599
www.hotel-scaletta.com
With warm tones, soft furnishings and a bright, playful feel, this small hotel near the Roman arena is the nicest place to stay in the centre. Rooms are decorated in yellow with soft, angled lights and the bathrooms have bright touches. The marine theme continues in the breakfast room, all blue and yellow, and a good spread.

718kn
12

fountain garden. From the rooftop loggia there are views over the old town and out to sea. Facilities include a sauna, jacuzzi, and a private boat and yacht for rent. There is no vehicle access.

Closed Jan, Feb
From €184
24

VODNJAN

STANCIJA NEGRIČANI

Stancija Negričani, Marčana
Tel 052 391084
www.stancijanegricani.com
A rural hotel that is a fine example of agrotourism, with rooms in an old stone farmhouse and excellent dinners of organic local produce. Bicycles are available and horse-riding can be arranged. The sea is just a short drive away.

€75–€130; breakfast 60kn per person
9
Outdoor
6km (4 miles) outside Vodnjan on road to Barban

KVARNER

Opatija is the undisputed tourist capital of Kvarner and one of the biggest holiday resorts in Croatia, whose seafront villas and hotels are busy throughout the year. Although it has its share of bland modern hotels, it also has some glorious relics of the Habsburg era, particularly along the Lungomare promenade between Opatija and Lovran. Villa Astra and Villa Ariston are two of the finest small hotels in Croatia, while to experience the faded grandeur of Opatija's golden age you must stay at the Hotel Kvarner. Elsewhere, the islands of Cres, Krk, Lošinj and Rab have numerous large beach hotels that are crowded in summer, but either closed or almost totally deserted in winter.

PRICES AND SYMBOLS

Prices are for a double room for one night, including breakfast. All hotels listed accept credit cards unless otherwise stated. For a key to the symbols, ▷ 2.

KRK

ZVONIMIR

Emila Geistlicha 38, Baška, Krk
Tel 051 656810
www.hotelibaska.hr
This large seaside hotel is separated by a promenade from the wide beach at Baška, with views across the water to the Velebit mountains. Completely renovated in 2003, it has indoor and outdoor pools and a number of interconnecting rooms which are suitable for families. Most rooms have a balcony with sea view.
🏊 From €114 or €120 (half-board)
🛏 70
🔆 🏊 Indoor and outdoor 🅿

LOŠINJ

APOKSIOMEN

Riva Lošinjskih Kapetana 1, Mali Lošinj
Tel 051 520820
www.apoksiomen.com
Located in a harbourside villa on the promenade, Hotel Apoksiomen is typical of the new breed of town-house hotels in Croatia, combining traditional ambience with modern comforts and standards of service.
Rooms are decorated with paintings by modern Croatian artists, and the palm-lined terrace café has lovely waterfront views.
🔆 Closed Nov–end Mar
🏊 From €120
🛏 25
🔆 🅿

LOVRAN

PARK

Šetalište Maršala Tita 60, Lovran
Tel 051 706200
www.hotel-park-lovran.com
This striking blue building by the harbour stands the end of the Lungomare promenade. Fully restored and reopened in 2005, it features a wellness centre over two floors with pool, jacuzzi, massage, gym and

MANORA

Mandalenska, Nerezine, Lošinj
Tel 051 237460
www.manora-losinj.hr

Opened in 2005 by the Spišić family, the Manora is striking from the outside, with cubic-style Mediterranean villas painted in the bright primary colours that are a feature of Lošinj. The funky boutique atmosphere continues inside, with light, spacious rooms offering views over the mountain or the sea. The restaurant serves some of the best food around, using island ingredients to produce creative dishes such as lamb cutlets with cream, steak with chocolate or ravioli with salmon, wild asparagus and ham.

From €98
22
Outdoor
Just outside Nerezine on the road to Mali Lošinj

beauty treatments. All of its facilities are accessible to visitors with disabilities.
All year
From €124
46
Indoor

OPATIJA

KVARNER

Pava Tomašića 1-4, Opatija
Tel 051 271233
www.liburnia.hr

Built in 1884 as the first hotel on the Adriatic coast, the Kvarner symbolizes Opatija's belle époque era. Although a little careworn, it is still the best place to recapture a bygone age. Tea and cakes are served at 5pm daily; there are grand dances in the Crystal Ballroom and on the summer terrace. The lush gardens of Villa Angiolina are a short stroll away, and the hotel has its own private bathing platform and heated seawater pool.

From €102
86
Indoor and outdoor

RAB

ZLATNI ZALAZ

Supetarska Draga 379, Rab
Tel 051 775150

This family-run guesthouse on the cliffs is known as the

The Kvarner Hotel in Opatija

'Golden Sunset' because of the wonderful sunset views from the terrace. The location on the road from Rab to Lopar is perfect, with pine woods on one side and a shimmering bay on the other. Steps lead down to a beach and private mooring for boats. The award-winning restaurant serves creative meat and fish dishes on the terrace in summer.

Closed Jan
From €66 (half-board)
18

VILLA ASTRA

Viktora Cara Emina 11, Lovran
Tel 051 704276
www.lovranske-vile.com

Villa Astra is a seafront villa on the road from Lovran to Opatija, commissioned in 1905 in floral Venetian Gothic style, with balustrades, stained glass, ornamental windows and gardens tumbling down towards the Lungomare promenade. Rooms are spacious and elegant, with rich fabrics and polished hardwood floors. The restaurant serves gourmet Istrian and Kvarner cuisine. During the winter Villa Astra offers themed weekend breaks.

From €248
6
Outdoor

RIJEKA

CONTINENTAL

Šetalište AK Miošića 1, Rijeka
Tel 051 372008
www.jadran-hoteli.hr

First opened in 1888, this imperial Austrian building overlooks a large riverside park near the foot of the steps leading up to Trsat. The high-ceilinged rooms have dark wooden furniture and most have views of the river. Although it is fairly basic, it makes an attractive place to stay within walking distance of the Korzo and city centre. The large café terrace, with tables beneath the chestnut trees, is a popular meeting place.

455kn
42

At junction of River Rječina and Mrtvi Kanal, near large Delta car park (parking lot)

STAYING

DALMATIA

Tourism in Dalmatia is seasonal in nature. Hotels in Zadar, Split and Trogir stay open throughout the year, but on the Makarska Riviera and particularly on the islands, almost everything shuts down in winter. Most of the hotels on the following pages are open year-round, but these are the exceptions and if you are travelling out of season, you may have to rely on private accommodation. Private rooms are numerous on the islands and can be booked through local agencies or directly with the owners. Islands such as Brač, Hvar and Korčula are incredibly popular in summer so it is always best to book in advance.

HVAR

RIVA YACHT HARBOUR
Riva, Hvar
Tel 021 750100
www.suncanihvar.com
The former Hotel Slavija was completely overhauled in 2006 and reopened as the Riva Yacht Harbour Hotel, the first Croatian member of Small Luxury Hotels of the World. The position is perfect, on the palm-lined promenade. Wireless internet access allows you to check your email on the terrace while enjoying the views. Roots restaurant serves creative Hvar-Mediterranean cuisine. There is no vehicle access.
🔱 From €69
ⓘ 54
🅢

PAG

BOŠKINAC
Stara Novalja, Pag
Tel 053 663500
www.boskinac.com
This small, luxury country house hotel is in vineyards in the wild, rocky scenery of northern Pag. The large bedrooms are decorated in bold colours and natural materials, and there is a restaurant and wine cellar offering tastings of Pag cheese and Dalmatian ham. Bicycle rental and horse-riding lessons are available.
🅒 Closed Jan and Feb
🔱 From €120
ⓘ 11
🅢 🅿
🚌 Signposted off the road from Novalja to Stara Novalja

SKRADIN

SKRADINSKI BUK
Burinovac, Skradin
Tel 022 771771
www.skradinskibuk.hr
If you want to explore the Krka National Park in depth, stay at this small town-house hotel on the central square, a short walk from the harbour and the national park boats. Rooms are simply furnished and

PALAČA DEŠKOVIĆ

Pučišća, Brač
Tel 021 778240
www.palaca-deskovic.com
A 15th-century
Renaissance mansion by
the harbour in Pučišća has
been converted into a
small luxury hotel that
makes an original place to
stay. Rooms and suites
are filled with antique
furniture and decorated
with Countess Dešković's
own paintings. If you want
to do it in style, arrive by
yacht—the hotel has its
own private moorings for
guests.
From €166
15

decorated in warm pastel
shades, and the top-floor
terrace has canyon views.
From €64
28

SPLIT

VESTIBUL PALACE

Iza Vestibula 4, Split
Tel 021 329329
www.vestibulpalace.com
This stylish hotel opened in
2005 inside Diocletian's
Palace. Mimimalism is the
rule here, with sleek lines,
glass ceilings, polished
wood floors and plain black
and white furniture blend-
ing in with ancient Roman
walls. The hotel may be a
little too self-consciously
trendy for some people's
tastes, but it is an oasis of
calm and contemporary
chic at the heart of the city.
There is no vehicle access.
From €190
7

TROGIR

TRAGOS

Budislavićeva 3, Trogir
Tel 021 884729
www.tragos.hr
The first hotel within the
walls of the old town was
opened by the Žunić family
in 2005. Set in an 18th-
century baroque palace a
few steps from the cathe-
dral square, its rooms are
decorated in warm colours
with original stone walls.
There is an attractive garden restaurant in summer.
600kn
12

Outside the Vestibul Palace

VIS

TAMARIS

Obala Sveti Jurja 30, Vis
Tel 021 711350
This elegant Habsburg villa
on the quayside is one of
the few places in Vis that
opens all year. Some rooms
have balconies and shutters
with views across the bay to
the Franciscan monastery
on the far side. The terrace
café is a good place for a
glass of Vugava while
watching the sailors tying
up their yachts and the sun
setting over the sea.

MARCO POLO

Obala 15, Gradac
Tel 021 697502
www.hotel-marcopolo.com
Unlike most hotels on the
Makarska Riviera, this chic
family-run boutique hotel
at the end of the prome-
nade in Gradac stays open
all year. From the rooftop
terrace, there are views
across the water to the
Pelješac mountains, and
the top-floor fitness centre
has a jacuzzi and looks out
to sea. The restaurant
serves dishes 'inspired by
Marco Polo's travels'. A
short walk along the promenade crosses a headland
on its way to the long
horseshoe beach at Brist.
From €72
30

600kn
27

ZADAR

FUNIMATION

Majstora Radovana 7, Zadar
Tel 023 206636
www.falkensteiner.com
The Austrian Falkensteiner
chain has brought its
concept to Croatia with the
opening of this all-inclusive
family resort. Tennis, beach
volleyball and an adventure
playground for kids are all
included in the price, along
with pools, waterslides and
a large aquapark by the
beach. Meals, drinks and
even ice-creams are in-
cluded too. Accommodation
ranges from single rooms
to large family suites.
From €160 (all-inclusive)
258
 Indoor and outdoor

DUBROVNIK AND BEYOND

Most large hotels in Dubrovnik are on the Lapad and Babin Kuk peninsulas, 5km (3 miles) west of the old town. Although this area has none of the character of the walled city, it has pine woods and beaches just a short bus ride from the centre. At the other end of town, upmarket hotels such as Villa Dubrovnik and Grand Villa Argentina are found outside Ploče Gate. There are two charming small hotels inside the city walls, but the best option for many visitors will be private accommodation. Rooms and apartments in the old city can be booked through local agencies or websites such as www.dubrovnik-apartments.com and www.dubrovnik-online.com. Budget travellers can stay in Dubrovnik's popular youth hostel (tel 020 423241, www.hfhs.hr), a 15-minute walk from Pile Gate. In summer another alternative is to stay in Cavtat or on the Elafiti Islands and travel into Dubrovnik by boat.

CAVTAT

CROATIA

Frankopanska 10, Cavtat
Tel 020 475555
www.hoteli-croatia.hr
This enormous beach hotel, surrounded by pine woods and gardens on the Sustjepan peninsula, has now been renovated and reopened as a five-star resort and one of the top seaside hotels in Croatia. Sports facilities include tennis, volleyball, watersports and an outdoor pool.

🏨 From €168
ⓘ 480 (some non-smoking)
🆒 🏊 Indoor and outdoor 🍸 🅿
🚌 10 to Cavtat
🔀 Fork left at the entrance to Cavtat

DUBROVNIK

GRAND VILLA ARGENTINA

Frana Supila 14, Dubrovnik
Tel 020 440555
www.gva.hr
Just outside Ploče Gate with magnificent views of the old town, the Argentina is traditionally the grandest address in town, with a guest list that has included Richard Burton, Elizabeth Taylor, Tito and Margaret Thatcher. As well as the main hotel building, there are four villas in the grounds, including the oriental-style folly, Villa Scheherezade, which can be hired by groups of ten people for €6,000 a day. Terraced gardens lead down to a private beach with views of the Old Port, while the Energy Clinic offers expensive spa and beauty treatments.

🏨 From €220
ⓘ 166 (some non-smoking)
🆒 🏊 Indoor and outdoor 🍸 🅿
🚌 5, 8

DUBROVNIK PALACE

Masarykov Put 20, Lapad,
Dubrovnik
Tel 020 430000
www.dubrovnikpalace.hr
The flagship of Goran
Štrok's Adriatic Luxury
Hotels, at the southwest-
ern tip of the Lapad
peninsula, was reopened
in 2004. The lobby sets the
tone, all sleek interior
design in glass, wood and
stone, and a Sunset Bar
with panoramic views of
the Elafiti Islands. Spread
over ten floors cascading
towards the beach, all the
rooms have sea-facing balconies. There are jogging
paths and footpaths in the
nearby pine woods.
From €317
308 (some non-smoking)
Indoor and outdoor
4

HILTON IMPERIAL

Ulica Marijana Blažića 2, Dubrovnik
Tel 020 320320
www.dubrovnik.hilton.com
The first Hilton in Croatia
opened in 2005 in this art
nouveau classic. Just outside Pile Gate, the rooms on
the top floors have views of
Lovrijenac fortress and the
sea. Although it has local
character, with prints of old
Ragusan argosies on the
walls, the hotel also has all
the hallmarks of the Hilton
brand, including the popular Hilton Breakfast buffet.
From €250
147 (some non-smoking)
Indoor
1, 2, 3, 4, 5, 6, 8, 9 to Pile

KARMEN

Bandureva 1, Dubrovnik
Tel 020 323433
www.karmendu.tk

These spacious apartments
beside the Old Port are
among the most attractive
places to stay in the old city.
Each has a kitchen, and
some have a balcony or terrace overlooking the port.
Breakfast is not included.
€75–€120
4

1, 2, 3, 4, 5, 6, 8, 9 to Pile

PETKA

Obala Stjepana Radića 38, Gruž,
Dubrovnik
Tel 020 410500
www.hotelpetka.hr

The Hilton Imperial Hotel

This high-rise hotel by Gruž
harbour is a good base for
early-morning departures
to the Elafiti Islands and
Mljet. It is worth paying
extra for a room with a
balcony and a view of
the harbour and the
Lapad peninsula.
From €120
104

1A, 1B, 3, 7, 8

SESAME INN

Don Frana Bulića 5, Dubrovnik
Tel 020 412910
www.sesame.hr

PUCIĆ PALACE

Od Puča 1, Dubrovnik
Tel 020 326200
www.thepucicpalace.com
With stone walls, dark oak
floors, original artworks
and handwoven rugs, this
stylish hotel in a baroque
palace on the market
square combines modern
comforts and antique
style. This was the first
hotel to open within the
walled city and its informal
luxury continues to set the
standard for boutique
townhouse hotels
throughout Croatia. All
rooms have DVD players
and wireless internet
access, with Bulgari
toiletries in the bathrooms.
There is even a private
yacht for guests to hire.
€479
19 (some non-smoking)

1, 2, 3, 4, 5, 6, 8, 9 to Pile

The friendly owner of the
Sesame restaurant (▷ 247)
has four rooms available on
the ground floor of a 200-
year-old family home in the
Pile district. Accommodation
is simple but comfortable,
with windows over a pretty
garden. For visitors on a
budget, this is among the
most affordable accommo-
dation within a close walk to
the old city.
390kn
4
1, 2, 3, 4, 5, 6, 8, 9 to Pile

STARI GRAD

Od Sigurate 4, Dubrovnik
Tel 020 322244
www.hotelstarigrad.com
This delightful small hotel
is in an 18th-century town-
house, whose antique

STAYING

SPECIAL IN DUBROVNIK
VILLA DUBROVNIK
Vlaha Bukovca 6, Dubrovnik
Tel 020 422933
www.villa-dubrovnik.hr
Known simply as 'the villa' by its fans, this hotel has acquired a cult following across the Mediterranean. Built as a rest home for Communist officials in 1958, it was used to house refugees during the 1991–2 war and then later as a military headquarters. The villa is showing its age and is scheduled for a major renovation in the next few years. Nothing, however, can detract from its setting, a bright white villa on a cliff, surrounded by rich gardens and terraces with views to the Old Port. Every room has a balcony with sea view. From the landing stage a private boat travels to the old city several times a day.

📅 Closed Nov–end Mar
💶 From €220; Mid-Jul to mid-Sep half board only
🛏 40
💳 🐾 🅿
🚌 5, 8
🚌 Take Frana Supila uphill from Ploče Gate and fork right beyond Grand Villa Argentina

ZAGREB
Šetalište Kralja Zvonimira 27, Lapad, Dubrovnik
Tel 020 438930
First opened as a hotel in 1932, this 19th-century villa guarded by stately palm trees stands at the start of the promenade that leads to Lapad bay and beach. The Zagreb is the best choice for mid-price comfort and is only a short bus ride from the old city.

💶 880kn
🛏 23
💳
🚌 2, 4, 5, 6, 7, 9

The exterior of the Zagreb Hotel

VILLA KVATERNIK
Kvaternikova 3, Cavtat
Tel 020 479800
www.hotelvillakvaternik.com
This small, attractive boutique hotel is owned by Croatian Australians. It is set in a 400-year-old stone house in the back streets of Cavtat, a short climb from the end of the seafront promenade. The owners can also offer eight rooms in the former Franciscan monastery, with simpler accommodation and breakfast served in the hotel.

SPECIAL IN PELJEŠAC
OSTREA
Ante Starčevića 9, Mali Ston
Tel 020 754555
www.ostrea.hr
Owned by the same family as Kapetanova Kuća restaurant (▷ 247), this stone house by the harbour in the village of Mali Ston makes a romantic place to stay, and is popular with honeymooners who come here to test the aphrodisiac qualities of the oysters. The waterside terrace is a lovely spot to sit and admire the views.

💶 From 890kn
🛏 10
💳 🅿
🚌 Take the Magistrala coast road north from Dubrovnik and turn left after around 40km (25 miles) to reach Mali Ston

💶 From €130 (€65 in monastery)
🛏 6
💳
🚌 10 to Cavtat

ELAFITSKI OTOCI
VILLA VILINA
Obala Iva Kuljevana 5, Lopud
Tel 020 759333
www.villa-vilina.hr
This stone house by the harbour at Lopud is owned by the Vilina family and offers comfortable accommodation in a peaceful setting, a short ferry ride from Dubrovnik. There are lovely walks along the promenade and over the summit of the island to Šunj. You can also sample owner's home-made rose-petal brandy.

📅 Closed Nov–end Apr
💶 From €140
🛏 18
💳 🏊 Outdoor
⛴ Lopud

furniture and handsome salons recreate the atmosphere of Ragusa's golden age. Wicker chairs and sofas on the tiny rooftop terrace make a lovely spot to enjoy the view across to the island of Lokrum.

💶 1,150kn
🛏 8
💳
🚌 1, 2, 3, 4, 5, 6, 8, 9 to Pile

HOTEL CHAINS

Name of Hotel Chain	Description	Number of Hotels in Croatia	Telephone Number and Website
Adriatic Luxury Hotels	Owned by Goran Štrok (▷ 11) as part of GS Hotels, this brand has four hotels in Dubrovnik and one in Rijeka.	5	+44 1753 838859 www.gshotelsresorts.com
Arenaturist	Former state-owned company managing hotels and resorts in Pula and Medulin.	8	052 529400 www.arenaturist.hr
Blue Sun	Large seaside hotels on the Makarska Riviera and near Zlatni Rat beach on Brač.	12	021 635210 www.bluesunhotels.com
Falkensteiner	Austrian-owned brand with family hotels in Kvarner and the all-inclusive Club Funimation at Zadar.	4	+39 047 297 8000 www.falkensteiner.com
Iberostar	This Spanish hotel chain has two large hotels in Cavtat and one on the island of Brač.	3	+34 922 070300 www.iberostar.com
Istraturist	In partnership with Spanish giant Sol Meliá, Istraturist manages hotels, campsites and tourist villages in Umag.	7	052 719000 www.istraturist.hr
Kempinski	This Swiss-based German chain plans to open two luxury golf, spa and marina resorts on the Istrian coast by 2009.	n/a	+49 69 66 41 96 16 www.kempinski.com
Korčula Hotels	This former state-owned company owns and operates hotels in Korčula Town.	5	020 726336 www.korcula-hotels.com
Liburnia Riviera	Hotels and villas on the Opatija Riviera, including Lovran and Mošćenička Draga.	15	051 710300 www.liburnia.hr
Maestral	A small group of seaside hotels on Dubrovnik's Lapad peninsula.	5	020 433600 www.hotelimaestral.com
Maistra	This company manages hotels in Rovinj, as well as the naturist camping village Koversada at Vrsar.	9	052 800300 www.maistra.hr
OMH	The Association of Small and Family Hotels includes characterful places to stay across Croatia.	73	021 317880 www.omh.hr
Plava Laguna	This former state-owned company manages hotels and campsites in the Istrian resort of Poreč.	14	052 410295 www.plavalaguna.hr
Starwood Hotels	The US business and leisure chain has three hotels in Zagreb under its Sheraton, Four Points and Westin brands, and a Le Meridien hotel in Split.	4	+1 888 625 5144 www.starwoodhotels.com
Suncani Hvar	This former state-owned company operates hotels in and around Hvar Town.	9	021 750750 www.suncanihvar.com
Riviera	Part of the Valamar brand which also features Rabac and Dubrovnik, Riviera has hotels and campsites in Poreč.	26	01 631 2777 www.riviera.hr

STAYING

Planning

BEFORE YOU GO

PASSPORTS AND VISAS

● Citizens of the UK, US, Canada, Australia and New Zealand need a valid passport to enter Croatia.

● Citizens of European Union countries require a passport or national identity card.

● Passport holders from the EU, US, Canada, Australia and New Zealand do not need a visa for stays of up to three months.

● Citizens of South Africa and most other countries require a visa, available in advance from the nearest Croatian embassy or consulate. For up-to-date details of visa requirements by country and a full list of Croatian embassies, see the Ministry of Foreign Affairs website at www.mfa.hr

● All foreign nationals must register with the police within 24 hours of arrival in Croatia. In practice this will usually be done for you by hotels, using a photocopy of your passport.

● Those passing through the Neum corridor (▷ 33) on their way to southern Dalmatia should check the visa requirements for Bosnia-Herzegovina as they may differ for some nationalities. Check the situation in advance at www.mvp.gov.ba

INSURANCE AND HEALTH

● Even if your country has a reciprocal health care agreement with Croatia (▷ 274), it is advisable to take out travel insurance covering medical emergencies as well as accidents, theft and personal liability.

● There are no compulsory vaccinations for Croatia but check that your anti-tetanus inoculations are up to date and consult your doctor or clinic to see whether any further vaccinations are recommended. Visitors to rural and forest areas of inland Croatia should seek advice on inoculation against tick-borne encephalitis.

CLIMATE

● Croatia has two distinct climatic zones. The coast and islands have a Mediterranean climate, with warm, dry summers and mild, wet winters. Temperatures on the Adriatic coast regularly exceed 25°C (77°F) in summer and rarely drop below 5°C (41°F) in winter. The inland regions have a more extreme continental climate, with hot summers and cold winters. In January the

WEATHER STATIONS

Rijeka 85m 279ft
Osijek 89m 292ft
Dubrovnik 164m 538ft

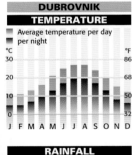

DUBROVNIK
TEMPERATURE

■ Average temperature per day
■ per night

°C 30 20 10 0 / °F 86 68 50 32

J F M A M J J A S O N D

RAINFALL

■ Average number of days with rainfall

20 15 10 5 0

J F M A M J J A S O N D

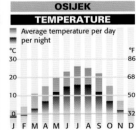

OSIJEK
TEMPERATURE

■ Average temperature per day
■ per night

°C 30 20 10 0 / °F 86 68 50 32

J F M A M J J A S O N D

RAINFALL

■ Average number of days with rainfall

20 15 10 5 0

J F M A M J J A S O N D

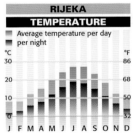

RIJEKA
TEMPERATURE

■ Average temperature per day
■ per night

°C 30 20 10 0 / °F 86 68 50 32

J F M A M J J A S O N D

RAINFALL

■ Average number of days with rainfall

20 15 10 5 0

J F M A M J J A S O N D

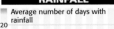

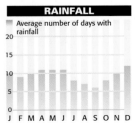

PLANNING

CITY	TIME DIFFERENCE	TIME AT 12 NOON ZAGREB
Auckland	+9	9pm
Dublin	-1	11am
London	-1	11am
New York	-6	6am
Sydney	+9	9pm

Croatia is on Central European Time (CET), one hour ahead of Greenwich Mean Time (GMT+1). Daylight saving time (GMT+2) operates from late March to late October. Clocks are put forward one hour on the last Sunday in March and put back one hour on the last Sunday in October.

CUSTOMS

From another EU country

The following maximum customs allowances apply to all travellers entering Croatia:

- **200 cigarettes or 50 cigars or 250g of tobacco**

- **1 litre of spirits**

- **2 litres of table wine**

- **250ml of toilet water**

- **2 litres of fortified wine or sparkling wine or liqueurs**

- **50ml of perfume**

- The alcohol and tobacco allowances cannot be used by travellers under 18 years of age.
- Boats are subject to a temporary importation procedure provided they are registered with customs at the nearest Port Authority on arrival.

- Valuable photographic and computer equipment should be declared on arrival.
- Pets may only be brought into Croatia if accompanied by an International Vaccination Certificate.
- The full customs regulations can be seen at www.carina.hr

temperature averages 0°C (32°F) in Zagreb and can reach −10°C (14°F) in highland areas. Snow is usual in the mountains.

● The *bora,* a fierce north-easterly wind, blows out to sea, striking fear into the hearts of sailors. At its strongest, it can force the closure of roads and ferries. It is most powerful in the Kvarner region in winter. Other winds are the *maestral*, a north-westerly sea breeze, and the *jugo*, a southerly wind bringing clouds and rain in winter.

● Long and short-range weather forecasts are available on the internet from the BBC, CNN, Weather Online and Yahoo. The Croatian Meteorological Office posts forecasts on its website (http://meteo.hr). In Croatia, you can get forecasts from local media, tourist offices and hotels or the weather forecast information line, tel 060 520520.

WHEN TO GO

● July and August are the peak holiday months. Hotel prices are at their highest and rooms are hard to find unless reserved. Roads are crowded and there are long waits for island ferries. On the plus side, the weather is reliable, and the sea is warm and the coastal towns are buzzing with life.

● Spring (May and June) and autumn (September and October) are pleasant, with mild weather but without the crowds. The sea is usually still warm for swimming, and these are good months for walking, cycling and sailing.

● Between November and April many hotels are shut and the islands virtually close. The weather can be cold, wet and windy and ferry services are minimal. This can be a good time for a break in Zagreb, with its cosy cafés and Christmas markets. On sunny days the coastal towns can be mild, but only Dubrovnik and Opatija are geared up for tourists year-round.

PLANNING

CROATIAN EMBASSIES AND CONSULATES ABROAD

EMBASSY	CONTACT DETAILS
Australia	Embassy of the Republic of Croatia 14 Jindalee Crescent, O'Malley, Canberra, ACT 2606; tel 02 6286 6988
Canada	Embassy of the Republic of Croatia 229 Chapel St, Ottawa, Ontario K1N 7Y6; tel 613 562 7820
Ireland	Embassy of the Republic of Croatia Adelaide Chambers, Peter St, Dublin 8; tel 01 476 7181
New Zealand	Consulate General of the Republic of Croatia 131 Lincoln Road, Edmonton, Auckland; tel 09 836 5581
South Africa	1160 Church St, 0083 Colbyn, Pretoria; tel 012 342 1206
UK	Embassy of the Republic of Croatia 21 Conway St, London W1T 6BN; tel 020 7387 2022
US	Embassy of the Republic of Croatia 2343 Massachusetts Ave NW, Washington DC, 20008; tel 202 588 5899

PRACTICALITIES

WHAT TO PACK

- Electrical adaptor
- First-aid kit
- Insect repellent
- Plastic sandals or flip-flops are a good idea on Croatian beaches, especially for children whose small feet can easily be hurt by pebbles or rocks. You can also buy waterproof swimming shoes for adults and children.
- Prescription drugs and medication, plus a copy of the prescription.
- Spare sets of glasses and contact lenses.
- Sun cream (sunscreen) and sunglasses.
- Swimwear and beach towel.
- Walking shoes, trainers (sneakers) or sandals. Even if you do not plan on trekking in the mountains, a good pair of shoes is useful for negotiating cobbled streets and uneven surfaces in towns.
- Warm and waterproof clothing. In summer on the coast a light sweater or jacket for the evenings should suffice, but in the mountains it can get cold at any time of year.
- Take photocopies of key documents such as passport, driver's licence and travel insurance, or send scanned copies to an email account that you can access while you are away. You should also make a separate note of your passport number, credit card numbers and emergency telephone numbers in the case of loss or theft.

ELECTRICITY

The electric power supply is 220V AC, 50Hz. Plugs have two round pins, in common with most of continental Europe. Visitors from the UK will need an adaptor and visitors from the US will need a transformer for appliances operating on 100–120V.

PUBLIC TOILETS

Public toilets (restrooms) exist in most towns and cities. There is usually a small charge for use, or you should leave some coins as a tip for the attendant. There are also public toilets at rail and bus stations. In an emergency, it is always possible to use the toilet in a bar or café, but it is polite to buy a drink first.

LOCAL CUSTOMS AND ETIQUETTE
Talking to strangers

Croatians are very sociable, and it is generally easy to strike up a conversation with strangers. Many young people speak excellent English and other foreign languages. It is best to avoid controversial topics such as politics, nationalism, the Homeland War and the trials of alleged war criminals at The Hague. You might find that people want to talk about these subjects, but it is often better to listen sensitively than to express strong opinions. Like everywhere else, football and sport always make good topics for conversation, especially among men.

CONVERSION CHART

FROM	TO	MULTIPLY BY
Inches	Centimetres	2.54
Centimetres	Inches	0.3937
Feet	Metres	0.3048
Metres	Feet	3.2810
Yards	Metres	0.9144
Metres	Yards	1.0940
Miles	Kilometres	1.6090
Kilometres	Miles	0.6214
Acres	Hectares	0.4047
Hectares	Acres	2.4710
Gallons	Litres	4.5460
Litres	Gallons	0.2200
Ounces	Grams	28.35
Grams	Ounces	0.0353
Pounds	Grams	453.6
Grams	Pounds	0.0022
Pounds	Kilograms	0.4536
Kilograms	Pounds	2.205
Tons	Tonnes	1.0160

CLOTHING SIZES

Use the clothing sizes chart below to convert the size you use at home.

UK	Metric	US	
36	46	36	SUITS
38	48	38	
40	50	40	
42	52	42	
44	54	44	
46	56	46	
48	58	48	
7	41	8	SHOES
7.5	42	8.5	
8.5	43	9.5	
9.5	44	10.5	
10.5	45	11.5	
11	46	12	
14.5	37	14.5	SHIRTS
15	38	15	
15.5	39/40	15.5	
16	41	16	
16.5	42	16.5	
17	43	17	
8	36	6	DRESSES
10	38	8	
12	40	10	
14	42	12	
16	44	14	
18	46	16	
20	46	18	
4.5	37.5	6	SHOES
5	38	6.5	
5.5	38.5	7	
6	39	7.5	
6.5	40	8	
7	41	8.5	

Dress

Formal clothing is rarely necessary in Croatia except for business, and casual dress is acceptable at all but the smartest restaurants. However, Croatians do like to dress up and look their best, and young women in particular can often be seen in the latest fashions. If you want to join in, put on your best casuals for the evening *korzo*, the Croatian equivalent of the ritual promenade which takes place all over the Mediterranean, when everyone strolls around in their latest outfit hoping to see and be seen. Do not wear beachwear or revealing clothing when visiting churches.

Nudism

Naturism has a long tradition in Croatia, and many beaches are officially designated FKK (free body culture). It is generally acceptable to take your clothes off at secluded beaches and bays. Non-naturists are

welcome to use naturist beaches, but you should behave sensitively and avoid taking photographs. Elsewhere, topless sunbathing is acceptable for both men and women on the majority of Croatian beaches.

Smoking

Cigarette smoking is widespread in Croatia, with few areas set aside for non-smokers. It is quite normal to see people smoking at restaurants. Smoking is banned on all forms of public transport, apart from certain carriages on long-distance trains.

What's in a name?

In towns and cities, especially Zagreb, you may notice that the names marked on street signs and addresses bear little resemblance to those used in conversation and on the map. For example, Ulica Gaja becomes Gajeva, Ulica Tesle becomes Teslina and Trg Maršala Tita becomes Titov Trg. This is due to the complexity of Croatian grammar, which changes word endings according to the case. Once you have grown accustomed to this, you can usually work out where you are by using a combination of logic, guesswork and common sense.

PLACES OF WORSHIP

- Croatia is predominantly Roman Catholic. There are Catholic churches in every town and village, but many of them are open only for Mass on Sunday mornings.
- Mass is held in English at 10.30am and Anglican services at noon on Sundays during term time at the Jesuit Seminary, Jordanovac 110, Zagreb.
- The Anglican Church in Vienna holds monthly services at the Jesuit Seminary in Zagreb. For details, see www.europe.anglican.org

PLACE OF WORSHIP	ADDRESS	TELEPHONE
Baptist Church	Radićeva 30, Zagreb	01 481 3167
Evangelical Lutheran Church	Gundulićeva 28, Zagreb	01 485 5622
Serbian Orthodox Church	Ilica 7, Zagreb	01 481 7531
Islamic Centre	Gavellina 40, Zagreb	01 613 7162
Jewish Community	Palmotićeva 16, Zagreb	01 492 2692

PLANNING

MONEY

Croatia's official currency is the kuna, abbreviated to HRK or kn. It takes its name from the pine marten, whose pelts were used for trading in medieval times. Banknotes are issued in denominations from 5kn to 1,000kn, with portraits of aristocratic poets and statesmen on one side and Croatian landmarks on the other. The kuna is divided into 100 lipa, though these are rarely used. Coins have a flowering linden tree (*lipa*) or pine marten (*kuna*) on one side, with native animals, birds and plants on the reverse. The only coins that are widely in circulation are 10 lipa, 20 lipa, 50 lipa, 1kn, 2kn and 5kn.

The euro (€), which is used by the majority of visitors to Croatia, is increasingly being adopted as a parallel currency and is expected to become the official currency by 2012. Prices for hotels and excursions are often quoted in euros but you can pay in either euros or Croatian kuna. Exchange rates vary from day to day but are usually around 8 kuna to the euro, 10 kuna to the British pound and 6 kuna to the US dollar.

CHANGING MONEY
● Cash and travellers' cheques can be exchanged at banks, post (mail) offices, exchange bureaux, travel agents, hotels, campsites and marinas.
● Commission charges vary from around 1 to 5 per cent.

● Euros are the most widely accepted foreign currency, but US dollars and sterling are also acceptable.
● Travellers' cheques bought in advance provide an extra degree of security but the commission for exchanging them is likely to be higher.
● The post office beside Zagreb railway station has currency exchange facilities and is open 24 hours a day.

ATMs
● The easiest, if not necessarily cheapest, way of getting Croatian kuna is by using your credit or debit card to withdraw cash from an ATM. These are found in all the main towns and resorts, as well as at railway and bus stations. Even on the islands, there is usually at least one ATM (*bankomat*) in all but the smallest villages.
● Most ATMs accept credit cards including Visa, Mastercard and Eurocard, and debit cards bearing the Cirrus, Maestro and Plus logos. American Express is less widely accepted.
● Instructions are given in a choice of languages.
● Before leaving home, make sure that you know your PIN (personal identification number). Never write it down in a way which could identify it, and never let anyone see you entering it into the machine.
● Your bank will probably make a charge for debit card withdrawals and levy interest payments for

credit card cash advances. Find out what the charges are before setting off to avoid any nasty surprises when you see your next statement.

CREDIT AND DEBIT CARDS
● Credit cards such as Visa, Mastercard, Diner's Club and American Express are widely accepted at hotels, shops, restaurants, petrol (gas) stations and car rental agencies.
● You can also pay using a debit card such as Cirrus or Maestro, which will debit the funds directly from your bank account.
● Chip-and-pin technology is becoming more widespread, so make sure that you know your PIN as you may have to enter it onto a keypad rather than using your signature as identification.
● Never rely on being able to use a credit or debit card, except in the bigger cities and international hotels. Croatia is still a largely

PLANNING

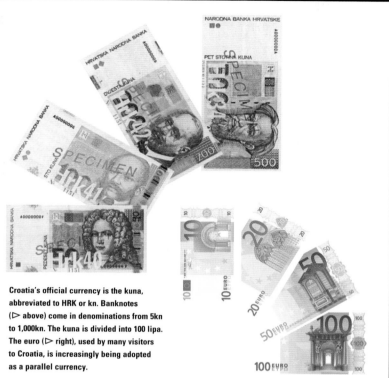

CROATIAN BANKNOTES AND EUROS

Croatia's official currency is the kuna, abbreviated to HRK or kn. Banknotes (▷ above) come in denominations from 5kn to 1,000kn. The kuna is divided into 100 lipa. The euro (▷ right), used by many visitors to Croatia, is increasingly being adopted as a parallel currency.

cash-based economy, and you should always carry enough cash to pay for everyday purchases such as food, drink and fuel. Many restaurants do not accept credit cards, and private accommodation (private rooms) should always be paid for in cash. Even where credit cards are accepted, you may get a discount for paying in cash.

WIRING MONEY
In an emergency, money can be wired from your home country by friends or relatives using a money transfer service such as Western Union (www.westernunion. com) or MoneyGram (www.moneygram.com). Payments can be made in

person, by telephone or online, and collected as little as 10 minutes later in Croatia. Post offices across Croatia act as agents for Western Union, while major branches of Atlas Travel act as agents for MoneyGram. This is a very expensive way of

acquiring money and should only be used as a last resort.

SALES TAX REFUNDS
See Shopping (▷ 162) for details of how to reclaim VAT (sales tax) on purchases over 500kn.

PRICES OF EVERYDAY ITEMS	
ITEM	**PRICE**
Coffee with milk	8kn
Ice-cream scoop	5kn
0.5 litre of beer	15kn
Litre of house wine	70kn
Litre of mineral water (in café)	15kn
Litre of mineral water (in shop)	5kn
Litre of unleaded fuel	8kn
10-minute telephone call to UK	36kn
Taxi from airport to Zagreb	200kn
Zagreb tram ticket	6.5kn

PLANNING

HEALTH

Public health services in Croatia are of a similar standard to those elsewhere in Europe. There are hospitals in all the main cities, and clinics on the islands and in smaller towns. There are also many private doctors and health centres. Most doctors speak English.

BEFORE YOU GO

● Make sure that you have a comprehensive travel insurance policy, including emergency medical assistance and repatriation. If you plan on doing any potentially hazardous sports and activities such as scuba-diving or skiing, check that these are covered by your insurance.

● EU citizens receive free medical care and hospital treatment on production of a passport or European Health Insurance Card (EHIC). However, you should still take out travel insurance as not all costs are covered and some treatment may only be available privately.

WHAT TO TAKE

● If you are taking any regular medication, bring enough for your stay. It is also a good idea to take a copy of the prescription.

● If you wear glasses or contact lenses, pack a spare set and bring your prescription in case you lose or break them.

● Pack a small first-aid kit including plasters (Band Aids), cotton wool, pain relief tablets, antihistamine tablets, anti-diarrhoea tablets and sea-sickness pills.

HEALTHY FLYING

● Visitors to Croatia from as far as the US, Australia or New Zealand may be concerned about the effect of long-haul flights on their health. The most widely publicized concern is Deep Vein Thrombosis, or DVT. Misleadingly called 'economy class syndrome', DVT is the forming of a blood clot in the body's deep veins, particularly in the legs. The clot can move around the bloodstream and could be fatal.

● Those most at risk include the elderly, pregnant women and those using the contraceptive pill, smokers and the overweight. If you are at increased risk of DVT see your doctor before departing. Flying increases the likelihood of DVT because passengers are often seated in a cramped position for long periods of time and may become dehydrated.

To minimize risk:

Drink water (not alcohol)

Don't stay immobile for hours at a time

Stretch and exercise your legs periodically

Do wear elastic flight socks, which support veins and reduce the chances of a clot forming

EXERCISES

1 ANKLE ROTATIONS **2 CALF STRETCHES** **3 KNEE LIFTS**

Lift feet off the floor. Draw a circle with the toes, moving one foot clockwise and the other counterclockwise

Start with heel on the floor and point foot upward as high as you can. Then lift heels high, keeping balls of feet on the floor

Lift leg with knee bent while contracting your thigh muscle. Then straighten leg, pressing foot flat to the floor

Other health hazards for flyers are airborne diseases and bugs spread by the plane's air-conditioning system. These are largely unavoidable but if you have a serious medical condition seek advice from a doctor before flying.

IF YOU NEED TREATMENT

● In an emergency, call an ambulance by dialling 94 from a public phone or 112 from a mobile phone.

● Alternatively, ask at your hotel or ask a taxi driver to take you to the nearest hospital (*bolnica*) or clinic (*klinika*).

● EU citizens should show the doctor their passport or EHIC card to receive free treatment. Travellers from other countries must pay according to a fixed scale of charges and keep the receipt to claim insurance. Contact your insurance company as soon as you can, preferably before receiving treatment.

PHARMACIES
● Pharmacies are indicated by the word *ljekarna* and a green cross, which is illuminated when they are open. In the larger towns and cities, there will always be at least one pharmacist on duty according to a rota system. The name of the duty chemist outside usual hours can be found on pharmacy doors.
● Pharmacies sell prescription and non-prescription medicines and drugs. The brand names of common products may vary, so it helps to take along the original packaging listing the active ingredients.

DENTAL TREATMENT
● EU citizens receive free emergency dental treatment, but other treatment has to be paid for. Most travel insurance policies only cover emergency treatment.
● The standard of dental care is high and costs are low in comparison with the European average.
● To find a dentist (*stomatološka klinika*), ask at your hotel or contact the Croatian Dental Chamber, Kurelčeva 3, Zagreb (tel 01 488 6710).
● The emergency dental clinic at Perkovčeva 3, Zagreb is open throughout the night and weekends (tel 01 482 8488).

HEALTH HAZARDS
● The sun can be very hot in summer, and skin

burns easily despite the deceptively cooling sea breezes. Apply a high-factor sun cream (sunscreen) regularly, especially after swimming. Other sensible precautions are to wear a sun hat and sunglasses, and drink plenty of water and non-alcoholic drinks.
● Look out for sea urchins, and wear plastic sandals to avoid getting the spikes in your feet.
● Snakes are frequently encountered when walking in the mountains. Most are harmless, but there are also venomous species such as the horn-nosed viper. Wear boots, thick socks and long trousers and seek medical advice immediately if you are bitten.
● Mosquitoes can be a nuisance in summer. Use an insect repellent and cover up with long-sleeved clothing and long trousers.

● More seriously, ticks are found in rural and forest areas of between April and October. Some of these carry tick-borne encephalitis, a potentially fatal viral disease. The precautions are the same as those for mosquitoes, so use an insect repellent and cover up bare skin. If you plan to walk, cycle or camp in forest regions seek advice on inoculation before travelling.
● Landmines are still a potential hazard in remote areas close to the borders with Serbia and Bosnia-Herzegovina. If you are travelling in former war zones, stick to main roads and marked footpaths and pay attention to warning signs. The usual sign is a red skull and crossbones accompanied by the words 'PAZI MINE'.

WATER
● Tap water is safe to drink, but bottled mineral water is widely available.

KEEPING CHILDREN SAFE
● Small children need to be well protected from the sun.
● A pair of plastic sandals provides protection on the beach against rocks, pebbles, sea urchins and jellyfish.
● Children under 16 must wear a helmet while cycling.

PHARMACIES IN CROATIA		
CITY	**PHARMACY**	**CONTACT DETAILS**
Zagreb	Gradska Ljekarna	Trg Bana Jelačića 3, tel 01 481 6198
		Open 24 hours a day
	Gradska Ljekarna	Ilica 301, tel 01 375 0321
		Open 24 hours a day
Dubrovnik	Gruž	Gruška Obala 9, tel 020 418990
	Ljekarna Dubrovnik	Stradun 4, tel 020 321133
One of the above pharmacies will always be on duty		

COMMUNICATION

TELEPHONES

● Telephone services are provided by Hrvatski Telekom, a subsidiary of T-Mobile.

● To call Croatia from abroad, dial the international access code (011 from the US and Canada, 00 from most other countries) followed by Croatia's country code 385. This should be followed by the full local number, omitting the initial 0 from the area code. For example, the number for Zagreb tourist information is 01 481 4051. To call this number from the UK/Europe you should dial 00 385 1 481 4051 or from the US/Canada you should dial 011 385 1 481 4051.

● To call the UK from Croatia, dial 00 44 followed by the local number, omitting the first 0 from the area code; to call the US, dial 00 1 followed by the full 10-figure number.

● To call other countries from Croatia, dial the international dialling code (▷ 277), followed by the number.

● For calls within Croatia, dial the area code and local number For calls within the same area, omit the area code and simply dial the seven-figure local number in Zagreb or six-figure number elsewhere.

● Numbers beginning 06 are charged at national rate, 08 are freephone numbers, and 09 are mobile phones.

PUBLIC TELEPHONES

● Public phone booths are a common sight in towns and cities, and there is usually at least one public phone even in small villages.

● Phones are blue, and

instructions are given in a choice of languages. To change language, press the button marked with a flag and the letter L.

● Calls cost 0.8kn per minute within Croatia, 3kn to most countries of Europe, 3.5kn to the UK and Ireland, and 5kn to the US, Canada and Australia. Calls to Croatian mobile numbers cost 2kn per minute.

● To use a public phone you must buy a phonecard (*telekarta*), from newsagents, kiosks or post offices. Cards are sold in denominations of 30, 50, 100kn and 200kn, and usually contain a bonus amount. For example, a 30kn card gives 33kn worth of calls and a 100kn card gives 115kn worth of calls.

● You can also make international calls from main post offices. Calls are metered and you pay afterwards.

MOBILE PHONES

● Mobile phone use is widespread in Croatia, with over 60 per cent of the population owning a mobile phone. The two main networks are VIPnet, a partner of Vodafone, and T-Com, owned by T-Mobile and Hrvatski Telekom. VIP numbers begin 091 and 092 and T-Com numbers begin 098 and 099.

● If you have a GSM phone, it will work in Croatia provided you have set it up for international roaming with your network operator before you leave home. Calls within Croatia could be expensive as they will be

USEFUL TELEPHONE NUMBERS	
Police	92
Fire	93
Ambulance	94
All emergencies	112
Directory enquiries	988
International directory enquiries	902

AREA CODES WITHIN CROATIA	
Dubrovnik	020
Osijek	031
Pula	052
Rijeka	051
Split	021
Varaždin	042
Zadar	023
Zagreb	01

INTERNATIONAL DIALLING CODES	
Australia	00 61
Canada	00 1
Germany	00 49
Ireland	00 353
Italy	00 39
New Zealand	00 64
UK	00 44
US	00 1

MAILING RATES		
DESTINATION	LETTER	POSTCARD
UK/Europe	7kn	5.50kn
US/Canada	8kn	6.50kn
Australia	9kn	7.50kn

routed through your home country. You may also be charged international rates for receiving calls and for sending and receiving text messages.

● For longer stays, consider buying a Croatian SIM card for your mobile phone. This will give you a local number and access to one of the networks within Croatia. SIM cards are available from phone shops and post offices with prices starting from around 300kn. You can buy top-up cards from news kiosks and post offices, or top up your phone at ATMs. If you do not have a GSM-enabled phone, you can buy mobile phone and pre-paid card packages for around 700kn.

INTERNET

● Internet access is widely available in Croatia. Bigger cities such as Zagreb and Dubrovnik have large internet cafés and computer centres, but even on the islands and in smaller inland towns you can usually find a travel agent or bar with a computer terminal to check your email.

● Most places offer high-speed internet access for around 20–30kn per hour. Internet cafés also offer printing, scanning and the option of burning your digital photos onto a CD.

● Larger hotels have business centres with high-speed internet connections. Smaller hotels often have a computer in the lobby, which is sometimes coin-operated and sometimes free for hotel guests.

● Croatian keyboards differ from those in other countries, so ask staff if you are not sure how to find characters. Croatian website and email addresses do not use accents.

USING A LAPTOP

● A number of hotels offer modem points for high-speed internet access from your room.

● Visitors from the UK will need an electricity adaptor and visitors from the US may need a transformer and surge protector for their laptop.

● If you need to use a dial-up connection, it is cheaper to dial up a local service provider than to make calls to your home network. You should also set your modem to ignore dial tones as these vary from country to country.

● Wireless internet access is becoming more common at airports, hotels and marinas. Rijeka was Croatia's first city to offer free wireless internet access, with a free wireless 'hot spot' along the Korzo.

POST

● Post offices (pošta) are open Monday to Friday 7–7 and Saturday 7–1. In villages and on the islands they may open mornings only. Main post offices in larger towns and cities are open longer hours.

● The post office beside the railway station in Zagreb is open 24 hours.

● Stamps can also be bought at news kiosks and tobacconists.

● Post boxes are yellow.

● Letters and postcards typically take 3–5 days in Europe and 7–10 days to North America.

PLANNING

FINDING HELP

PERSONAL SECURITY

● Crime rates are low in Croatia but you should still take the same precautions as you would anywhere else to avoid becoming a victim of theft or petty crime.

● Keep money, credit cards and valuables in a hotel safe and avoid carrying around large amounts of cash.

● Keep a passport or identity card on you at all times, with a photocopy in your hotel safe. The police have the power to ask for your passport at any time, and it will also help to identify you in the case of an accident.

● Make a note of the serial numbers of travellers' cheques and keep it separate from the cheques in case of loss.

● Never let anyone see you entering your PIN when withdrawing cash from an ATM, or at a chip-and-pin terminal.

● Beware of pickpockets on crowded buses and trams in cities such as Zagreb, Split, Rijeka and Dubrovnik.

● Never leave money or valuables unattended on a beach or poolside.

● Always lock your car and keep all valuables out of sight in the boot (trunk), or better still take them with you.

● If you are driving a rental car, take the rental documents out of the car whenever it is left unattended.

● Avoid discussing the war in sensitive areas, particularly in the former war zones close to the Bosnian and Serbian borders.

IF YOU NEED HELP

● In an emergency you can call the police by dialling 92 from a public phone or 112 from a mobile phone.

● If something is stolen you must report it to the police and obtain a crime report for your insurance company.

● If you lose your passport, contact your embassy or consulate to arrange a replacement.

● If you are arrested, ask to speak to your embassy or consulate.

EMBASSIES AND CONSULATES IN ZAGREB

COUNTRY	ADDRESS	TELEPHONE NUMBER
Australia	Centar Kaptol III, Nova Ves 11	01 489 1200
Canada	Prilaz Gjure Deželića 4	01 488 1200
France	Hebrangova 2	01 489 3600
Germany	Ulica Grada Vukovara 64	01 630 0100
Ireland	Miramarska 23	01 631 0025
Italy	Medulićeva 22	01 484 6386
New Zealand	Vlaška 50A	01 615 1382
UK	Ulica Ivana Lučića 4	01 600 9100
US	Ulica Thomasa Jeffersona 2	01 661 2200

PLANNING

OPENING TIMES AND NATIONAL HOLIDAYS

BUSINESS HOURS

● Office hours are Monday to Friday 8–4.

● Working hours vary throughout the year, especially on the coast. During the summer months some shops and offices close for a few hours during the afternoon and reopen in the evening until 10pm.

● Tourist offices and private travel agencies (▷ 280) have widely varying opening hours depending on the season. In winter many are open only on weekday mornings from 8 to 2. In summer tourist offices in the major cities and coastal resorts stay open for very long hours, typically 8am–10pm daily between June and the end of September.

● Churches in main towns and cities are open from around 7am to 7pm daily, but village churches are usually kept closed except for times of Mass.

● Museums are usually closed on Sunday afternoons and Mondays, but this varies around the country so check individual opening hours.

● Meal times are typically around 12–3 for lunch and 7–10 for dinner, but many restaurants stay open throughout the day from noon to midnight.

● The Croatian attitude to time is quite flexible and you should not rely on fixed opening hours. Although most museums, restaurants and tourist offices have official opening hours they vary from season to season and are always liable to change at short notice due to weather, local festivals or unexpected circumstances. If you are going out of your way, it is always best to check in advance by telephone.

NATIONAL HOLIDAYS	
1 January	New Year's Day
6 January	Epiphany
March/April	Easter Sunday and Monday
1 May	Labour Day
May/June	Corpus Christi (60 days after Easter)
22 June	Anti-Fascist Resistance Day
25 June	Croatian National Day
5 August	Victory Day
15 August	Feast of the Assumption
8 October	Independence Day
1 November	All Saints' Day
25–26 December	Christmas

In addition, there are numerous local and regional festivals and saints' days, when museums, shops and offices will be closed to coincide with local festivities.

OPENING TIMES	
Banks	Mon–Fri 7–7, Sat 7–1
	Outside these hours money can be changed at exchange bureaux, travel agents and hotels, or you can withdraw cash at ATMs.
Pharmacies	Mon–Fri 8–8, Sat 8–2
	In larger towns and cities there will always be at least one pharmacist on duty at night and weekends.
Post offices	Mon–Fri 7–7, Sat 7–1
	In villages and on the islands many post offices are only open in the morning. Main post offices in the bigger cities operate longer hours, with some staying open until 10pm.
Shops	Mon–Fri 8–8, Sat 8–2
	Supermarkets and department stores in Zagreb and Split may open on Saturday afternoons and Sundays. Some smaller shops close for a siesta on weekday afternoons. Shops in tourist resorts on the islands and coast work long hours in summer, with some staying open from 8am–10pm daily to meet demand. Markets are busiest early in the morning, from 8am to noon Monday to Saturday, and sometimes on Sunday as well.

TOURIST INFORMATION

Croatia has a network of tourist information offices, together with private travel agencies offering places to stay, excursions and information.

BEFORE YOU GO
The Croatian National Tourist Board has offices in Europe and the US that will send out information and maps to help you plan your visit. As well as general tourist information, the CNTB publishes an annual hotel directory and brochures in various languages on camping, diving, fishing, sailing and adventure travel. Visit their website www.croatia.hr

TOURIST OFFICES IN CROATIA
● You will find official tourist offices in all towns and cities, operated by the local tourist board (*turistiška zajednica*). In major cities such as Zagreb and Dubrovnik, these open for long hours all year, but on the coast and islands they operate reduced hours or close down in winter. Between June and September tourist offices in coastal towns and resorts are open daily from around 8am to 10pm.
● The quality of information varies widely, but most tourist offices can provide maps and leaflets. Staff can usually speak some English and German.
● Travel agents in the main towns and resorts are also good sources of tourist information. Although these are private businesses, they are usually happy to provide advice. Staff generally speak English and German, and have knowledge of local attractions and events.

Most travel agencies also offer excursions, private accommodation, souvenirs and currency exchange. The biggest agency is Atlas (www.atlas.hr).

CROATIAN NATIONAL TOURIST BOARD OFFICES	
Croatia	Iblerov Trg 10/4, Zagreb
	Tel 01 469 9333
France	Avenue Victor Hugo 48, 75116 Paris
	Tel 01 45 00 99 55
Germany	Kaiserstrasse 23, 60311 Frankfurt
	Tel 069 238 5350
Italy	Via dell'Oca 48, 00186 Roma
	Tel 06 3211 0396
Netherlands	Nijenburg 2F, 1081 Amsterdam
	Tel 020 661 6422
Spain	Calle Claudio Coello 22/Ese B/IoC, 28001 Madrid
	Tel 91 781 5514
Sweden	Kungsgatan 24, 11135 Stockholm
	Tel 08 5348 2080
UK and Ireland	2 The Lanchesters, 162–164 Fulham Palace Rd, London W6 9ER
	Tel 020 8563 7979
US	350 Fifth Avenue, Suite 4003, New York, NY 10118
	Tel 212 279 8672

TOURIST INFORMATION OFFICES IN CROATIA	
Dubrovnik	Stradun, Dubrovnik
	Tel 020 321561; www.tzdubrovnik.hr
Hvar	Trg Svetog Stjepana, Hvar Town
	Tel 021 741059; www.tzhvar.hr
Korčula	Obala Franje Tuđmana, Korčula Town
	Tel 020 715701; www.visitkorcula.com
Osijek	Županijska 2, Osijek
	Tel 031 203755; www.tzosijek.hr
Pula	Forum 3, Pula
	Tel 052 219197; www.pulainfo.hr
Rab	Trg Municipium Arbe, Rab Town
	Tel 051 771111; www.tzg-rab.hr
Rijeka	Korzo 33, Rijeka
	Tel 051 335882; www.tz-rijeka.hr
Šibenik	Obala Franje Tuđmana 5, Šibenik
	Tel 022 214411; www.sibenik-tourism.hr
Split	Peristil, Split
	Tel 021 345606; www.visitsplit.com
Varaždin	Ulica Padovca 3, Varaždin
	Tel 042 210987; www.tourism-varazdin.hr
Zadar	Ilije Smiljanića, Zadar
	Tel 023 316166; www.tzzadar.hr
Zagreb	Trg Bana Jelačića 11, Zagreb
	Tel 01 481 4051; www.zagreb-touristinfo.hr

PLANNING

MEDIA

For decades the press in Croatia was used as a political mouthpiece. It is only since the election of President Mesić that press freedom has been encouraged, and Croatia now has a lively and independent media expressing a wide range of views and styles.

NEWSPAPERS AND MAGAZINES

● Newspapers can be bought at kiosks, or read for free in cafés and bars. The most popular dailies are *24 Sata*, *Jutarnji List* and *Večernji List*, all of which have news, sport, weather and showbiz gossip.

● *Globus* and *Nacional* are weekly glossy news magazines, similar to *Time* or *Newsweek* in the US. Nacional also publishes an online edition in English, available by subscription (www.nacional.hr). *Feral Tribune* is a popular satirical weekly in Split.

● Foreign newspapers and magazines are sold at bookshops in Zagreb and Dubrovnik, also in coastal resorts in summer.

DAILY NEWSPAPERS

Glas Istre In Istria
Glas Slavonije In Slavonia
Jutarnji List The most popular national daily
La Voce del Popolo Italian-language paper for Istria and Kvarner
Novi List In Rijeka
Slobodna Dalmacije In Split
Sportske Novosti National daily sports paper
Večernji List Popular national evening paper
24 Sata News and gossip.

TOURIST PUBLICATIONS

● The *In Your Pocket* series of city guides have attracted a cult following throughout Eastern Europe for their irreverent, no-nonsense approach and opinionated reviews of restaurants, nightlife and shops. Published every two months for Zagreb and annually for Dubrovnik, Osijek, Rijeka and Zadar, they are an excellent source of up-to-date information on everything from concert listings to public transport maps. They fit in your pocket and can be picked up free of charge from tourist offices, cafés and hotels, or downloaded from www.inyourpocket.com

● *Welcome to Zagreb* and *Welcome to Dubrovnik* are full-size free magazines produced three or four times a year by the city tourist boards, with articles on city life and traditions in Croatian and English.

TELEVISION

● The main national TV and radio stations are operated by public service broadcaster Hrvatski Radiotelevizija (HRT).

● HRT1 broadcasts news, chat and game shows, including Croatian versions of *The Weakest Link* and *Who Wants to be a Millionaire?*

● HRT2 shows sport, soap operas and foreign drama and films, many broadcast in English with Croatian subtitles.

● RTL and Nova are nationwide commercial channels.

● A range of cable, digital and satellite channels are available on subscription. Most hotel rooms have access to satellite TV channels such as BBC and CNN.

RADIO

● HRT operates three national and eight regional radio channels. HR1 broadcasts news and talk, HR2 popular music and entertainment, and HR3 broadcasts classical music.

● There are daily news bulletins in English on HR1 (92.1 FM) at 8.05pm Monday to Saturday. Between July and the end of September, HR2 (98.5 FM) has regular updates on traffic and sailing conditions in English, German and Italian.

BOOKS AND MUSIC

HISTORY AND WAR

- *Croatia: A Nation Forged in War* (1997) by Marcus Tanner is a comprehensive and highly readable account of 2,000 years of Croatian history by a journalist who covered the Balkan wars for the London-based *Independent*.
- *The Fall of Yugoslavia* (1996) by Misha Glenny is an eyewitness account written by a former BBC correspondent.
- *Madness Visible* (2004) by Janine di Giovanni is a powerful portrait of the Balkan wars by a writer for the London-based *Times*. Although it focuses on Bosnia and Kosovo and there is little on Croatia, it is a harrowing, compelling account of the horrors of war.
- *They Would Never Hurt A Fly* (2005) by Croatian exile Slavenka Drakulić tells the stories of some of the people charged with war crimes in the Hague, and asks how war can turn ordinary people into monsters. The same author became known for her books of essays on everyday life in Eastern Europe, including *How We Survived Communism And Even Laughed* (1991), *Balkan Express* (1993) and *Café Europa: Life After Communism* (1996).
- *Dubrovnik: A History* (2003) by Robin Harris is a scholarly account, from the medieval origins of Ragusa to the 1991 siege.

TRAVELOGUES

- *Black Lamb And Grey Falcon* (1942) by Rebecca West is a 1,000-page epic volume describing a series of journeys through Yugoslavia in the 1930s, beginning with Croatia. Outdated and prejudiced in places, it is still worth reading for its quirky observations, entertaining character sketches and understanding of Balkan history and culture.
- *Through The Embers Of Chaos: Balkan Journeys* (2002) by veteran travel writer Dervla Murphy is an enjoyable account of a journey by bicycle through the newly independent states of former Yugoslavia.
- *Another Fool In The Balkans: In The Footsteps of Rebecca West* (2005) by Tony White describes a series of visits to Zagreb, Belgrade and Istria by a young British writer.

FICTION

- *The Bridge Over The Drina* (1959) is the masterpiece by Nobel prizewinning author Ivo Andrić (1892–1975). Born in Bosnia to Croatian parents and writing in the Serbian language, Andrić embodies the contradictions of the Balkans. Set in the Bosnian town of Višegrad over a period of 500 years, the novel tells the story of Balkan and Ottoman history through a series of sketches set on the bridge of the title.
- *The Ministry of Pain* (2005) by Dubravka Ugrešić is a novel set in Amsterdam among a group of ex-Yugoslav exiles, by a Croatian author who left during the war. Her earlier books include *The Culture of Lies* (1998), a set of essays attacking the rise of nationalism in Croatia.

MUSIC

- Bookstores and souvenir shops sell CDs of Croatian folk music, including the *tamburica* (mandolin) music of Slavonia and the *klapa* (male voice choirs) of Dalmatia. Reliable names to look out for include the Lado ensemble from Zagreb and the Linđo ensemble from Dubrovnik.
- *The Rough Guide to the Music of the Balkans* (2003) is a good introduction to the region, featuring two Croatian groups alongside brass bands and gypsy music.
- Tamara Obrovac is a singer and flautist who combines jazz with traditional Istrian folk songs, including some in the Istriot dialect, on her albums *Transhistria* (2001), *Sve Pasiva* (2003) and *Daleko je...* (2005).
- Darko Rundek is a singer and actor from Zagreb who blends Balkan rhythms, jazz and cabaret sounds with his Cargo Orkestar on albums such as *La Comedie des Sens* (2004) and *Mhm A-Ha Oh Yeah Da-Da: Migration Stories and Love Songs* (2006).
- US jazz siren Helen Merrill was born Jelena Ana Milčetić to Croatian immigrants. She explores her Croatian roots on the autobiographical *Jelena Ana Milčetić aka Helen Merrill* (2000).

USEFUL WEBSITES

GENERAL INFORMATION

www.croatia.hr
Information in Croatian, English and German, with links to national tourist board sites in other languages.

www.hr Croatian Homepage, with over 17,000 links in 700 categories. Croatian and English.

www.croatiatraveller.com
English only.

www.visit-croatia.co.uk
Information, advice and readers' tips. English only.

www.inyourpocket.com
Savvy advice and listings for urban travellers. English only.

NEWS

www.hina.hr Official Croatian news agency. Croatian and English.

www.hic.hr
English and Spanish.

www.balkantimes.com
News and comment. English and nine Balkan languages.

TRAVEL AND WEATHER

www.croatiaairlines.hr
Croatian, English and German.

www.hznet.hr Croatian Railways. Croatian, English and German.

www.jadrolinija.hr Ferry travel. Croatian, English, German and Italian.

www.hak.hr Croatian Auto Club. Croatian, English, German and Italian.

www.hac.hr Croatian Motorways site. Croatian and English.

www.dhmz.htnet.hr or **meteo.hr** Weather forecasts. Croatian and English.

MISCELLANEOUS

www.dubrovnik-festival.hr
Croatian and English.

www.mdc.hr Museums. Croatian and English.

REGIONAL TOURIST BOARDS	
Zagreb	www.zagreb-touristinfo.hr
Zagreb County	www.tzzz.hr
Istria	www.istra.hr
Kvarner	www.kvarner.hr
Zadar and northern Dalmatia	www.zadar.hr
Split and central Dalmatia	www.dalmatia.hr
Dubrovnik	www.tzdubrovnik.hr
Dubrovnik County	www.visitdubrovnik.hr

KEY SIGHTS QUICK WEBSITE FINDER		
SIGHT/TOWN	WEBSITE	PAGE
Brač	www.bol.hr	114–115
Brijuni	www.brijuni.hr	86–87
Cavtat	www.tzcavtat-konavle.hr	155
Cres	www.tzg-cres.hr	104
Dubrovnik	www.tzdubrovnik.hr	142–160
Hvar	www.tzhvar.hr	116–119
Kopački Rit	www.kopacki-rit.com	64
Korčula	www.korculainfo.com	120–123
Krk	www.krk.hr	105
Krka	www.npkrka.hr	124–125
Kumrovec	www.mdc.hr/kumrovec	65
Lokrum	www.lokrum.hr	157
Lonjsko Polje	www.pp-lonjsko-polje.hr	66–67
Mljet	www.np-mljet.hr	158–159
Opatija	www.opatija-tourism.hr	107
Osijek	www.tzosijek.hr	68–69
Plitvička Jezera	www.np-plitvicka-jezera.hr	70–73
Poreč	www.istra.com/porec	92–93
Pula	www.pulainfo.hr	94–97
Rab	www.tzg-rab.hr	108–109
Rijeka	www.tz-rijeka.hr	110–111
Rovinj	www.tzgrovinj.hr	98–101
Samobor	www.samobor.hr	74
Šibenik	www.sibenik-tourism.hr	131
Split	www.visitsplit.com	132–137
Trogir	www.trogir-online.com	138
Varaždin	www.tourism-varazdin.hr	76–79
Vis	www.tz-vis.hr	139
Zadar	www.zadar.hr	140–141
Zagorje	www.tz-zagorje.hr	80–83
Zagreb	www.zagreb-touristinfo.hr	46–59

WORDS AND PHRASES

Croatian is one of the most phonetic of all European languages and, unlike English, particular combinations of letters are nearly always pronounced the same way.

Vowels are pronounced as follows:

a	as in	c**a**r, but shorter
e	as in	v**e**t
i	as in	b**i**t
o	as in	n**o**t
u	as in	b**oo**k

Note also these combinations:

aj	'ai' as in h**igh**
ej	'ei' as in m**ay**
oj	'oi' as in t**oy**

Consonants as in English except:

c	as **ts** in ma**ts**
č	as **ch** in **ch**at
ć	as **t** in over**t**ure
dž	as **g** in ca**g**e
đ	as **d** in **d**uration
h	in the back of the throat like the Scottish lo**ch**
j	as **y** in **y**es
lj	as **ll** in mi**ll**ion
nj	as **ny** in ca**ny**on
r	harder than the English **r**, more similar to the Scottish **r**
š	as **sh** in **sh**are
ž	as **s** in plea**s**ure

All Croatian nouns are either masculine, feminine or neuter. They also have case endings that change according to how the noun is used in a sentence. An adjective's ending changes to match the ending of the noun. Verbs are also marked masculine, feminine or neuter as well as singular or plural. It is therefore easier to treat basic phrases as a whole, but different options of a basic form are given when necessary (e.g. masculine or feminine verb endings, marked as 'masc/fem').

Personal pronouns (e.g. I, you, they) are usually omitted from the beginning of the sentence, unless it is important to stress who the subject is. The personal pronoun 'you' has two forms, polite 'vi' and informal 'ti' and the verb endings change according to which form is used. The context requires the use of the polite form in most of the phrases here, but the informal option is also given when appropriate (marked as 'pol/inf').

CONVERSATION

I don't speak Croatian
Ne govorim hrvatski

I only speak a little Croatian
Govorim samo malo hrvatski

Do you speak English?
Govorite li engleski?

I don't understand
Ne razumijem

Please repeat that
Molim vas ponovite

Please speak more slowly
Govorite sporije, molim vas

What does this mean?
Što to znači?

Write that down for me, please
Napišite mi to, molim

My name is
Zovem se

What's your name?
Kako se zovete/zoveš? (pol/inf)

Hello, pleased to meet you
Zdravo, drago mi je da smo se upoznali

This is my friend
Ovo je moj prijatelj/moja prijateljica (male/female)

This is my wife/husband/daughter/son
Ovo je moja supruga/moj muž /moja kći/moj sin

Where do you live?
Gdje živite/živiš? (pol/inf)

I live in...
Živim u...

What is the time?
Koliko je sati?

When do you open/close?
Kad otvarate/zatvarate?

Good morning/afternoon/evening
Dobro jutro/dobar dan/dobra večer

Goodbye/Bye-bye
Doviđenja/Ćao

See you tomorrow
Vidimo se sutra

How are you?
Kako ste/si? (pol/inf)

Fine, thank you
Dobro, hvala

That's alright
U redu je

USEFUL WORDS

yes **da**	thank you **hvala**	where **gdje**	when **kad**	why **zašto**
no **ne**	you're welcome **nema na čemu**	here **ovdje**	now **sad**	who **tko**
please **molim**	excuse me/sorry! **oprostite!**	there **tamo**	later **kasnije**	may I/can I **smijem li/mogu li**

Could you help me, please?
Možete li mi pomoći, molim?

How much is this?
Koliko stoji?

I'm looking for...
Tražim...

Where can I buy...?
Gdje mogu kupiti...?

How much is this/that?
Koliko stoji ovo/to?

When does the shop open/close?
Kad se prodavaonica otvara/zatvara?

I'm just looking, thank you
Samo razgledam, hvala

This isn't what I want
To nije ono što želim

I'll take this
Uzet ću ovo

Do you have anything less expensive/smaller/larger?
Imate li što jeftinije/manje/veće?

Are the instructions included?
Jesu li upute priložene?

Do you have a bag for this?
Imate li vrećicu za ovo?

I'm looking for a present
Tražim poklon

Can you gift wrap this please?
Možete li mi ovo umotati, molim?

Do you accept credit cards?
Prihvaćate li kreditne kartice?

I'd like a kilo of...
Molim kilu...

Do you have shoes to match this?
Imate li cipele koje idu s ovim?

This is the right size
Ovo je prava veličina

Can you measure me please?
Možete li me izmjeriti molim?

Do you have this in...?
Imate li ovo u...?

Is there a market?
Ima li ovdje tržnica?

0 **nula**	6 **šest**	12 **dvanaest**	18 **osamnaest**	30 **trideset**	90 **devedeset**
1 **jedan**	7 **sedam**	13 **trinaest**	19 **devetnaest**	40 **četrdeset**	100 **sto**
2 **dva**	8 **osam**	14 **četrnaest**	20 **dvadeset**	50 **pedeset**	1,000 **tisuću**
3 **tri**	9 **devet**	15 **petnaest**	21 **dvadeset jedan**	60 **šezdeset**	million **milijun**
4 **četiri**	10 **deset**	16 **šesnaest**	22 **dvadeset dva**	70 **sedamdeset**	quarter **četvrt**
5 **pet**	11 **jedanest**	17 **sedamnaest**		80 **osamdeset**	half **pol**

Where is the nearest post office/mail box?
Gdje je najbliža pošta/najbliži poštanski sandučić?

What is the postage to...?
Koliko je poštarina za...?

One stamp, please
Jednu marku, molim

I'd like to send this by air mail/registered mail
Želim ovo poslati zrakoplovom/preporučeno

Can you direct me to a public phone?
Možete li me uputiti k najbližoj telefonskoj govornici?

Where can I buy a phone card?
Gdje mogu kupiti telefonsku karticu?

What is the charge per minute?
Koliko stoji jedna minuta?

Can I dial direct to...?
Mogu li direktno zvati...?

Do I need to dial 0 first?
Moram li prvo okrenuti nulu?

Where can I find a phone directory?
Gdje mogu naći telefonski imenik?

What is the number for directory enquiries?
Koji je broj službe za telefonske informacije?

Please put me through to...
Molim spojite me s...

Have there been any calls for me?
Je li bilo telefonskih poziva za mene?

Hello, this is...
Halo, ovdje...

Who is this speaking please?
Tko je na telefonu molim?

I'd like to speak to...
Htio/htjela (masc/fem) bih govoriti s...

Extension ... please
Interni broj ... molim

Please ask him/her to call me back
Molim vas recite mu/joj da me nazove

Is there a bank/currency exchange office nearby?
Ima li u blizini banka/mjenjačnica?

What is the exchange rate today?
Koji je današnji tečaj?

I'd like to change sterling/dollars
into kunas (Croatian currency)
**Želim promijeniti britanske
funte /američke dolare u
hrvatske kune**

Can I use my credit card to
withdraw cash?
**Mogu li podići gotovinu
svojom kreditnom karticom?**

I'd like to cash this traveller's
cheque
**Želim unovčiti ovaj putnički
ček**

GETTING AROUND

Where is the train/bus station?
**Gdje je željeznički/autobusni
kolodvor?**

Does this train/bus stop at...?
Staje li ovaj vlak/autobus u...?

Please stop at the next stop
**Molim zaustavite na
sljedećem stajalištu**

Where are we?
Gdje smo?

Do I have to get off here?
Moram li sići ovdje?

Where can I buy a ticket?
Gdje mogu kupiti kartu?

Where can I reserve a seat?
**Gdje mogu rezervirati
mjesto?**

Please can I have a single/return
(one-way/round-trip) ticket to...
**Molim vas jednosmjernu/
povratnu kartu za...**

When is the first/last bus to...?
**Kad ide prvi/zadnji autobus
za...?**

COLOURS

black	blue
crna	**plava**
brown	purple
smeđa	**grimizna**
pink	white
ružičasta	**bijela**
red	gold
crvena	**zlatna**
orange	silver
narančasta	**srebrna**
yellow	grey
žuta	**siva**
green	turquoise
zelena	**tirkizna**

SHOPS

baker's	fishmonger's	launderette
pekarnica	**ribarnica**	**praonica rublja**
bookshop	florist	newsagent's
knjižara	**cvjećarna**	**trafika**
butcher's	gift shop	photographic shop
mesnica	**prodavaonica suvenira**	**fotografska radionica**
cake shop		
slastičarna	grocer's	shoe shop
	trgovina	**prodavaonica**
clothes shop	**mješovitom**	**obuće**
prodavaonica odjeće	**robom**	
		sports shop
	hairdresser's	**prodavaonica**
delicatessen	**frizerski salon**	**sportske robe**
prodavaonica delikatesne robe	jeweller's	tobacconist's
dry-cleaner's	**prodavaonica nakita**	**prodavaonica duhana**
kemijska čistionica		

I would like to standard/first-class
ticket to...
**Molim jednu kartu za
drugi/prvi razred za...**

Where is the information desk?
Gdje su informacije?

Where is the timetable?
Gdje je vozni red?

Do you have a metro/bus map?
**Imate li kartu podzemne
željeznice/autobusa?**

Where can I find a taxi (rank)?
**Gdje mogu naći taksi
(stajalište)?**

Please take me to...
...(address), molim

How much is the journey?
Koliko stoji ova vožnja?

Please turn on the meter
**Molim vas uključite
taksimetar**

I'd like to get out here please
Želim ovdje izaći, molim vas

Could you wait for me, please?
**Možete li me pričekati, molim
vas?**

Excuse me, I think I am lost
**Oprostite, mislim da sam se
izgubio/ izgubila (masc/fem)**

TOURIST INFORMATION

Where is the tourist information
office/tourist information desk,
please?
**Gdje je ured za turističke
informacije /gdje su turističke
informacije, molim?**

Do you have a city map?
Imate li plan grada?

Can you give me some
information about...?
**Možete li mi dati informacije
o ...?**

What is the admission price?
Koliko stoji ulaz?

Is there a discount for senior
citizens/students?
**Imate li popust za starije
osobe/studente?**

Are there guided tours?
Imate li ekskurzije s vodičem?

Are there boat trips?
Imate li izlete brodicom?

Is there an English-speaking
guide?
Imate li engleskog vodiča?

Are there organized excursions?
**Imate li organizirane
ekskurzije?**

Can we make reservations
here?
**Možemo li ovdje napraviti
rezervaciju?**

What time does it open/close?
**U koliko sati
otvarate/zatvarate?**

Is photography allowed?
Smije li se fotografirati?

Do you have a brochure in
English?
**Imate li brošuru na
engleskom?**

Monday **ponedjeljak**	morning (until about 10 am) **ujutro**	year **godina**	April **travanj**	November **studeni**	National Holiday **državni blagdan**
Tuesday **utorak**	(the rest of the morning) **prije podne**	today **danas**	May **svibanj**	December **prosinac**	
Wednesday **srijeda**	afternoon **poslije podne**	yesterday **jučer**	June **lipanj**	spring **proljeće**	Christmas **Božić**
Thursday **četvrtak**	evening **večer**	tomorrow **sutra**	July **srpanj**	summer **ljeto**	26 December **Sveti Stjepan**
Friday **petak**	night **noć**	January **siječanj**	August **kolovoz**	autumn **jesen**	New Year's Eve **Novogodišnja noć/ Silvestrovo**
Saturday **subota**	day **dan**	February **veljača**	September **rujan**	winter **zima**	
Sunday **nedjelja**	month **mjesec**	March **ožujak**	October **listopad**	Easter **Uskrs**	New Year's Day **Nova godina**

Where can I find a good nightclub?
Gdje mogu naći dobar noćni klub?

What time does the show start?
U koliko sati počinje predstava?

Could you reserve tickets for me?
Možete li mi rezervirati karte?

How much is a ticket?
Koliko stoji jedna karta?

Should we dress smartly?
Trebamo li se odjenuti elegantno?

IN TROUBLE

Help!
Upomoć!

Stop, thief!
Stani, lopov!

Can you help me, please?
Možete li mi pomoći, molim vas?

Call the fire brigade/police/an ambulance
Zovite vatrogasce/policiju/ hitnu pomoć

I have lost my passport/wallet/ purse/handbag
Izgubio/izgubila (masc/fem) samputovnicu/lisnicu/ novčanik/tašnu

Is there a lost property office?
Ima li ovdje ured za izgubljeno-nađeno?

Where is the police station?
Gdje je policijska postaja?

I have been robbed
Pokraden/pokradena (masc/fem) sam

I have had an accident
Imao/imala (masc/fem) sam nezgodu

Here is my name and address
Ovdje su moje ime i adresa

Did you see the accident?
Jeste li vidjeli nezgodu?

Are you insured?
Jeste li osigurani?

Please can I have your name and address?
Mogu li dobiti Vaše ime i adresu molim?

I need information for my insurance company
Trebam informacije za moje osiguranje

ILLNESS

I don't feel well
Ne osjećam se dobro

Is there a doctor/pharmacist on duty?
Ima li ovdje dežurnog liječnika/ljekarnika?

I need to see a doctor/dentist
Trebam liječnika/zubara

Where is the hospital?
Gdje je bolnica?

When is the surgery open?
Kad je ordinacija otvorena?

I need to make an emergency appointment
Trebam hitno vidjeti liječnika

I feel sick
Zlo mi je

I am allergic to...
Alergičan/alergična (masc/fem) sam na...

I have a heart condition
Imam slabo srce

I am diabetic
Imam dijabetes

I'm asthmatic
Imam astmu

I've been stung by a wasp/bee
Ubola me osa/pčela

Can I have a painkiller?
Mogu li dobiti tabletu protiv bolova?

How many tablets a day should I take?
Koliko tableta dnevno trebam uzeti?

How long will I have to stay in bed/hospital?
Koliko dugo moram ostati u krevetu/bolnici?

I have bad toothache
Jako me boli zub

I have broken my tooth/crown
Slomio mi se zub/slomila mi se krunica

A filling has come out
Ispala mi je plomba

Can you repair my dentures?
Možete li mi popraviti zubnu protezu?

on/to the right **na desno/** **desno**	north **sjever**	daily **dnevno**	town/old town **grad/stari grad**	bridge **most**
on/to the left **na lijevo/lijevo**	south **jug**	cathedral **katedrala**	town hall **gradska** **vijećnica**	no entry **zabranjen** **pristup**
opposite **nasuprot**	east **istok**	church **crkva**	square **trg**	entrance **ulaz**
straight on **ravno**	west **zapad**	castle **tvrđava**	street **ulica**	exit **izlaz**
near **blizu**	free **besplatno**	museum **muzej**	island **otok**	lavatories – men/women **zahodi (WC) –** **muški/ženski**
in front of **pred**	donation **prilog**	monument **spomenik**	river **rijeka**	
behind **iza**	open **otvoreno**	palace **palača**	lake **jezero**	Theatre **Kazalište**
	closed **zatvoreno**	gallery **galerija**		Garden **Vrt**

I'd like to reserve a table for ... people at ...
Želim rezervirati stol za ... osoba u ... sati

A table for ..., please
Stol za ..., molim

Could we sit there?
Možemo li sjesti tamo?

We would like to wait for a table
Htjeli bismo sačekati slobodan stol

Could we see the menu/drinks list?
Možemo li pogledati jelovnik/cjenik pića?

Is there a dish of the day?
Imate li specijalitet dana?

Do you have the menu in English?
Imate li jelovnik na engleskom?

Where are the lavatories?
Gdje su zahodi?

I can't eat wheat/sugar/salt/ pork/beef/dairy
Ne smijem jesti pšenicu/ šećer/sol/svinjetinu/govedinu/ mlijeko i mliječne proizvode

I am a vegetarian
Ja sam vegetarijanac

Could I have bottled still/ sparkling water?
Molim bocu negazirane/ mineralne vode

The food is cold
Jelo je hladno

The meat is overcooked/too rare
Meso je prepečeno/ nedovoljno pečeno

I ordered...
Naručio/naručila (masc/fem) sam...

This is not what I ordered
Ovo nisam naručio/naručila (masc/fem)

Can I have the bill, please?
Račun, molim

Is service included?
Je li napojnica uključena u cijenu?

I have made a reservation for ... nights
Imam rezervaciju za ... noći

Do you have a room?
Imate li sobu?

How much per night?
Koliko stoji jedna noć?

Double/single room
Dvokrevetna/jednokrevetna soba

Twin room
Soba s dva odvojena kreveta

With bath/shower
S kupaonicom/tušem

May I see the room?
Mogu li vidjeti sobu?

Could I have another room?
Mogu li dobiti drugu sobu?

Is there a lift in the hotel?
Ima li u hotelu dizalo?

Are the rooms air-conditioned/ heated?
Jesu li sobe klimatizirane/s grijanjem?

Is breakfast included in the price?
Je li zajutrak uključen u cijenu?

Do you have room service?
Imate li sobno posluživanje?

I need an alarm call at...
Trebam naručiti buđenje u ... sati

The room is too hot/too cold/ dirty
U sobi je prevruće/ prehladno/soba je prljava

Please can I pay my bill?
Mogu li platiti račun, molim?

Please order a taxi for me
Naručite mi taksi, molim

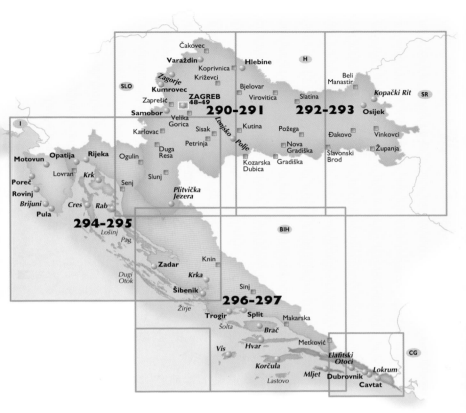

Čakovec
Varaždin
Koprivnica
Hlebine
H
Zagorje
Križevci
Beli
Manastir
SLO
Kumrovec
Bjelovar
Kopački Rit
SR
Zaprešić
Virovitica
Slatina
ZAGREB
Samobor
48-49
290-291
292-293
Osijek
Velika
Gorica
Kutina
Požega
Đakovo
Vinkovci
Karlovac
Sisak
Nova
Gradiška
Slavonski
Brod
Županja
Duga
Resa
Petrinja
Kozarska
Dubica
Gradiška
Ogulin
Motovun
Opatija
Rijeka
Lovran
Krk
Senj
Slunj
Poreč
Rovinj
Plitvička
Jezera
Brijuni
Cres
Rab
Pula
294-295
Lošinj
BIH
Pag
Knin
Zadar
Dugi
Otok
Krka
Sinj
Šibenik
296-297
Žirje
Trogir
Split
Makarska
Šolta
Brač
Metković
CG
Vis
Hvar
Elafitski
Otoci
Lokrum
Korčula
Mljet
Dubrovnik
Lastovo
Cavtat

Motorway (Expressway)

National road

Regional road

Minor road

Railway

International boundary

■ City / Town / Village

National park / Nature park

Built-up area

● Featured place of interest

✈ Airport

621
▲ Height in metres

290-297

0   20 km
0   10 miles

Maps

Nagykanizsa

I

61

Nagyatád

H

PÉCS

6

Drnje Gola
ivnica Hlebine Ždala

Szigetvár

6

vljani Novigrad Podravski
Virje Đurđevac

Barcs

Gyöngyös

Harkány

akitnica
ki Kloštar
c Podravski Pitomača Drava N Gradac
kovac 43 Prugovac Terezino Moslavina
stveni Veliko 288 Rogovac Polje Budakovac Podravska Donji
Trojstvo Sedlarica Korija Gradina Miholjac
Šandrovac Krčenik Rakitovica
r 2 Virovitica Novaki Sopje Ćađavica Črnkovci
Severin Lasovac Suhopolje 34 Karašica 53
Velika Pisanica Medinci Miljevci Milanovac Benićanci Marijar
Međurača 28 Lončarica Bistrica Slatina 2 Harkanovc
Berek Veliki Grubišno Pivnica Čačinci Zdenci Klokočevci Koška
Pavlovac Grđevac Polje Hum Aleksandrovac Đurđenovac
Hercegovac Ilova Đulovac Voćin Ćeralije Lu
Gornji Veliki Bastaji 830 Orahovica Feričanci Subotič
Garešnica 45 Zdenci 5 E661 Dujanova Slatinski 953 Našice
Rogoža Dežanovac Daruvar Kosa Drenovac Papuk Gazije Podgorač Borovik
ka Garešnica 291 Novo Velika Vetovo Kutjevo 53
Kutina 237 Uljanik Bučje Zvečevo Kula Levanjska Kond
užilovčiča Ilova Badljevina S L A V O N I J A Varoš Hrkanovci
Gaj Dragović Jakšić 51 Čaglin 423 Klokočevi
Poljе Banova Pakrac Lipik 984 Strmac Požega Kuzmica 53 Garč
Lonja Jaruga Lipovljani Korita Brezovo 51 Baničevac Pleternica Bilice Slavonski
Puska Krapje Novska Polje Cernik Rešetari Koprivnica Sibinj A3 E70 Brod
inci Jasenovac Trnakovac Nova Gradiška St Petrovo Batrina Srpski D Bebrina
Drenov 47 Mlaka Okučani Selo Zapolje Pričac Brod
Bok A3 E70 N Varoš Visoka Vrbje Davor Bebrina
Baćin Hrvatska Sava Greda Gradiška
Dubica St Gradiška

Kozarska
Dubica

4

16

Vrbas

Ukrina

Doboj

BIH

4

17

17

Banja
Luka

Bosna

E73

5

292 F G 297 H

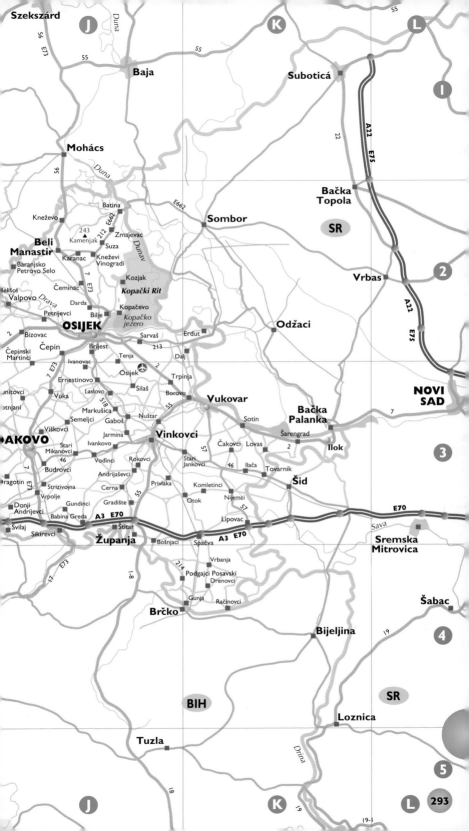

Janjina	297 H9	Kravarsko	290 E3
Jarmina	293 J3	Krcenik	292 H2
Jasenak	295 C4	Kricke	296 F7
Jasenice	295 D6	Krizevci	290 F2
Jasenovac	291 F3	Krizpolje	295 D4
Jastrebarsko	295 D3	Krk	294 C4
Jelsa	297 G8	Krnjak	295 D4
Jesenice	297 F8	Krsan	294 B4
Jezerane	295 D4	Krstinja	290 D4
Jezerce	290 D5	Kruge	296 E5
Jezero	295 D4	Krupa	296 E6
Jezevo	290 E2	Kuce	290 E3
Josani	296 E5	Kucice	297 G8
Josipdol	295 D4	Kula	292 H3
Jovici	295 D6	Kumrovec	290 D2
Jurandvor	294 C4	Kupari	296 J9
Jurovski Brod	295 D3	Kupinec	290 D3
Jursici	294 B5	Kupinecki Kraljevec	290 E3
		Kupiredci	296 E6
K		Kupjak	295 C4
Kabal	291 F2	Kutina	291 F3
Kali	295 D6	Kutjevo	292 H3
Kamensko	297 G2	Kuzmica	292 H3
Kampor	294 C5		
Kandarola	294 C5	**L**	
Karanac	293 J2	Labin	294 B4
Karlobag	295 D5	Laktec	290 E2
Karlovac	295 D3	Lasinja	290 E3
Kasce	297 H8	Laslovo	293 J3
Kasina	290 E2	Lasovac	291 F2
Kastel Stari	296 F7	Lastovo	297 G9
Kastel Sucurac	296 F7	Lecevica	296 F7
Kastel zegarski	296 E6	Lekenik	290 E3
Kistanje	296 E7	Lepavina	291 F2
Kladnice	296 F7	Lepoglava	290 E1
Klana	294 B3	Levanjska Varos	292 H3
Klanac	295 D5	Licki Novi	295 D5
Klanjec	290 D2	Licko Lesce	295 D5
Klapavica	296 E6	Lipik	291 G3
Klek	297 H9	Lipovac	293 K3
Klenovnik	290 E1	Lipovljani	291 F3
Klinca Sela	290 D3	Lipovo Polje	295 D5
Klis	297 F7	Lokva	297 G8
Klokocevci	292 H2	Lokve	294 C4
Klokocevik	292 H3	Loncarica	291 G2
Klostar Ivanic	290 E2	Lonja	291 F3
Klostar	294 A4	Lopar	294 C5
Klostar Podravski	291 F2	Lovas	293 K3
Knezevi Vinogradi	293 J2	Lovca	290 E4
Knezevo	293 J2	Lovinac	296 E6
Knin	296 F6	Lovran	294 B4
Kolan	295 C6	Lovrec	297 G7
Koljane	297 F7	Lovrecica	294 A4
Kom	296 E6	Lozice	295 D6
Komiza	296 F9	Lozisca	297 F8
Komletinci	293 K3	Lozovac	296 E7
Kompator	291 F3	Lubenice	294 B5
Kondric	292 H3	Lucica	295 D7
Kopacevo	293 J2	Ludbreg	290 F1
Koprivnica	291 F1	Lug Suboticki	292 H3
Koprivnica	292 H3	Luka	295 D7
Korcula	297 G9	Lukovo	295 C5
Korenica	290 E5	Lukovo sugarje	295 D6
Korija	291 G2	Lumbarda	297 G9
Korita	291 G3	Lun	294 C5
Koromacno	294 B5		
Koska	292 H2	**M**	
Kostanjevac	295 D3	Mahicno	295 D3
Kotarani	290 E4	Mahovo	290 E3
Kotoriba	291 F1	Maja	290 E4
Kozarac	290 E3	Majurec	290 F2
Kozica	297 G8	Makarska	297 G8
Kozjak	293 J2	Mala Cista	296 E7
Kozjan	295 D5	Mali Iz	295 D7
Kraljevica	294 C4	Mali Losinj	294 C6
Krapina	290 D2	Malinska	294 C4
Krapje	291 F3	Maljkovo	297 F7
Krasic	295 D3	Maranovici	296 H9
Krasno Polje	295 C5	Marcana	294 B5

Marija Bistrica	290 E2	Omisalj	294 C4
Marijanci	292 H2	Opatija	294 B4
Marina	296 F8	Opuzen	297 H8
Markovac Trojstveni	291 F2	Orahovica	292 H3
Markusica	293 J3	Orasac	296 J9
Maslinica	296 F8	Orebic	297 G9
Masvina	290 D4	Orlec	294 B5
Matulji	294 B4	Orlic	296 F6
Mazin	296 E5	Osijek	293 J2
M Buna	290 E3	Osor	294 B5
Medak	295 D6	Osredci	296 E6
Medinci	292 G2	Ostarije	295 D4
Medulin	294 B5	Otavice	296 F7
Medumajdan	290 E4	Otocac	295 D5
Meduraca	291 F2	Otok	293 K3
Merag	294 B5	Otok	297 G7
Metajna	295 C5	Ozalj	295 D3
Metkovic	297 H8		
Mihovljan	290 E2	**P**	
Milanovac	292 H2	Padene	296 E6
Miljevci	292 H2	Pag	295 D6
Milna	297 F8	Pakostane	295 D7
Mlaka	291 F3	Pakrac	291 G3
Mocile	295 C3	Pasman	295 D7
Modrus	295 D4	Pavlovac	291 F2
Molat	295 C6	Pazin	294 B4
Moravice	295 C3	Pecane	296 E5
Moscenica	290 E3	Perna	290 E4
Moscenice	294 B4	Perusic	295 D5
Moscenicka Draga	294 B4	Petrcane	295 D6
Moslavina Podravska	292 H2	Petricko Selo	290 D3
Mostari	290 E2	Petrijevci	293 J2
Motovun	294 A4	Petrinja	290 E3
M Prolog	297 H8	Pican	294 B4
Mravnica	296 J9	Pirovac	296 E7
Mrkopalj	294 C4	Pisarovina	290 E3
M Ston	296 H9	Pitomaca	291 G2
Muntic	294 B5	Pivnica	292 G2
Mursko Sredisce	290 E1	Planjane	296 F7
Murter	296 E7	Plaski	295 D4
Murvica	295 D6	Plavno	296 E6
Murvica	297 F8	Plesivica	290 D3
Muzilovcica	291 F3	Pleternica	292 H3
		Ploce	297 H8
N		Plocice	296 K9
Narta	291 F2	Pocitelj	295 D6
Nasice	292 H3	Podgajci Posavski	293 K4
Nebljusi	290 E5	Podgora	297 G8
Nebljusi	296 E5	Podgorac	292 H3
Nedelisce	290 E1	Podhumlje	296 F9
Neum	297 H9	Podlapaca	295 D5
N Gradac	292 G2	Podorljak	296 E8
Nijemci	293 K3	Podstrana	297 F7
Nin	295 D6	Podstrazje	297 F9
Njivice	294 C4	Podturen	290 E1
Nova Gradiska	292 G3	Pojatno	290 D2
Novaki	292 G2	Pokupsko	290 E3
Novalja	295 C5	Polaca	295 D7
Nova Sela	297 H8	Polaca	296 F6
Novigrad	294 A4	Polace	297 H9
Novigrad	295 D6	Policnik	295 D6
Novigrad Podravski	291 F2	Poljanak	290 D4
Novi Marof	290 E1	Poljica	295 D6
Novi Vinodolski	294 C4	Pomena	297 H9
Novo Zvecevo	292 G3	Popovaca	291 F3
Novska	291 F3	Porat	295 C6
Nustar	293 J3	Porec	294 A4
N Varos	291 G4	Porozina	294 B4
		Posedarje	295 D6
O		Postira	297 F8
Oborovo	290 E3	Potnjani	293 J3
Obrez	290 E3	Potomje	297 H9
Obrovac	296 E6	Povljana	295 D6
Ogulin	295 D4	Pozega	292 H3
Oklaj	296 E7	Poznanovec	290 E2
Okucani	291 G3	Praznica	297 G8
Olib	295 C6	Pregrada	290 D2
Omis	297 G8	Prekopa	290 E3
		Prelog	290 F1

ACKNOWLEDGMENTS

Abbreviations for the credits are as follows:
AA = AA World Travel Library, **t** (top), **b** (bottom or below), **c** (centre), **l** (left),
r (right), **a** (above), **bg** (background), **CNTO** = Croatian National Tourist Office

Every effort has been made to trace the copyright holders, and we apologise in advance for any unintentional errors or omissions.
We would be pleased to apply any corrections in any future edition of this publication.

UNDERSTANDING CROATIA
4 AA/P Bennett; 5cl AA/P Bennett; 5ccl AA/J Smith; 5ccr AA/P Bennett; 5cr AA/P Bennett; 7t AA/P Bennett; 7ct AA/J Smith; 7cb AA/P Bennett; 7b AA/P Bennett; 8t AA/P Bennett; 8ct AA/P Bennett; 8cb AA/J Smith; 8b AA/P Bennett

LIVING CROATIA
9 AA/P Bennett; 10tl Courtesy of CNTO; 10tc AA/P Bennett; 10tr Courtesy of CNTO; 10/11 bg AA/P Bennett; 11tl ©Reuters/Corbis; 11tr ©Nikola Solic/Reuters/Corbis; 11c AA/P Bennett; 12tl AA/P Bennett; 12tr Peter Weimann/Still Pictures; 12/13bg AA/J Smith; 13tl Courtesy of CNTO; 13tc AA/P Bennett; 13c AA/P Bennett; 13tr AA/P Bennett; 14tl ©Greg Newton/Corbis; 14tr ©Stoyan Nenov/Reuters/ Corbis; 14/15bg AA/K Paterson, 15tl ©Susan Mullane/New Sport/Corbis; 15tr ©Tim de Waele/Corbis; 16tl ©2006 K J Historical/Corbis; 16tc AA/P Bennett; 16tr Rex Features; 16lc Courtesy of CNTO; 16bg AA/P Bennett

THE STORY OF CROATIA
17 AA/P Bennett; 18/19bg AA/P Bennett; 18tl AA/P Bennett; 18bl AA/ P Bennett; 18cr AA/P Bennett; 18/19b Courtesy of CNTO; 19cr AA/P Bennett; 19cb Courtesy of CNTO; 19br AA/P Bennett; 20/21bg AA/P Bennett; 20tl AA/ P Bennett; 20bl AA/P Bennett; 20cr AA/P Bennett; 20/21b AKG-Images; 21c ©EO Hoppe/Corbis; 21bl Getty Images/Hulton Archive; 21br Mary Evans Picture Library; 22/3bg AA/P Bennett; 22tl AA/P Bennett; 22cr Time Life Pictures/Getty Images; 22bl AA/P Bennett; 22/23b ©Antoine Gyori/Corbis Sygma; 23c © Bernard Bisson/Corbis Sygma; 23bl ©Juan Vrijdag/Pool/Reuters/Corbis; 23br Time Life Pictures/Getty Images; 24bg AA/P Bennett; 24bl ©Ray Stubblebine/Reuters/Corbis; 24bc ©Reuters/Corbis; 24br ©Nikola Solic/Pool/Reuters/Corbis

ON THE MOVE
25 AA/J Smith; 26/28t Digitalvision; 27c AA/J Smith; 28c AA/J Smith; 29 AA/J Smith; 30/35t Digitalvision; 31c AA/J Smith; 32b AA/J Smith; 33c AA/J Smith; 34b AA/J Smith; 36t AA/J Smith; 36c AA/J Smith; 37 AA/J Smith; 38/39t AA/J Smith; 39b AA/P Bennett; 40/42t Digitalvision; 40c AA/P Bennett; 43 AA/J Smith; 44 AA/J Smith

THE SIGHTS
45 AA/P Bennett; 46 AA/J Smith; 47cr AA/P Bennett; 50cl Archaeological Museum Zagreb; 50t Archaeological Museum Zagreb; 51tl AA/P Bennett; 51tr AA/P Bennett; 52t AA/P Bennett; 52cl AA/P Bennett; 52c AA/P Bennett; 52cr AA/P Bennett; 52bl AA/P Bennett; 53l AA/P Bennett; 53r AA/P Bennett; 54 AA/P Bennett; 54/55 AA/ P Bennett; 55 AA/P Bennett; 56l Courtesy of Medvednica Nature Park; 56r AA/P Bennett; 57l AA/P Bennett; 57r AA/P Bennett; 58l AA/P Bennett; 58c AA/P Bennett; 58r Courtesy of Strossmayer Gallery of Old Masters, Zagreb; 59t AA/P Bennett; 59b AA/P Bennett; 61l AA/P Bennett; 61r AA/P Bennett; 62 Courtesy Muzej grada Koprivnica/Galerija Hlebine; 63l AA/P Bennett; 63r AA/J Smith; 64cl AA/P Bennett; 64tr AA/P Bennett; 65tl AA/P Bennett; 65cr AA/P Bennett; 66t AA/P Bennett; 66cl Courtesy of Lonjsko Polje Nature Park; 66c AA/J Smith; 66cr AA/P Bennett; 67l AA/J Smith; 67r Courtesy of Lonjsko Polje Nature Park; 68t AA/P Bennett; 68cl AA/P Bennett; 68ccl Courtesy of CNTO; 68 ccr AA/P Bennett; 68cr AA/P Bennett; 69l AA/P Bennett; 69r AA/P Bennett; 70t AA/P Bennett; 70cl AA/P Bennett; 70c AA/P Bennett; 70cr AA/P Bennett; 71 AA/P Bennett; 72/73 AA/P Bennett; 73 AA/P Bennett; 74tr AA/J Smith; 74cl AA/J Smith; 75l AA/P Bennett; 75r AA/P Bennett; 76 AA/P Bennett; 77t AA/P Bennett; 77cl AA/P Bennett; 77c AA/P Bennett; 77cr AA/P Bennett; 78l AA/P Bennett; 78r AA/P Bennett; 79l AA/P Bennett; 79cl AA/P Bennett; 79cr AA/P Bennett; 79r AA/P Bennett; 80t AA/P Bennett; 80cl AA/P Bennett; 80ccl AA/P Bennett; 80ccr AA/P Bennett; 80cr AA/P Bennett; 81 AA/P Bennett; 82cl AA/P Bennett; 82ccl AA/P Bennett; 82ccr AA/P Bennett; 82cr AA/P Bennett; 83l AA/P Bennett; 83r AA/P Bennett; 85l AA/P Bennett; 85r AA/J Smith; 86t AA/P Bennett; 86cl AA/P Bennett; 86c AA/P Bennett; 86cr AA/P Bennett; 87l Courtesy of CNTO (Milan Babic); 87r AA/P Bennett; 88l AA/P Bennett; 88r AA/J Smith; 89l AA/P Bennett; 89c AA/P Bennett; 89r AA/P Bennett; 90t AA/J Smith; 90cl AA/J Smith; 91l AA/J Smith; 91r AA/J Smith; 92t AA/P Bennett; 92cl AA/P Bennett; 92c AA/P Bennett; 92/93 AA/P Bennett; 93l AA/P Bennett; 93c AA/P Bennett; 94 AA/P Bennett; 95t AA/P Bennett; 95cl AA/P Bennett; 95ccl AA/P Bennett; 95ccr AA/P Bennett; 95cr AA/P Bennett; 96 AA/P Bennett; 96/97 AA/P Bennett; 97 AA/P Bennett; 98t AA/P Bennett; 98cl AA/P Bennett; 98c AA/P Bennett; 98cr AA/P Bennett; 99l AA/P Bennett; 99r AA/P Bennett; 100l AA/P Bennett; 100r AA/P Bennett; 101l AA/P Bennett; 101r AA/P Bennett; 102l AA/P Bennett; 102c AA/P Bennett; 102r AA/P Bennett; 104tr AA/P Bennett; 104cl AA/P Bennett; 105tl AA/P Bennett; 105cr AA/P Bennett; 106l AA/P Bennett; 106r AA/P Bennett; 107t AA/P Bennett; 107cr AA/P Bennett; 108t AA/P Bennett; 108cl Courtesy of CNTO (Juvaj Kopac); 108ccl Courtesy of CNTO (Juvaj Kopac); 108ccr P Bennett; 108cr

AA/P Bennett; 108cr AA/P Bennett; 109l AA/P
Bennett; 109r AA/P Bennett; 110t AA/J Smith;
110cl AA/J Smith; 110ccl AA/J Smith; 110ccr
AA/J Smith; 110cr AA/J Smith; 111l AA/J Smith;
111c AA/J Smith; 111r AA/J Smith; 112l AA/P
Bennett; 112c AA/J Smith; 112r AA/J Smith; 114t
AA/P Bennett; 114cl AA/P Bennett; 114ccl AA/P
Bennett; 114ccr AA/P Bennett; 114cr AA/P
Bennett; 115l AA/P Bennett; 115r AA/P Bennett;
116t AA/P Bennett; 116cl AA/P Bennett; 116c
AA/P Bennett; 116cr AA/P Bennett; 117 AA/P
Bennett; 118l AA/P Bennett; 118c AA/P Bennett;
118r AA/P Bennett; 119l Courtesy of CNTO (Juvaj
Kopac); 119r AA/P Bennett; 120t AA/J Smith;
120cl AA/J Smith; 120c AA/J Smith; 120cr AA/J
Smith; 121 AA/J Smith; 122c AA/J Smith; 122r
AA/J Smith; 123l AA/J Smith; 123c AA/J Smith;
123r AA/J Smith; 124t AA/P Bennett; 124cl AA/P
Bennett; 124c AA/P Bennett; 124cr AA/P
Bennett; 125l AA/P Bennett; 125r AA/P Bennett;
126l AA/J Smith; 126r AA/P Bennett; 127l
Courtesy of Lastovo Island Tourist Office; 127c
AA/P Bennett; 127r AA/J Smith; 128l AA/J Smith;
128r AA/P Bennett; 129l AA/P Bennett; 129c
AA/P Bennett; 129r Courtesy of CNTO; 130l AA/P
Bennett; 130c AA/J Smith; 130r AA/J Smith;
131tl AA/P Bennett; 131cr AA/P Bennett; 132
AA/J Smith; 133t AA/ J Smith; 133cl AA/J Smith;
133c AA/J Smith; 133cr AA/J Smith; 134l AA/J
Smith; 134r AA/J Smith; 135l AA/J Smith; 135r
AA/J Smith; 136l AA/J Smith; 136r AA/J Smith;
136/137 AA/J Smith; 137cl AA/J Smith; 137c
AA/J Smith; 137cr AA/J Smith; 137br AA/J
Smith; 138 AA/P Bennett; 139 AA/J Smith; 140t
AA/J Smith; 140cl AA/J Smith; 140c AA/J Smith;
140cr AA/J Smith; 140cr AA/J Smith; 141l AA/J
Smith; 141c AA/J Smith; 141r AA/J Smith; 142
AA/ P Bennett; 144cl AA/J Smith; 144b AA/P
Bennett; 146l AA/P Bennett; 146r AA/J Smith;
147t AA/P Bennett; 147cr AA/J Smith; 148t
AA/P Bennett; 148cl AA/P Bennett; 148ccl AA/J
Smith; 148ccr AA/P Bennett; 148cr AA/P
Bennett; 149 AA/P Bennett; 150l AA/P Bennett;
150r AA/J Smith; 151 AA/J Smith; 152t AA/P
Bennett; 152cl AA/P Bennett; 152ccl AA/P
Bennett; 152 ccr AA/P Bennett; 152cr AA/P
Bennett; 153 AA/P Bennett; 154l AA/J Smith;
154r AA/J Smith; 155t AA/P Bennett; 155cr AA/P
Bennett; 156t AA/J Smith; 156cl AA/J Smith; 157
AA/P Bennett; 158t Courtesy of Mljet Tourist
Office; 158cl Courtesy of Mljet Tourist Office;
158c ©Wayne Walton/Lonely Planet Images;
158cr Courtesy of Mljet Tourist Office; 159
Courtesy of Mljet Tourist Office; 160l AA/P
Bennett; 160r AA/P Bennett

WHAT TO DO

161 AA/P Bennett; 162/163t AA/J Smith; 163c
AA/J Smith; 164/165t AA/J Smith; 164c
Digitalvision; 165c AA/P Bennett; 166/167t AA/J
Smith; 166cl AA/P Bennett; 166cr AA/P Bennett;
167c AA/J Smith; 168 Image 100; 169 AA/M
Lynch; 170/176t AA/P Bennett; 170c AA/P
Bennett; 171c AA/P Bennett; 172c AA/P Bennett;
173c AA/P Bennett; 174c AA/P Bennett; 175c
©Corbis; 176c Digitalvision; 177/180t AA/P
Bennett; 177c AA/P Bennett; 178c AA/P Bennett;
179c AA/T Kelly; 181/185t AA/P Bennett;
181c AA/P Bennett; 182c AA/P Bennett; 183c
AA/P Bennett; 184c AA/P Bennett; 186/189t
AA/P Bennett; 186c AA/P Bennett; 187c AA/J
Smith; 188c AA/P Bennett; 190/194t AA/P
Bennett; 190c AA/P Bennett; 191c AA/P Bennett;
192c AA/J Smith; 193c AA/P Bennett; 195/198t
AA/J Smith; 195c AA/P Bennett; 196c AA/J
Smith; 197c AA/J Smith; 198 Digital Vision

OUT AND ABOUT

199 AA/P Bennett; 200bl AA/P Bennett; 200cr
AA/P Bennett; 201 AA/J Smith; 202l AA/P
Bennett; 202c AA/P Bennett; 202r AA/P Bennett;
203 AA/P Bennett; 204 AA/P Bennett; 206 AA/P
Bennett; 207 AA/P Bennett; 208 AA/P Bennett;
209bl AA/P Bennett; 209cr AA/T Kelly; 210 AA/P
Bennett; 211 AA/P Bennett; 212 AA/P Bennett;
213t AA/P Bennett; 213c AA/P Bennett; 213b
AA/P Bennett; 214 ©Art Kowalsky/Alamy
Images; 215c AA/P Bennett; 215b AA/P Bennett;
216 AA/P Bennett; 217c AA/P Bennett; 217b
AA/P Bennett; 218 AA/P Bennett; 219 AA/P
Bennett; 220 AA/P Bennett; 221t AA/P Bennett;
221cr AA/P Bennett; 221cbr AA/P Bennett; 221b
AA/P Bennett; 222 AA/P Bennett; 223 AA/P
Bennett; 224 AA/P Bennett; 225t AA/P Bennett;
225b AA/P Bennett; 226 AA/P Bennett; 226/227
AA/P/ Bennett; 228l AA/P Bennett; 228c AA/P
Bennett; 228r AA/P Bennett

EATING AND STAYING

229 AA/P Bennett; 230l AA/P Bennett; 230c AA/P
Bennett; 230/231 AA/P Bennett; 231c AA/J
Smith; 231r AA/P Bennett; 234/247t AA/C
Sawyer; 234 AA/T Kelly; 235 AA/T Kelly; 236
AA/T Kelly; 237 AA/T Kelly; 238 AA/T Kelly; 239
AA/T Kelly; 240 AA/T Kelly; 241 AA/T Kelly; 242
AA/T Kelly; 243 AA/P Bennett; 244 AA/P Bennett;
245 AA/T Kelly; 246 AA/T Kelly; 247 AA/T Kelly;
248l AA/T Kelly; 248c AA/T Kelly; 248/249 AA/T
Kelly; 249c AA/T Kelly; 249cr AA/T Kelly; 249br
AA/T Kelly; 250cl AA/T Kelly; 250c AA/T Kelly;
250cr AA/T Kelly; 250bl AA/T Kelly; 251l AA/T
Kelly; 251c AA/T Kelly; 251r AA/T Kelly; 252/263t
AA/C Sawyer; 252 AA/T Kelly; 253 AA/T Kelly;
254 AA/T Kelly; 255 AA/T Kelly; 256 AA/T Kelly;
257 AA/T Kelly; 258 AA/T Kelly; 259 AA/T Kelly;
260 AA/T Kelly; 261 AA/T Kelly; 262 AA/T Kelly;
263 AA/T Kelly; 264 AA/T Kelly; 265 AA/T Kelly

PLANNING

267 AA/C Sawyer; 271t AA/P Bennett; 271l AA/P
Bennett; 273t Currency information courtesy of
MRI Bankers Guide to Foreign Currency, Houston,
USA; 273c www.euro.ecb.int/; 275 AA/J Smith;
276t AA/J Smith; 276b AA/J Smith; 277 AA/P
Bennett; 278 AA/J Smith; 279 AA/J Smith;
281 AA/J Smith

Project editor
Cathy Hatley

Interior design
Kate Harling

Picture research
Kathy Lockley

Cover design
Tigist Getachew

Internal repro work
Michael Moody, Sarah Butler, Ian Little

Production
Helen Brown, Lyn Kirby

Mapping
Maps produced by the Cartography Department of AA Publishing

Cartographic editor
Anna Thompson

Main contributors
Tony Kelly (author); Lindsay Bennett (verifier); Marie-Claire Jefferies, Marilynne Lanng, Penny
Phenix (editorial work); Marie Lorimer (indexer); Sheila Hawkins (proofreader)

Copy editor
Stephanie Smith

See It Croatia
ISBN 978-1-4000-1853-6

Published in the United States by Fodor's Travel and simultaneously
in Canada by Random House of Canada Limited, Toronto.
Published in the United Kingdom by AA Publishing.

Fodor's is a registered trademark of Random House Inc, and Fodor's See It
is a trademark of Random House, Inc.
Fodor's Travel is a division of Random House, Inc.

Color separation by Keenes, UK
Printed and bound by Leo, China
10 9 8 7 6 5 4 3 2 1

Special Sales: This book is available for special discounts for bulk purchsases for sales
promotions or premiums. Special editions, including personalized covers, excerpts of
existing books, and corporate imprints, can be created in large quantities for special needs.
For more information, write to Special Markets/Premium Sales, 1745 Broadway,
MD 6-2, New York, NY 10019 or e-mail specialmarkets@randomhouse.com.

A02770
Maps in this title produced from data supplied by Global Mapping, Brackley, UK.
Copyright © Global Mapping/Hibernia
Relief map images supplied by Mountain High Maps® Copyright © 1993 Digital Wisdom, Inc
Weather chart statistics supplied by Weatherbase © Copyright 2006 Canty and Associates, LLC
Transport map © Communicarta Ltd, UK

Important Note: Time inevitably brings changes, so always confirm prices, travel facts,
and other perishable information when it matters. Although Fodor's cannot accept
responsibility for errors, you can use this guide in the confidence that we have
taken every care to ensure its accuracy.

Fodor's Key to the Guides

AMERICA'S **GUIDEBOOK LEADER** PUBLISHES GUIDES FOR **EVERY KIND OF TRAVELER**. CHECK OUT OUR MANY SERIES AND FIND YOUR **PERFECT MATCH**.

GOLD GUIDES
Built for today's travelers with unique graphics and maps for easy planning and advice on quintessential local experiences, along with Fodor's Choice rated hotels, restaurants, and sights to guarantee an exceptional vacation.

EXPLORING GUIDES
Splendid color photography paired with exquisitely written articles on history, culture, art, and architecture; suggested walks and excursions; and full-color maps allow you to experience a destination like a well-informed local.

COMPASS AMERICAN GUIDES
Long-time resident writers and photographers reveal the culture and character of American cities, states, and regions through intelligently written essays, literary excerpts, and stunning color imagery.

AROUND THE CITY WITH KIDS
68 great ideas for family fun in and around the city, hand-picked by resident parents, with age-appropriate ratings, entertaining trivia, and nearby kid-friendly snack spots.

SEE IT GUIDES
Colorful and practical, these illustrated guides feature smart writing on history and culture, rich photography, *and* practical travel information. Complete dining and restaurant reviews, exact admission fees, kid-friendly ratings, and everything from sightseeing and shopping, to nightlife, performing arts, and outdoor activities.

25 BEST
Compact city guides of must-see sights and the best dining, shopping, and activities; with a detailed, full-size street map conveniently built-in so you can confidently navigate the city.

FLASHMAPS
Easy-to-follow maps perfect for residents or visitors who want to quickly locate restaurants, shops, museums, movie theaters, subway and bus routes, and more.

LANGUAGES FOR TRAVELERS
All the words and phrases you need for greeting locals, dining out, and getting around in a handy phrasebook along with two CDs for pronunciation practice.

Available at bookstores everywhere.
For a complete list of more than 300 guidebooks,
visit **Fodors.com/shop**.

Dear Traveler

From buying a plane ticket to booking a room and seeing
the sights, a trip goes much more smoothly when you have
a good travel guide. Dozens of writers, editors, designers,
and cartographers have worked hard to make the book
you hold in your hands a good one. Was it everything you
expected? Were our descriptions accurate? Were our
recommendations on target? And did you find our tips and
practical advice helpful? Your ideas and experiences
matter to us. If we have missed or misstated something,
we'd love to hear about it. Fill out our survey at
www.fodors.com/feedback or e-mail us at
seeit@fodors.com. Or you can snail mail to the See It
Editor at Fodor's, 1745 Broadway, New York, New York
10019. We'll look forward to hearing from you.

Tim Jarrell
Publisher